PILLAGING THE EMPIRE

Between 1500 and 1750, European expansion and global interaction produced vast wealth. As goods traveled by ship along new global trade routes, piracy also flourished on the world's seas. *Pillaging the Empire* tells the fascinating story of maritime predation in this period, including the perspectives of both pirates and their victims. Brushing aside the romantic legends of piracy, Kris Lane pays careful attention to the varied circumstances and motives that led to the rise of this bloodthirsty pursuit of riches, and places the history of piracy in the context of early modern empire building.

This second edition of *Pillaging the Empire* has been revised and expanded to incorporate the latest scholarship on piracy, maritime law, and early modern state formation. With a new chapter on piracy in East and Southeast Asia, Lane considers piracy as a global phenomenon. Filled with colorful details and stories of individual pirates from Francis Drake to the women pirates Ann Bonny and Mary Read, this engaging narrative will be of interest to all those studying the history of Latin America, the Atlantic world, and the global empires of the early modern era.

Kris Lane holds the France V. Scholes Chair in Colonial Latin American History at Tulane University. He is the author of *Colour of Paradise: The Emerald in the Age of Gunpowder Empires* and *Quito 1599: City and Colony in Transition*. He is currently writing a book on the colonial history of Potosí, Bolivia.

PILLAGING THE EMPIRE

Global Piracy on the High Seas, 1500–1750

Second Edition

Kris Lane

Routledge
Taylor & Francis Group

NEW YORK AND LONDON

Second edition published 2016
by Routledge
711 Third Avenue, New York, NY 10017

And by Routledge
2 Park Square, Milton Park, Abingdon, Oxon OX14 4RN

Routledge is an imprint of the Taylor & Francis Group, an informa business

© 2016 Taylor & Francis

The right of Kris Lane to be identified as author of this work has been asserted by him in accordance with sections 77 and 78 of the Copyright, Designs and Patents Act 1988.

First edition published by Routledge, 1998

Library of Congress Cataloging-in-Publication Data
Lane, Kris E., 1967–
   Pillaging the empire : global piracy on the high seas, 1500–1750 / Kris Lane. — Second edition.
      pages cm
   Includes bibliographical references and index.
   1. Pirates—America—History. 2. Privateering—America—History. 3. America—History, Naval. 4. Pirates—History. 5. Privateering—History. 6. Naval history, Modern. I. Title.
   E18.75.L36 2015
   364.16'4—dc23
   2015006441

ISBN: 978-0-7656-3841-0 (hbk)
ISBN: 978-0-7656-3842-7 (pbk)
ISBN: 978-1-315-72226-9 (ebk)

Typeset in Bembo
by Apex CoVantage, LLC

For what is history, in fact, but a kind of Newgate calendar, a register of the crimes and miseries that man has inflicted on his fellow man? It is a huge libel on human nature, to which we industriously add page after page, volume after volume, as if we were building up a monument to the honor, rather than the infamy of the species.

—Washington Irving, *The Knickerbocker's History of New York*

CONTENTS

TABLES, MAPS, AND FIGURES

Tables

Maps

Figures

PREFACE AND ACKNOWLEDGMENTS

In 1502, on his fourth and final voyage, Christopher Columbus happened upon a great trading canoe just off the coast of Honduras. It was "long as a galley," as Ferdinand, the Admiral's thirteen-year-old son recalled, and carved from one great tree trunk. Neither its twenty-five naked paddlers nor the richly clad men who appeared to be their masters offered any resistance as the Spaniards seized the craft, and they remained paralyzed with fright as the bearded strangers rifled through the cargo. It was only when some cacao beans were allowed to spill from their containers in the course of the looting that they momentarily forgot their fear, scrambling to retrieve them "as if they were their eyes."[1]

In this passage from *Ambivalent Conquests*, Inga Clendinnen's remarkable reinterpretation of the history of the Spanish conquest of Yucatán, we catch not only a glimpse of the beginnings of European piracy in the Americas but also an early clashing of two vastly different value systems. The Columbus incident cited here constituted a simple act of "piracy on the high seas"—certainly Spain's enemies would have described it as such—and the Maya traders would have most likely agreed (though they were probably stunned to be left with their cacao beans in favor of the odd greenstones and gold work). Indeed, a literal interpretation of our current legal and dictionary definitions of piracy could cast much of the European conquest of the Americas as piracy, a grand larceny "on or by descent from the sea." Plunder is plunder, might is wrong. In typical late-comer fashion, Spain's northern European enemies created the so-called Black Legend with just such literal definitions of "unjust war" in mind, then treated indigenous Americans with stunningly hypocritical cruelty themselves. Meanwhile, they excused acts of piracy against Spanish subjects as "robbing the robbers." Were they not pirates all?

Defining piracy, as these examples suggest, has always been problematical, always subject to multiple perspectives, always plastic in the hands of nationalist historians. As with all "concise narratives," this one attempts to avoid partisanship, accommodate multiple points of view, celebrate nothing, condemn no one, and, in short, simply try to make some "objective" sense out of apparent chaos. Though revisionist in some ways, the present text follows the more traditional history of piracy in that it focuses primarily on the activities of Spain's, and to a lesser extent Portugal's, post-conquest enemies in the Americas. It is less traditional in its attempt to place the seaborne attackers of these Iberian powers in a broader, world-historical context and to view most of their acts as pecuniary rather than nationalistic in nature. In this regard, I hope the book attains a kind of structural and perspectival coherence.

Given the enduring popularity of the topic, old and new books on piracy abound. Some of these works are wonderfully detailed and well researched, and the true enthusiast should consult them rather than this volume for the nitty-gritty of pirate life (several of the better ones are listed in the bibliography). Even better, and of easier access than ever with electronic advances, are the several pirate journals published in the late seventeenth and early eighteenth centuries and reissued in various forms to the present day. For the interested lay reader and perhaps the undergraduate student, however, few scholarly treatments of piracy in history have offered a general, concise overview of the phenomenon as it developed in American waters, including the Pacific, during the early modern era (c. 1450–1750). There are a few exceptions, but in general these works tend to lack in depth what they possess in breadth; either the pirates themselves are romanticized and reduced to caricatures, or Spain's seaborne empire, the usual victim of pirate attacks, is misrepresented or its pivotal role is simply downplayed. The present study has benefited greatly from the work of many conscientious scholars who over the years have recognized these deficiencies in the literature and have worked to flesh out both the Spanish side of the story and the social complexities of pirate and privateering crews of varying nationalities. These more narrowly focused works, usually restricted to one region and time period, have been invaluable informants to the present project, and in order to avoid any hint of literary piracy on my own part, I have attempted to give them full and accurate credit wherever it is due.

The central narrative of this book owes much to the careful scholarship of numerous historians, most notably Kenneth Andrews, Paul Hoffman, Cornelis Goslinga, David Cordingly, Peter Earle, David Marley, and Clarence Haring for the Caribbean region and Peter Bradley and Peter Gerhard for the Pacific; without their work this study would have taken a lifetime of archival research and at least nine lifetimes of accumulated wisdom. Other first-rate sources exploited include the works of Tonio Andrade, Charles Boxer, Giancarlo Casale, Cheng Wei-Chung, J.H. Parry, John B. Wolf, Carla Rahn Phillips, Marcus Rediker, Robert Ritchie,

Mendel Peterson, and the pirate historian's pirate historian, Philip Gosse. Outside of a few primary pirate bits encountered by me in South American and Spanish archives, the present volume makes no attempt at originality beyond the general aim of producing a companion text on piracy suitable for World History or similar courses. For the reader interested in reconstructing pirate life (without, it is hoped, reviving pirate atrocities), I have included such sidelights as instruction in dice throwing, seventeenth-century style, and select (modern) recipes for pirate dishes and drinks.

The pirates were often superb storytellers, and while the following narrative drifts into analysis from time to time, it is the pirates' stories, along with those of their victims, that make up the core of this book. I have tried to leave moral, legal, and psychological reflections to the reader whenever possible, but a confession of bias should help to clear up potential ambiguities. Like the great historian Carlo Cipolla, who in the course of his studies accumulated more knowledge of cannons and warships than any other specialist of early modern Europe, I am a self-proclaimed pacifist and landlubber—beyond this my specialty is early modern Spanish American history. Thus, in the course of the following narrative I may appear to side with the people being beaten up and robbed or those getting seasick and drowning. With these confessions in mind, the reader will discover that I view the pirates of this period much as the vegetarian views the butcher shop, with an uneasy combination of fascination and horror.

The more mundane horror of long nights at the word processor was mitigated by the constant support of my wife, who carried our first child just as this book was gestating. In her long-suffering way she unintentionally reminded me that her task was infinitely more challenging than my own—certainly the product of her labors, a beautiful little girl named Ximena, has proved to be more entertaining. She will be going to college as this second edition goes to press, and I may not be the first parent driven to piracy by the high cost of post-secondary tuition. Other sources of encouragement included the late Robert Levine of the University of Miami History Department and Stephen Dalphin, former executive editor at M.E. Sharpe. For this second edition, I offer special thanks to M.E. Sharpe editors Steve Drummond and Irene Bunnell and to the kind and helpful staff at Routledge. As for outside readers and other partners in crime, I wish to thank the indefatigable John Crocitti at the University of Miami and Joan Campbell and Creston Long at the College of William & Mary; their insights and criticisms were much appreciated. Arne Bialuschewski offered many helpful comments and suggestions for the second edition. In the spirit of American individualism, on the other hand, I am proud to announce that this book was produced with absolutely no financial assistance from state, federal, municipal, or private foundations—a fact that gave rise to the unfortunate rumor that I had discovered a cache of pirate loot among the Florida Keys. If only it had been so. I would like to credit the History Department of the University of Miami, however, for allowing me to develop my thoughts on early modern piracy during my year-long visitorship in an experimental course entitled "Piracy in the West Indies." Finally, many thanks to the students of that course for their enthusiasm and curiosity; they and the many others I have taught since, at William & Mary and now at Tulane University (both founded with pirate loot), reminded me that in spite of such painfully overwrought films as *Cutthroat Island*, the spirit of piracy in the Americas is alive and well.

Crimes such as piracy may not pay in the long run, but they certainly offer scholars and other writers plenty to chew on and, it must be said, to regurgitate. One could even say that piracy provides another kind of parasitical livelihood, that of pirate scholar. Speaking of parasites, this new edition of *Pillaging the Empire*, much like the first, clings like a leach upon the scholarship of others. Even so, in the intervening years since the book first appeared in 1998, I have had the good fortune to come across many more original documents in European and Latin American archives relating to pirate attacks and reprisals. I have not attempted to rewrite this book, but rather to expand its geographical scope, to update its bibliography, to insert a few choice findings, and to correct some lamentable errors. My gut feeling about the subject has not changed: I remain fascinated and repulsed in equal measure.

A General Note on Racial-Ethnic Terms and Place Names

In the text I have chosen to use the term "Native American" rather than "Indian" whenever possible—and more precise terms, such as "Taíno" or "Mapuche," when appropriate. Though one reader has suggested that the term "Native American" is anachronistic, my feeling is that "Indian" remains erroneous and misleading (especially in a text that also deals with native peoples of the Indian subcontinent) no matter how common it was in early modern usage. Clearly no native peoples of the Western Hemisphere recognized a pan-American ethnic identity prior to the twentieth century, no matter how they may be grouped in general today. Peoples of sub-Saharan African origin, enslaved or free, are referred to as either "Africans" or "blacks." As with "Native American," the former term is hopelessly vague and the latter suggests a uniformity of color that did not exist. Given the European tendency to omit precise African ethnic or language group origins in common usage, however, I have had to resort to these terms for the most part. I do not subscribe to any distinctions of "race" beyond the human, but early modern Europeans were not so inclined (though their views differed somewhat from the modern). Hence peoples of "mixed" heritage are referred to by their often unfortunate contemporary monikers, e.g. "mulatto," "mestizo," and so forth. That these terms still circulate without reflection is a chilling reminder of the enduring nature of colonial racist dogma, Spanish, Portuguese, and otherwise.

Spanish-American place names were not perfectly standardized in the colonial period, and I have chosen to use modern terms in most cases; the most likely candidates for reader confusion are: "Riohacha" for "Río de la Hacha," "Portobelo" for "Porto Bello" (or "Puerto Bello"), and "Lima" for "Ciudad de los Reyes."

In current English usage, "West Indies" refers to islands in the Caribbean Basin; I have attempted to keep to this distinction although in Spanish colonial terms "The Indies" referred to all of the American colonies (and to overseas colonies in general, including "East Indian" places such as the Philippines).

Note

1 Inga Clendinnen, *Ambivalent Conquests: Maya and Spaniard in Yucatan, 1517–1570* (Cambridge: Cambridge University Press, 1987), 3.

A CHRONOLOGY OF EARLY MODERN PIRACY

1556	Ottoman corsair Sefer Reis raids coast of India
1559	Treaty of Cateau-Cambrésis; Martin Cote takes Santa Marta, Cartagena (1560); anonymous pirate attack on Campeche; Wang Zhi captured and executed by Ming authorities
1561	Spanish fleet system regularized
1562	First slaving and contraband expedition of John Hawkins to Santo Domingo; first French Huguenot expedition to Florida under Ribault
1564	Second Hawkins expedition to Caribbean (Burburata, Santa Marta); second and third French expeditions to Florida (Laudonnière and Ribault); Sefer Reis launches raid on Swahili Coast
1565	Menéndez Avilés destroys French outposts in Florida
1566	Lovell and Drake engage in contraband trade at Burburata and Riohacha
1567	Drake and Hawkins's third slaving and contraband mission to Tierra Firme, punished by returning fleet at San Juan de Ulúa (1568)
1571	Don Juan of Austria and Christian allies defeat Ottomans at Lepanto (Greece)
1572	Drake returns to Caribbean, attacks Panama
1574	Uluç Ali Pasa captures Spanish *presidio* of La Goletta; Limahon (Lin Feng) attacks Manila
1575	Cervantes captured by Berber corsairs
1577–80	Drake's circumnavigation, includes taking of prize *Cacafuego* off coast of Peru (1579)
1584	First Raleigh expedition to Virginia
1586	Drake returns to Caribbean to take Santo Domingo, Cartagena; Cavendish sets out on circumnavigation voyage; Mir Ali Beg raids Swahili Coast
1587	Raleigh returns to Virginia; Cavendish takes Manila galleon
1588	Anglo-Dutch defeat of the Invincible Armada
1594–95	Richard Hawkins's South Sea voyage (captured off modern Ecuador)
1595	Last expedition of Drake and Hawkins, attacks on San Juan (P.R.), Riohacha, both succumb to disease and die off Panama coast (1596)
1598	Death of Philip II; Peace of Vervins between Spain and France; Cumberland attacks San Juan (P.R.)
1599	First fleet of Dutch salt-gatherers lands at Punta de Araya (Venezuela); Portuguese attack Malabar
1600	Olivier van Noort enters Spanish South Pacific
1603	Death of Elizabeth I; peace with Spain under James I (1604)
1605	Fajardo expedition punishes Dutch at Punta de Araya; policy of depopulation instituted in northern Hispaniola
1609	Beginning of Twelve-Year Truce between Spain and Dutch rebels; Grotius publishes *Mare Liberum*
1615	Speilbergen destroys South Sea Fleet off Cañete (Peru)

1617–18   Raleigh's disastrous El Dorado expedition
1621   Twelve-Year Truce ends; Dutch found West India Company
1624   Jacques l'Hermite blockades Callao, Guayaquil sacked; Jakob Willekens and Piet Heyn capture Bahia (Brazil); English establish settlements in Windward Islands; Dutch drive Spanish from Taiwan
1628   Piet Heyn takes New Spain Fleet off Matanzas Bay, Cuba; pirate Zheng Zhilong joins Ming forces
1629   Cornelis Jol (Pie de Palo) fails to take Havana, joined by Diego el Mulato; Toledo takes Nevis, St. Kitts
1630   Hauspater takes Santa Marta; Spanish drive buccaneer-pirates from Tortuga
1633   Cornelis Jol and Diego el Mulato take Campeche
1642   William Jackson sacks Maracaibo
1648   Peace of Westphalia ends eighty-year Spanish war with Dutch
1654   Second Spanish raid on Tortuga, temporary garrison established
1655   English take Jamaica
1659   Myngs destroys Cumaná, attacks Puerto Cabello and Coro (Venezuela)
1661   Koxinga (Zheng Chenggong) defeats Dutch at Taiwan
1662   Myngs takes Santiago de Cuba, Campeche; Mansfield sacks Santiago de Cuba
1663   Mansfield and Morgan sack Campeche; Barnard sacks San Tomé
1665   Mansfield sacks Sancti Spiritus and takes Santa Catalina (Providence Island)
1667   Morgan assaults Puerto Príncipe, Portobelo
1668   L'Ollonais takes Maracaibo and Gibraltar (Venezuela)
1669   Morgan takes Maracaibo and Gibraltar; Cox and Duncan take Santa Marta, ransom bishop
1670   Treaty of Madrid establishes peace between England and Spain
1671   Morgan captures and burns Panama; amnesty offered to repentant buccaneers
1672   Laurens de Graaf (Lorencillo) takes Campeche
1674   First "Corsair Ordinances" issued to punish Spanish renegades; breakup of Dutch West India Company
1678   Scott assaults Campeche; de Grammont sacks, occupies Maracaibo, Gibraltar
1679   Franquesnay fails to take Santiago de Cuba
1680   Portobelo taken by Sharp, Coxon, et al.; Sharp enters Pacific; de Grammont takes Cumaná and La Guaira
1681   Sharp and Ringrose capture South Sea charts (*derrotero*)
1683   Laurens de Graaf, de Grammont, and van Hoorn take Veracruz
1685   Laurens de Graaf and de Grammont take Campeche
1687   Grogniet and filibusters take Guayaquil; Phips salvages treasure ship off Hispaniola

1690   De Cussy attacks Santiago de los Caballeros; Strong expedition to South Sea

1691   Spanish and English attack Cap François (Hispaniola), filibuster haven

1692   Earthquake destroys Port Royal, Jamaica

1694   Ducasse and filibusters attack southeast Jamaica

1695   Henry Avery captures treasure-laden pilgrim fleet in Indian Ocean

1697   Baron de Pointis and filibusters take Cartagena; Peace of Ryswick signed

1701   William Kidd tried and hanged for piracy in England

1710–11   French Attack Rio de Janeiro

1702–13   War of Spanish Succession ends with Treaty of Utrecht

1715   Wreck of Spanish treasure fleet off Cape Canaveral, Florida

1718   Blackbeard dies off North Carolina in gun battle

1721   Ann Bonny, Mary Read, and "Calico Jack" Rackham captured

1722   Bartholomew "Black Bart" Roberts dies off West Africa in gun battle

INTRODUCTION

Fifteen men on the dead man's chest—
Yo ho ho, and a bottle of rum!
Drink and the devil had done for the rest—
Yo ho ho, and a bottle of rum!

For many readers whose first language is English, the word "piracy" brings to mind these verses from Robert Louis Stevenson's *Treasure Island*. Stevenson's Long John Silver, Ben Gunn, Israel Hands, Captain Flint, and other colorful pirate characters had analogues and even namesakes in the early modern past, but these characters, at least as we know them, were essentially products of a late nineteenth-century literary imagination. For historians of the early modern world, and of early Spanish America in particular, a striking feature of many English-language pirate novels such as *Treasure Island*, and even some pirate histories, is the conspicuous absence of the Spanish and their colonial subjects, the pirates' principal victims in the Americas for more than two centuries. Pirates certainly fought amongst themselves, but "pieces of eight" and "Spanish doubloons" were usually taken from Spanish towns and Spanish ships. While the omission of the Spanish side of the story may be harmless at the level of fiction, it distorts history. As will be seen, piracy in the Americas took many forms during the long period between Columbus's landfall and the great pirate trials of the early eighteenth century—these will be explored in chronological order and in some detail. From the Spanish point of view, the pirates, mostly men of French, English, and Dutch heritage who preferred to call themselves merchants, privateers, "gentlemen of fortune," and so on, were simply foreign criminals, and as such deserved no quarter. In the long run, defense against these interlopers cost Spain's empire dearly.

The present study is not intended to deflate the romantic image that pirates have enjoyed in the popular imagination, even, it should be noted, among Spanish and Spanish American readers. The pirates need not be debunked, exposed, or judged at this late stage. Rather, as there is a growing interest among historians of the early modern world in activities that tied very distant regions together for the first time—among them long-distance trade, mass migration, and religious proselytization—a world-history approach to piracy might also serve a purpose. Pirates have been studied in particular regions and time periods in the Americas, but they remain to be treated in the aggregate in terms of their larger historical context, and this study is an attempt in that direction.

A word on definitions is in order. From the Spanish view, and often the Portuguese as well, northern European and other interlopers in American, African and Asian waters they claimed were pirates (*piratas*), or unsanctioned sea-raiders. This was often the case, but as will be seen there were also many acts of "privateering," or raids carried out under license from a monarch (or other governing body) during wartime. Other interlopers often referred to as pirates by the Spanish were actually smugglers, though often well-armed and aggressive ones. These are the basic distinctions, but numerous synonyms for pirate, such as "buccaneer" and "freebooter," arose in the seventeenth century—for these I refer the reader to the glossary. The key to all such terms is point of view, of course, but to the pacifist the majority approach the universal, or at least classical, *hostis humani generis*; the pirates were "enemies of humankind."

The basic features of the Spanish empire in the Americas will be outlined first, as an understanding of what the pirates were after, and were up against, is necessary to tracing their trajectories in American waters. Chapter 1 will focus on the activities of mostly French corsairs (from the contemporary Spanish term, *corsario*) in the Spanish Caribbean between 1500 and 1559, but a short treatment of sixteenth-century piracy in the Mediterranean and East Atlantic is included to give context to the French problem. The French threat in the Americas coincided with a rise in anti-Spanish piracy along the so-called Barbary, or Berber, Coast of North Africa, a substantial phenomenon of long duration. Spanish expansion into North Africa after the so-called Iberian Reconquest (711–1492) led to a chronic pirate problem that would outlast the early modern period, always affecting Spanish views toward piracy in the Americas.

Chapter 2 treats the rise of the English "Elizabethan" pirates, a bold group that included such notable figures as John Hawkins and Francis Drake. The Elizabethans, as the name suggests, were active during the long reign of Queen Elizabeth I (1558–1603), a period that also saw Spain, under the equally long-lived Philip II (1556–1598), rise to preeminence in Europe. As in other cases, the Elizabethan pirates often became privateers, or crown-sanctioned mercenaries, during wartime, in this case after 1585. War or no war, however, from the Spanish point of view Drake and his compatriots were still pirates when attacking Iberian targets "beyond the line," that is, in waters claimed by Spain or Portugal.

The next wave consisted largely of Dutch pirates—or privateers, since most were sanctioned by an incipient Dutch state—active from about 1570 to 1648. They are the subject of Chapter 3. As with many of the Elizabethans and even some of the earlier Protestant French corsairs, the Dutch resented Spain's religious orthodoxy almost as much as its political power. Much of the northern Netherlands, under radical Protestant leadership by the late 1560s, was engaged in a massive rebellion against Catholic Spanish control, and the animosity spread from land to sea. Thus Dutch activities against Spanish and Portuguese dominions in the Americas and elsewhere during this period might be seen as an extension of the so-called Eighty Years War (1568–1648), which ended with Spain's recognition of Dutch independence. Dutch maritime intrusion into American waters had serious commercial aims as well, however, and these helped to blur the lines between trade, war, and criminal piracy. In the long run, Dutch predation in Spanish waters was not as damaging as that of the Elizabethans, but the temporary loss of northeastern Brazil was a huge blow to Portuguese interests, formally united with Spain between 1580 and 1640. An exception to this trend was a raid led by Piet Heyn, a veteran of the Brazil conflicts and an outstanding sea captain who managed to take a legendary treasure from the Spanish in Matanzas Bay, Cuba, in 1628. Heyn was well armed and openly sponsored by the Dutch West India Company, and was thus a respected naval officer rather than a criminal in his homeland. His return to Amsterdam with 15 million guilders' worth of American treasure upset European financial markets and deeply wounded Spain's international credit. Unsurprisingly the Spanish remember Piet Heyn as a pirate.

Chapter 4 introduces the first sea predators in the Americas universally recognized as pirates: the seventeenth-century buccaneers. This motley group of English, French, Dutch, Danish, and even renegade Spanish and Portuguese subjects harried Spanish—and later English, Dutch, and French—shipping in the Caribbean Sea after about 1630. Their origins and major exploits, including Henry Morgan's sack of Panama in 1671, will be detailed up to the early 1680s. The era of the buccaneers might be considered the "golden age" of piracy in the Americas, but, perhaps paradoxically, it coincided with Spain's financial and political decline. The buccaneers were only one of many problems faced by the ailing empire, and were thus often weakly countered, but emerging English, French, Dutch, and Danish colonies in the Caribbean joined in the fight to suppress the buccaneers after about 1683. Many pirates were forced to raid elsewhere due to growing merchant and planter interests, and Chapter 5 follows a number of these same Caribbean pirates into the Spanish Pacific, or South Sea, as it was then called, where they were active between 1680 and 1694. The South Sea buccaneers included some of the most famous journal-writing pirates of the period, among them the English Basil Ringrose and the French Raveneau de Lussan. Their exploits included the capture of a Spanish book of sea-charts in 1681 and the sack of Guayaquil (in present day Ecuador) in 1687.

Chapter 6 moves to eastern seas, first treating piracy and attempts to suppress it in the Indian Ocean, and then similarly in the western Pacific. Historians disagree as to whether European expansion into these eastern waters after 1500 constituted piracy or created it as a new category, or whether piracy had long existed but had never been so widespread or violent. New monopoly trading claims, weapons, and capital investment certainly raised the stakes. For the Indian Ocean, the chapter traces the sixteenth-century rivalry between the Portuguese and Ottomans that led to mutual accusations of piracy before turning to the case of the Malabar pirates of southwest India. The chapter then shifts to the South China Seas to examine large-scale piracy cycles involving Chinese, Japanese, and Southeast Asian perpetrators and victims as well as European interlopers. The chapter ends with the incursion of the South Sea buccaneers of the previous chapter.

Chapter 7 treats the end of buccaneering and the last of the early modern pirates in the Americas, a group of mostly Anglo-American sea-robbers often referred to as "freebooters." These pirates were essentially the remnants of the seventeenth-century buccaneers, now forced to seek a living in an increasingly hostile legal and political environment. Among the most notable individuals of this group are Captain William Kidd, who was executed in London in 1701, and Edward Teach, aka "Blackbeard," who was killed off North Carolina in 1718. Pirate suppression had been under way in the Caribbean since the 1680s, but it was during the years 1713–26, the decade or so following the War of the Spanish Succession (1702–13), that piracy came under fierce attack from all sides. The Spanish had always tried to fight sea predators, of course, but not until this period did other nations or kingdoms with colonial interests in the Americas see fit to suppress piracy once and for all (or so they hoped). A genuine extermination campaign ensued and some 500 pirates were tried and executed between 1716 and 1726, mostly in English colonial outposts. To reinforce the terror, all trade or close contact with such persons was criminalized, particularly in the English colonies, and made subject to capital punishment. Thus, though pirate activity would continue to appear from time to time in American waters after 1730, never again would it thrive in the atmosphere of freedom and seemingly endless plunder that marked the late seventeenth century.

The chapters that follow are a condensed chronicle of the pirates' own exploits compiled from various sources, but their overall subtext is Spanish response. How did over two centuries of piracy in the Americas affect colonial settlements on the Caribbean and Pacific islands and coasts? How severely did piracy disrupt trans-Atlantic and trans-Pacific shipping? How effective were the various defensive measures employed over the years by Spain and its colonial subjects? These sorts of questions will be addressed where information is available in order to make clear the deep impact of piracy on its principal victims. As will be seen, the Spanish in America were both greatly despised and greatly envied by European rivals in the wake of Columbus's voyages; Spain's treasures in gold and silver and the extent of mistreatment of native peoples were both exaggerated. As a result the pirates often missed great opportunities for plunder and misjudged indigenous peoples and other potential allies due to poor information.

For their part, the Spanish also routinely overestimated the threat they faced from foreign enemies. This sort of mutual misunderstanding and "out-imagining of the other" was not so costly for Spain's pirate enemies, but it led to massive Spanish expenditures on fortifications and garrisons, as at San Juan de Puerto Rico, Havana, Veracruz, Portobelo, Cartagena, and Santa Marta, and to the construction of costly patrol squadrons and quasi-navies (*armadillas*). Though occasionally effective in defending coasts and shipping lanes from pirate attacks, these devices, paid for overwhelmingly by the already overtaxed citizens of Spanish America, were a drain on local economies, as well as on the crown's limited resources. In other cases valuable lands were abandoned due to short-term indefensibility, but with long-term consequences, including permanent loss to foreign rivals. Thus it can be seen that the imaginations of both aggressors and victims in this story had manifold and unexpected effects on the long-term history of the region; in numerous cases better intelligence would have been worth its weight in gold.

As individuals, some of the pirates certainly approached the romantic image that has been applied to them in literature, and a fair number of the historical actors we call pirates were no doubt remarkable, and even at times honorable and compassionate people. Just as often, perhaps, the pirates were products of their time, status-obsessed and avaricious, as unscrupulous in their dealings with Africans and Native Americans as they were with fellow Europeans. Some were genuine psychopaths. Others were freethinkers and sexual rebels, among them the only two women known to be pirates in this period, Ann Bonny and Mary Read (captured in 1721). European life, or more often life in the European overseas colonies, was nasty, brutish, and short for all but the wealthiest in the early modern era, and running off to join a pirate crew offered escape, adventure, and possibly even wealth and fame. Indeed the pirates' motives, and in some cases their fates, might be compared with those of the early Spanish conquistadors. All would take great risks, most would die penniless, and only a chosen few would enjoy their share of the great elusive prizes to be had in the Americas. And as with the conquistadors of the sixteenth century, many of the great pirates of the seventeenth would just as quickly forfeit all their winnings in a game of cards, a duel, or an outrageous, rum-soaked debauch. Perhaps it is precisely this reckless spirit of adventure and amoral abandon, not the pirates' life histories in and of themselves, that manages to intrigue us after so many centuries.

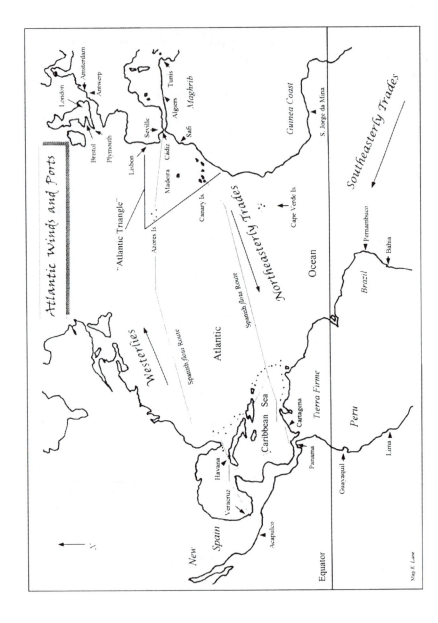

MAP 1 Atlantic Winds and Ports

1

SPAIN AND THE SIXTEENTH-CENTURY CORSAIRS

In the late fifteenth century, well before the rise of modern nation-states in northwestern Europe, the newly united kingdoms of Castile and Aragon were competing with the neighboring kingdom of Portugal for control over a burgeoning overseas trade. Both realms were more centralized than their northern neighbors, and better poised for expansion into the Atlantic than their competitors in the Mediterranean, mostly merchant interests based in the Italian city-states of Venice, Florence, and Genoa. The Portuguese and Spanish were initially interested in the spices and fine fabrics of Asia, then available only by way of Muslim middlemen, but they also sought to monopolize access to African gold, ivory, pepper, and, after 1441, slaves. Early sugar colonies were established on several East Atlantic islands, the Portuguese focusing on the Madeiras, Cape Verdes, and São Tomé, and the Spanish on the Canaries, or Fortunate Isles. Improved sailing technology made long-distance sea travel more feasible than ever before and in 1492 the Genoese Christopher Columbus sailed west across the Atlantic, or Ocean Sea as it was then called, thereby opening up a whole new world of possibilities for his Spanish sponsors. The Portuguese–Spanish rivalry now included the Americas, but the dispute was settled for the time being by a papal dispensation and the subsequent Treaty of Tordesillas in 1494, effectively dividing the known world into halves, one for each realm. "The line" beyond which European peace treaties would often prove ineffective was placed at 370 leagues (c. 2,000 km) west of the Cape Verde Islands.

Other emerging European seafaring nations, along with virtually everyone else besides the Spanish and Portuguese, treated this division of the earth's spoils as an act of contemptible arrogance. Thus, as the seaborne empires of Spain and Portugal developed in the late fifteenth and early sixteenth centuries, so too did the phenomenon of maritime predation, often in the form of piracy, or criminal sea raiding. The Spanish and Portuguese called the interlopers—some North African in origin, others French, English, or Irish—"corsairs" (*corsarios*), and quickly set about developing defensive measures to face them. Piracy had been a problem in the Mediterranean and North Atlantic for centuries, but the prey, prior to the windfall of American discovery and conquest, had been only moderately attractive. Now a regular sea traffic in gold, silver, gems, and sugar, compact and valuable items that nearly everyone wanted, was growing ripe for the picking.

The region of greatest risk for the Spanish, whose only connection to the wealth of the Americas was the transoceanic route opened by Columbus, was the so-called Atlantic Triangle, the East Atlantic Ocean bounded by the Iberian Peninsula and Moroccan coast of Africa, the Azores, Canary, and Madeira Islands. The threat to Spanish and Portuguese shipping in this region, mostly originating in France and the British Isles, but also the north coast of Africa, was real and immediately felt. Upon returning from his third voyage to the so-called New World in 1498, Columbus already feared French attackers near Madeira and took precautions to avoid an encounter. The multinational corsairs would in time spread beyond this region, entering American waters by the 1530s, just as the Spanish conquistadors were consolidating their control over the great interior empires of Mexico and Peru. But before the corsair threat reached the Caribbean Sea, the first American theater of pirate conflict, Spain faced other, more traditional enemies to its growing maritime empire in the Mediterranean. Indeed, since the problem of piracy in the Mediterranean drained Spanish wealth and military resources throughout the early modern period (c. 1450–1750), a brief consideration of this phenomenon will help to clarify Spain's subsequent pirate policies in the Americas.

The Brothers Barbarossa and the Barbary Coast Corsairs

The famous voyage of Christopher Columbus coincided with another important event in Spanish history, the completion of the *reconquista* (AD 711–1492), or Christian Reconquest of the Iberian Peninsula from descendants of early Muslim conquerors, or "Moors." Much of Iberia had been in Christian hands for centuries, but it was only during the reign of Isabella of Castile and Ferdinand of Aragon that Granada, the last Islamic kingdom on the peninsula, fell. The conquest of Granada was completed in 1492, followed by the staggered expulsion of many Muslim and Jewish refugees, a diaspora that scattered these peoples throughout the Mediterranean basin and into various parts of Europe. The united kingdoms of Spain, under the so-called *Reyes Católicos*, or Catholic Monarchs, were vehemently intolerant of heterodox religious beliefs, particularly Islam and Judaism, and some factions even pressed for a counter-conquest, an extended crusade of sorts, against the Muslim and Jewish inhabitants of North Africa. Following the advice of one such militant, Francisco Cardinal Jiménez de Cisneros, Archbishop of Toledo, King Ferdinand began a program of conquest, focusing on the ports of the Maghrib, or Barbary (really "Berber") Coast. Ferdinand's campaigns between 1497 and 1510 led to the capture of the coastal settlements of Melilla, Mers el-Kebir, El Peñón de Vélez, Oran, Bougie, and Tripoli. Also in 1510, the Berbers surrendered control of an island off Algiers to the Christians, and the key fort of El Peñón (The Rock) was built upon it soon after. The Spanish were essentially following in the footsteps of the Portuguese, who had captured the key North African port of Ceuta in 1415.

In addition to its Reconquest elements, the Spanish advance into North Africa was also in part a symbolic drive against the advances of the Turkish Ottoman Empire, which had stunned Christian Europe by taking Constantinople in 1453. The Ottomans backed the Berbers, and also the Iberian Muslim exiles who lived among them, and a sustained resistance to Spanish hegemony in the Mediter-ranean developed.[1] The Barbary Coast might have been fully subjected to Span-ish control, but the discovery of the Americas and coincidental political changes in Europe distracted from the purpose. Spain under the Holy Roman Emperor Charles V (1516–56), known in Spain as Carlos I, turned away from fighting Mus-lim pirates in favor of mainland European concerns, and with this shift in interest and resources the military outposts, or *presidios*, established by Ferdinand in the Maghrib became vulnerable. Resentment of the Spanish presence led Algerian Berbers to court the Ottomans, and an affiliate corsair by the name of Oruç, a native of the Greek island of Lesbos, took control of Algiers in 1516. Oruç had made a name for himself among the Ottomans as early as 1504 by capturing two richly laden papal galleys traveling from Genoa to Civita Vecchia, on the Italian coast near Rome, but he preferred to remain semi-independent of the Turkish sultan's orders. Known to Europeans as Barbarossa (Italian for "Red-beard"), Oruç was followed in the pirate trade by his similarly red-bearded brother, Hayreddin, in 1518, and these Barbary corsairs, the Barbarossa brothers, soon became legend-ary figures.

Oruç had initially secured the sponsorship of the governor, or *bey*, of Tunis by offering him a tribute of twenty percent of any booty or ransom taken. Com-mission agreements allowed both parties some independence from one another, along with mutual gains, and would be followed by pirates and island governors in the Caribbean in the next century. The downside of such agreements, of course, was that the governors had little direct power over the corsairs. The consequences of this weakness could be taxing, as, for example, when Oruç became powerful enough that he lowered the *bey's* tribute to ten percent of his take. Oruç Bar-barossa continued to harry Christian, and particularly Spanish, shipping in the Mediterranean for about a decade, but his attempts to recapture the Spanish tribu-tary cities of North Africa were unsuccessful. In a 1512 attempt on Bougie he lost an arm to an arquebus (or primitive matchlock) shot, and in 1518, two years after the death of King Ferdinand, he was killed by Spanish forces outside Tilimsan (Algeria). In spite of these failures, the first Barbarossa had proved a real menace to the Catholic kings. In what was perhaps Oruç's greatest victory, a fleet carrying

FIGURE 1.1 An Early Modern Mediterranean Galley

Source: Jacques Gérol du Pas, *Recueil de veues les diférens bastimens de la mer Mediteranée et l'ocean*, Paris: 1710 (courtesy of the James Ford Bell Library, University of Minnesota).

7,000 veteran Spanish soldiers sent to relieve the fort of El Peñón in 1517 was all but annihilated by the one-armed corsair and his followers.[2]

The younger Barbarossa, Hayreddin, sought greater political legitimacy and firmer backing from the Ottoman sultan. He was named *beylerbey*, or regent-governor of Algiers, and already in 1519 Hayreddin was forced to defend his capital from an attack by a fleet of fifty Spanish warships under command of Hugo de Moncada. Barbarossa's forces routed Moncada's, and a number of similarly spectacular defeats of Christian armies and navies ensued. With the aid of Turkish reinforcements, including 2,000 of the famed janissary corps, the second Barbarossa finally drove the Spanish from their fortress at El Peñón in 1529. As a titled subject of the sultan, Hayreddin became more governor than pirate, leaving the business of sea raiding to a group of trusted captains, known as *reis*. Among the most prominent of these reis were Turgut (known to Europeans as Dragut), a Rhodes-born Muslim; Sinan, a Jewish pirate from Smyrna; and Aydin (or "Drub-devil"), a renegade Christian and possibly a Spaniard. The various reis and their crews rarely ventured into East Atlantic waters, the favorite haunt of French corsairs in this period, preferring instead to focus their efforts on Spain's Mediterranean coast and the Balearic Islands. In 1529, the year of Hayreddin's capture of El Peñón, Aydin Reis managed to rout a Spanish *armadilla*, or small fleet, of eight galleys off the island of Formentara. The armadilla's commander, General Portundo, was killed in the fire-fight, and most of the surviving crewmembers were taken as slaves to Algiers. Perhaps anxious to share in the glories of the reis, the younger Barbarossa returned to the sea in 1534, now at the head of a fleet of sixty-one galleys. His principal objectives were in Italy, and included the capture of a famous young duchess named Julia Gonzaga, whom he hoped to seize at Fondi and offer as a present to the sultan. The duchess's last-minute escape from the Berber corsair became a folktale in her own lifetime, and a disappointed Hayreddin was forced to turn his energies instead on Tunis, which he captured in a day.[3]

Spain continued a sporadic campaign against the likes of Hayreddin and his followers, sending the famous Genoese admiral Andrea Doria to recapture Tunis in 1535. A garrisoned fort, or *presidio*, was subsequently established at La Goletta, but diplomatic ties with local elites were weak and all of the Spanish presidios of North Africa were dangerously undermanned. A large fleet under Andrea Doria's command was defeated by the Berbers off the distant Albanian coast in 1538, and a new attempt on Algiers in 1541 failed miserably, though more as a result of storms than of organized resistance. Among the many notable participants in the battle of Algiers was Hernán Cortés, the famed conquistador of Mexico, then in Spain fighting to maintain title to his American holdings. The equally famous Barbarossa the younger went on to form an ambiguous alliance with Francis I (1515–47), Spain's enemy and king of France, before his death in 1546. The Ottomans did not neglect their promises to the Berbers after the death of the Hayreddin, and in 1551 they sent Turgut Reis (Dragut) to recapture Tripoli from the Knights of Malta. The knights had been established in Tripoli since 1530, dispatched by Charles V, but they proved to be no match for Dragut and his seasoned corsairs.[4]

No individual pirates rose to the legendary status of the Barbarossa brothers after the mid-sixteenth century, but Barbary Coast piracy was by no means dead. Forced Muslim converts to Christianity in Spain, known as *moriscos*, were unhappy with a variety of discriminatory measures used against them, and many rebelled in 1569. The governor of Algiers, Uluç Ali Pasa, took advantage of the distracting Morisco uprising in Spain to recapture Tunis. Things could still go both ways, however, as Don Juan of Austria, a young admiral fresh from a resounding victory over the Ottoman naval forces at Lepanto in 1571, managed to retake Tunis for the Christians in 1573. It was a hollow victory, however, as Uluç Ali Pasa soon recaptured the city, along with the important Spanish presidio of La Goletta, in 1574. Thus the fight for the North African coast in the sixteenth century resembled a tug-of-war, with neither side victorious. The disastrous defeat at Lepanto, however, led the Ottomans to seek a peace with the Christians, and an agreement signed in 1580 lessened the importance of the Maghrib as a theater of Turkish–European conflict. What the region became instead was a pirate nursery, a permanent home for corsairs and disgruntled Muslim-Jewish exiles, and a constant thorn in Spain's side.

Berber piracy after the Battle of Lepanto and resulting treaties was a kind of *guerrilla*, or "little war," with mostly Muslim corsairs preying on Spanish and other

European shipping in the Mediterranean until the 1810s, when this activity was finally suppressed by allied forces and the fledgling U.S. Navy. Robbery was certainly an important feature of Berber piracy, but more often it consisted of *rescate*, or bargaining to ransom captives based on their wealth and status. (Rescate in the Caribbean and other American contexts, as will be seen, referred to the practice of contraband trading, or forcibly breaking Spain's monopoly arrangements with its colonies. Portuguese *resgate* was somewhere in between the Mediterranean and American forms, usually referring to the "ransoming" of sub-Saharan African captives, a cover for slave trading.) The ransoming of Christian captives, most of them Spaniards, from the *bagnios*, or jails, of Algiers and other cities of the Muslim Maghrib became highly formalized in the sixteenth century. This form of rescate involved many notable personages, including Spain's most famous writer of fiction, Miguel de Cervantes. Cervantes, a veteran of the Battle of Lepanto, was taken hostage by Berber corsairs in 1575, and he seems to have drawn on his personal experiences in describing the captive's life in the following passage from *Don Quixote* (1614):

> So I passed my life, shut up in a prison-house, called by the Turks a *bagnio*, where they keep their Christian prisoners: those belonging to the King and those belonging to private people, and also those who are called the slaves of the *Almazen*—that is to say, of the township—who are employed in the public works of the city and in other communal employment. Slaves of this kind have great difficulty in gaining their liberty because, as they belong to the community and have no master of their own, there is no one with whom to bargain for their ransom, even if they have the money. To these *bagnios*, as I have said, some private people of the city take their prisoners, particularly when they are waiting to be redeemed. For they are kept here in idleness and safety until their ransom comes. The King's captives, if they are to be ransomed, do not go out to work with the rest of the gang either, except if their ransom is delayed; in which case, to spur them to write more urgently for it, they make them work and fetch firewood with the others, which is no light job.[5]

Fortunately for posterity, Cervantes was ransomed for some 500 *escudos* (worth about 700 silver pesos, see Box 1) in 1579. Meanwhile, the business of captivity among the pirates of North Africa entered into the popular imagination of most Spaniards, becoming a topic of countless sermons and folktales. Since the Spanish crown was chronically short of cash, ransoming became the special mission of the Trinitarian and Mercedarian religious orders, a cause for which they raised funds even in the distant American colonies.[6] Clearly the religious and widely felt aspects of this continued "little war" against the North African corsairs, a sort of mini-crusade, gave the conflict an intimate and even personal aspect rarely seen in American waters. Nevertheless, as will be demonstrated later, the confessional differences that developed in the sixteenth century among European Christians, particularly the great rift between Protestants and Catholics after the appearance of Martin Luther and John Calvin, greatly influenced pirate activity in the Americas. As in the Mediterranean, piracy in the Western Hemisphere both reflected and exacerbated broader religious and political tensions. Whether religious and political motives outweighed economic ones, however, would always be open to question.

Jambe de Bois and the First Caribbean Corsairs

Reliable information on the earliest pirates in the Americas is slim, but it is clear that French corsairs predominated in the first half of the sixteenth century, especially in the years 1530–60. Some Protestant French corsairs, somewhat like their counterparts in the Mediterranean, were motivated by religious or confessional animosity. Most, however, simply regarded Spain's weakly defended New World fleets as enticing economic prey. The French were first active in the Atlantic Triangle in the period of Columbus's famous voyages, but it was not until Cortés's conquest of Mexico (1519–21) that large amounts of American treasure began to flow back to Spain. The gold, sugar, and tobacco of Hispaniola, along with the pearls of Cubagua and Margarita, islands off the north coast of Venezuela, had been objects of envy for some time, but the volume of compact treasure was to increase dramatically in the era of the conquistadors.

A prelude to pirate acts to come occurred in 1523, when a Norman corsair named Jean Florin (or Fleury) captured several Spanish ships off Cape St. Vincent (southwest Portugal). The ships, which were carrying a portion of the treasure stolen from the Aztec, or Mexica, ruler Moctezuma, had encountered other French corsairs near the Azores and had lost some valuables. Florin, however, ended up with the lion's share of the booty; by some accounts his opportune attack yielded 62,000 ducats in gold, 600 marks (c. 140 kg) of pearls, and several tons of sugar.[7] One of Cortés's ambassadors in charge of the treasure, Alonso de Ávila, was also captured and held prisoner by the French until 1525, when he was ransomed in the manner of the Berber captives. Although the Florin raid occurred in the Atlantic Triangle, for all practical purposes the great age of piracy in the Americas had begun.

Spain was for the first time forced to protect itself from sea predators on American trade, and its responses, though not always effective, and certainly not mindful of panicked requests from merchants and colonists, were entirely practical. In an era of Spanish expansion in Europe, cost was key. Fleets were made to travel in convoys as early as 1525, and by 1552 merchant ships were ordered to travel armed, at their own expense. By 1561 the bi-annual *flota*, or fleet system, leaving Spain in January and August, was in place. Ships left Sanlúcar de Barrameda or Cádiz, near the mouth of the Guadalquivir, sailed south along the Moroccan coast to the Canaries to take on water, caught the northeasterly trades

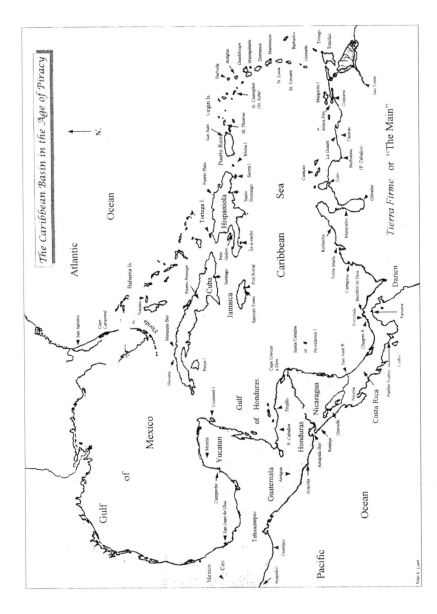

MAP 2 The Caribbean Basin in the Age of Piracy

across the Atlantic, and arrived in the Caribbean Sea within about a month's time, usually entering among the Windward Islands (Dominica and Guadeloupe). Return fleets left Cartagena de Indias and Veracruz to join at Havana, whence they caught the Gulf Stream, passed the treacherous Florida Strait and found southwesterly trades to Europe. Barring attacks from pirates or hurricanes, the return voyage from Havana to Spain took two to three months, often broken by a stop at the Azores.

Though practical in light of fiscal pressures, Spain's reluctance to finance a professional navy in the waters it claimed "beyond the line" had lasting effects. Straggling merchant ships, like wounded herd animals picked out by wolves, would continue to fall prey to packs of pirates unavenged. Smugglers would likewise come and go virtually at leisure, and Caribbean towns not deemed worthy of fortifying were of necessity abandoned. Still, given Spain's already notoriously overstretched exchequer, the static approach to American defense was the only option. If merchants and colonists wanted to protect their gains, they would have to pay for it themselves. Onerous "pirate taxes," such as the ad valorem *avería*, ensued, and the practice of delegating defense responsibilities to the victims sowed the seeds of dissent, and ultimately rebellion, in some regions. Eventually most creoles (Spanish *criollos*), or colonial-born elites, came to view themselves as double victims—attacked in their own homes by free-roving corsairs on the one hand, and on the other slowly bled to death by an increasingly desperate and ungrateful peninsular government.

Early French visitors to American waters initially cruised the Brazilian coast, only recently claimed by Portugal in 1500 when it was first visited by accident by the East India–bound Pedro Álvares Cabral. The French sought to trade with coastal indigenous groups for dyewood, or *brazil*-wood, from which the modern nation takes its name, but the Portuguese, though far more interested in their African and East Indian ventures, did not tolerate the encroachment. One early French interloper was Captain Gonneville of Honfleur, who traded goods with indigenous Brazilians in 1503–4 from his ship *l'Espoir*. Though France's Francis I (1515–47) and his supporters rejected the notion, the Portuguese claimed Brazil under the Treaty of Tordesillas, and João III (1521–57) eventually responded with colonization efforts and active defense measures. An important feature of Martim Afonso de Sousa's critical 1530–33 expedition was to crush French corsairs, and thus the founding of Brazil could be said to have resulted in large part from a pirate threat.[8] In spite of increasing Portuguese hostility, attempts to plant an "Antarctic France" in Brazil continued into the 1560s, when the last colonists, most of them Protestant refugees, or Huguenots, were finally driven from the region. French corsairs, some of them Protestants but others Roman Catholics like their Iberian enemies, quickly learned that something better than dyewood could be had in the Spanish Caribbean. Compared with Brazil's still-modest wealth, Spain's American treasures, consisting of gold, pearls, and precious stones, glittered like a fishing lure.

Though probably not the first North European pirate to appear in the Caribbean, an anonymous French corsair raided a Spanish relief ship near the Chagres River, on the north coast of the Panamanian Isthmus, in November of 1536. The corsair stole the vessel and abandoned its crew onshore after throwing the cargo, a number of much-prized horses on their way from Santo Domingo to Peru, into the sea. The same French corsairs then made their way to the north coast of Cuba, hoping to attack ships setting off for Spain from Havana. Their small numbers prevented a direct attack on the harbor, and as they waited offshore a group of wealthy citizens of Havana offered to back a punitive expedition, and soon three 200-ton Spanish ships set sail. The French, in their stolen *patache* (English patax, a small, deckless sailing ship), managed to stay ahead of their pursuers, and as luck would have it the larger Spanish vessels were overcome by high seas and subsequently abandoned by their crews, who escaped in small rowboats. The corsairs returned to the abandoned ships, set fire to two of them, and took the third for themselves. Having found little treasure but causing some damage, they disappeared, presumably to Europe, through the Florida Strait.

In 1537 French corsairs harried Spanish shipping and settlements once again, including the growing Tierra Firme—or mainland South American ports of Cartagena and Nombre de Dios (Panama), Havana, and Santo Domingo, port of the island of Hispaniola (which was blockaded). Elsewhere on Hispaniola the small settlement of La Yaguana was burned, the first in a long series of attacks that proved so damaging that the site was eventually abandoned. Contemporary Spanish observers, such as the historian and castle-keeper of Santo Domingo, Gonzalo Fernández de Oviedo, recommended a plan of fortification and active resistance to the Emperor Charles V. The king, busy with numerous Old World political struggles, chose not to fund those of the New. As noted in the Mediterranean case, a generally static defense policy, which the Spanish would follow for over a century in both the Caribbean and the Pacific, was only logical under the circumstances. Spanish settlements in the vastness of the Antilles and American continents were far too scattered and too thinly populated, and the corsair threat still too mercurial, to justify expensive fortifications, a navy, or standing armies. Outside of the key provisioning ports of Santo Domingo, Havana, San Juan de Puerto Rico, Cartagena, San Juan de Ulúa (Mexico), and a few others, the merchants and settlers of Spain's American empire were on their own.

Settlers did not readily give up their livelihoods to the pirates, however, and at times they developed unusual local defense plans. In the following passage, a French corsair landing at Cubagua Island (c. late 1530s) is described by a Milanese traveler, Girolamo Benzoni, in his *Historia del Mondo Nuovo* (1565):

> [O]ne of the [French corsair] ships arrived at Cubagua during the time when pearl fishing flourished; the Spaniards, on discovering them, took two vessels from the place and put fifty Indians in them with bows and arrows [and] sent them out to the ship after making them believe that

the occupants were sodomites, and that if they did not try to kill them they would land, capturing many [Indians] and making them serve them as women. Convinced, the Indians approached the ship, whose occupants contemplated these nude, new people [*gente nueva, desnuda*], perhaps thinking they had come to view them or to trade some pearls; but, while they were close by, the Indians began to shoot their arrows and wounded several. The French, who evidently had better news of the pearls fished from those seas than of the poisonous herbs used by the natives of that land, upon feeling themselves wounded and seeing that those arrows were deadly, without delay they hoisted sail and left. And from what I understand, not one more ship of theirs has come near that island; in this manner and with this ruse the Spaniards, formerly full of fear, liberated themselves from the French.[9]

Benzoni's account of these events at Cubagua may have been embellished, but it demonstrates how the actions of the French corsairs in the Caribbean, and settlers' reactions to them, were already a serious matter (and in the process of becoming legend) by the middle of the sixteenth century. It also demonstrates the early participation of Native Americans in piratical struggles.[10]

A brief peace with France from 1538 to 1542 was quickly reversed and French raiders, possibly aided by a renegade Spanish subject, returned to capture Cartagena de Indias in 1544. The renegade, according to Benzoni, was a sailor who had been publicly whipped in Cartagena some years earlier and had returned from Europe with French allies to seek revenge. Always fond of a good story, Benzoni claims the wronged mariner located the judge who had ordered his punishment and stabbed him to death.[11] Between booty and Barbary-style ransoms the raid yielded 150,000 ducats' worth of gold. In the same year the corsairs failed to take Santiago de Cuba, however, at the time a larger and more important settlement than Havana. The Cuban repulse was led by a native of Seville named Diego Pérez, and, like pirate fighters throughout the Spanish Indies from this time on, Pérez appealed for recognition from the crown.[12] As these two cases demonstrate, Spanish subjects could make use of the foreign threat in various ways, most notably as traitors or heroes. Piracy, like war, was generally a negative phenomenon for its victims, but in lieu of formal navies or coast guards, the distribution of titles and other honors motivated crown subjects of all sorts to fight valiantly. Military titles were less accessible for low-born individuals like the abused mariner, but political rewards would become the principal fringe benefit of the two-and-a-half-century war on piracy in the Americas. More in the spirit of the hero Diego Pérez than the whipped sailor of Cartagena, Spanish settlers repulsed a new French attack in October of 1544. This engagement, near the town of Santa María de los Remedios, a pearling post on the Tierra Firme coast near Cabo de la Vela (northeastern Colombia), was one of several successful local responses. As Paul Hoffman has demonstrated, the corsairs attempted some twenty-two land raids in the Indies between 1535 and 1547, but only fifteen succeeded. More importantly by far, the Spanish lost some sixty-six ships to French corsairs during these twelve years. Even so, of this total forty-one, or more than half, were taken off the coast of Spain rather than in the Indies.[13] Thus, while clearly a growing menace in American waters, piracy and privateering in the first half of the sixteenth century remained most damaging in the Atlantic Triangle and Mediterranean.

In spite of the growing danger, Spain's merchants and officials responded with half-hearted and ad hoc measures. Mandates to travel in convoys were not always followed, and certainly not enforced, and the order to arm all merchant ships was practically disregarded. Just the same, frightened merchants demanded armed protection from the crown, and occasional armed escorts, such as those headed by Blasco Núñez Vela and Martín Alonso de los Ríos, were provided. However, merchant pressure drove the avería tax, which financed these escorts, downward from 6 to 2.5 percent by the mid-sixteenth century. Thus, though Spain was engaged in a damaging war with France throughout the 1540s and 1550s, no one, least of all the merchants of the newly formed Seville Merchant Guild (or Consulado, est. 1543), wanted to foot the bill. A second official peace lasted from 1544 to 1552, but evidence suggests the corsairs acted more often as pirates than

FIGURE 1.2 French Corsairs Raiding a Spanish Settlement

Source: Theodor de Bry, *Historia.America* VI (courtesy of the Mariners' Museum, Newport News, VA).

as privateers. Members of the Audiencia of Santo Domingo, the Spanish circuit court in the Caribbean, observed in the truce year of 1549: "Although there is peace [the French] do not stop such robberies so long as such rich prizes are on offer at such small risk."[14] In that year the corsairs cruised for stray Spanish ships off the islands of San Juan, Mona, and Saona, near Puerto Rico, then turned their attentions to the south coast of Hispaniola. Other ships were taken off Cabo de la Vela, Santa Marta, and Cartagena. Next came raids on the towns of Havana, San Germán in western Puerto Rico, and La Yaguana on Hispaniola. Corsairs also harassed pearlers at Cubagua Island. Citizens of Santo Domingo organized a small punitive force, a kind of seaborne militia of the sort typical of anti-pirate raids into the eighteenth century, but to little effect. The corsair ships, being unpredictable moving targets manned by experienced seamen, would always have the upper hand in such encounters.

In 1552 official hostilities between France and Spain were resumed, and as one historian has described it, "the Caribbean became for the first time a significant theater of international warfare."[15] Indeed, it was for the first time that French squadrons, with royal warships among them, appeared in the Spanish Caribbean.

FIGURE 1.3 French Raiders Attacked by Native Americans off Margarita Island

Source: Theodor de Bry, *HistoriaAmericae VI* (courtesy of the Mariners' Museum, Newport News, VA).

As might be expected, these fleets began their activities in the Atlantic Triangle, where François Le Clerc, alias "Jambe de Bois" (literally "Leg of Wood," or "Peg-Leg") raided Puerto Santo on the Portuguese island of Madeira in 1552. le Clerc, the first known peg-legged pirate of the early modern era, was at this time officially sanctioned, and hence a privateer. He and his squadron cruised the waters around the port of Cádiz and the mouth of the Guadalquivir River in southern Spain before sailing for the Canaries and Azores. Here the French pursued the West Indies treasure fleets for a time, without success, before sailing westward to seek booty in the Caribbean. It was in these seas that they caused the Spanish to regret their passive defense strategy.

Thus, it was during this period of heightened alert and genuine warfare that French corsair captains such as Jambe de Bois and Jacques de Sores carried out their boldest and most punishing raids in the Spanish West Indies. Squadrons of small but quick-sailing ships, among them a number of rowable and hence maneuverable pinnaces, descended on the small islands of Mona and Saona, and then on Puerto Rico and the Hispaniola port towns of La Yaguana and Monte Christi. In 1554 le Clerc and his followers nearly razed Santiago de Cuba, and Sores did the same to Havana after capturing the town in 1555. The Havana raid was no mere pirate sortie, but rather a full-scale military assault. Sores landed some 200 trained and well-armed men, a sight not seen before in the Spanish Caribbean, and thus one for which the defenders of the city and its rudimentary castle (El Morro) were unprepared.[16] The Spanish settlers and their slaves were also unprepared for the seemingly fundamentalist behavior of the Protestant Sores; he was a Huguenot from Normandy and hence no friend of Catholic Spain and its inquisitors. After some intrigues and apparent misunderstandings with the local governor, Sores proceeded to murder a number of captives, many of them African slaves and hence innocent bystanders in the whole business. He and his men then set fire to the town and whatever vessels were left anchored in the harbor and made off with a small amount of treasure extorted from hapless citizens. In this manner, the French corsair captains Sores and Le Clerc unwittingly set the standard for pirate cruelties in the Americas; from the 1550s onward Spanish subjects could expect to be tortured, murdered, and extorted at random by foreign raiders from the sea.

The Spanish quickly discovered that their cheapest means of defense against such depredations was to abandon vulnerable coastal settlements until the marauders had had their fill. No official "scorched-earth" policy appeared until the first decade of the seventeenth century, but in the interim the uneasy settlers of the Spanish Caribbean could do little but petition the Council of the Indies, Spain's colonial oversight committee, for aid. Building forts and arming fleets, as the war-weary crown well knew, were enormously expensive endeavors—they were to be avoided in all but the most desperate situations. It seems that compared with the loss of Milan or the Netherlands, among other European problems, the defense of the Indies did not figure.

FIGURE 1.4 A Sailor's Revenge in Cartagena, 1544

Source: Theodor de Bry, *HistoriaAmericae VI* (courtesy of the Mariners' Museum, Newport News, VA).

In this regard it is important to keep in mind the scale of Spanish settlement in the sixteenth-century Caribbean. Most of the towns that the early French corsairs raided were just that, towns, often with fewer than 500 permanent residents. Though they would grow significantly in subsequent years, the "cities" of Havana, Santo Domingo, San Juan, and Cartagena were little more than hamlets in the mid-sixteenth century; by 1550 the bulk of Spain's American subject population was already concentrated in the protected interiors of Mexico and Peru. Even as late as 1570, Santo Domingo, seat of the *audiencia*, was said to have no more than 500 *vecinos*, or Spanish heads of household. All of Puerto Rico was home to only 200 or 300 vecinos. Havana was said to have had only sixty households in 1570, and all of Cuba only 322 vecinos around 1550. Cartagena, though growing rapidly, counted only about 300 Spanish vecinos in 1570.[17] These population estimates for Spanish settlers do not reflect totals, as household heads might preside over four or five family members, and African slaves and Native American wards made up the majority population of virtually every settlement. Still, rapid declines in the indigenous population in the Caribbean preceded the French corsairs, and the raiders encountered a region already approaching a black majority in several places. Benzoni noted as early as the 1540s that on some islands fortified villages of *cimarrones*, or runaway African slaves, were already a major security concern.[18] Though Native Americans, slaves, and free persons of color helped settlers more often than corsairs, they also constituted a volatile sector in the eyes of Spanish officials.

In the later 1550s, French corsairs returned to the still more weakly defended ports of Tierra Firme and neighboring islands, sacking the pearling settlements, or *rancherías*, of Margarita and Cubagua (apparently native arrows were no longer sufficient defense), before sailing west to Riohacha, Santa Marta, and Cartagena. In a midnight attack on Santa Marta in April 1555 the iconoclastic Sores allegedly ordered soldiers to hack the arms off a statue of the Virgin Mary with halberds, saying that if she were the mother of God she ought to be able to defend herself.[19] The corsairs were not content with sacking these by-now common targets, and launched an expedition to cruise the Gulf of Honduras and other unfamiliar coasts. One squadron left the Basque ports of Bayonne and St. Jean de Luz in 1558 and attacked the Honduran mining outlet of Puerto Caballos. Direct losses to these French raiders prior to the Treaty of Cateau-Cambrésis in the following year were not huge, at least in terms of stolen bullion, but it was clear to the Spanish by now that in spite of prominent Huguenot participation their northern neighbor was motivated more by treasure envy than religious fundamentalism. The predators were unlikely to disappear no matter what diplomats decided, and indeed, even as the terms of peace were being negotiated, the French were planning a series of raids on Nombre de Dios, Santo Domingo, and Puerto Rico. Ignoring the official cessation of hostilities "beyond the line," the corsair–privateers planned to cap this bold post-war offensive with a seizure of the New Spain treasure fleet between Veracruz and Havana. In the end, no such plan was carried out, but the threat of state-sanctioned piracy on this scale forced the Spanish under Philip II (1556–98) to reconfigure defenses.

The French Corsair Threat in Brazil

Spain and its colonies were not the only victims of French aggression. As we have already seen, French corsairs were a longstanding problem for the Portuguese throughout the Atlantic, but particularly in Brazil. One pretext for plunder was the official French claim to portions of this vast South American region dating to the first years of the sixteenth century. As early as 1503, as noted above, French merchants bartered axes, combs, and other items with native Tupi-speakers for dyewood along Brazil's enormous coast, and some traders also engaged in piracy when the opportunity arose. The pattern of mixed trade and plunder continued in cycles across two centuries.

Assigning blame in such a vast and lawless place could be complicated. The German captive and gunner Hans Staden, who for a time was employed by

Portuguese shippers, described a violent encounter with a French vessel in 1547 off the coast of Paraíba, in northeastern Brazil, in his 1557 memoir:

> We sailed for . . . Potiguaras . . . where we meant to load a cargo of brazil wood and to raid the natives for more provisions. As we arrived there, we found a ship from France that was loading wood, and we attacked it, hoping to capture it. However, they destroyed our mainmast with one shot and sailed away; several on our ship were killed or wounded.[20]

Clearly, acts of piracy could go both, or even three, ways. The Portuguese routinely called the French "pirates" even as they attacked them, and both groups of European interlopers had few scruples when it came to robbing native Brazilians "at or by descent from the sea," the standard definition of piracy. Staden, who was later captured much farther south by native Brazilians in canoes, goes on to describe an attack by his Portuguese vessel on a French "pirate ship" near the Azores. His blithe summary consists of one sentence: "The ship contained lots of wine and bread, which refreshed us."[21]

The cherished dream of an "Antarctic France" was never realized, in part due to the self-inflicted Wars of Religion. The Portuguese did not sit by, however. From Lisbon and Salvador they sent three expeditions to destroy the incipient colony established by the chevalier de Villegagnon in Guanabara Bay. Antarctic France was dismantled between 1560 and 1567, giving rise to the future metropolis of Rio de Janeiro. Some historians have questioned the Portuguese claim that the French intended to use their Brazilian colony as a base for piracy, but evidence suggests they did so from the start, and without regard for confessional or even national differences.

French Protestant missionary Jean de Léry captured the carefree corsairing spirit of the age in describing his passage to Brazil in 1556, the year after Villegagnon established his base on an island that still bears his name in Guanabara Bay. Léry narrates an early encounter with unarmed English merchant vessels near the coast of Spain that he says were "nearly pillaged" by the crew of his well-armed ship. It is an ambiguous passage, but Léry follows with this pithy observation:

> I must say . . . that I have seen practiced on the sea what is also done most often on land: that is, he who has weapons in his fist, and who is strongest, carries the day, and imposes the law on his companion. The way it goes is that these mariner gentlemen, striking sail, and meeting with the poor merchant ships, usually claim that they have been unable to approach any land or port because of tempests and calms, and that they are consequently short of supplies, for which they are willing to pay. But if, under this pretext, they can set foot on board their neighbor's ship, you need hardly ask whether, as an alternative to scuttling their vessel, they relieve it of whatever takes their

fancy. And if one protests (as in fact we always did) that no order has been given to pillage indiscriminately, friends as well as enemies, they give you the common cant of our land soldiers, who in such cases offer as sole reason that it's war and custom, and that you have to get used to it.[22]

In subsequent pages Léry describes in detail how his vessel's crew seized and pillaged several unarmed Spanish and Portuguese vessels near the Canary Islands, mostly relieving them of such ordinary "treasures" as fish, salt, and sailcloth, before continuing across the Atlantic to Brazil. One stout vessel was also taken, but most were destroyed for spite. According to the Protestant preacher, piracy was the prerogative of the strong, and wanton acts of cruelty were to be expected by anyone who dared to set sail.

Contraband Trade and the Treaty of Cateau-Cambrésis

Official war with France was halted by the Treaty of Cateau-Cambrésis in 1559, but not all of France's subjects were of one mind. As we have just seen, the Huguenots, with the backing of the French Admiral Coligny, among others, set out to develop Franco-American colonies right in the midst of territories claimed by Spain and Portugal. Jean Ribault proposed at least one settlement along the east coast of what the Spanish called La Florida (including present-day Georgia and South Carolina), and by 1563 several struggling outposts had been planted. The choice of Florida for a settlement was no accident, as Spanish treasure galleons now almost universally passed through the narrow Florida Strait on their way to Spain from Havana. Philip II could not suffer such a menacing foreign presence to take root so close to his lifeline, and by 1565 he agreed to support a punitive expedition headed by the renowned captain-general of the Spanish *Armada de la carrera*, or Indies Squadron, Pedro Menéndez de Avilés. Well-armed and tightly organized, Menéndez's marines quickly routed the French, killing Ribault and his followers and destroying all remnants of the Huguenot colonies within a month of landing.

Huguenot settlements in the vicinity of Rio de Janeiro, Brazil, met with similar reactions from the Portuguese in the 1560s, and for the time being the Iberian kingdoms clung to and enforced the terms of Tordesillas. Ribault, like his compatriots in Brazil, was no corsair, to be sure, but his projects were viewed by the Spanish (quite realistically, in fact) as future bases for French raids on Spanish shipping and settlements. The Florida campaign was thus seen as little more than the nipping of a pirate base in the bud. As with all defense efforts in the Americas, however, the Spanish defense of Florida was a mixed blessing. Though strategically necessary, in the long term it would become an expensive liability. The region offered little in the way of minerals or agriculture and was home to few potential Indian tributaries. Since it was immediately clear that Spanish Florida could not support itself, the garrison at St. Augustine was kept small, an absolute dependency paid for once again by reluctant merchants and colonists living elsewhere. There seemed to be no alternative; by the early 1560s the threat of French piracy in Spanish American waters had reached crisis proportions, and the Spanish were forced to respond with expensive, long-term defense measures for the first time.

Iberian removal of the Huguenot bases of Florida and Brazil did not cause French corsairs to disappear from the West Indies. Instead, the French turned to strong-armed contraband trading, breaking into Spain's (and to a lesser extent Portugal's) tightly held colonial markets at every opportunity. These smugglers brought slaves, Rouen cloth, lace, and other goods to remote Spanish colonies in the Caribbean, and they were often welcomed by monopoly-weary colonists. After the punitive raids of Menéndez, however, this was not always so; certainly no one wanted to be denounced as a traitor for dealing with the French. One post-treaty trade incident from 1568, when the English were already active in the Caribbean, concerned a certain Captain Borgoing of le Havre. Borgoing, apparently an experienced *rescatador*, or contraband trader, who even carried a license on this journey, put in at Margarita Island (north of Venezuela) to truck for pearls. A Spanish vecino, or urban householder, named Carillo, said to have ordinarily engaged in such trade, invited the French ashore with guarantees of safety for their persons, merchandise, and ships. Apparently out of pure capriciousness, but possibly due to some particular insult, Carillo and the Margarita settlers attacked the French "corsairs" some ten or twelve days later, killing sixteen or seventeen of them and stringing up their bodies along the coast for show. The incident, which ended in the total despoiling of the French visitors, was recorded by Spanish observers rather than French survivors, and reveals the two-sided nature of risk in smuggling. Just as foreign contrabandists could easily shift from peaceful, if tense, trade to violence and robbery, so also could the colonist-consumers, if the odds favored them.[23]

More such strong-armed trading was to follow, as will be seen in the next chapter, but it was increasingly in the hands of English rather than French adventurers. Elizabethan smugglers such as John Hawkins and Francis Drake followed in the wake of the French corsairs, sometimes joining their remnant bands, and they adapted handily to Spain's new defense policies under Philip II. For purposes of future reference, the main patterns established during the Berber and French corsair periods may be summarized as follows: (1) as active war on the North African coast or Maghrib faded into a hostage-taking guerrilla ("little war"), Spain was forced to implement more and more costly defense measures against French corsairs and colonists in the West Indies—they raised taxes, outfitted naval squadrons, and fortified new garrisons; (2) the difference between piracy and privateering remained vague, but the use of local governors' commissions, as in the case of Oruç Barbarossa and the bey of Tunis, gave sea-robbers a sense of extra-territorial legitimacy in the absence of a monarch's decree; and (3) Spanish elites in the thinly populated Caribbean discovered to their chagrin that defense against pirates was in their hands, but they turned this apparent disadvantage around by participating in punitive raids in exchange for military promotion and other entitlements—the pirate threat, they discovered, could be a source of local power. All three of these early-established patterns would reappear, though in somewhat changed form, throughout the early modern period of American piracy.

marco: common measure for silver bars based on the mark of Cologne and equivalent to c. 1/2 lb. (230 g). Fineness was expressed as a fraction of 2,400 (e.g., 2,350/2,400 = 0.98 fine, an extension of the gold karat fraction of $x/24$).

Note: Relative values of gold and silver changed markedly over the course of the early modern period due to inflation, fears of debasement, relative scarcity (silver, for example, became less scarce relative to gold, and thus less valuable), and so on. Cacao beans, as some pirates noted, continued to be used as currency in parts of New Spain and Central America during our period—in the later sixteenth century fifty cacao beans equaled roughly one real. Pearl and gemstone values, like those for jewelry and other worked objects, were subjective and thus could not be easily reduced to weight measures. For further discussion see Pierre Vilar, *A History of Gold and Money, 1450–1820*, trans. J. White (London: Verso, 1991 [1960]), and Clarence H. Haring, "American Gold and Silver Production in the First Half of the Sixteenth Century," *Quarterly Journal of Economics* 29 (May 1915): 433–79.

Notes

1 Ellen G. Friedman, *Spanish Captives in North Africa in the Early Modern Age* (Madison: University of Wisconsin Press, 1983), xix–xxiii. Regarding the importance of exiles (xix): "Their presence [in North Africa] not only strengthened the ideological prop for corsairing, but also provided for the corsairs a group of embittered exiles who had an intimate knowledge of Spanish coastal regions and who could frequently pass as Spaniards."

2 Philip Gosse, *The History of Piracy* (London: Longman, Green, 1932), 15.

3 Ibid., 21. See also Jacques Heers, *The Barbary Corsairs: Warfare in the Mediterranean, 1480–1580* (London: Stackpole, 2003).

4 On the Knights' corsairing exploits, see historian Molly Greene's *Catholic Pirates and Greek Merchants: A Maritime History of the Mediterranean* (Princeton: Princeton University Press, 2010), and also maritime archaeologist Ayse Devrim Atauz's *Eight Thousand Years of Maltese Maritime History: Trade, Piracy, and Naval Warfare in the Central Mediterranean* (Gainesville: University Press of Florida, 2008).

5 Miguel de Cervantes, "The Captive's Tale Continued," in *Don Quixote*, trans. J.M. Cohen (New York: Penguin Classics, 1950), 355. For a provocative quantitative assessment of the larger phenomenon, see Robert C. Davis, *Christian Slaves, Muslim Masters: White Slavery in the Mediterranean, the Barbary Coast, and Italy, 1500–1800* (New York: Palgrave Macmillan, 2003).

6 Friedman, *Spanish Captives*, 114–15, notes that New World contributions, or *limosnas*, for redemption of captives in North Africa went from under 30 percent of the total collected in 1648 to over 70 percent in 1667.

7 See Anthony Pagden, ed. and trans., *Hernán Cortés: Letters from Mexico* (New Haven: Yale University Press, 1986), 329–30, fn. 509–10. Anne Pérotin-Dumon, "The Pirate and the Emperor: Power and the Law on the Seas, 1450–1850," in James D. Tracy, ed., *The Political Economy of Merchant Empires: State Power and World Trade, 1350–1750* (Cambridge: Cambridge University Press, 1991), 203, notes that the stained glass windows of the church of Villequier, where Florin was lord, commemorate his feat. For more biographical details on the earliest French corsairs in the Caribbean, see Jean Pierre Moreau, *Pirates: flibuste et piraterie dans la Caraïbe et les mers du sud, 1522–1725* (Paris: Tallandier, 2006).

8 H.B. Johnson, "Portuguese Settlement, 1500–1580," in Leslie Bethell, ed., *Colonial Brazil* (Cambridge: Cambridge University Press, 1987), 12.

9 Girolamo Benzoni, *La Historia del Nuevo Mundo* (Caracas: Academia Nacional de la Historia, 1967 [orig. published as *Historia del Mondo Nuovo*, 1565]), 126 (my translation).

10 Native corsairing overlapped with other criminal charges in these years; see Kris Lane, "Punishing the Sea Wolf: Corsairs and Cannibals in the Early Modern Caribbean," *New West India Guide* 77:3-4 (2003): 201–20.

11 Benzoni, *Historia del Nuevo Mundo*, 125.

12 Clarence H. Haring, *The Buccaneers in the West Indies in the XVII Century* (London: Methuen, 1910), 44.

13 Paul Hoffman, *The Spanish Crown and the Defense of the Caribbean, 1535–1585: Precedent, Patrimonialism, and Royal Parsimony* (Baton Rouge: Louisiana State University Press, 1980), 25.

14 Quoted in Kenneth Andrews, *The Spanish Caribbean: Trade and Plunder, 1530–1630* (New Haven: Yale University Press, 1978), 82.

15 Ibid.

16 Alejandro de la Fuente, *Havana and the Atlantic in the Sixteenth Century* (Chapel Hill: University of North Carolina Press, 2008), 1–2, 70–80.

17 Andrews, *Spanish Caribbean*, 14–21. Cuba was said to have counted only 1,200 vecinos by 1630.

18 Benzoni, *Historia*, 113–15; Benzoni notes an estimate of 7,000 cimarrones on Hispaniola alone (115).

19 See the original documents on this attack in Colombia's Archivo General de la Nación, Bogotá, Section Historia Civil 22:19. Begging crown officials for forts, a local official claimed also that Sores's men sought alliances with neighboring Tairona Indians.

20 Hans Staden. *Hans Staden's True Story: An Account of Cannibal Captivity in Brazil.* 1557. Neil L. Whitehead and Michael Harbsmeier, eds. and trans. (Durham: Duke University Press, 2008), 29.

21 Ibid., 30.

22 Jean de Léry. *History of a Voyage to the Land of Brazil.* 1578. Janet Whatley, ed. and trans. (Berkeley: University of California Press, 1990), 9.

23 Andrews, *Spanish Caribbean*, 79.

2

SMUGGLERS, PIRATES, AND PRIVATEERS

The Elizabethans

In the wake of Henry VIII's rejection of Catholic authority, and ultimately Catholicism itself, England joined the list of potential Protestant enemies of Spain in 1534. The confessional issue would not be resolved for another twenty-five years, however, and England was not yet in a league with Spain in the mid-sixteenth century; to test Castilian power directly would have been suicidal. Still, a group of intrepid merchant families living in southwestern England began to engage in long-distance trade of the kind already much practiced by the French corsairs and smugglers. In some cases these merchant families, the most famous being the Hawkinses of Plymouth, would ally with French interlopers in their efforts to break into Iberian trade monopolies. These early English smugglers, who would soon become pirates and privateers, were most active during the reign of the fiercely Protestant Elizabeth I (1558–1603), and are thus referred to as the Elizabethan corsairs. In the interest of clarity, their activities in the Americas may be classified as follows: (1) contraband slave trading from 1558 to 1568; (2) piracy from 1568 to 1585; and (3) privateering from 1585 to 1603. The Elizabethans included John Hawkins, Francis Drake, John Oxenham, and Thomas Cavendish, and their exploits in Spanish American waters were generally better documented than those of their French predecessors. A selective narrative of their sea raiding and trading activities follows.

West Country Slave Traders

In spite of centuries of whitewash and legendizing, Francis Drake and the Hawkinses first entered the Caribbean as slave traders. How this unsavory business developed, along with its largely unpredicted consequences, is a story worth recounting. Still, we must not forget that the Portuguese had been capturing sub-Saharan Africans and transporting them to the European and East Atlantic Island markets for over a century by the time Elizabeth I acceded to the throne of England. With the development of sugar and gold mining operations in the Caribbean, first staffed by indigenous laborers but soon demanding new inputs from abroad, the Portuguese began to trade slaves to their Spanish neighbors. This was legally accomplished only through the merchant guild of Seville (the Consulado), but some wily traders skipped this long and expensive detour and began to trade directly with the colonists of Hispaniola, Cuba, Puerto Rico, and Tierra Firme. The traffic in human beings, whether taken by force or barter from the African coast, was as profitable as it was barbaric—only the gold trade yielded higher returns. And while Spanish moralists such as Bartolomé de las Casas argued vehemently and effectively against the enslavement of Native Americans in the early sixteenth century, no European effectively questioned the morality of enslaving Africans, branding them like cattle, and transporting them to plantations and mines.

Such was the early modern spirit of enterprise, and the English would not be left out of any such lucrative trade. Little wonder then that some pirates, when later forced to testify, pointed out the striking similarities (though at a different scale) between their own occupation and that of the merchant empires that they felt persecuted them. Outrage, they argued, was a matter of perspective. To return to the Elizabethans, recall that Portuguese slavers controlled a number of trading forts, called *feitorias*, from the Guinea Coast south to Angola, around the Cape to Mozambique and other points in the Indian Ocean. Intrigued by the possibility of rupturing this Portuguese monopoly, the Englishman John Hawkins, scion of a prominent West Country merchant family, set sail from Plymouth in October of 1562 with three small vessels. His aim was to sail to the Canary Islands, meet a business associate by the name of Pedro de Ponte who had contacts in Hispaniola, pick up a Spanish pilot familiar with the Indies Route, and then make his way to the West African coast to raid, rather than trade, for slaves. Hawkins later mentioned the slaving raid, albeit vaguely, suggesting that he and his men had attacked African settlements on the coast. In reality, they had stolen some 300 slaves already in Portuguese custody off Sierra Leone and taken them to sell illegally along the north coast of Hispaniola. The whole business outraged both Portuguese and Spanish officials, but as with French smuggling, they were all but powerless to stop it.

John Hawkins was more smuggler than pirate at this stage. He wanted a piece of the Indies trade, a means of bypassing the Seville and Lisbon monopolists and selling, presumably in England, his cargoes of Antillean hides, sugar, ginger, and pearls. However, the trade goods gathered on these early voyages were not sent to England, or even France, but rather to Spain and Portugal. As a part of his complex ruse, Hawkins had arranged for an English factor in Seville, one Hugh Tipton, to receive goods from one of the smugglers' ships in order to legalize their entry. Spanish customs officials took the cargo instead. Another of Hawkins's ships was searched at Lisbon and its contents likewise confiscated. This arrangement seems rather unusual and highly risky—apparently Hawkins thought, as Kenneth Andrews has argued, that he could slip by Spanish customs and beat the Consulado at its own game. In any case, like Hawkins and his shady associates, the settlers of Hispaniola and other parts of the Caribbean knew well the illegality of such commerce, but they themselves were victims of monopoly practices. Lessons learned, Hawkins, the *rescatadores* (as the outlaw Spanish factors were called), and the isolated colonists tried again.

John Hawkins's second voyage, which set sail in early 1564, was larger and better organized than the first. Relations between Spain and England had deteriorated, however, and confessional tensions were on the rise. English pirates were actively harassing Spanish shipping in the North Atlantic, and Spain's ambassador loudly protested the outfitting of any new West Indies voyage. A number of high-ranking English individuals, including both courtiers and London merchants, invested nonetheless, and the queen donated a cumbersome, carrack-type ship of 700 tons, the *Jesus of Lübeck*. Hawkins followed his old plan, contacting the Canary Island-based rescatador Pedro de Ponte, raiding the West African coast, this time for some 400 African captives, then sailing to the Caribbean to seek his profit. At the pearling island of Margarita the contrabandists were refused license to trade. Their subsequent reception at the Tierra Firme settlement of Burburata (on the east coast of Golfo Triste, Venezuela) was not much warmer. The citizens of this rather remote port, a popular stop for French corsairs and smugglers in the 1550s, sent for approval from the governor at Coro, holding Hawkins impatiently at bay for some ten days. When the governor arrived, a trade license was granted, but under conditions unappealing to the English. A tax of 7.5 percent (the normal customs duty, or *almojarifazgo*) on all merchandise was to be topped by a levy of thirty ducats per slave. Since slaves were the principal items of trade, totaling 156 individuals, Hawkins not only balked at the terms but also put ashore 100 armed men to force the elimination of this tax. The resulting slave sale yielded some 11,055 *pesos de oro* (see Box 1, in Chapter 1), representing an average price of seventy-one pesos per slave. The remainder of the merchandise, less than 1,500 pesos worth, consisted primarily of Rouen and Dutch linens.[1]

Hawkins then proceeded westward to Riohacha to sell the remaining slaves and other goods to the pearling operators of the region. Again the Spanish feared trading without permission, particularly in light of an order sent from Santo Domingo that expressly forbade any commerce with the interloper. Again Hawkins threatened to use force and thus unloaded his cargo on the semi-willing colonists. There may have been some corruption and collusion on the part of the local treasury official, Miguel de Castellanos, but the threat of force at Riohacha and Burburata is more illustrative of the terms of such trading ventures in the Elizabethan era. As with the Portuguese in Africa, and more especially Asia, trade across cultures was not generally an amicable affair; there were no international courts in which to enforce contracts, and no laws among smugglers other than those of supply and demand. Sometimes demand had to be encouraged, and prices were agreed upon under duress from the stronger party. Might made prices "right," and Hawkins left Riohacha's citizens happy that their town had not been looted and razed. Hawkins's second and more successful American voyage ended with an uneventful visit to the soon-to-be-destroyed French settlement of Fort Caroline, on the east coast of Florida.

Despite continued Spanish diplomatic pressure, John Hawkins sponsored a third voyage, now captained by a stand-in, John Lovell. Lovell set out from Plymouth in 1566 and followed Hawkins's general pattern, picking up slaves along the Guinea Coast and putting in first at Margarita Island in the Caribbean. Here Lovell joined a French slaver and smuggler, Jean Bontemps, and the two tried in vain to repeat forced sales at Burburata and Riohacha. In both instances hostages were taken as a means of enforcing the terms of trade, but to little effect; apparently the market for slaves in these tiny settlements was saturated. In any case, the same treasury official at Riohacha, Miguel de Castellanos, seems to have gotten the better of Lovell and his companions in an exchange of ninety-two African captives. These poor individuals, who were said to be infirm—no doubt from the deprivations of the Middle Passage—were treated by both sides as mere bargaining chips. As was normal in Spanish correspondence, the captive Africans were referred to as *piezas de negros*, black units of capital.

San Juan de Ulúa and Aftermath

John Hawkins's third slaving voyage, the fourth of the series including the Lovell venture, was a large gamble and it lost large. Like the others, this joint-stock operation began with the outfitting of ships, namely the *Minion*, *William & John*, *Swallow*, *Judith*, *Angel*, and the lumbering veteran *Jesus of Lübeck*, totaling over 1,300 tons capacity. Spanish diplomats again protested the business loudly, but no one listened, least of all Hawkins, who claimed he was the personal object of Spanish "hate."[2] A brief but violent encounter with some of Philip II's ships putting in at Plymouth from Flanders in August of 1567 set the tone for the voyage. Here Hawkins insulted the unsuspecting visitors with noise and gunfire, but the Spanish would have their revenge soon enough. Hawkins set sail, putting in at the Canaries and presumably arranging some business with his old rescatador contacts. The ships then made their way to the West African coast between Cape Verde and Sierra Leone, where the crewmembers stole a number of Africans from their Portuguese captors before involving themselves in some sort of dispute on land. Hawkins and his crew apparently arranged to fight on behalf of one coastal African group against another, offering armed assistance in exchange for whatever prisoners were taken. This engagement lasted three months and yielded approximately 470 slaves, probably only one-half to two-thirds of whom survived a long, fifty-two-day trip to the Caribbean.

Once in American waters, Hawkins followed a predictable pattern, stopping first at Margarita, where he was coolly received. His force was large enough to demand some measure of respect and goods were exchanged, but there was apparently no joy on either side. The next stop was Burburata, and here the English discovered that their old allies in government had been removed for welcoming them on previous visits. As a result of this change of affairs no licenses were granted, but again, probably due to the imposing force that Hawkins commanded (not to mention his much-desired cargo of human laborers), the colonists gave in. The past also came back to haunt the English at Riohacha, where the now-exasperated treasurer, Castellanos, met them with zealous refusals. Hawkins had sent a young captain, a relative named Francis Drake, with the *Judith* and *Angel* to begin bargaining with the townsfolk of Riohacha while taking on food and water at Curaçao. The Spanish immediately fired on Drake's ships, and he replied in kind, his gunners managing to blast the governor's own house to bits. In the midst of this hostility a packet-boat from Santo Domingo arrived and was immediately driven ashore by the English in a hail of arquebus fire. Drake then landed some of his men and a few large guns and drove the terrified citizens of the town into the hills. The English lost only one man in this engagement, a Thomas Surgeon (probably his occupation); Spanish casualties are not known. This violent incident at Riohacha, which was followed by robbery and hostage-taking, set the terms of trade and most of Drake's African cargo was successfully bartered for pearls and local produce.

Farther west along the Tierra Firme coast, Santa Marta's citizens were similarly bullied, though with less direct violence, and more slaves were unladed. Cartagena de Indias, the next stop, was a sore disappointment. Here Hawkins was either out of his league or badly misinformed. Cartagena was the main port of New Granada and the usual stop for licensed Spanish and Portuguese slavers; its merchant community was in no need of Hawkins's goods and the city was too well protected to be pressured by smugglers. Having little merchandise and few slaves left to trade anyway (one witness later claimed that only forty slaves remained unsold), Hawkins opted to set sail for England.[3] It was now late July and hurricane season was at hand. In the Florida Strait Hawkins's fleet ran into bad weather, though not probably a genuine hurricane (which would have genuinely destroyed them), and confusion ensued. The *William & John* became separated from the other five ships and limped home to England. The giant *Jesus*, technically the queen's vessel, was badly damaged. In light of this accident, and finding themselves drifting in the Gulf of Mexico, Hawkins and his followers decided to attempt a landing at Veracruz, principal port of New Spain, for repairs. The sentinels of the fort of San Juan de Ulúa, a small island opposite Veracruz, allowed the ships to dock, mistaking them for the expected fleet from Spain. A routine exchange of hostages took place (a normal precaution with unexpected, storm-driven foreign ships during this period) and the English were allowed to refit their vessels.

As luck would have it, the Spanish fleet arrived the very next day and its commander, don Martín Enríquez, newly appointed viceroy of New Spain, was not amused. More hostages were exchanged, and Hawkins thought for a time that

FIGURE 2.1 The *Jesus of Lübeck*

Source: From a sixteenth-century manuscript, in J.S. Corbett, *Drake and the Tudor Navy*, London: 1898.

he might be allowed peaceful leave. It soon became clear, however, that Enríquez had other plans. Following a sudden arrest of English sailors and some scuffling, a fierce battle broke out and the English managed to sink two Spanish vessels and burn another. The Spanish, meanwhile, made use of their shore battery guns on the island and began hammering away at the already storm-damaged English ships. The *Jesus* was abandoned almost immediately, and only the *Judith*, under Drake, and the *Minion*, under an angry and embarrassed Hawkins, managed to escape. These two ships lost sight of one another almost immediately, barely managing to make their separate returns to England. Drake's voyage was no pleasure cruise, but Hawkins and his men on the *Minion* seem to have had the worse time of it, being forced to abandon some crewmembers on the coast of Mexico and losing many more to disease and injury on board during the trip home. The 1568 Hawkins voyage was an unmitigated disaster, with the loss of three-quarters of its 400-man crew and, along with the *Swallow*, the largest of its ships, the *Jesus of Lübeck*.

Kenneth Andrews has argued convincingly that English interest in the Caribbean slave trade declined in the aftermath of the battle of San Juan de Ulúa not so much as a result of the direct losses incurred in this engagement, but rather because of the low profitability of the Hawkins ventures. The English, unlike their Portuguese and French competitors, had moved too far in the direction of armed, belligerent trade. Thus the costs of outfitting their expeditions, especially after adding such unnecessarily large ships as the *Jesus of Lübeck*, began to eat into gains.[4] Arms were necessary, as evidenced by the engagements with large Portuguese vessels off the Guinea Coast, and English actions in these waters had lasting consequences. Indeed, as a result of continued English marauding in Portuguese-controlled West Africa, including seaway robbery and interloping in the gold and slave trades, Lisbon broke off diplomatic relations with England in 1568. Still, as Andrews suggests, the English might have stayed competitive in the nasty game of slave smuggling longer had they avoided direct confrontation and followed a more stealthy approach. Whatever their reasons, the English did not re-emerge as important Caribbean traders until the next century. In the meantime, they would become important as pirates.

Drake and Elizabethan Piracy

The period following the disaster at San Juan de Ulúa, at least to the turn of the seventeenth century, was one of piracy (to 1585) and privateering (to 1603). As noted earlier, piracy and privateering differed only in that the latter activity was officially sanctioned by a monarch—involving letters of marque and reprisal or similar documents—and was carried out in time of war. Of the fourteen known unsanctioned intrusions into Caribbean waters between 1568 and 1585, none seems to have been outfitted for trade; piracy was their unequivocal purpose. Another notable development was the tendency of English raiders in this period, the best known of them being Francis Drake, to ally themselves with similarly seasoned French corsairs in their attacks on Spanish ships and ports. The French and English were differently motivated, but they shared a sense of outrage. Drake and his compatriots claimed to be motivated by "gentlemanly" revenge, primarily for insults received at San Juan de Ulúa, and John Hawkins even continued to back these missions in hopes of recouping his losses, if not his honor. For their part, many of the remaining French corsairs were motivated by religious or confessional revenge, mostly for the massacres of Huguenots in Florida and Brazil. For a brief period, then, these traditionally opposed nationalities joined forces against a common Catholic foe.

Then again, the pirates' prime motive was plunder, not preaching, and the English–French alliances in the Caribbean were born of the same pragmatism that led Drake to seek the aid of indigenous and runaway African enemies of the Spaniards. Indeed, in the long run it was the *cimarrones*, as the runaway slaves of the Spanish were called, and to a lesser extent indigenous groups like the Cuna Cuna of eastern Panama, who made the greater difference. The period from 1570 to 1574 was particularly active, and some ten pirating expeditions harried Spanish Caribbean ports and ships to an unprecedented extent. French corsairs were engaged in suspicious activities on the north coast of Panama by 1570, and Drake and the English soon followed. The French set the tone for future exploits in the region by capturing two pilots, one Spanish and one of African descent, from the mouth of the Chagres River. The captives, like many hundreds to follow in the next century and a half of piracy, were duly squeezed of all useful "intelligence." Indeed, spying and hostage-taking remained important pirate tactics well into the eighteenth century, and the cimarrones of the Vallano (or Bayano) country of eastern Panama were consummate spies and stealthy masters of ambush and man-trapping in their adopted terrain.

The communities of African runaways in the circum-Caribbean region, and to a lesser extent in spots along the Pacific Coast, would be of great importance to the French and English pirates, particularly since these European interlopers had no bases of their own. Most of the cimarrones lived in ordered settlements—usually surrounded by wood-and-earth stockades, which the Spanish called *palenques*, a term later applied to maroon settlements in general. Having established themselves in parts of Hispaniola, Mexico, Panama, and elsewhere as early as the 1520s, they shared a deep distrust of the Spanish. Partly as a result of the long-standing feud between the Panama cimarrones and their Spanish neighbors, which was often punctuated by mutual, punishing raids, well-armed allies such as Drake and the French corsairs were welcomed. These alliances with non-Spanish Europeans should not be considered as entirely natural but rather the result of a timely exigency. The cimarrones knew all too well the slaving past of the French and English, but they realized that these potential enslavers—armed and angry as they were—could be used effectively against the Spaniards in the short term, a worthwhile compromise. One Vallano maroon settlement was described by a member of the Drake band in 1572 as follows:

> The third day of our journey they brought us to a town of their own, seated near a fair river, on the side of a hill, environed with a dyke of eight foot broad and a thick mud wall of ten foot high, sufficient to stop a sudden surpriser. It had one long and broad street, lying east and west, and two other cross streets of less breadth and length. There were in it some five or six and fifty households, which were kept so clean and sweet that not only the houses, but the very streets, were very pleasant to behold. In this town we saw they lived very civilly and cleanly, for as soon as we came thither they washed themselves in the river, and changed their apparel, which was very fine and fitly made (as also their women do wear) somewhat after the Spanish fashion, though nothing so costly. This town is distant thirty-five leagues from Nombre de Dios and forty-five from Panama. It is plentifully stored with many sorts of beasts and fowl, with plenty of maize and sundry fruits.[5]

Panama's maroon communities were such a threat in the 1570s that Spanish viceregal authorities organized a series of high-profile punitive expeditions to search out and destroy them. Before these raids proved effective, however, as happened in the 1577 Vallano War, the cimarrones aided a number of French and English interlopers. In 1572–73 Drake set out to capture Nombre de Dios, on Panama's north coast, but his force was too small; he left Plymouth with seventy-three men in mid-1572 and only thirty or so survived to see the new year in the tropics. With the help of certain maroons, however, Drake managed to cross much of the isthmus by stealth, finally setting up an ambush near the Casa de Cruces (or Venta Cruz) on the upper Chagres. The first joint English–cimarrón attempt on the treasure-laden mule train, or *regua*, coming north from Panama failed, but other allies were soon to arrive. A French Huguenot corsair and master cartographer by the name of Guillaume le Testu, who happened to be cruising the Caribbean under Italian sponsorship, arrived on the Panama coast in March of 1573. Le Testu joined forces with Drake and the maroons and a second attack on the mule train yielded considerable treasure. The sortie was not without cost for the pirates, however, as le Testu and several other treasure-laden French and Englishmen were captured and killed by the Spanish rearguard. The maroons, according to surviving allies, chose freedom over cumbersome silver bars.

Spanish officials were, as was often the case in other pirate situations, overly concerned. The small size of the 1572–73 Drake mission has been noted, but contemporary rumor had it that Drake, the French, and the maroons had established a large and permanent foothold to the east of Nombre de Dios. These particular *corsarios luteranos*, or "Lutheran corsairs," as the Spanish liked to call them, were hardly capable of maintaining such outposts, even with maroon help. As Andrews has noted, the pirates had almost no official support in Europe: le Testu's old friend Coligny, the most likely supporter of anti-Spanish actions in the Caribbean, was killed in the St. Bartholomew's Eve Massacre of 24 August 1572, and Elizabeth I's court had no interest in financing further Caribbean enterprises after the Hawkins debacle of 1568.[6] The Dutch Sea-Beggars were active in the Atlantic during this period (c. 1570–72) as well, but in spite of their Protestant fervor and animosity toward Philip II, they were far too occupied with home affairs to consider large-scale Caribbean voyages.

True or false, these rumors of war and even full-scale invasion were a great aid to small-time Elizabethan adventurers like John Oxenham, a companion of Drake in the 1572–73 raid. Oxenham was another West Country seaman of middling status, but rather than wait for Drake's great voyage of circumnavigation in 1577, he set out again for Panama from Plymouth in April 1576 with some fifty-seven men in a small frigate. Again allying with the cimarrones of Vallano, Oxenham and his men crossed the Panamanian Isthmus and built a forty-five-foot pinnace in the Gulf of San Miguel. There he began menacing the Spanish in the Pacific, the first enemy European to do so. A lucky hit on an unsuspecting ship coming into the Gulf of Panama yielded 60,000 pesos in gold from the Audiencia of Quito and an unknown quantity of silver. Wiser pirates might have sailed home with such a large take, but Oxenham was overcome either by greed or pride (or drink, perhaps), and soon found himself in Spanish hands. His temporary base on the north coast, at Acla, was taken by a Spanish force before he could return to it, and Oxenham and many of his maroon allies were captured by a force sent into the Vallano country. Still fearful of a large-scale English or French attack, the Spanish transported Oxenham to Lima, where he was tried by the Inquisition for heresy and hanged in 1580 (as a Protestant and hence heretic, Oxenham's body was probably burned rather than buried, giving rise to the legend that he was burned at the stake).

Whether or not Oxenham deserved such a bad end is open to question, but he had certainly set a new standard for pirate behavior during his raids on the small settlements of the Pearl Islands, in the Gulf of Panama. There Oxenham and his men had desecrated and burned a church, defiled several religious paintings and sculptures, and even made ugly sport of a Franciscan friar by crowning him with a chamber pot. Aside from this, Oxenham made all sorts of outrageous claims about a coming English invasion, which he said would consist of at least 2,000 fighting men. As before, no such support was forthcoming, but rumors of it terrified Spanish officials who knew just how weak their own position was. As mentioned earlier, the Vallano maroons were largely reduced by a force sent from Lima in 1577, but other Englishmen lurked off the north shore, near the Chagres River. One such potential ally of Oxenham was Andrew Barker, who left Bristol sponsored by the Earl of Leicester with his ships *Ragged Staff* and *Bear*, but Barker failed both to meet up with Oxenham and to take any Spanish prizes.[7] Francis Drake would have a chance to try to ransom the unfortunate Oxenham in Lima in 1579, but without success.

Drake left England on what was to become known as the "Famous Voyage" on 13 December 1577 with 164 men and boys and four relatively small ships and a pinnace. He would return to England from the Orient almost three years later, the first of his countrymen to circumnavigate the globe. This expedition, headed by the seventy-foot, 120-ton flagship *Pelican* (later renamed *Golden Hind*, after the crest of Drake's patron, Sir Christopher Hatton), was apparently aimed at nothing more than piratical raids on Spanish shipping in the South Sea, as the Pacific Ocean was then called. Drake may have also had an interest in the East Asian spice trade and in discovering the western opening of the imaginary Strait of Anian (the Northwest Passage linking the north Atlantic and north Pacific), but these were secondary objectives at best. The expedition, a joint-stock operation like most pirate ventures of its time, was made up mostly of Englishmen, but with an important complement of foreigners experienced in navigation and even two or three African ex-slaves taken in the Panama raids of the early 1570s. One of these, a man named Diego, had defected to the English at Nombre de Dios and had aided Drake on many occasions.[8] The ships were well armed and well provisioned, and, given the spirit of the times, the *Pelican* was lavishly decorated and even supplied with chamber musicians. The flagship was also outfitted with fourteen cannon, seven on either side, along with several smaller, deck-mounted guns called bow-chasers, and a variety of small arms, including arquebuses, crossbows, and even longbows.

By the time Drake had passed through the Strait of Magellan and begun heading north along the coast of Chile in September of 1578, the *Pelican* was alone. Two ships had been intentionally destroyed in Atlantic waters due to their slowness, and a third had turned back to England in storms encountered at the mouth of the Strait. The fourth ship was wrecked in the same heavy weather. Drake reconnoitered the south Pacific coast, finding little of interest before reaching Valparaíso, port of Santiago de Chile. Valparaíso in 1578 was little more than a hamlet, but a vessel carrying sea-charts for other parts north was robbed in the harbor. Farther north the *Golden Hind* was careened, or hauled over and cleaned from the underside, an operation taking some weeks. Eventually Arica, the Pacific outlet for the famed silver mines of Potosí, was reached and two ships in the harbor attacked. One of these gave Drake his first taste of Spanish treasure on this voyage, and more would come his way. A quick raid on ships lading at Callao, port of the Peruvian capital of Lima (called by the Spanish the City of Kings, or Ciudad de los Reyes), rendered little booty, but it was discovered by a captive that a treasure-laden ship had just left for Panama.

Leaving his old comrade Oxenham, one of twelve English captives previously taken on the Isthmus, to meet his fate at the hands of Lima's inquisitors, Drake set off in pursuit of the silver ship, officially called the *Nuestra Señora de la Concepción*. The *Concepción* was known to sailors by the far more secular moniker *Cacafuego*, or "Shitfire," but this colorfully named ship's fateful encounter with Drake was not yet imminent. In the meantime Drake's men overtook a small ship sailing out of Guayaquil, belonging to one Benito Díaz Bravo and carrying 18,000–20,000 gold pesos (between 75 and 84 kg of gold bullion, presumably from the inland mines of Zaruma, Zamora, and Popayán) along with a good deal of *pita-* or agave-fiber cordage and tackle. The ship's clerk, Francisco Jácome, was suspected of hiding yet more gold, so Drake's crew put a rope around his neck and pushed him from a yardarm. Instead of hanging the unfortunate Jácome, however, he was allowed to drop alive into the sea, and was then recovered by sailors in a launch. Terrorized but clearly clean of conscience, Jácome was released, later to testify as to his actions before a Spanish magistrate. On 1 March 1579, off Cabo San Francisco, on the Audiencia of Quito coast and just south of the equator, Drake and his crew attacked their slow-moving prey, the *Cacafuego*.

According to contemporary accounts, the Spanish captain of the *Cacafuego*, Juan de Antón, was so surprised to see a foreign ship coming alongside him that he doubted it was possible. Drake commanded him (apparently through an interpreter) to "strike sail" and yield, to which Antón replied, "Come on board to strike [the sails] yourselves!"[9] Drake's men responded with a volley of arquebus shot and arrows, accompanied by a series of chainballs (cannonballs connected by a chain, for maximum damage to rigging) from the larger ordnance, which tore the mizzenmast and lateen yard of the Spanish vessel clean off, a near crippling blow. The English boarded without incident after this exchange, with the *Golden*

Hind at starboard and a stolen pinnace at port. According to an anonymous relation of the voyage:

> We found in her some fruit, conserves, sugars, meal, and other victuals, and (that which was the especialest cause of her heavy and slow sailing) a certain quantity of jewels and precious stones, 13 chests of rials [reales] of plate, 80 pound weight in gold, 26 ton of uncoined silver, two very fair gilt silver drinking bowls, and the like trifles, valued in all at about 360,000 pesos. We gave the master a little linen and the like commodities, and at the end of six days we bade farewell and parted. He hastening somewhat lighter than before to Panama, we plying off to sea. . . . [10]

Short of the substantial feat of circumnavigation this was as good as it would get for Drake. Another prize was taken off Caño Island (Costa Rica) by the crew's pinnace on 20 March 1579 while the *Golden Hind* was being careened. As luck would have it, the small vessel, though carrying little of value in its hold, had aboard two pilots of the Manila galleon route. These men, Alonso Sánchez Colchero and Martín de Aguirre, just happened to have their chart-books, or *derroteros*, along with them. Only Sánchez Colchero was detained, the others having been let go to sail the pirates' own pinnace back to Nicoya, whence they had come. The *Hind* was repaired and part of the treasure moved to the newly stolen bark, and Drake and his followers sailed northward. Word of the "Lutheran corsairs" traveled quickly along the Pacific coast of New Spain, and well inland, and the panic that ensued even led the president of the Audiencia of Guatemala to order church bells melted down to found cannon. A Spanish army officer writing to Philip II from Cartagena summed up the mood of the colonies by noting that news of Drake's Pacific raids "has spread much melancholy throughout these realms." [11] The small port of Realejo was passed up when the captive pilot, Sánchez Colchero, denied Drake his expertise in finding a safe approach. His resistance was repaid by dunking in the manner practiced on Jácome, the clerk of Guayaquil, and afterward he seems to have been cooperative.

A prize was taken, encountered almost by accident off Acajutla, in the early morning hours of 4 April. This ship, containing a potentially illegal cargo of Chinese merchandise headed to Peru from Acapulco, belonged to a Spanish nobleman named Francisco de Zárate. Zárate's later testimony provides the best description of Drake and his shipboard life during this voyage:

> He is called Francisco Drak, and is a man of about 35 years of age, low of stature, with a fair beard, and is one of the greatest mariners that sails the seas, both as a navigator and as a commander. His vessel is . . . a perfect sailer. She is manned with a hundred men [an overestimate] all of service and of an age for warfare, and all are as practiced therein as old soldiers could be. Each one takes particular pains to keep his arquebus clean. He treats them

Caca Fogo.

Caca Plata.

FIGURE 2.2 Engagement between *Golden Hind* (*Cacaplata*) and *Cacafuego*

Source: Levinus Hulsius, *Kurtze Warhafftige*, Nürnburg, 1603.

Note: After Theodor de Bry, *HistoriaAmericae VIII*, compare to Figure 3.1.

with affection and they treat him with respect. He carries with him nine or ten cavaliers, cadets of English noblemen. These form a part of his council, which he calls together for even the most trivial matter, although he takes advice from no one. But he enjoys hearing what they say and afterwards issues his orders. He has no favorite. . . . The aforesaid gentlemen sit at his table, as well as a Portuguese pilot. . . . He is served on silver dishes with gold borders and gilded garlands, in which are his arms. He carries all possible dainties and perfumed waters. . . . He dines and sups to the music of viols. . . . I understood that all the men he carries with him receive wages, because, when our ship was sacked, no man dared take anything without his orders. He shows them great favor, but punishes the least fault. He also carries painters who paint for him pictures of the coast in its exact colors. This I was most grieved to see, for each thing is so naturally depicted that no one who guides himself according to these paintings can possibly go astray. . . .[12]

Thus we see that Drake's idea of a pirate voyage was hardly democratic, but rather highly aristocratic. High living aboard the *Golden Hind* was not restricted entirely to Drake's person, apparently, and discord seems to have been minimized by his conspicuous noblesse oblige (in practice for his later knighthood, perhaps).

Early on 13 April 1579 Drake put in at Guatulco, a tiny Mexican port on the west end of the Gulf of Tehuantepec and occasional provisioning post for the Peru ships. There was not much booty to be had here, but the pirates went ashore against little resistance and took what they could. Stores of water in casks and some food items were found, probably considered worth their weight in gold by this time since Drake had, after all, some ninety mouths to feed besides his own. As good militant Protestants, Drake's men desecrated a small chapel and whatever religious articles they could lay hands on. One Spanish witness, Francisco Gómez Rengifo, later claimed that an unnamed boatswain, "small, with a scant, fair beard and his face . . . pitted with pock-marks" broke a crucifix against a table, saying, "You ought indeed to be grieved, for you are not Christians, but idolators who adore sticks and stones."[13] This self-righteous scolding continued aboard the *Golden Hind* after the pirates had unleashed still more aggression on a small ship lying at anchor. After this scuttling Drake invited, or rather coerced, his prisoners, and later a local crown official, or *alcalde mayor*, to join him in a Protestant worship service. The witnesses variously described the pious English captain as remarkably competent in the business of navigation and remarkably arrogant and boastful, reminding them often that he could do with them as he pleased. Drake claimed that unlike the Spanish officials who had insulted him and his cousin, John Hawkins, at San Juan de Ulúa some ten years previous, he was magnanimous and civilized; the present mission was simply aimed at settling that score in a gentlemanly fashion.[14]

The Guatulco raid would be Drake's last along the west coast of New Spain, but his enemies hardly knew this; rumor was that an entire English fleet lurked offshore, ready at any moment to launch an invasion of Acapulco, or worse. Messengers dispatched from Guatulco to Mexico City and Acapulco by the local alcalde had already spread the panic far and wide. Quickly organized forces, often made up of unseasoned elites intent on making a name for themselves in the fight against the pirate-heretics, made their way to the coast to meet the invaders. One such group of 200 or so highlanders was accompanied by the captive interpreter

Miles Philips, an Englishman taken at San Juan de Ulúa back in 1568. This expedition put out to sea at Acapulco, sailing southeastward in search of Drake, but the gentlemanly pirate was nowhere to be found. A similar search mission had been launched by the Audiencia of Guatemala, but with similar results. Having learned from the various pilots he had interviewed that the Manila galleon, the famously rich China ship that came once a year to Acapulco, was not due for some months, and not wanting to face even a disorganized armada besides, Drake headed far to the west, where he found winds sufficient to take him to the northwest coast of North America.

At perhaps forty-eight degrees north latitude the *Golden Hind* encountered freezing weather and Drake decided to follow the coastline southward in search of a careenage. The search for the Northwest Passage, or the Strait of Anian, was thus simply abandoned. Drake's careening spot, in any case, may well have been somewhere in San Francisco Bay, and here he and his company stayed for over a month. Drake called the place "New Albion," making the acquaintance of indigenous peoples, and, with the casual, acquisitive arrogance typical of the times, claimed it for the queen. On 23 July 1579 the crew took leave of "New Albion" and its friendly inhabitants. Lucky winds took the *Golden Hind* to the Caroline Islands (near Guam) by 13 October, an unusually quick passage across the broad Pacific Ocean.

The long voyage home included stops in the Spice Islands, most notably at Ternate, where some uneasy negotiations for cloves were carried on with one Sultan Babullah, rival of the Portuguese at nearby Tidore. It should be noted also, however, that Drake, after careening his vessel in these seas, left three Spanish-speaking Africans on an island in the Banggai Archipelago (south of the Celebes), one a man who had been taken off Paita (northwest Peru) and another from Guatulco, along with a female slave named Maria, taken from Francisco Zárate off Nicaragua in December of 1579. These three castaways, along with the child to whom Maria was to give birth, having been "gotten with child between the captain and his pirates," were left with "rice, seeds and means of making a fire."[15] Such a gesture can hardly have been considered friendly or even charitable under the circumstances, and it is quite possible that Drake aimed to jettison any persons that might soil his gentlemanly reputation (the incident is not mentioned in *The World Encompassed*, but was decried by William Camden in his *Annales*).

Elizabethan Privateers

Affairs between Spain and England took a rather sudden turn for the worse in 1585 and Drake was at the forefront of the aggression. His two large expeditions to the West Indies during this period, however, though sponsored by the queen, were not typical of the times. As Andrews has shown, some seventy-six English expeditions made their way to the Caribbean during the eighteen-year period of hostilities ending with Elizabeth I's death in 1603. Excluding Drake's ventures, this leaves seventy-four expeditions, most small, all of them privately financed, comprised of 183 individual voyages.[10] This sharp rise in maritime predation was enough to drive Spain's officials in the Caribbean to distraction, and it ended with a costly series of responses by the turn of the century. These included regular naval patrols, increased armament of merchant vessels, and the amazingly massive—and still visible—fortification of major ports like Cartagena, Havana, and San Juan de Puerto Rico. Elizabethan corsairs were everywhere in sight during the long Anglo-Spanish War; they hovered around every Caribbean port like flocks of vultures, casually grouping together and breaking apart in a way that made them impossible to counter. Compared to this sort of uncertainty, organized naval engagements back in Europe, such as the famous Anglo-Dutch meeting with Philip II's Invincible Armada in the English Channel in 1588, were at least fathomable, if not predictable in their outcomes.

So many Elizabethan raiders found their way to Caribbean waters during the period after 1585 that the stories of only a few can be recounted briefly here. Some attention will be given to Drake's 1585 voyage, since it was quite large and set the tone for subsequent adventures, but the less-studied Pacific raids of Thomas Cavendish and Richard Hawkins in the mid-1580s and mid-1590s, respectively, will also be reviewed. These latter corsairs are noteworthy for different reasons, the first for managing to capture a Manila galleon before repeating

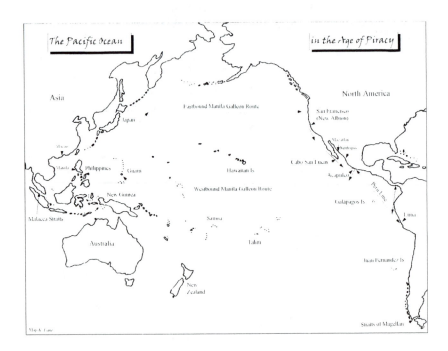

MAP 3 The Pacific Basin in the Age of Piracy

Drake's feat of circumnavigation, and the second for attempting new alliances with certain maroon communities along the Pacific coast of South America. It should be remembered, as several historians have pointed out, that England in the age of Elizabeth I was not terribly wealthy, and at this point had relatively modest international ambitions. Many of the corsairs, including Drake, to be sure, were big talkers, and the Spanish sometimes believed them, but England's later-developing maritime and imperial traditions should not be projected back to this early period. In reality the first great wave of English marauding in the Caribbean was a series of business ventures, always excused rather than commanded by a monarch whose power was more symbolic than material.

Thus, with only a marginal blessing from the queen, Drake left England with a massive fleet of twenty-two vessels of varying size and 2,300 men, including several companies of trained soldiers. The fleet made a show of force off Spain's north coast, then sailed south toward the mouth of the Guadalquivir and Cádiz but failed to catch the treasure fleet arriving from the Caribbean. This missed opportunity was followed by a major mishap, an inopportune sack of Santiago, in the Cape Verde Islands. So many English contracted some sort of contagious fever in this landing that the expedition nearly fell apart. Just the same, the raiders made their way to the Caribbean within a month and sacked Santo Domingo without much difficulty. The city yielded little booty, only about 25,000 ducats' worth, but the incident, as was becoming customary, spread panic throughout the Spanish and Portuguese Indies. In early 1586 Drake took Cartagena with equal ease, but while this was a more notable feat, the booty taken was similarly disappointing (and even if the crew was dying quickly from fevers the loot had to be split a lot of ways). From Cartagena Drake hoped to launch an expedition against Panama, but high mortality and dissension among his officers led him to begin the return trip to England instead. Thus, after six weeks looting and convalescing in Cartagena, the sickly and disappointed raiders made their way to the Florida Strait. Given the condition of the crew, Havana was bypassed, but the small Spanish settlement of St. Augustine, on the north Florida coast, was nearly destroyed in a brief raid.

Drake's 1585–86 venture was not a resounding loss, but it was certainly no great success given its size and armaments. Even the St. Augustine raid proved nearly inconsequential; panic or no, the settlers and soldiers of the town and fort came out of the woods and rebuilt as soon as English sails disappeared from view. Subsequent attempts to evacuate Ralph Lane and his struggling English colonists from Roanoke yielded similarly mixed results—the colonists were removed, but several ships were destroyed by storm—and Drake returned to England with a decimated and disappointed crew, the outlay of capital for the adventure, like those of John Hawkins some twenty years earlier, exceeding its returns in booty. Still, as Andrews and other historians of the period have noted, the effect of the 1585–86 voyage was to encourage and even force Spain to acknowledge the new scale of the English threat in its colonial waters. With just a bit more luck an enemy fleet of this size could have captured a treasure fleet, sacked Panama

or Havana, or even established a permanent base of operations in the Caribbean. Such was not the case at this stage, but all the petty Elizabethan privateers to follow in the wake of Drake's 1585–86 expedition profited from the fear it sowed. Spain, for its part, tried to improve the safety of its treasure shipments by means of faster and better-armed ships, most notably the expensive but necessary war frigates, or *galibrazas*. The tax applied to all merchandise in the Indies trade in return for protection, the *avería*, was raised precipitously, from just under 2 percent in 1585 to 4 percent in 1587, and to 8 percent in 1591.[17] When customs duties and sales taxes were added, generalized price rises were inevitable, especially in the colonies, but also in Spain.

Other Spanish reactions to the Drake venture included the construction of new galleys (Drake had destroyed the old ones) for the protection of Santo Domingo, Cartagena, and Havana, and the beginnings of the stone fortification of the same cities. Two prominent military architect-engineers were sent to the Caribbean in 1586, Juan de Tejeda and Juan Bautista Antoneli, and by the end of Elizabeth's reign they had managed to fortify Cartagena, the mouth of the Chagres, Panama, San Juan de Ulúa, Havana, Santo Domingo, and Puerto Rico. Modern, star-shaped fortresses were enormously expensive to build, with outlays in stone, tools, and most of all, slaves, and were nearly as costly to maintain. Soldiers demanded wages, arms, and victualing the year round, yet most of the time they faced no enemies. As in the Old World, New World galleys and *castillos* were manned with an odd assortment of condemned criminals, slaves, and other social outcasts in order to cut costs. All this was fine for the towns that got forts and for the ships that enjoyed escorts, but for everyone else—local townsfolk and intra-colonial shippers, in particular—the situation was as bad as before.

One such unprotected seaway, even after Drake and Oxenham's audacious intrusions in the 1570s, was the Peru–Panama–Mexico route on the Pacific coast. On 31 July 1586 a young gentleman of Suffolk, Thomas Cavendish, set out to repeat Drake's exploits in the South Sea. At his command were three ships, led by the 120-ton *Desire*, and 123 men, some of them veterans of Drake's "famous voyage" of 1577–80. The sole purpose of the trip was plunder, partly to rebuild the declining fortunes of its spendthrift leader, though any intelligence gained along the way was to be duly noted and presented at court. As with Drake's disappointing 1585 voyage to the Caribbean, the expedition made an unwise stop along the west coast of Africa shortly after setting out, leading to a deadly outbreak of disease (possibly scurvy, but more likely malaria), which decimated the crew. Thus it was a weather-beaten and sickly band of Englishmen that passed the Strait of Magellan and entered Pacific waters on 6 March 1587. A few brief raids along the southern coasts of the Viceroyalty of Peru netted little loot, and one of Cavendish's ships, the bark *Hugh Gallant*, was scuttled off the coast of the Audiencia of Quito.

The west coast of New Spain, least protected of all Spanish America since it counted no cannons, no forts, no armies, nor navies—the so-called Armada del Mar del Sur was not a navy at all—would offer even this hapless privateering crew

a chance at glory. A 120-ton prize was taken off Acajutla (Guatemala) on 19 July, but it yielded no booty aside from a pilot who knew the Manila route, Miguel Sánchez. Sánchez turned out to be a valuable prize himself, and was soon coerced into revealing the approximate return time of two galleons, which he claimed would be sometime in November. Unsurprisingly, Cavendish and his men were greatly encouraged by the prospect of taking one of the famed China ships, or *naos de la China*, as they were commonly called. The Acajutla prize was burned, and likewise a packet-boat taken on 20 July, the latter sent by Guatemalan officials to warn parts north of the intruders' arrival. The English then proceeded to follow Drake's example in landing at Guatulco, which offered no resistance and even less booty. A small cacao vessel was robbed and an assault on the town launched. The usual Protestant revenge was wreaked on the small adobe-and-thatch church of Guatulco, but one religious incident (not mentioned by Cavendish's chronicler, Francis Pretty) would be regarded by many in New Spain as a miracle. Apparently some of Cavendish's men attempted to pull down a large wooden cross overlooking the bay by all means possible, from hatchets and saws to fire, to a line tied to their ship. The cross held firm and the pirates went on their way, but the incident was hardly forgotten. Indeed, Cavendish's attempted sacrilege led to the long-term veneration of the so-called Santa Cruz de Guatulco by rich and poor throughout southern Mexico. Pieces of the cross were removed as relics and eventually some splinters were made into a smaller cross now housed in a side chapel of the Oaxaca cathedral. Problems in pregnancy and speech impediments were said to be cured by remnants of the cross the pirate heretics could not defile.[18]

Cavendish would gain even more renown for his subsequent actions, however, and for some months he and his crew bided their time, waiting for the Manila galleons' return. The Spanish were not inactive in the Pacific during this time, but two attempts to locate and capture the Elizabethan intruders ended in quarrels and ultimate failure. A small force under command of one Cristóbal de Mendoza left Panama and reached Acapulco by mid-October, where it was to join with other ships under command of a Mexican *audiencia* judge, Diego García del Palacio. A personal dispute between the two captains led to the dissolution of what might have been a fleet, and Cavendish and his men were left free to raid the north Mexican coast, which they obligingly did. A few barks were seized and some tiny villages, such as Navidad and Acatlán, to the west and south of Guadalajara, were raided and despoiled. On 19 October 1587 Cavendish and his crew sailed from the vicinity of Mazatlán northwestward to Cabo San Lucas, at the southern tip of Baja California. There the crew took on fresh water, fished, hunted fowls and other small game, and waited for the arrival of the China ships.

There were two galleons arriving from Manila that year, the *Nuestra Señora de la Esperanza* (Our Lady of Hope) and the *Santa Ana*. The first passed Cabo San Lucas without being sighted by Cavendish and his men in early November, but the second, under command of Tomás de Alzola, was not so lucky. Like most of the large vessels that crossed the Pacific during this period, the *Santa Ana* was

was led by Richard Hawkins, only son of the famous John Hawkins; it entered the South Sea in early 1594. After some small-scale pillage off Chile and Peru, Hawkins and his flagship *Dainty* were taken captive off the Audiencia of Quito coast by a small Spanish squadron commanded by Beltrán de Castro. Whereas Oxenham had been tried for heresy and executed, the wounded Hawkins and his crewmembers were transported to Spain, ransomed, and allowed to return to England by mid-1603. This last of the Elizabethan voyages to the South Sea was for the Spanish an important victory, but there was little time to celebrate, since the Dutch were already following in their wake. It would in any case be nearly a century before English raiders returned to these waters.

In his memoir, *Voyage into the South Sea* (1622), Sir Richard Hawkins recounted his experiences in great detail, and his work reminds us of the remarkable interest the early pirates and privateers showed for things other than booty. Indeed, the greater part of Hawkins's treatise regards natural history and geography, along with technical and detailed discussions of the necessities of outfitting long-distance expeditions, the particulars of law in a "just war," and the maintenance of discipline aboard ship. All this talk was perhaps a way of beating around the bush, since he had lost his flagship to the "papist enemy," but it shows both the corsairs and their Spanish captors in a relatively positive light. Hawkins seems to have been a harsher judge of his own rowdy and sometimes incompetent crewmembers than of the "temperate" and "gentle" Spaniards who captured them off the Esmeraldas coast of the Audiencia of Quito. For example, after hearing news of a Spanish trap laid for him, Hawkins claimed, "But the enemy I feared not so much as the Wine; which, notwithstanding all the diligence and prevention I could use day and night, overthrew many of my people."[20] Temperance concerns aside, Hawkins left fine descriptions of life on board ship, pirate military tactics, and of autonomous coastal peoples of the Spanish Pacific, such as the famed "Molatoes" (actually Afro-Native American maroons) of Esmeraldas, in present-day Ecuador.[21]

Although several important voyages followed, Francis Drake's last one will serve as an end for this discussion of Elizabethan piracy and privateering in Spanish American waters. Piracy was a dangerous business in the sixteenth century, and most of the Elizabethans who had had some measure of success in their ventures—usually due to a boldness that bordered on folly—ended their lives in pursuit of yet more booty. As noted, Oxenham was killed by the Spanish for his audacity and poor judgment, but more typical were the deaths of Cavendish, Drake, and John Hawkins. Cavendish succumbed to disease at the age of thirty-one while trying to return to England from a botched crossing of the Strait of Magellan in 1591. Drake and Hawkins, in their last big gamble, likewise died of fevers off the Panama coast in 1596 and were buried at sea after a series of low-yield raids throughout the Spanish Caribbean. The only other expedition of this scale to set out during Elizabethan times was that of the Earl of Cumberland, who sacked and pillaged Puerto Rico in 1598. The city of San Juan and its new fort (another "El Morro") fell easily to the English, but fever forced the captors to abandon their plans to seize the island for the queen. Sporadic raids continued for a few more years and some renegades were active throughout the reign of James I (1603–25), but the first wave of English piracy in the Americas was essentially over by the turn of the seventeenth century.

Corsairs, Cod, and the Northwest Passage

As we have seen, the great mineral treasures of the early modern Americas were limited to territories claimed by Spain and Portugal. This led sea predators to naturally focus on Spanish and Portuguese towns and vessels, either in the tropics or on their way home. Or in any case this remained a strong preference since Iberian targets were most likely to yield ready cash. Yet European overseas expansion was a much larger project, and wherever sea traffic grew, piracy followed. Thus, pirates and privateers haunted the frigid North Atlantic on occasion and according to season, usually raiding for supplies.

The vast cod banks of Newfoundland had drawn European fishermen since late medieval times, and by the early sixteenth century Basque sailors had established temporary bases in the Canadian Maritimes. Portuguese, English, Flemish, French, and Danish fishermen also exploited the banks, and some such men preyed on each other from time to time, although this seems to have been rare. These were vast seas famous for heavy weather, and it made more sense not to do violence to one's competitors in case of emergency survival needs. Whalers followed a similar path, preferring to hunt the world's largest mammals rather than those of their own kind.

The case of Elizabethan corsair Martin Frobisher stands out in this context, as he was among the first Europeans to make recorded contact with the Inuit inhabitants of Baffin Island. He was not a fisherman, but rather a fisher of men. In a series of three expeditions from 1576–78, Frobisher searched in vain for the Northwest Passage, probing rocky island shores amid icebergs above 60 degrees north latitude. Fearless and well hated, even by his closest associates, the physically imposing Frobisher had made his name as a pirate in the English Channel. But the 1576–78 mission had peaceful intentions, ultimately aiming to open direct English commerce with China via a sea passage around North America.[22]

What happened instead was a strange blend of treasure-hunting and kidnapping, piracy of the sort first practiced by Christopher Columbus almost a century earlier in the Caribbean. Upon encountering Inuits in their kayaks and on land, Frobisher and his men captured several women, children, and men as prizes to show Queen Elizabeth and the investors. They also made signs that they were searching for gold, and before long they located an outcrop of metallic mineral that they excavated to the tune of several tons. The Inuit prisoners died of disease in England, and the ore turned out to be a worthless mix of galena and pyrite. A return trip found the Inuit ready to defend themselves, and the entire mission was aborted.

The search for the Northwest Passage, first proposed in 1537, continued throughout the early modern period, and one of Frobisher's discoveries, later called Hudson's Strait, was a popular entry point. John Davis was first to follow Frobisher, but it was Henry Hudson, frequently in Dutch employ, who was credited with discovering his namesake bay in 1610. William Baffin shot farther north in 1616, reaching an astonishing 78 degrees north latitude. These explorations fell under the peacetime rule of England's King James I, who died in 1625, but many of the participants were old corsair hands from Elizabeth's heyday.

Another early seventeenth-century English explorer who knew a thing or two about piracy was John Smith, famous founder of Virginia. Smith had spent considerable time in the Mediterranean, where he saw firsthand how many Englishmen went "renegade" and joined the Barbary corsairs. Smith made the early observation that peace, a kind of Devil's workshop, tended to make formerly honest sailors and marines break bad. Salé, on the west coast of Morocco, became a staging point for audacious north Atlantic raids, some of which plundered vulnerable towns in Ireland. English pirate Peter Easton attacked fishermen off Newfoundland for provisions and extra hands in 1611, and the infamous Henry Mainwaring followed in 1614. "Moroccan" corsairs in these years comprised a tangle of proto-national and confessional identities, as made clear in the case of Jewish merchant, corsair sponsor, and spy Samuel Pallache. Mainwaring, rather like William Kidd almost a century later, also played both sides.[23]

The Elizabethan period of corsairing in the Americas may be summarized as follows: (1) independent English merchants challenged Spain's monopoly trade practices by smuggling African slaves to the Americas after 1559 and were treated with increasing hostility, culminating in the attack on John Hawkins and Francis Drake at San Juan de Ulúa (Mexico) in 1568; (2) the San Juan de Ulúa incident led to nearly two decades of English piracy, including Drake's raid on Panama in 1572–73, John Oxenham's entry into Pacific waters in 1576–77, and Drake's circumnavigation and raiding of Spanish shipping in the South Sea (1577–80); and (3) open war with Spain after 1585 led to an unprecedented level of English privateering, or officially commissioned sea raiding, in Spanish American waters until the death of Elizabeth I in 1603.

English pirates would be overshadowed by their Dutch neighbors after the peace established by James I in 1604, but they would later return to prominence among the late-seventeenth-century buccaneers. For the Spanish the most notable general patterns of the Elizabethan era included the novelty of periodic foreign raids in Pacific waters, the growing need to fortify Caribbean ports such as Havana, Cartagena, and San Juan de Puerto Rico, and the inevitability of raising local taxes to fund naval defense. By the end of this period the general shift was toward active rather than passive defense throughout the Americas, a very costly trend that would continue in the following decades. The Elizabethan era coincided with Spain's rise under the Prudent King, Philip II, and after unification with Portugal in 1580 Spain became the center of the world's most wealthy and powerful overseas empire. England, in spite of important naval victories and a great deal of privately financed sea-raiding, appeared little more than a bit player on the world scene by comparison. Meanwhile, another upstart Protestant nation would begin to prick Spain's side in the Indies, sometimes with veteran English corsairs at the helm. These were the Dutch sea-rovers, and they are the subject of the following chapter.

BOX 2 ELIZABETHAN-ERA NAVIGATION

Francis Drake and a number of his contemporaries were said to be excellent navigators, and indeed they were. Most of their knowledge, however, was derived from the work and experience of Spanish and Portuguese mariners and hydrographers, some of whom published their observations, such as Pedro Nunes (1537), Pedro de Medina (1547), Martín Cortés (1551), and others who simply passed on their knowledge by word of mouth. Some pilots, as has been seen, shared information only when coerced, usually by pirates or corsairs like Drake. Pilotage was only one aspect of navigation, albeit an important one, and it consisted essentially of knowing water depths along approaches to harbors, bays, and river mouths. Good pilots knew how to avoid rocks and sandbars, and depths were sounded by plumb line, knotted at every fathom and dropped often. In some cases the plumb, or lead bar, was hollowed and filled with tallow at the bottom end to pick up traces of sand or muck on the sea floor, the absence of which might indicate rocks or coral reefs—the sort of things that could wreck a ship while entering or leaving an estuary. Experienced pilots also knew how tides affected a given channel and used their knowledge to make use of inward and outward flowing streams.

Several types of compasses were in use by Elizabethan times, all of them helpful in finding steerage direction in overcast conditions or open seas. One compass type consisted of a wooden box containing a pivoting iron needle that was periodically rubbed with a lodestone, or natural magnet. The needle was attached to a card of paper or hide marked with the standard thirty-two directional divisions. The problems of variation and dip due to the actual location of magnetic north were partially solved with the introduction of the adjustable variation compass, invented in 1597, and hence too late to be of use to Drake and his contemporaries. (A compass maker named Robert Norman invented a means of measuring dip by 1581, but it is not clear how widespread this knowledge was before 1600). Routes traveled were often marked on prepared sheepskins, known as portulan charts (*portolani*), many of which survive in university and private collections, and time was measured by means of half-hour sandglasses, preferably turned by alert cabin boys, and much later (mid-1700s) by finely crafted mechanical clocks.

Given that the earth is round, a fact known to most mariners well before Columbus's day, distances marked on flat maps and charts were difficult to square with spherical reality, especially in extreme northern latitudes. The Flemish cartographer Gerard Mercator developed a projection map that accounted for curvature by 1569, and his earlier designs were copied in England by John Dee in the 1540s. Still, the Mercator projection was not mathematically understood until the late 1580s, and no means of adapting it for practical use at sea became available until 1599, when the mathematician Edward Wright published his *Certaine Errors in Navigation Detected and Corrected*. Globes that might have been adapted for establishing directional lines over a curved surface were available before this time, but they do not seem to have been used on board ships.

Once European ships left the relatively familiar waters of the East Atlantic and Mediterranean, navigation became somewhat more important than pilotage. The first problem in north–south sailing, of course, was the determination of latitude, how to find one's position on the globe relative to the equator or the poles. For this purpose early navigators relied on observations of the sun's altitude at midday (meridian altitude) and, in the northern hemisphere at least, on the altitude of the star Polaris, aided by one or two measuring devices. Among the most common of these were the cross-staff, back-staff, and astrolabe, and readings were checked against an almanac or chart giving the sun's declination at the celestial equator for every day of the year. The Portuguese seem to have first developed the cross-staff and astrolabe for long-distance travel, but their true origins remain obscure (Arabic astronomers used astrolabes in medieval times, for instance). The astrolabe consisted of a brass wheel marked precisely for degrees (sometimes down to 1/4 degree) around the edges, a rotating pointer, or alidade, with aligned pinholes at either end, and a ring by which the instrument could be suspended. The navigator, preferably at a landing rather than on a moving ship, would hang the astrolabe from his thumb (they were heavy enough to hang level, ideally) at midday and adjust the alidade to point the sun's rays through the pinholes (see Figure 2.3). When sunlight passed through to the ground, the day's altitude reading, given by the pointer against the vertical, could be compared with the predicted solar declination at the equator. The cross-staff was much simpler, but required the user to look at the sun directly, a cause of blindness among more than a few sixteenth-century navigators. This problem was remedied by the development of the back-staff, which followed the same principle of measuring altitude by means of a sliding transom along a graduated ruler, but allowed the user to sight the horizon and gauge the sun's shadow. The back-staff was developed in the 1590s by an English captain, John Davis, and thus came to be known as the Davis quadrant.

If figuring latitude with some precision was fairly easy for the Elizabethans, longitude was another matter. In fact, no method of calculating longitude

FIGURE 2.3 Measuring the Sun's Meridian Altitude with an Astrolabe

Source: Pedro de Medina, *Arte de navegar,* 1545 (courtesy of the James Ford Bell Library, University of Minnesota).

within ten degrees of accuracy was developed during the period of piracy treated by this book. East–west measurements dogged early long-distance mariners like Columbus, and it soon became clear that the earth was substantially wider than ancient cosmographers like Ptolemy had predicted. Thus pirate mariners in the Elizabethan period and after did their best to latch on to experienced Portuguese and Spanish pilots, individuals who knew trans-oceanic winds and currents (and hence expected travel times), could recognize islands and shorelines, and so on. With time the English, French, and Dutch became just as experienced as their often unwilling Spanish and Portuguese teachers, and eventually surpassed them in navigational expertise. Early modern navigators did try to measure east–west progress by means of logs thrown alongside ship from the front and allowed to pass to the rear before being reeled in. The ever-alert cabin boy or grommet would have turned his half-minute sandglass carefully while the ship passed the log, thus measuring the ship's speed—using the known length of the ship against the time required to pass the log (calculated in "knots," as per a knotted rope attached to the log). This method of measuring speed, ingenious though it was, could not account for currents, sideways motion, and other contingencies, and furthermore had to be repeated with every perceived wind change. Later pirates tried various methods to remedy this problem, including the observation of lunar eclipses, but until the mid-eighteenth century longitude was the holy grail of European navigation.

Source: Adapted from David Waters, "Elizabethan Navigation," in ed. Norman J. Thrower, *Sir Francis Drake and the Famous Voyage, 1577–1580: Essays Commemorating the Quadricentennial of Drake's Circumnavigation of the World* (Berkeley: University of California Press, 1984), 12–32; and J.H. Parry, *The Age of Reconnaissance* (New York: Mentor Books, 1964) 98–115. On the problem of longitude in the eighteenth century, see Dava Sobel, *Longitude* (New York: Walker, 1995).

Notes

1 Kenneth Andrews, *The Spanish Caribbean: Trade and Plunder, 1530–1630* (New Haven: Yale University Press, 1978), 109.

2 Ibid., 123. See also Harry Kelsey, *Sir John Hawkins: The Queen's Slave Trader* (New Haven: Yale University Press, 2003), and *Francis Drake: The Queen's Pirate* (New Haven: Yale University Press, 2000).

3 Ibid., 130. Hawkins' own account of this voyage is reprinted in John Hampden, ed., *Francis Drake, Privateer: Contemporary Narratives and Documents* (Tuscaloosa: University of Alabama Press, 1972), 31–39.

4 Ibid., 129–30. Andrews estimates that even if Hawkins had returned directly to London from Cartagena his profits would not have exceeded 10 percent due to high outfitting costs.

5 Anonymous, *Sir Francis Drake Revived*, reprinted in Hampden, *Francis Drake*, 83.

6 Andrews, *Spanish Caribbean*, 141.

7 Ibid., 143. See also J.S. Dean, "Bearding the Spaniard: Capt. John Oxnam in the Pacific," *Northern Mariner/le marin du nord* 19:4 (Oct. 2009): 379–92, and Kris Lane, *Quito 1599: City and Colony in Transition* (Albuquerque: University of New Mexico Press, 2002), 195–96.

8 Hampden notes this in *Francis Drake*, 70.

9 Ibid., 213.

10 Ibid., 170.

11 Don Miguel de Eraso y Águilar quoted in Zelia Nuttall, ed., *New Light on Drake: A Collection of Documents Relating to His Voyage of Circumnavigation, 1577–1580* (London: Hakluyt Society, 1914), 119. On church bells, see Peter Gerhard, *Pirates on the West Coast of New Spain, 1575–1742* (Cleveland: Arthur H. Clark, 1960), 67.

12 Hampden, *Francis Drake*, 214–15. For an example of Drake's thorough incorporation into Spanish literature at this time, see Lope de Vega's 1598 epic poem *La Dragontea*, ed. Antonio Sánchez Jiménez (Madrid: Cátedra, 2007). See also Nina Gerassi-Navarro, *Pirate Novels: Fictions of Nation Building in Spanish America* (Durham: Duke University Press, 1999), chap. 2.

13 Ibid., 217.

14 Ibid., 216. See also William A. Lessa, "Drake in the South Seas," in Norman J. Thrower, ed., *Sir Francis Drake and the Famous Voyage, 1577–1580: Essays Commemorating the Quadricentennial of Drake's Circumnavigation of the Earth* (Berkeley: University of California Press, 1984), 60–77.

15 Hampden, *Francis Drake*, 196, 215. See also the first declaration of John Drake, Francis Drake's cousin, taken at Santa Fe, on the River Plate, in March of 1584 (in Nuttall, *New Light on Drake*, 31).

16 Andrews, *Spanish Caribbean*, 156.

17 Ibid., 153.

18 Gerhard, *Pirates on the West Coast of New Spain*, 85.

19 Gerhard quoting Francis Pretty, *Pirates on the West Coast of New Spain*, 92. Pretty's account is in Richard Hakluyt's *Principal Navigations*, 12 vols. (New York: AMS, 1965 [1600]), vol. 3.

20 Richard Hawkins, *Voyage into the South Sea* (New York: Da Capo Press, 1968 [facsimile of 1622 ed.]), 103.

21 Ibid., 124–25. This was the Illescas group of San Mateo Bay, later recognized by the Audiencia of Quito as semi-autonomous in exchange for a promise not to ally with pirates (1599).

22 See James McDermott's magnificent *Martin Frobisher: Elizabethan Privateer* (New Haven: Yale University Press, 2001).

23 Mercedes García Arenal and Gerard Wiegers, *A Man of Three Worlds: Samuel Pallache, a Moroccan Jew in Catholic and Protestant Europe*, Martin Beagles, trans. (Baltimore: Johns Hopkins University Press, 2003).

3

FROM THE LOW COUNTRIES TO THE HIGH SEAS

The Dutch Sea-Rovers

Well before the death of Elizabethan piracy and the establishment of peace under England's James I in 1604, a new threat to Spanish and Portuguese sea sovereignty was on the rise. After 1566 Philip II faced an uprising in the Low Countries, or Netherlands, a region he had inherited from his father, the former Emperor Charles V. Militantly Protestant Hollanders, among them the so-called Sea Beggars, were harassing the Spanish and others in the early 1570s; after 1580, the year that Philip added Portugal to his ample domain, a number of Low Country provinces had declared themselves independent of Hapsburg rule. The Dutch would continue to fight Spain and Portugal, both at home and abroad, until the Peace of Münster (Westphalia) in 1648. Thus, though most Dutch depredations on Luso-Hispanic shipping and settlements in the West Indies were called "piracy" by Philip II and his successors, in truth they were an outgrowth of a generalized state of war and rebellion. What came to be known afterward as the Eighty Years War (1568–1648) was, like Elizabeth's war with Spain, an on-again, off-again affair, and by no means always "on." Similar also was the method of fighting "beyond the line" by means of privately financed ventures aimed at trade, plunder, or settlement, loosely approved by a fractious central government. After the turn of the seventeenth century, Dutch corsairing, or piracy, was a business, but it was also almost universally affiliated with one or both of the great Dutch trading corporations of the early modern period, the East India Company (or VOC, after its Dutch acronym, chartered in 1602) and the West India Company (established in 1621). Dutch sea-rovers, as will be seen, posed the first serious threat to Spanish and Portuguese sovereignty in the Americas, capturing northeastern Brazil in 1630 and attempting to plant colonies in Chile by 1642. In the Caribbean the Dutch capped years of piracy and smuggling with the capture of the New Spain treasure fleet off the north coast of Cuba in 1628, and followed with the establishment of permanent colonies at Curaçao (1634) and other minor islands, and Suriname, on the Wild Coast of South America.

Calvinism and Competition at Sea

The historian Charles Boxer suggested that the rise of Dutch sea supremacy in the seventeenth century rested on one basic principle: thrift. Certainly force played a part as well, as did sharp trade practices, low taxes, a bourgeois state leadership, surplus population and hence low labor costs, and so on, but it was Dutch economizing, a source of endless jokes and proverbs, that made money—and prompted expansion—first. By the mid-sixteenth century, if not earlier, Dutch shippers dominated the salt fish and bulk goods trades of the North Atlantic, particularly the routes connecting Baltic ports with the Iberian kingdoms of Spain and Portugal. Fat-hulled Dutch herring buses and fly-boats (see ship descriptions in Box 3) were everywhere in these seas by the time of the first revolt against Spain in 1566, and Dutch freight rates were considered the cheapest available. Dutch ships, stripped down and inexpensive to build, as Boxer noted, were manned with skeleton crews who received minimal rations and wages.[1] By cutting corners in these and other ways—making no friends among the working classes—Low Country merchants, based first in Antwerp and later in Amsterdam, soon dominated Europe's merchandising and financial markets. As fickle monarchs in France, England, Spain, and elsewhere struggled for political supremacy in an increasingly heterodox continent, the lowly "cheese-mongers" of Amsterdam carved out their own niche, a Calvinist commoner's republic, and set about building a worldwide merchant empire.

Dutch thrift, Dutch discipline, Dutch Calvinism, all these aspects of a peculiarly Dutch sea culture had direct and visible consequences in the fight against Spain and Portugal. For instance, it is difficult to deny that the Dutch were able to accumulate massive amounts of liquid capital by surpassing their rivals first in short-run, low-cost shipping in bulk goods, then in the long-distance trade in spices, slaves, and other high-value items. To this efficiency in shipping was added an austere lifestyle among the burgher-oligarchs (at least until 1650 or so) that encouraged reinvestment and savings rather than conspicuous consumption. Also, as will be seen, confessional animosity toward Catholic Spain was even more evident among the Dutch abroad than it had been for the Elizabethans, although not even a clear majority of Dutch citizens were Protestants. If these aspects of Dutch culture encouraged a spirit of competition and even outright hostility toward the Spanish and Portuguese, it also became apparent that Dutch economizing in more than a few cases alienated corsair crews to the extent that they refused to risk their lives against their supposed Catholic enemies. The fledgling Dutch Republic was no democracy, and what was good for the shareholders was not necessarily good for the common seaman. Hence, as will be seen, Dutch corsairs often underachieved in spite of their great numbers and superior armament.

Protestant ethic or no, the Dutch abroad were a force to be reckoned with. Sea Beggars were said to be cruising the Spanish Caribbean as early as 1569, but Low Country traders and privateers were not common in these seas until the last decade or so of the sixteenth century.[2] This growing Dutch presence in American waters was not born of anger, however, but rather of need. The rebellion against Spain, and by extension Portugal, meant that Dutch herring preservers needed a new source of salt by the mid-1580s. The prized salt of Setúbal, in southern Portugal, was now off limits, and attempts to exploit the salt pans of the Cape Verde Islands were sharply rebuffed. Dutch traders, finding themselves in a pickle, soon turned to an American alternative.

Salt and Sovereignty in the Caribbean

Dutch merchants were already active in the West Indies, often in concert with French and English adventurers like Drake and Hawkins, well before the end of the sixteenth century. Like the French before them, they grew fond of smuggling along the coast of Brazil by the 1580s, and were known to have been processing Brazilian dyewood and raw sugar at home by this time. Still, they did not ignore the Spanish Caribbean. Much to the consternation of Spanish officials, who were busily attempting to fortify major ports and protect valuable bullion fleets against Elizabethan privateers, cargoes of less easily controlled items, such as sugar, ginger, *cassia fistula* (a purgative drug resembling Old World senna), and hides were being sent to the Netherlands illegally from the Greater Antilles by the 1590s. Some of this trade was "colored," or partially legitimized by cover agents in Seville, the Canaries, and Hispaniola (like John Hawkins's early ventures), but as tensions rose in Europe, particularly with increased Spanish seizures of Dutch ships in the East Atlantic, pure smuggling came to dominate. Between 1592 and 1596 some seven Dutch contrabanding ships were said to have stopped at Margarita Island, off Venezuela.[3] It was about time for the Spanish to take notice.

It was also in this region, along Venezuela's coast at the salt deposits of Punta de Araya, that Dutch ships, most of them only lightly armed, first challenged Spanish sovereignty. The interlopers treated the salt pans, which the Spanish ignored but claimed, as a pure gift of nature, and between 1599 and 1605 Dutch cargo hulks of 200–400 tons capacity were swarming around the Araya Peninsula on the order of 100 ships a year. The Spanish, exasperated by this affront on their sovereignty, launched a punitive expedition in 1605 under the command of Luis Fajardo. Fajardo arrived at Punta de Araya in September with fourteen galleons, accompanied by four smaller ships and a force of 2,500 men. The Spanish easily routed their targets, most of them Dutch but including a few English and French vessels, capturing nine ships in the first assault and seven in the second.[4] The Dutch, like the other foreigners, had also been engaged in contraband trade along the coast at Cumaná and elsewhere, mostly for tobacco, but they apparently had not done any raiding. Still, Fajardo treated his captives as "pirates and corsairs," following a *cédula*, or royal edict of 6 July 1605, and beheaded or hanged most of them without trial. Fajardo and his second in command, Juan Alvarez de Avilés, went on to engage some twenty-four Dutch vessels (again accompanied by a few English and French vessels) off the south coast of Cuba in early 1606. After some losses on both sides, but no decisive resolution, the pirate enemies and salt diggers temporarily left the Caribbean.

This harsh reprisal, seemingly coming out of nowhere, was actually typical of Spanish foreign policy in the Caribbean, or even of its colonial policy more generally. Such a far-flung empire could not affordably be policed and manned with salaried magistrates at every juncture, so the Spanish state relied on two means of keeping a lid on illegal activities such as piracy and smuggling. One method, as seen here, was to shift unexpectedly from an apparent laissez-faire approach to one of almost capricious state-sponsored terror. In this way, twenty years or more of law-by-local-custom could be suddenly and tragically reversed. This means of control by swift and exemplary punishment was likewise turned on wayward Spanish officials and colonists from time to time, and was more than a passing source of creole animosity toward crown officials. The second tactic used by the Spanish, with somewhat less obvious results, was the more or less institutionalized practice of paying informants and other intelligence gatherers for "ratting" on their peers. As might be imagined, this policy, though very helpful to otherwise uninformed officials fresh from Spain, or even Mexico City, sowed seeds of distrust among coastal settlers, further undermining Spanish sovereignty by preventing settler cohesion.

The Fajardo expeditions of 1605–6 dampened the enthusiasm of some Dutch investors in the Caribbean contraband trade, but not for long. Though the salts of Araya were abandoned for the time being (Portuguese salt was available after 1605, though not cheaply), Dutch traders were soon bartering for tobacco farther east, on the island of Trinidad and at San Tomé, on the Orinoco River. This eastward shift in tobacco trading was also related to the Fajardo raids; in addition to ordering northern Hispaniola and other vulnerable coasts depopulated (their inhabitants removed to established centers such as Santo Domingo), Venezuelan tobacco cultivation was entirely outlawed. As will be seen in the next chapter, Spain's "scorched earth" policy in indefensible Caribbean regions would lead to the rise of buccaneers and other foreign interlopers on Hispaniola, but the ban on tobacco farming in Venezuela also had significant consequences. Tobacco was becoming a hugely popular drug in northern Europe during the first decades of the seventeenth century and prices in London and Amsterdam were soaring. As a result, northern European contrabandists sought suppliers throughout the Americas, even trading small arms with unconquered "Carib Cannibals" in the Windward Islands for cured leaves.

This early drug trade, since it bypassed Spain's Seville monopoly, was considered unlawful and a threat to state security—some of the smugglers were also pirates, as it turned out. The foreigners proved difficult to catch given Spain's weak navy, so the government sought to root out the suppliers on the mainland instead. A number of Venezuelan growers, whom the Spanish Crown considered equivalent to traitors, or apostates (*gente perdida*), were forced to give up their lucrative profession or face imprisonment after 1606. As with the modern contraband drug trade, however, the power of international demand encouraged growers to explore other options. Some simply moved to more remote locations, such as the Orinoco River basin, where they continued to fuel the seemingly limitless addictions of English, Dutch, French, and other European smokers. The goods they took in exchange, duty-free, were traded as far south as Upper Peru. The tobacco trade in the early seventeenth century was sufficiently attractive that the Dutch and others sought to establish their own American plantations, which they soon attempted in the Orinoco and eastward. Spanish and Portuguese raids on these incipient colonies, especially after 1621, however, drove the foreigners to seek yet newer ground, the English redoubling their efforts at Jamestown, Virginia (1607), and on Caribbean islands such as Nevis (1628) and St. Kitts, the French at Tortuga (by 1630), and the Dutch in northernmost Brazil (by 1620).[5] Tobacco thus displaced salt as the principal bone of Dutch–Spanish contention in the Caribbean, but it turned out to be only one of many aspects of a new commercial war.

Spain's Philip III (1598–1621) and his ministers soon discovered that the expensive Caribbean defense strategy of the first decade of the seventeenth century could not be sustained, and by the time the Twelve-Years Truce (1609–21) with the United Provinces of the Netherlands expired, Dutch smugglers, privateers, and pirates faced little resistance. In 1621 some intrepid Hollanders even began to exploit the Araya salt pans once again, though mindful not to lose their heads doing it. The end of the truce also coincided with another more important development, namely the formation of the Dutch West India Company. This organization, headed by a board of directors called the Heeren XIX, or "Nineteen Gentlemen," was chartered with belligerent commerce in mind. This was business of the variety practiced by John Hawkins and his type over half a century earlier, but the Dutch traders went the further step of arming for conquest in order to guarantee a high rate of return to shareholders. Furthermore, West India Company employees, like the famously Calvinist admiral and former pirate Piet Heyn, were not prohibited from stealing the enemy's most prized possessions in lieu of a forced sale. From the Spanish Crown's point of view, this was simply piracy on a grand scale, and hence the post-truce aggressions of the Dutch trading firms would be met with the first large-scale Spanish naval expeditions seen in the Americas (1625–40).

Piet Heyn and the Dutch West India Company

As will be seen later in the case of Chile and Peru, the Dutch did not restrict themselves to the Caribbean Sea when harassing the Luso-Hispanic Americas, but it was in the Caribbean, in the waters off northern Cuba, where Dutch interlopers—pirates from one perspective, privateers from another—took their most memorable prize, a Spanish silver fleet. There would be other American prizes, however. Brazil was considered a plum by the West India Company's directors, and Portugal seemed too weak to prevent its loss, even with Spain's very conspicuous aid. Portuguese outposts in the East Indies, now being attacked or displaced by agents of the VOC, were considered of greater overall importance to Dutch commerce, but if parts of the West Indies (and Atlantic Africa) could be had as well, all the better. Armed for conquest and occupation rather than simple strong-armed trade by 1623, Admiral Piet Heyn and a massive fleet made up of twenty-six ships and carrying 3,300 men set out for Bahia de Todos os Santos, or All Saints Bay, on the northeast coast of Brazil, and took control of it without much struggle in 1624. A combined Spanish-Portuguese fleet under command of Fadrique de Toledo quickly won back Bahia by 1625, but the Dutch had made their point; they would return to play for keeps in the more northerly sugar-growing region of Pernambuco soon afterward.

In the Caribbean the Spanish feared a Dutch assault on Havana, but none materialized. A West India Company reconnaissance mission under Pieter Schouten cruised Spanish waters from Barbados westward with three ships in 1624, capturing a galleon from Honduras, but accomplished little more. In 1625 the Bahia relief fleet, commanded by Boudewijn Hendricksz, made its way to Puerto Rico after careening at the Virgin Islands. Hendricksz laid siege to San Juan and its fort on 24 September, taking the former but not the latter and paying dearly for this shortcoming; his ships retreated, badly damaged, under punishing fire from the castle. (Apparently the Spanish fortification strategy of the late sixteenth century was beginning to pay off.) The Dutch left for the smaller islands after five weeks of interspersed pillage and bombardment, but failed to sack Margarita in February of 1626. While waiting near Havana for the passing of the New Spain fleet later that year, Captain Hendricksz died and his followers returned to Holland with little to show the shareholders and directors of the company. A few semi-independent Dutch raiding expeditions from these years did notable damage, though with little gain, among them a squadron led by the frighteningly named Hendrick Jacobszoon Lucifer in 1627.[6]

Pieter Pieterszoon Heyn, who has often been mistakenly called Peg-leg, or Pie de Palo, like his French predecessor François Le Clerc, entered Caribbean waters in 1627 also, but quickly left for Brazil (the real Dutch Peg-leg [Houtebeen] of this era was Cornelis Jol, famous for his raids on Campeche in the 1630s).[7] Heyn's fleet returned to the West Indies in 1628, however, with thirty-two ships, 700 cannon, and some 3,500 men; he was looking for a haul of Spanish treasure big enough to placate the West India Company stockholders disappointed by the Hendricksz mission. On 8 September, in the midst of hurricane season, Heyn encountered the New Spain treasure convoy as it made for Havana. The unusually small, fifteen-ship Spanish flota, commanded by Juan de Benavides, tried to avoid an encounter by shooting into Matanzas Bay, just east of Havana. Benavides's

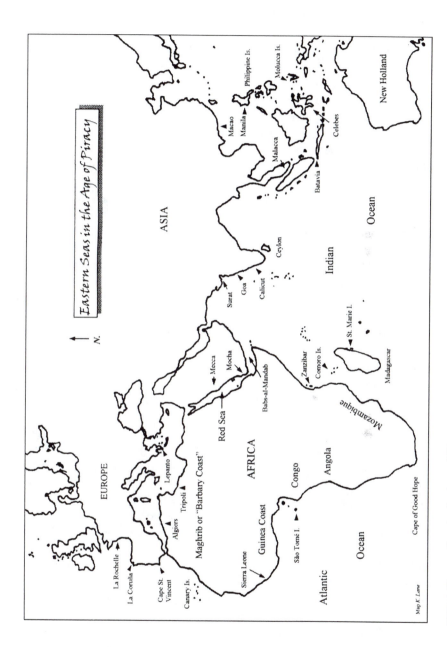

Eastern Seas in the Age of Piracy

N.

EUROPE

La Rochelle
La Coruña
Cape St. Vincent
Canary Is.
Algiers
Tripoli
Lepanto

Maghrib or "Barbary Coast"

Sierra Leone
Guinea Coast
São Tomé I.

AFRICA

Congo
Angola

Atlantic
Ocean

Cape of Good Hope

Mecca
Mocha
Red Sea
Babs-al-Mandab

Zanzibar
Comoro Is.
Mozambique

St. Marie I.
Madagascar

ASIA

Surat
Goa
Calicut
Ceylon

Indian
Ocean

Macao
Manila
Philippine Is.
Molucca Is.
Malacca
Celebes
Batavia

New Holland

Map K. Lane

MAP 4 Eastern Seas in the Age of Piracy

pilots were apparently less familiar with this bay's shoals than they had claimed, and several of the large ships foundered, stranding the treasure well offshore and leaving most of the ships' guns pointed the wrong way. Heyn and his men seized the opportunity and captured all fifteen vessels, taking half for prizes and setting fire to the rest. Benavides was imprisoned, not by the Dutch, but rather the Spanish, and was eventually executed for negligence and abandonment of duty in Seville in May of 1634.[8] Heyn, meanwhile, took gold, silver, silks, dyestuffs, and other valuables worth some 12 million florins (c. 4.8 million silver pesos). Later, as the underpaid sailors and soldiers who had participated in the raid rioted in the streets of Amsterdam, burgher shareholders enjoyed dividends of over 75 percent, the highest ever paid by the West India Company.[9] Clearly the notion of "pirate democracy," at least in terms of the division of spoils, had not advanced much since Drake's time.

Piet Heyn's great theft hurt Spain's pride and purse in equal measure but it was an act not to be repeated. In the aftermath other Dutch raiders cleaned up Caribbean leftovers as best they could. A force of twelve ships commanded by Pieter Adriaenz Ita took two Honduras galleons, and Adrian Janszoon Pater managed similar feats soon after. Indeed, the period 1628–35 saw such relentless Dutch activity that Spain's sovereignty in the Caribbean, in spite of the victories of Fadrique de Toledo in 1629–30 at Nevis and St. Kitts (Spanish San Cristóbal) and the Marquis de Cadereyta's capture of Dutch San Martín in 1633, seemed to be slipping inexorably away.[10] The island of Curaçao was planted with a permanent Dutch settlement by 1634, and trading posts and salt mines were established on several of the Lesser Antilles in subsequent years. Dutch privateering and piracy would continue from these bases until well after the Peace of Münster in 1648, but with decreasing vigor as merchant interests in the Americas developed. The Spanish continued to fear large-scale Dutch attacks for some years after Matanzas, however, and thus spent enormous sums outfitting naval escorts for the treasure ships. Carla Rahn Phillips, who has studied the post-Heyn period Spanish fleets in great detail, has shown how one round-trip voyage for the newly outfitted Armada de la Guardia could cost upward of one million ducats (1.4 million silver pesos). Such expenses were incurred in the 1632–33 voyage, when the fleet met up with no enemies and lost no ships to storms. Little wonder, then, that merchants, forced to pay averías of 23 to almost 40 percent and more to fund these fleets, preferred to take their chances with pirates.[11]

For their part, the Dutch began to experience the sort of problems by now all too familiar to their Spanish and Portuguese prey: colonies, always thought to be the milch cows of empire, were in fact hugely expensive to defend and administer. Some Dutch resources were diverted to Pacific waters in these years, as will be seen in the next section, but Brazil proved to be the West India Company's overseas quagmire. After a quick conquest and the establishment of an energetic administration, northeast Brazil turned from asset to liability in less than a decade.

The region remained in Dutch hands until 1654, but was beset by persistent and costly settler rebellions after 1645. Compared with unrewarding company service, the life of the freelance pirate appealed more and more to Dutch seamen, and their numbers grew in the Caribbean, particularly after 1630. One outstanding leader of Dutch sea-rovers in this period was Diego el Mulato, a former slave of Havana who went renegade in 1629. This part-African pirate was Diego de Los Reyes, described in the following passage by the English Dominican Thomas Gage, who met (and was robbed by) him in 1637 near Portobelo and later spoke with his mother in Havana. Gage describes his own capture by this adopted Dutch pirate as follows:

> My further thoughts were soon interrupted by the Hollanders, who came aboard our frigate with more speed than we desired. Though their swords, muskets, and pistols did not a little terrify, yet we were somewhat comforted when we understood who was their chief captain and commander. We hoped for more mercy from him, for he had been brought up amongst Spaniards, than from the Hollanders, for as they were little bound unto the Spanish nation for mercy, so did we expect little from them. The captain of this Holland ship which took us was a mulatto, born and bred in Havana, whose mother I saw and spoke with afterwards that same year, when the galleons struck into that port to expect there the rest that were to come from Veracruz. This mulatto, for some wrongs which had been offered unto him from some commanding Spaniards in Havana, ventured himself desperately in a boat out to sea, where were some Holland ships waiting for a prize. With God's help getting unto them, he yielded himself to their mercy, which he esteemed far better than that of his own countrymen, promising to serve them faithfully against his own nation, which had most injuriously and wrongfully abused, yea, and whipped him in Havana, as I was afterwards informed.[12]

That Diego el Mulato was elevated to the post of captain within eight years of joining the pirates suggests the Dutch valued merit over color and nationality, at least when it came to war. Certainly not all European pirates were as color-blind as these, but Diego of Havana was symbolic of the mixed-heritage rebels who would make up an ever larger proportion of pirate crews by the mid-seventeenth century. In the succeeding buccaneer era, particularly, European indentured servants and seamen had much in common with slaves and mixed-heritage Spanish subjects, and a sort of class camaraderie could at times override color prejudice. From the Spanish point of view, renegades of any color were the most dangerous sort of enemy; like the disgruntled mariner who led the French corsairs into Cartagena harbor in 1544 (see Chapter 1), "apostate" Spanish subjects like Diego el Mulato were Judas figures, treacherous men who knew too much.

Dutch Intruders in the Pacific

The decade 1590–1600 witnessed the great worldwide expansion of the Dutch Republic. As we have seen, it was Portugal's place in the East Indies that the Dutch coveted most; the West Indies, Spanish or otherwise, were only a secondary or tertiary objective. It was the quest for silks and spices, and to a lesser extent slaves, that pushed explorers like Cornelis Houtman to the East Indies by way of the Cape of Good Hope in 1594, and drove a new trade in information gathered previously by English circumnavigators like Drake and Cavendish, along with Spanish and Portuguese spies and renegades. By 1600 the Dutch had made contact with the newly established Tokugawa Shogunate in Japan, and had formed the beginnings of what would become an exclusive European trading arrangement with those islands. Well before the great East and West India companies were formed in the early seventeenth century, investors in Amsterdam were clamoring for permission to seek trade in distant parts of the globe.

One such company of traders—they were smugglers, it should be noted, not pirates—was organized in 1598 by Pieter van der Haghen with the intention of entering the Spanish Pacific, or South Sea. The expedition, which was to explore trading and even settlement possibilities along the coast of Chile before heading on to the East Indies, was made up of some 500 men in five large vessels, headed by the 500-ton *Hope*, commanded by Jacob Mahu. The saleable cargo consisted of cloth from the Netherlands and Rouen (France) and dry goods such as glassware and tools, but a great deal of armament seems to have been carried as well. Indeed, the ships were so heavily armed that much of the cargo, at least by weight, consisted of arquebuses, muskets, chain-mail armor, and cannon, some for protection of the crew and some to be traded to potential indigenous or runaway African and mixed-heritage allies.[13] The war with Spain was ongoing, and investors understood that intimidation might have to accompany any exchanges in Spanish dominions if a profit was to be realized. Not being familiar with the difficult southern passage from the Atlantic to the Pacific, the Mahu expedition employed several English pilots, one of them, Timothy Shotten, a veteran of Cavendish's 1587 circumnavigation.

Mahu's fleet left the Netherlands in late June of 1598 for the Cape Verde Islands, but found the Portuguese unwilling (with good reason, no doubt) to sell them supplies. Mahu himself died while cruising the west coast of Africa in search of water and food; local inhabitants apparently took the Dutch for slave traders, which they could easily have been, and fled from their landing parties. Fruit and cattle were at last found on Annobon Island (off equatorial Africa), and the voyage to the Strait of Magellan was begun under command of Simon de Cordes in early January 1599. The passage was reached in spite of the crew's general discontent—they had been informed rather suddenly that they were going "the long way" to the East Indies—on 6 April. The anger and bitterness provoked by this deception, the type of which was to be repeated in subsequent Dutch South

Sea voyages, was compounded by a punishing passage through the Strait. Cordes apparently misjudged the winds and ignored the advice of his English companions, thus stranding the fleet in Great Bay (or Cordes Bay) through the winter season. By the time the passage could be completed safely at least 120 men had died. During their sojourn many had succumbed to hunger, disease, and exposure,

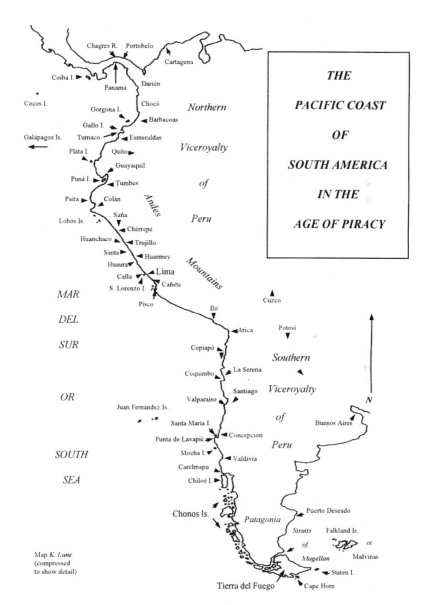

MAP 5 The Pacific Coast of South America in the Age of Piracy

but some of the expedition's members had been killed by local indigenous bands, variously described by witnesses as ten- to eleven-foot-tall giants (Magellan's legendary *patagones*, or "bigfeet," hence Patagonia) and "people small in body dressed in skins."[14] Hardship and delusions of the other's grandeur went together well, it seems.

Cordes established a sort of officers' club called the Order of the Unchained Lion before leaving the Strait for the Pacific, promising in a pompous manner to do damage to the king of Spain in the name of the United Provinces (by sacking the supposed source of Spain's war treasury). The Dutch would have little opportunity to effect such damage during this voyage, however, as the fleet became permanently separated upon trying to enter Pacific waters. Cordes and the misnamed flagship *Hope*, along with the 300-ton *Charity*, eventually reached Santa María Island, off Concepción, Chile, in early November. Unaware that one ship, the 150-ton *Glad Tidings*, had suffered an accident on leaving the Strait and was being helped by two other vessels, the *Faith* and *Fidelity*, Cordes had spent a month cruising the southern Chile coast in search of friendly Native Americans. In most cases the few indigenous peoples encountered among the Chonos Islands had been cordial, but farther north, at Punta de Lavapié, a landing party of twenty-three Dutchmen was attacked and annihilated without so much as a chance for discussion. The indigenous inhabitants of this region, as in other parts of the Americas, were not to be automatic allies of Spain's European enemies, evidenced further by the *Charity*'s loss of a party of twenty-seven on Mocha Island to a similar attack. By this time less than half of the expedition's original 500-man crew was still alive, and further bad luck drove the *Faith*, commanded by Sebald de Weert, to abandon the others and sail back to Europe via the Strait. De Weert's consolation upon arriving with only thirty-six weary and sick survivors at Goeree on 13 July 1600 was that his would be the only ship from the Mahu expedition to return to Europe at all.[15]

Meanwhile the *Hope* and *Charity* found the Spanish authorities of the coast near Santa María to be unwelcoming, not even allowing them to trade for much-needed foodstuffs. Cordes and his remaining followers made for the East Indies on 27 November 1599, the *Hope* arriving in Japan to yet another hostile reception after some months; the *Charity* was lost at sea. The *Glad Tidings* meanwhile, after being repaired, again tried to leave the Strait of Magellan only to be blown south by storms beyond sixty degrees latitude. Eventually struggling northward again, the twenty-three bedraggled crewmembers, under Dirck Gerritsz, surrendered to the Spanish at Valparaíso on 17 November 1599. The *corregidor*, or crown official of Santiago de Chile, Jerónimo de Molina, took the prisoners for questioning, sending a few on to Lima and eventually Spain but keeping most of them in custody locally. One of the survivors, whom the Spanish called Adrián Rodríguez, would play the spy in a later Dutch venture to the Pacific under Jacques l'Hermite, but for now he was just another sailor in prison.[16] Lastly, the crew of the *Fidelity*, under Simon de Cordes's brother Baltasar, managed to organize a combined Dutch-indigenous attack on the Spanish post at Chiloé in April of 1600. Here the native inhabitants had been willing allies, but the Spanish quickly retook the island, killing all but twenty-three Dutch and perhaps 300 Native Americans. This loss served as a strong disincentive for indigenous Chileans to join with foreign interlopers in the future. Amazingly, the *Fidelity* was sailed to the Portuguese East Indies spice outpost of Tidore, where the crew was imprisoned in January 1601.

Rather less disastrous was the almost simultaneous but more plodding Dutch South Sea expedition commanded by Olivier van Noort, a former tavern keeper from Utrecht. Funded by the merchants Pieter van Beveren, Huyg Gerritsz van der Buys, and Jan Benning, van Noort's flagship, the 250-ton *Maurice*, followed by the 300-ton *Hendrick Frederick* and two fifty-ton barks called *Hope* and *Concord*, left Holland on 13 September 1598. After unpleasant brushes with the Portuguese off the coast of Guinea and at Rio de Janeiro, Brazil, van Noort's fleet attempted to locate one of the tiny South Atlantic Islands, St. Helena or Ascensión, for wintering. It was too late to pass the Strait of Magellan and neither of the two islands appeared on the horizon, so the fleet made for the northeast Patagonia coast, landing near Puerto Deseado in an already desperate state. The original crew of some 248 was now reduced by almost a third, one of the barks was barely seaworthy, and the only food to be had in this desolate place was the meat and eggs of penguins. By mid-November van Noort began to drive through the Strait, only to be met with fierce contrary winds. After a near-mutiny, an unprovoked slaughter of Penguin Island natives, and a brief and uneventful rendezvous with the departing *Faith*, under Sebald de Weert—each side, being short of supplies, apparently left the other to "go Dutch"—the fleet entered the South Pacific at the end of February 1600. As had happened to the Mahu–Cordes fleet, the ships simply could not manage to stay together in these stormy seas; the *Hendrick Frederick* was on its own from here on, and van Noort, meanwhile, headed north in the *Maurice*.

Although van Noort's luck had been at best mixed to this point, he did find the indigenous inhabitants of Mocha Island less hostile than they had been to his predecessors. A small exchange of knives and hatchets for food took place in late March of 1600, and van Noort's refreshed crew set sail for Santa María, where they were supposed to rendezvous with the crew of the *Hendrick Frederick*. On the way they overtook the *Buen Jesús*, a small bark under don Francisco de Ibarra, who was part of a reconnaissance squadron sent south from Callao in January. In lieu of booty—a cargo of gold from Chile was said to have been thrown overboard before capture—the *Buen Jesús* yielded information and a pilot. Acting very much like a pirate ship by now, the *Maurice* took a second prize with the picturesque name of *Los Picos* near Valparaíso on 28 March. This vessel yielded a welcome cargo of wine, olives, and fruit, along with some leather and some letters regarding the Mahu captives. The letters, written by the captive Dirck Gerritsz, reminded van Noort of Spanish disapproval of his presence in the South Sea. A landing at Huasco on 1 April added to the ships' stores of fruit and meat, the

Buen Jesús was released, *Los Picos* burned, and the borrowed pilot thrown overboard for complaining that he had been poisoned. Van Noort had decided to try his luck in the East Indies, and the *Maurice* set sail by mid-year for the Ladrones and Philippine Islands.[17]

Van Noort appears to have continued with his piratical intentions against the Spanish in the Philippines, where he arrived in late 1600 to search for an incoming Manila galleon. Soon the *Maurice* closed in on Manila, harrying small trading vessels in the vicinity of the Bisayas Islands along the way. Dutch vessels were a novelty in the Philippines at this time and consequently the resident Spanish were not well prepared for a sea attack. The city center of Manila was walled, but few fighting vessels were on hand to counter piracy—those that did exist were currently engaged, along with most of the Spanish fighting men of the Philippines, with the Muslim Malay rebels of the southern islands. A quick solution was needed and a galley commander named Pedro Ronquillo de Castillo was charged with constructing two fighting ships at the port of Cavite by the Spanish governor. Some sort of quarrel developed between Ronquillo and a senior judge of the audiencia (and future president of the Audiencia of Quito), Antonio de Morga, and Ronquillo was dismissed. An untested but ambitious *letrado*, or man of letters, Morga himself replaced Ronquillo and set out to face van Noort a month later in the freshly built *San Diego*, a formidable ship at 200-odd tons, but only lightly armed. A smaller vessel, the *San Bartolomé*, under Captain Juan de Alcega, was to accompany Morga but soon fell behind. The *San Diego* and *Maurice* engaged in battle on 14 December 1600, and for a time it appeared that the victory would fall to the Spanish. Morga's men grappled and boarded the larger Dutch vessel, very nearly overwhelming the tired crew, but a well-aimed shot to the hull of the *San Diego* from van Noort's ship forced the judge to abandon the attack and seek a landing. The *San Diego* sank quickly, killing almost 200 men while trying to reach the nearby island of Fortuna.

Morga was lucky enough to be among the few survivors, but van Noort's *Maurice* would always haunt him as the one pirate ship that got away. As will be seen later, Morga would have another chance to confront the Dutch in the Pacific, at Guayaquil in 1624, but he would never fully avenge this embarrassing loss in the Philippines.[18] Alcega and the crew of the *San Bartolomé*, meanwhile, had failed to follow Morga's orders to stay by the flagship, instead opting to chase the *Concord*, which was successfully captured and taken for a prize to Manila; all crewmembers were executed. A bruised van Noort took his crew to Borneo to repair the *Maurice*, which then made its way west across the Indian Ocean, rounding the Cape of Good Hope and arriving in Rotterdam on 27 August 1601, the first Dutch and only the fourth European expedition to circumnavigate the globe.

Back in Peru, the *Hendrick Frederick*, under command of Pieter Esaiasz de Lint, cruised alone, vainly searching for the *Maurice*. Several inconsequential engagements with the Spanish occurred in May and June of 1600 at Santa María, Concepción, and Arica, followed by a quick dumping of prisoners and an unhappy

Dutchman named Christian Haese off Guayaquil, port of the Audiencia of Quito.[19] De Lint continued north to the Gulf of Panama and beyond, landing at Coiba Island to careen and victual in early August. On 11 August he took a small maize carrier near Caño Island, imprisoning a Franciscan friar named Agustín de Cavallos, who left the only surviving account of the *Hendrick Frederick*'s crew and intentions. He and several other captives were put ashore near Realejo sixteen days later, but during his sojourn among the "Calvinist heretics" Cavallos noted that the crew of fifty-four Dutchmen, most of them able Spanish speakers, aimed to meet up with van Noort near Cabo San Lucas and seize a Manila galleon. They would then sail together to the East Indies. Cavallos also noted that de Lint carried a copy of Cavendish's detailed ship's log, and thus had little trouble finding his way around these seas. After taking another small vessel and incorporating three African slaves and a Dutchman (then in the employ of a Portuguese ship owner) into the crew, the *Hendrick Frederick* disappeared.[20]

It is unclear what path de Lint followed from here, but he was not sighted by the Spanish again, and does not appear anywhere in the historical record until April or May of 1601 in the East Indies, when his crew entered the service of the VOC at Ternate, the new Dutch post in the Molucca Islands. Gerhard suggests that the *Hendrick Frederick* landed at Cocos Island, well to the west of Costa Rica, to careen and victual before setting off across the vast Pacific.[21] This is a likely and interesting possibility, given the island's remoteness, but whatever their last stop these first serious Dutch intruders in the Spanish South Sea caused great consternation all up and down the west coast of New Spain and Peru. Partly as a result of this panic, a fleet of three galleons, including Richard Hawkins's captured *Dainty*, rechristened the *Inglesa* (or "Englishwoman"), and several smaller warships left Callao in early 1600 under Juan de Velasco, nephew of the Peruvian viceroy. After patrolling the waters around Pisco, a famous wine-producing center in southern Peru, Velasco's task was to deliver the annual bullion shipment from Callao to Panama, which he did without incident. Afterward he was ordered to cruise the coast of New Spain as far as Cabo San Lucas looking for the pirates, but the Dutch never appeared, and Velasco had the misfortune of encountering a hurricane near Salagua in mid-August of 1600. He was never heard from again, presumably killed in the wreck of the *capitana*, or flagship.

The next Dutch enterprise to wreak havoc in the Spanish South Sea—one which would destroy the better part of Peru's sea defenses—was commanded by a veteran East Indies sailor, Joris van Speilbergen (or Spilbergen), and sponsored by the States-General and VOC. Speilbergen left the Netherlands on 8 August 1614, in the midst of the Twelve-Years Truce with Spain (1609–21), with four large ships, two yachts, and approximately 700 men. The men, among them some 350 soldiers and including some Germans and Frenchmen, were told that India was their destination, not a lie, perhaps, but as with van Noort's crew no one suspected that they would have to cross both the Atlantic and Pacific to get there. This deception may have been wise for security purposes in Europe, but it made for

FIGURE 3.1 Antonio de Morga's *San Diego* Meets Olivier van Noort's *Maurice* off the Philippines, 14 December 1600

Source: Theodor de Bry, *Historia Americae VIII* (courtesy of the James Ford Bell Library, University of Minnesota).

great unhappiness among the crew, some of whom later deserted to the Spanish and informed on their superiors. Along with a fair amount of war matériel, as in the Mahu expedition, the Speilbergen fleet carried enough preserved rations to last three years; they hoped to avoid the sorts of hardships faced by their predecessors. Still, water and fresh fruits were needed along the way, and before reaching the Strait they made stops at the Canary and Cape Verde Islands, followed by Ilha Grande and São Vicente, Brazil. An agreement to trade for supplies in late January 1615 at São Vicente went sour due to a sudden shift in Portuguese policy, and the Dutch responded by burning a church and a sugar mill, and also taking and looting a small vessel on its way to Angola. Word of these actions was sent overland via the provinces of Río de la Plata and Charcas to Lima, where the Peruvian viceroy Montesclaros began preparing his ill-fated defense fleet.

Now fully victualed, the Dutch ships *Great Sun, Great Moon, Morning Star, Aeolus,* and *Huntsman* made their way to the Strait of Magellan. At São Vicente Speilbergen had faced some of the same problems of officer and crew insubordination as van Noort and Mahu, but he seems to have dealt with them more effectively. The yacht *Gull* had in fact deserted entirely after Speilbergen had two officers hanged for treason, but the majority of the expedition's leaders seem to have happily partaken in celebratory feasts in Cordes Bay in mid-April. Not everyone celebrated equally here in the cold wastes of Tierra del Fuego, however, and in spite of the much-celebrated Dutch tradition of thrift and exemplary austerity, Speilbergen and his officers dined like kings on this particular occasion. While the common seamen and soldiers made do with a diet of scrounged herbs, mussels, and berries, the officers filled themselves—accompanied by chamber music—with beef, pork, fowl, citrus fruits, preserves, olives, capers, wine, and beer.[22] As might be imagined, this conspicuous inequality in the distribution of rations led to considerable unhappiness among those not included in the feast. Two Germans who later deserted at Papudo, Chile—Andreas Heinrich of Emden and Philip Hansen of Königsberg—claimed that this, not harsh discipline or deception regarding India, was their principal motivation for leaving the expedition.

After a little over a month spent passing the Strait, Speilbergen's fleet made north along the coast of Chile, reaching Mocha on 26 May 1615. Here a number of indigenous *caciques,* or chieftains, were entertained on the flagship, followed by a small exchange of dry goods and hardware for food supplies. The next port of call was the island of Santa María, where Speilbergen's men repeated their experience at São Vicente; a Spanish invitation to trade turned out to be a trap, so the settlement was ordered burned and looted. An informant captured on this occasion, Juan Cornejo, revealed the presence in these seas of a Spanish naval squadron sent with precise orders to search out and destroy Speilbergen's fleet. The fleet had in fact already returned northward after cruising the Chilean coast but Speilbergen, undaunted, made careful plans for an engagement. The Dutch anchored off Concepción on 3 June but did not attempt a landing, possibly due to the defensive posture of the Spanish assembled there (they were led by Chile's governor, Alonso de Ribera, an experienced military man). Speilbergen continued north to Valparaíso, where a landing force of 200 tore up what was left of the intentionally burned and abandoned town on 12 June. While watering at Papudo, two prisoners taken at São Vicente were released and the two unhappy Germans deserted to seek better rations.

Hoping to find a pile of silver awaiting the treasure galleons from Callao, Speilbergen and his men put in at Arica on 2 July. They must have found out that the year's shipment had departed in mid-May, however, for no engagement took place, much to the relief of the poorly armed and undertrained citizenry.

A trading vessel was overtaken near Pisco on 16 July, yielding a modest cargo of olives and 7,000 silver pesos, and late the next day, off Cañete, just south of Lima, the viceroy's fleet hove into view. The Peruvian *armadilla*, or "little navy," consisted of seven ships, two crown galleons, and five conscripted merchant vessels, fitted out with a total of fifty-six guns and carrying some 620 armed men. The Spanish had a clear advantage in terms of armed individuals, but the Dutch carried twice as many big guns. A brief engagement that evening between Speilbergen's flagship *Great Sun* and one of the unarmed merchantmen, the *San Francisco*, ended in disaster for the latter. About ninety men are said to have drowned, but the ship's captain miraculously survived by latching onto a Dutch drum.[23]

The long-anticipated sea battle with the Dutch had started off badly for the Spanish, and it would only worsen on the following day. At daybreak on 18 July 1615 the Spanish armadilla's commander, Rodrigo de Mendoza, found his ships in disarray. Perhaps frightened by the experience of the *San Francisco* the night before, the various merchantmen had sailed away, and most stayed out of the battle altogether. This left Mendoza in the 400-ton *Jesús María* and Captain Pedro Alvarez de Pulgar in the 250-ton *Santa Ana* to face the full brunt of the Dutch attack. After several hours of battering from Speilbergen's guns Mendoza put up the flag of surrender, only to flee to Pisco. This left Alvarez de Pulgar and the *Santa Ana* (which on an earlier occasion he had called "heavy and a poor sailer") in a vulnerable position. She was shot through below the water line and sunk, along with her stubbornly resistant captain, in short order. One survivor of this engagement, the crossed-dressed Basque soldier and notorious "*picara*," Catalina de Erauso, described this dramatic incident in her memoirs as follows:

> We went out to meet them from the port of Callao in five ships, and for a long time it went well for us, but then the Dutch began hammering away at our flagship and in the end she heaved over and only three of us managed to escape—me, a barefoot Franciscan friar, and a soldier—paddling around until an enemy ship took us up. The Dutch treated us like dirt, jeering and scoffing. All the others who had been on the flagship had drowned. Four ships remained under General Rodrigo de Mendoza, and when they got back to Callao the next morning at least nine hundred men were reckoned as missing, myself included, because I'd been on the flagship. . . . For twenty-six days I was in enemy hands, thinking they meant to deal with me by carting me off to Holland. But in the end they flung me and my two companions out on the Paita coast, a good hundred leagues from Lima, and after several days and no end of trouble a good man took pity on our naked state, gave us some clothes and gear and pointed us in the direction of Lima, and we finally made it back.[24]

Spanish losses in this disastrous encounter were said to number between 400 and 500 killed or drowned, along with the two ships, one a brand-new frigate worth over 100,000 pesos. The Dutch ships sustained no significant damage, though casualties amounted to some thirty to forty killed and fifty wounded. Speilbergen intended to make the most of this victory by closing in on Callao and Lima, but his greatest achievement was already behind him.[25]

The viceroy, Montesclaros, may have been embarrassed by the poor performance of his little navy, but he was not crippled by the loss. By the time Speilbergen and his fleet reached Callao on 20 July he had mustered a strong-looking series of militia companies, some made up of completely untrained clergymen and students from the University of San Marcos. The defenses of Lima were much weaker than they appeared—a lucky shot that hit the *Huntsman* came from one of only three guns left at Callao, for example—but the ad hoc show of force seems to have worked. The Dutch pirates set sail by 26 July, hoping for easier prey farther north. A small prize carrying salt and honey was taken off Huaura and the deserted town of Huarmey was sacked for food stores on 28 July. Some prisoners were also dropped here, joined by another deserter, this time a Frenchman named Nicolas de la Porte. The north Peruvian port of Paita was attacked on 9 August, falling to the pirates the next day after a spirited resistance. Speilbergen and his men quickly sacked and burned the town, but finding the site agreeable they spent nearly two weeks around Paita victualing and resting. The Dutch spoke amicably with indigenous and black fishermen working from balsa rafts offshore and near the Lobos Islands and an exchange of food for prisoners was effected with the local corregidor, Juan Colmenero de Andrade, and his wife, "Doña Paula." From here Speilbergen planned his next bold venture, the seizure of the incoming viceroy, the Prince of Esquilache.

As luck would have it, the viceroy's escort had received word of the Dutch presence beforehand, and had put in at Manta, well to the north of Guayaquil, to allow the famous passenger to make his journey to the capital overland. This opportunity missed, another chance for famous prey came on the evening of 27 August, when one of Speilbergen's men spied a sail off Punta Santa Elena. This ship, the *Nuestra Señora del Rosario*, out of Acapulco, made a lucky escape and landed safely at Guayaquil. This close call was in fact more fortunate for the Spanish than the Dutch could possibly have realized. The *Rosario*, as it happened, carried the very ransomable personage of Antonio de Morga, Quito's new president and veteran pirate fighter, along with a handsome cargo of contraband silks—worth some one million pesos—fresh from Manila.[26] Ignorant of all this Manila contraband floating by under his nose, Speilbergen and his fleet sailed north to the coast of New Spain in hopes of surprising an actual Manila galleon.

The Dutch cruised Central American waters with minimal effect, spending most of their time searching for supplies. Speilbergen's crew put in near Amapala Bay on 20 September, continued northwestward along the coast to Guatulco, weathering a hurricane along the way, and finally arrived at Acapulco on 11 October. Speilbergen's crew was now desperate for supplies, especially scurvy-fighting citrus fruits, and was willing to fight for whatever it could lay hands on. A strange

FIGURE 3.2 View of Paita, Peru

Source: Joris van Speilbergen, *The East and West India Mirror* (1619).

incident followed their arrival, however: a Dutch party went ashore under a flag of truce, promising to release prisoners in exchange for food. The Spanish accepted the offer, holding fire from their new shore-mounted guns while both sides entertained one another. Spanish officers were allowed aboard the Dutch vessels to inspect their rigging and armament, and Speilbergen's own son was treated to the hospitality of the local alcalde mayor. Following this strangely pleasant interlude, proof that nationalist and confessional animosity could be at least temporarily cast aside, Speilbergen left Acapulco on 18 October and cruised northward. A pearling vessel from California was taken, its crew imprisoned, and an attack on the hamlet of Salagua attempted. Having expected the Dutch to land, the Spanish took the day, but losses on both sides were minimal, largely due to the superior firearms of the Dutch.[27] The Salagua incident was followed by an apparently enjoyable period of rest and relaxation near Navidad, at the bay of Tenacatita. The Dutch lingered in these waters until 2 December 1615, when they at last decided to make the Pacific crossing from Cape Corrientes. Speilbergen passed by Manila and the Moluccas before returning to the Netherlands on 1 July 1617.

As Peter Bradley has shown, Speilbergen's raids and the appearance of the Viceroy Esquilache signaled a watershed in Spanish South Sea defense strategy. As in the Caribbean and Atlantic Triangle, this shift would entail a vast increase in military expenditures, and hence higher taxes, particularly on merchant shipping.

The crown was as wary as the merchant sector of a defense buildup in Peru, however, and tried to put a damper on the viceroy's plans; from the perspective of central authorities, local defenses could not be allowed to siphon away crucial bullion in the midst of multiple European crises. Esquilache nevertheless went ahead with his projects, which included the construction of forts around Callao, the formation of a salaried army of 500 men (and perhaps the occasional woman like Catalina de Erauso), and the reconstruction of the Armada del Mar del Sur. By 1621 two galleons and one patax carried treasure from Callao to Panama while a similar contingent patrolled the south Peruvian and Chilean coasts.[28] This shift to active defense in the Pacific was modest by Atlantic standards, but it could only become larger and more costly from here onward.

Despite Spanish fears and expensive defense measures in the wake of Speilbergen's raids, Dutch privateers were not to return to the Pacific for almost a decade. In the meantime, the Thirty Years War had begun in Europe (in 1618), the truce between the United Provinces and Spain had expired, and the Dutch West India Company was chartered (on 3 June 1621). As noted earlier, the political climate in the Netherlands now favored outright hostility against the colonial dominions and shipping of Spain and Portugal, and the West India Company outfitted and armed a number of post-truce expeditions with this sentiment in mind. Brazil, of course, turned out to be the first choice of most of the company's investors, but Peru and Mexico were not forgotten. Though more closely connected to the older East India Company (VOC) than the West India Company in the end, a substantial fleet of Dutch ships was sent to the Pacific with the blessing of Count Maurits of Nassau in 1623. This massive expedition, consisting of eleven ships, most between 300 and 800 tons and fitted out with a total of 294 guns and some 1,630 men, was commanded by Admiral Jacques l'Hermite. The so-called Nassau Fleet left the Netherlands on 29 April and took almost a year—in spite of new knowledge from both Dutch and Spanish sources to aid in the passage around Cape Horn via the Strait of Lemaire—to reach the coast of Chile, which was first sighted on 28 March 1624. Its fortunes would range from ill to mixed, but the Nassau Fleet would be remembered in Peru for its blockade of Lima's port of Callao and for sacking the city of Guayaquil in 1624.

From the beginning l'Hermite's fleet seemed to suffer from its unwieldy size. It was difficult enough to coordinate the movements of so many large ships, but in addition to these expected difficulties, major leaks were discovered in several vessels while still in the English Channel. Two other ships collided soon after, causing significant damage to one another, and the flagship *Amsterdam* experienced an explosion of its signal gun. All these incidents caused delays and unease—every day was precious with 1,600 mouths to feed. A brief reversal of fortune came in the form of several weakly defended sugar carriers from Brazil, captured off the coast of Spain. The sugar was transferred to a Dutch trader at the Moroccan port of Safi, but bad luck returned near the island of Annobon with the discovery of eight feet of water in the hold of the *Maurice*, due not to war damage but rather to crew negligence while careening. Aside from these continued technical difficulties, the crew was now suffering horribly from scurvy. What was variously called the *mal de Olanda* (Dutch sickness) and the *mal de Luanda* (Angolan sickness) by later Spanish interrogators took some 200 lives before the Atlantic was crossed. Further medical problems would take their toll—l'Hermite himself fell ill with gout shortly after arriving in the Pacific—and were complicated by the machinations of a surgeon who was found to be poisoning rather than curing his fellow crewmembers. The surgeon was said to have been wearing a pouch around his neck containing the body parts of snakes and was subsequently tortured by dunking. He confessed to witchcraft, to the terror of all aboard, and was beheaded.[29]

In spite of these myriad and at times bizarre tribulations, the Nassau Fleet eventually managed to sail around Cape Horn and link up at the Juan Fernández Islands in early April 1624, now effectively under the command of Vice-Admiral Hugo Schapenham, who permanently replaced l'Hermite after his death in June. The Dutch left the islands for Arica on 13 April, hoping to seize a shipment of silver and possibly move inland to the mining country of the high interior of Peru. The fleet was well armed, carrying all sort of grenades, muskets, anti-cavalry spikes, and so on, but the idea of an overland march to Potosí or some such place was outrageously naïve. These notions of an attack on the interior were quickly abandoned when a Spanish *chinchorro*, or launch, was captured offshore. The Dutch smelled silver nearby, but the boat's captain, Martín de Larrea, was clever enough to misinform his captors when interrogated about recent shipments. Though contradicted by black slave crewmembers (to whom the Dutch appear to have promised freedom and other incentives), Larrea convinced Schapenham and his men that the silver fleet had departed for Panama thirteen rather than three days earlier ("trece días" rather than the "tres" claimed by the slaves).[30] The black crewmembers were listened to on other matters, however, leading the Dutch to believe that an attack on Lima would easily succeed, guaranteed by the aid of some 4,000 slaves who would gladly join in attacking their Spanish tormentors. Besides, only half the year's treasure had been sent northward; the other half, belonging to Lima's merchants, could be found aboard the *Nuestra Señora de Loreto*, now riding off Callao.

Thus the Nassau Fleet was drawn to Callao, which the Dutch blockaded in mid-May after some abortive attempts to land a large force at Bocanegra, several kilometers north of Lima. A number of vessels were burned in Callao harbor, an action that backfired since the burning wrecks began to float out toward the Dutch ships, putting them in great danger. During this endeavor a German crewmember named Carsten Carstens was captured by the Spanish and interrogated severely before being burned at the stake ("for being a pirate," not for being a heretic).[31] Due to this series of events, along with an apparent lack of firm leadership, the Dutch missed a good opportunity to attack Lima. The city's defenses were almost as weak as the slaves had testified—although the slave population might not have joined the Dutch as willingly as claimed. The efforts of Viceroy

Esquilache had not been continued with equal fervor by his successor, the Marquis of Guadalcázar, and many of the most able fighting men of the city had sailed with the silver fleet to Panama. Only about 2,000 soldiers were on hand in Lima at the time, most with questionable military experience, and Callao's three forts, one still in foundations, had only twenty-four guns among them. Had the Dutch known the level of panic among Lima's citizenry in the first days of the blockade—a panic resembling that caused by Speilbergen almost a decade earlier—things might have gone differently.

Instead, parts of the Nassau Fleet hived off to attempt other targets, north and south. Four ships under command of Cornelisz Jacobsz sailed southward on 14 May to Pisco and Arica, but due to cowardice or a general lack of resolve failed to take either. A more modest party of 200 sailed northward to Guayaquil on 23 May, commanded by Rear-Admiral Johan Willemsz Verschoor. A surprise attack on ships and buildings on the island of Puná was quickly followed on 6 June by a successful attack on the city of Guayaquil. The Guayaquileños were unprepared, and the Dutch under Verschoor faced only eighty gun-toting resisters among a total of 200. Here, for the first time since leaving Holland, some of the frustrated crewmembers of the Nassau Fleet were allowed to vent their rage. They did at Guayaquil what all notorious pirates were wont to do; namely, they pillaged, burned, and desecrated the town, killing between thirty-five and fifty-five Spanish residents in the most cruel ways possible. Special torments were reserved for friars, one of whom was disemboweled and allowed to watch his entrails spill out. Others were hanged or thrown overboard, along with recalcitrant secular prisoners, tied back-to-back like mutinous sailors.[32] After tiring of this mayhem and finding little in the way of silver or other valuables, Verschoor and his men returned to join the blockade of Callao by 5 August.

In their absence l'Hermite had died, replaced by the unreliable Hugo Schapenham on 2 June. Also, and perhaps more importantly, the viceroy had managed to muster a much larger though still dubiously trained defense force, now totaling some 4,600, mostly drawn from the interior (some from as far away as Cuzco). In addition to their increased numbers, the Limeños had constructed a number of small rowboats and a barge mounted with cannon to protect the inner harbor, and more particularly the flagship *Loreto*, which had evaded the Dutch throughout the blockade. Also, shoreline gun placements and temporary fortifications had been augmented. Schapenham and his followers had set up camp on San Lorenzo Island, facing the bay, and had only managed to take a few small trading vessels, which arrived unaware of the blockade from Guayaquil, Trujillo, Pisco, and elsewhere. Growing desperate, the Dutch attempted an exchange of prisoners, which was promptly rejected by the viceroy. To the horror of observers on shore, twenty-one of the thirty Spanish captives were promptly hanged on the island, but the effect of this terror was to work against rather than for the Dutch.

The crew of the Nassau Fleet was growing mutinous, even suffering some desertions, and at last Schapenham opted to give up the blockade on 14 August.

An unsuccessful second raid on Guayaquil, now guarded by fresh reinforcements from the highlands (at President Morga's bidding), was followed by a brief visit to the coast of New Spain in October. An attempt to exchange prisoners for provisions as Speilbergen had done some years earlier failed at Acapulco on the 28th, and Schapenham's fleet dispersed along the coast.[33] After taking on water and vainly searching for a Manila galleon, the Nassau ships sailed to the East Indies. Many more crewmembers succumbed to scurvy in the trans-Pacific passage, and Schapenham himself died near Java in late 1625. As several historians have noted, the Spanish got off easily considering the size and armament of this fleet. It was, after all, the largest enemy force to reach the South Sea in colonial times.

Considering the costly failure of the Nassau Fleet, the Dutch West India Company was not quick to organize a new South Sea expedition. Instead, the company took advantage of the privateering raids of Piet Heyn and others in the Caribbean and expanded its influence in northeastern Brazil, conquering much of the region by 1641. Even here the Dutch found, however, that the costs of occupation were barely offset by the spoils of war. Thus in the midst of a financially cloudy situation regarding the East and West India Companies, Hendrick Brouwer was sent to Valdivia, Chile, in 1642. The Brouwer expedition was to be much smaller in scale than that of l'Hermite, and it had the advantage of using Recife, in northeastern Brazil, as a provisioning base. The Dutch governor of Brazil, Count Maurits, hoped to establish a foothold on the coast of Chile, a base from which future attacks on the mineral-rich interior could be launched. The West India Company did not have the funds to send an occupying force like that used to take Brazil, but it was thought that the soldiers accompanying Brouwer would be aided by indigenous allies. The Mapuche, or "Araucanians," of southern Chile had at times been helpful in the past, and it was well known that they had forced the Spanish to abandon Valdivia after a revolt in 1599. Brouwer was to find that in spite of this apparently favorable situation, Native American alliances with the Dutch, even if they could be formed, did not ensure success.

Thus inspired by dreams of multitudes of gold-bearing rivers and friendly native peoples, Hendrick Brouwer set sail from the Netherlands on 6 November 1642. The fleet, which consisted of three ships and two yachts, headed by Brouwer in the *Amsterdam*, carried about 250 men and a cargo destined to aid soldiers and settlers more than petty traders. Alongside guns and pikes the expedition carried a wide variety of farming, mining, and blacksmithing equipment. At Recife water and food were taken on, along with 350 soldiers, and the fleet set sail for the Strait of Magellan on 15 January 1643. As in previous Dutch expeditions to the Peruvian coast, Brouwer's men had been deceived as to the voyage's true objectives. As might be expected by now, this deception was not taken well by most crewmembers, but Brouwer's mixture of harsh discipline and fair rationing of food and clothing seems to have offset thoughts of mutiny. The list of rations quoted by Bradley implies that these sailors lived rather well compared with their contemporaries (see pirate food descriptions in Box 7, Chapter 7):

> a good cheese for the whole voyage; three pounds of biscuit, half a pound of butter, and a quatern of vinegar per week; about a pint of fresh water per diem; every Sunday three quarters of a pound of flesh; six ounces of salted cod every Monday and Wednesday; a quarter of pound stock-fish for every Tuesday and Saturday; grey pease, and three quarters of a pound of bacon, for Thursday and Friday: Besides this, as much oatmeal boiled in water as they could eat.[34]

No mention of beer or wine is made here, but it is unlikely that the officers of the voyage managed to monopolize the entire supply of these beverages. A rationing of woolen clothes helped fight the southern cold as well, and the fleet rounded Cape Horn via open seas around Staten Island during the months of March and April. Food would in fact become a serious problem, however, as the supply ship *Orange Tree* disappeared in a storm, eventually to limp back to Recife with a broken mast.

Brouwer and his followers reconnoitered the coast around Chiloé Island from May to August of 1643, finding little of note besides burned Spanish encampments. An attack on the small settlement of Carelmapu on 20 May yielded some much-needed food supplies, along with a letter to the local corregidor informing him of a coming Dutch expedition and advising him to pursue a scorched-earth defense strategy. The much hoped-for element of surprise had been compromised again by the Spanish overland intelligence network, and the Dutch crew, now finding out for the first time the long-term commitments of their captain in this cold and thinly populated region, began to sour on the whole voyage. Supplies had become so dear that stealing food or tobacco was made a capital offense. The only positive experience of the voyage was to occur upon returning to Carelmapu in early July; here 470 Native Americans, carrying coveted food stores, were persuaded to remove to Valdivia to aid the Dutch in establishing a settlement. A small cache of plate and coin was also discovered, but it was not sufficient to do more than whet the appetites of the adventurers.[35]

While preparing to sail to Valdivia, Brouwer died—he was about sixty-two years of age, apparently—and leadership was conferred on Elias Herckmans, captain of the ship *Vlissingen* (named for the port from which the unlikely Spanish term for Dutch seamen, "Pechelingue," derives). Brouwer's corpse was gutted in order to preserve it for burial at Valdivia, and the crew left Carelmapu on 21 August. Valdivia was reached in three days and amicable relations with local indigenous peoples, mostly under leadership of the cacique Manquipillan, were established by the end of the month. As van Baerle's account shows, the Dutch appear to have made a sincere effort to learn the local language. A general feeling of optimism seemed to reign at this time, and Captain Elbert Crispijnsen was sent back to Brazil on 25 September to report on the expedition's progress and request supplies. This good feeling quickly wore off, however, as the nearly 500 men remaining began to go hungry. The Native Americans, who had initially welcomed the Dutch, were now unsure of the true intentions of these intruders who snooped around desperately for gold mines and seemed to be settling in for a long stay. Another cacique named Manqueante provided relief to the Dutch in early October in the form of livestock, but it was clear that this was intended as a farewell gift, not a renewed invitation.

Herckmans, concerned that his men were beginning to desert due to short rations, informed Manqueante of his intentions to return to Brazil. The Dutch captain promised to come back to Valdivia as soon as possible with more men and supplies, and, interestingly, 1,000 African slaves to spare the Native Americans the hard labor of mining and farming in the new Dutch colony.[40] All these promises were to come to nothing, as it turned out, and the remaining ships left Valdivia for the last time on 28 October 1643. Herckmans reached Recife by 28 December after rounding Cape Horn and found Count Maurits gravely disappointed; the governor had already outfitted the relief force requested by Crispijnsen. Thus, just prior to the Brazil uprisings of 1645, ended Dutch pretensions in the Spanish South Sea.

If this was the end of Dutch incursions along the Pacific coast of the Americas, the Spanish did not know it. In fact, they immediately began to respond to the pirate threat with more expense and effort than ever before. The cacique Manqueante, now claiming to be a friend of the Spanish (for self-protection, no doubt), informed on his old allies, mentioning Herckmans's promise to return. Thus Peru's viceroy prepared the largest maritime reconnaissance mission yet seen in these waters. By late 1644 a fleet under command of Antonio Sebastián de Toledo, another viceroy's son, left Callao with close to twenty ships—a total of twenty-two finally rendezvoused in Chile—and over 1,000 men. Another force of 2,000 was said to be marching overland toward Valdivia. The land forces commanded by Chile's governor failed to arrive, apparently due to indigenous resistance in the interior, but the seaborne forces began work on fortifications at Valdivia, led by Maestre de Campo ("Field Marshal") Alonso Villanueva de Soberal, and continued throughout the southern hemisphere summer of 1645. Toledo left for Arica at the beginning of April to carry Potosí's silver to Panama, but 700 men remained to suffer through the winter and guard against the elusive and now illusory Dutch enemy. In their spare time, and perhaps for want of live foes, the soldiers of the new garrison revived the spirit of the counter-reformation by disinterring and burning Brouwer's heretical and already much-abused corpse.

Even though a peace with the Dutch was pending, the Peruvian viceroy, Mancera, continued to develop a defensive network along the coast. Local initiative still carried the majority of the burden of financing militia arms, small fortifications, and so on, but the crown was becoming more and more directly responsible. The Valdivia expedition had cost some 348,000 pesos, and maintenance of the garrison would cost at least 20,000 pesos annually. These expenses were borne largely by the royal exchequer, though transferred in reality onto the backs of Indian tribute payers and Spanish merchants and property owners. The difference from the point of view of Spain, which was in the midst of a seemingly interminable financial crisis anyway, was a sharp reduction in bullion remissions from Peru. The fortification of Callao alone cost almost one million silver pesos, and warship construction, artillery manufacture, and soldiers' pay together added another half million. The Dutch corsairs had thus cost their enemies much more than they themselves realized.

The Treaty of Münster in 1648 ended the Eighty Years War with Spain, but it did not end Dutch piracy. As with their English and French counterparts in the later seventeenth century, Dutch pirates would pay little heed to treaties and truces signed by high officials in Europe; indeed, a number of prominent future buccaneers, such as Laurens de Graaf, would be of Dutch nationality. Others would engage in smuggling, often entering the Río de la Plata with slaves poached from the Portuguese. On examining this earlier period of Dutch maritime predation, however, one can see patterns that distinguish state- or company-sponsored activities between 1568 and 1648 from those that followed. The theft of much of Brazil was no small affair, of course, but the principal novelty of the Dutch era of piracy in the Americas was the sustained effort to attack Spanish settlements in the Pacific. As has been noted, it was the aftermath of Dutch raids such as Speilbergen's and l'Hermite's that cost the Spanish treasury most dearly in the end. Spanish success against Dutch interlopers on the other side of the Pacific, mostly attempts to hold Portuguese spice outposts during the period of unification (1580–1640), were only marginally more successful, but they also had to be paid for with Peruvian silver.

Piet Heyn's Caribbean raid, on the other hand, though notable for its stupendous haul of booty, was a one-of-a-kind event, not to be compared with the cumulative damage inflicted later by buccaneers such as Henry Morgan. Indeed, most of the sailors who participated in Dutch company expeditions to the Americas in the early seventeenth century were unlike the later pirates in two regards: first, they were not organized in a loose or "democratic" fashion on board ship (they were not self-styled adventurers but rather *varendvolk*, or common seafarers of a proletarian sort), and second, they could not expect an equal share of any booty recovered. These factors were probably the most significant causes for Dutch failures against the Spanish, especially in the Pacific, but elsewhere as well. Piet Heyn's success off Cuba was therefore anomalous and in the end, as noted earlier, his crew rioted in the vain hope of receiving part of their hard-won loot. If Dutch piracy was a business, then a conflict between labor and management was as inevitable as in any factory. Thus part of the core of rebellious Dutch privateering crews from this era would form the nucleus of the next wave, the Caribbean buccaneers.

BOX 3 SHIPBUILDING IN THE SEVENTEENTH CENTURY

The Dutch raiders discussed earlier sailed mostly Dutch-built vessels, but later buccaneers often sailed ships stolen from Spanish and colonial traders. The pirates themselves, Dutch, French, English, or otherwise, were rarely shipbuilders, but they almost always included a few carpenters and other artisans and seem to have known how to maintain and even improve the ships they stole or were loaned. A basic overview of ship design in this era will help to illustrate the capabilities and limitations faced by pirates and their mostly Spanish prey by the time of Piet Heyn. By the early seventeenth century, ships capable of long-distance travel were divided into two basic types, the Mediterranean galley and the Atlantic full-rigger. The former type, used by the pirate Barbarossas and their Christian opponents alike, was a long and narrow vessel propelled almost exclusively by means of oars, with up to twenty rows of prisoners heaving in unison (see Figure 1.1). The galley was an excellent fighting vessel, especially in calm seas and in shallow bays and estuaries, but it was not suitable for the rigors of the stormy Atlantic, and less suited still to the cargo needs of merchants. Thus the full-rigged ship was developed in western Europe, most likely by Basques, and was common in the North Atlantic by the early fifteenth century. Crossovers between Mediterranean and Atlantic ship design occurred before Columbus's time (some credit fourteenth-century Basque pirates with the first borrowing), improving the performance of Atlantic-style ships for long-distance sailing. Among the improvements to full-rigged ships borrowed from the Mediterranean were the triangular, or "lateen" sail, usually added to the rearmost, or mizzen-mast, and the "carvel" method of hull construction. The lateen sail added sail surface and aided in balance, especially in driving winds, and the carvel method of laying planks end to end over an internal skeleton—seams sealed with pitch and rope—made ships more rigid and thus seaworthy for long voyages. Steerage was by means of a hinged, sternpost rudder, in general use by the mid-fourteenth century.

Square-rigged, ocean-going vessels capable of trans-Atlantic or East Indies voyages developed in at least two directions from here, one toward tub-like, high-capacity hulls, some with high castles fore and aft, as in the Portuguese carrack, and the other toward longer, "Y"-shaped hulls and lower-slung beakheads and forecastles, as in the sixteenth century and later Spanish galleon. One of the predecessors of the galleon, which followed the second, sleeker design was the much smaller caravel (Spanish *carabela redonda*), Columbus's *Niña* and *Pinta* serving as examples of this type (the *Santa María* was a carrack, or *nao*, as the Spanish called it). With the development of an extensive overseas empire the Spanish shifted toward almost

Gations d'Espagne, Grands Vaisseaux, hauts de l'arriere, pour les Voyages des Indes Occidentales. Gueroult fec. 3º

FIGURE 3.3 A Seventeenth–Century Spanish Galleon

Source: Jacques Gérol du Pas, *Recüeil de veües les diferens bastimens de la mer Mediteranée et l'ocean,* Paris: 1710 (Courtesy of the James Ford Bell Library, University of Minnesota).

exclusive use of galleons (see Figure 3.3) after the mid-sixteenth century, both as cargo and military vessels. Judging from contemporary descriptions of the *Golden Hind* and similar ships, the Elizabethan pirates such as Drake apparently sailed English copies of the basic galleon in their American and trans-world voyages. A variety of smaller dispatch vessels (*barcos, pataches,* and so on) accompanied the semi-annual Spanish flotas, or convoys, but only a few Mediterranean-style patrol galleys (*galeras*) were introduced to colonial waters after the mid-sixteenth century to root out pirates—with generally poor results. Spanish vessels were built in European, American, and Asian shipyards, the most prominent of the former being the Basque ports of the Bay of Biscay and the latter including Havana, Guayaquil, Guatulco (Pacific New Spain), and Cavite (Philippines). Due to the relative scarcity of skilled labor in the colonies, European-built ships were considered superior through-out the early modern period. Spanish ships captured by pirates in the Pacific, however, were almost all of local manufacture (often derided as poor sailers).

In the midst of Spain's maritime expansion, North Atlantic traders and fishermen, among them the Dutch, developed the shorter, tub-like hull form in short-run cargo vessels known as hulks. In spite of their relative small-ness (c. 100 tons capacity), cog-like fatness, and shallow draft, these vessels, eventually modified to a form known as the *vlieboot,* or fly-boat, were rou-tinely sailed to the Americas, and were present at the salt-pans of the Araya

Peninsula around 1600. The economical Dutch *fluyt*, developed around 1595, was a longer and larger descendant of the fly-boat, but continued to be nearly flat-bottomed and of shallow draft. As with the Spanish full-riggers of the period, Dutch fluyts generally carried three masts, the fore, main, and mizzen, the first two fitted with graduated sets of square sails and the last with a lateen sail. Occasionally a fourth mast was placed behind the mizzen, called the bonaventure mizzen-mast, and outfitted like its partner with a lateen sail. A last feature common to Spanish galleons, Portuguese carracks, and Dutch fluyts was the spritsail, a small, rectangular sail hung below the bowsprit, well in front of the main body of the ship. In all cases the objective was to maximize sail area and hence speed. Dutch traders were always looking for ways to cut costs, and fluyts met the bill by maximizing cargo space and minimizing crew size (mostly by means of extensive block and tackle). These features may have helped Dutch burghers maximize profits in the North Atlantic, but they made fluyts unsuitable for war purposes, or even self-defense. Dutch warships, increasingly common worldwide after 1600, consisted of either modified fluyts, called *pinnances* (not to be confused with the English pinnace) or Flemish-style frigates, which somewhat resembled the sturdier galleons of the Spanish. Piet Heyn and his contemporaries appear to have sailed in these latter types of ships, expensive but considered necessary to the expansionist plans of the Dutch East and West India Companies. All Dutch expeditions included numerous dispatch vessels, particularly of the versatile "yacht" type.

Armaments were as much a factor in pirate engagements with the Spanish as ship design, and here the defenders often found themselves at a disadvantage. As Carlo Cipolla and others have noted, Spain was surprisingly reliant on foreign manufacturers for large guns, which in the sixteenth and seventeenth centuries consisted mostly of cast iron or bronze muzzle-loading cannon. Due to problems of oxidation and brittleness iron was generally considered inferior to bronze, though it was always cheaper (hence the pirates' incessant stealing of bronze church bells). The English of Drake's time nevertheless perfected iron gun-making to such an extent that an important export industry developed, and even Spain was counted as a major, if often contraband, buyer of these weapons. Large guns in this period were only marginally standardized by caliber, and often had to be supplied with custom-made stone or iron shot. Other types of projectiles included spiked, chained, exploding, incendiary, and shrapnel, or "dice," shot. Shipboard guns were mostly arranged on the lower decks for broadside engagement, and though not terribly accurate at any distance they could be very destructive at close range (recall van Noort's sinking of Morga's brand-new ship in 1600 off the Philippines). Privateers and pirates in the Americas took great pains to outfit themselves with substantial guns, powder, and shot, and almost always exceeded the firepower of their colonial prey; the Spanish

Crown simply could not afford to arm its far-flung peripheries, and merchants were thus asked to arm themselves. Perhaps in the economical spirit of their Dutch counterparts, they almost universally failed to do so.

For more details, see Carla Rahn Phillips, *Six Galleons for the King of Spain: Imperial Defense in the Early Seventeenth Century* (Baltimore: Johns Hopkins University Press, 1986); Richard Unger, *Dutch Shipbuilding before 1800* (Amsterdam: Van Gorcum, 1978); and Carlo Cipolla, *Guns Sails, and Empires: Technological Innovation and the Early Phases of European Expansion, 1400–1700* (New York: Pantheon, 1965).

Notes

1 Charles R. Boxer, *The Dutch Seaborne Empire, 1600–1800* (London: Hutchinson, 1965).

2 Kenneth Andrews, *The Spanish Caribbean: Trade and Plunder, 1530–1630* (New Haven: Yale University Press, 1978), 136.

3 Ibid., 174.

4 Ibid., 202. See J.I. Israel, *Dutch Primacy in World Trade, 1585–1740* (Oxford: Clarendon Press, 1989), 87–99, for figures on the salt trade. Note that the Basque transvestite Catalina de Erauso described an engagement with Dutch vessels off Punta de Araya in 1603; see Catalina de Erauso, *Lieutenant Nun: Memoirs of a Basque Transvestite in the New World*, Michele Stepto and Gabriel Stepto, trans. (Boston: Beacon Press, 1996 [c. 1626]), 8.

5 Andrews, *Spanish Caribbean*, 234.

6 Ibid., 247.

7 Biographical details on Cornelis Jol may be found in Cornelis Goslinga, *The Dutch in the Caribbean and on the Wild Coast, 1580–1680* (Gainesville: University of Florida Press, 1971), 176–77. The English traveler Thomas Gage claimed that Heyn was called "Pie de Palo" in Mexico around 1635. See J. Eric S. Thompson, ed., *Thomas Gage's Travels in the New World* (Norman: University of Oklahoma Press, 1958 [1648]), 98.

8 For a detailed overview of Matanzas and its aftermath, see Carla Rahn Phillips, *Six Galleons for the King of Spain: Imperial Defense in the Early Seventeenth Century* (Baltimore: Johns Hopkins University Press, 1986), 3–9.

9 Boxer, *Dutch Seaborne Empire*, 77.

10 Andrews, *Spanish Caribbean*, 248.

11 Phillips, *Six Galleons for the King of Spain*, 192–94. The cost of wintering the fleet in Cartagena alone was more than 523,000 ducats (194). The avería, though exorbitant, paid only about 20 percent of the costs incurred; the royal treasury was forced to pay the remainder.

12 Thompson, *Thomas Gage's Travels*, 315.

13 Peter T. Bradley, *The Lure of Peru: Maritime Intrusion into the South Sea, 1598–1701* (New York: St. Martin's Press, 1989), 11.

14 Gerritsz quoted in Bradley, *The Lure of Peru*, 15. Though the incorporation of manuscript and published Spanish sources sets the excellent work of Bradley and Gerhard apart from other writers on piracy in the Pacific, both draw also from James Burney, *A Chronological History of the Voyages and Discoveries in the South Sea or Pacific Ocean*, 6 vols. (New York: Da Capo, 1967 [facsimile of 1806 ed.]), especially vols. 2: 186–234,

328–53, and 3: 1–36, 113–45. Engel Sluiter's fine Ph.D. dissertation, "The Dutch on the Pacific Coast of America, 1598–1621" (History Ph.D., University of California at Berkeley, 1937), also incorporated Spanish sources and covers Dutch intrusions in the Pacific up to Speilbergen's voyage. Sluiter's work also provides a concise summary of early Dutch activity in the Caribbean.

15 Bradley, *The Lure of Peru*, 17.

16 Ibid., 18.

17 Ibid., 22.

18 This account of Morga's Philippine fight is drawn largely from John Leddy Phelan, *The Kingdom of Quito in the Seventeenth Century* (Madison: University of Wisconsin Press, 1967), 95–97; and Henry Stanley, ed. and trans., *The Philippine Islands, Moluccas, Siam, Cambodia, Japan, and China at the Close of the 16th Century* [by Antonio de Morga] (London: Hakluyt Society, 1868), 155–98.

19 Bradley, *Lure of Peru*, 22.

20 Peter Gerhard, *Pirates on the West Coast of New Spain, 1575–1742* (Cleveland: Arthur H. Clark, 1960), 106.

21 Ibid., 107, fn.

22 Bradley, *Lure of Peru*, 34. An English translation of Speilbergen's journal is in *The East and West Indian Mirror, Being an Account of Joris Van Speilbergen's Voyage Round the World, 1614–17* (London: Hakluyt Society, 1906).

23 Bradley, *Lure of Peru*, 40.

24 Catalina de Erauso, *Lieutenant Nun*, 52–53. See also Bradley, *Lure of Peru*, 206, fn 19.

25 Bradley, *Lure of Peru*, 40.

26 Ibid., 44.

27 Gerhard, *Pirates on the West Coast of New Spain*, 119.

28 Bradley, *Lure of Peru*, 48.

29 Ibid., 54.

30 Ibid., 56.

31 Ibid., 60.

32 Ibid., 59.

33 Gerhard, *Pirates of the West Coast of New Spain*, 128.

34 Quoted in Bradley, *Lure of Peru*, 76. For a contemporary account of this misguided enterprise, see Caspar van Baerle, *The History of Brazil under the Governorship of Count Johan Maurits of Nassau, 1636–1644*, Blanche T. van Berckel-Ebeling Koning, trans. and ed. (Gainesville: University Press of Florida, 2011), 251–75. On the Dutch aims and misperceptions so evident in this and other South Sea ventures, see Benjamin Schmidt, *Innocence Abroad: The Dutch Imagination and the New World, 1570–1670* (New York: Cambridge University Press, 2006).

35 Bradley, *Lure of Peru*, 78.

36 Ibid., 80.

4

THE SEVENTEENTH-CENTURY CARIBBEAN BUCCANEERS

No other pirates in history have been more celebrated, hated, romanticized, demonized, or otherwise misrepresented than the late seventeenth-century buccaneers. This is not surprising since it was in this period more than any other, before or after, that individuals of many nationalities could come together freely in loose bands, embark from a variety of Caribbean bases, and make a living, virtually unhindered, by pillage. It was a time of opportunity for embittered Dutch sailors, for abandoned French colonists, for abused English, Scots, and Irish indentures, even for indebted sea captains and naval officers who had little other excuse to turn to crime to solve their problems. The rise of the buccaneers coincided with the decline of Spain, first as the preeminent political player in Europe and the Mediterranean, then as an economic superpower. The decline meant that Spain's American colonies were weaker both as consumer markets and as suppliers of hard money. The age of the buccaneers also coincided with the Cromwell dictatorship in England and the subsequent Restoration of Charles II and the Stuart Dynasty, the rise of the "Sun King," Louis XIV, in France, and the consolidation of Dutch independence from Spain. The timing of the rise of the buccaneers was also closely tied to the development of non-Spanish colonial bases in the Caribbean, namely the islands of St. Kitts (St. Christopher), St. Thomas, Barbados, Nevis, Antigua, Curaçao, Tortuga, Jamaica, and the northern and western regions of Hispaniola. By mid-century, pirates of all ethnic backgrounds and social classes could claim a base in one part or another of these American seas. Here, now at Tortuga, now at Port Royal, Jamaica, now at Danish St. Thomas, they could put in at friendly ports to sell stolen merchandise, find drink or other pleasure, rest and recover strength, and seek letters of marque for further "privateering" ventures against the Spanish. It was an unusual window in the history of the West Indies, and it lasted for several decades.

Renegades and Runaways on Hispaniola and Tortuga

Life was hard for a poor commoner in the West Indies. Almost as soon as systems of indentured servitude, with periods of duty ranging from eighteen months to seven years, were established in the French and English Caribbean colonies, the unhappy indentures, or *engagés*, rebelled. These renegade Europeans, along with marooned sailors and other marginal individuals, seem to have made up the core of the group that would later be called buccaneers. Their first calling was not piracy, and indeed the term applied to them seems a misnomer. The buccaneers were first of all hunters of feral cattle on the north coast of Hispaniola, their sustenance a kind of beef jerky grilled on a Taíno-style wooden grate called a *boucan*. The French thus termed the jerky *viande boucanée*, and the jerky-makers *boucaniers*. Compared to the servant's life on St. Kitts or Barbados, or even Curaçao, the life of the "buccaneers," as the English called them, was very good. A base was established off Hispaniola's northwest shore on the rocky island of Tortuga by the late 1620s, and soon the buccaneers established regular trade ties, mostly in hides and cured meat, but also in tobacco and crude sugar, with passing French, Dutch, and English smugglers and would-be colonialists.

The buccaneers got their start in these uninhabited regions due to two factors that they themselves probably failed to realize. First, the Native Americans who had once filled these islands, most of them peaceful Taínos, had nearly disappeared over a century before, killed by disease, mine work, forced migration, or other excesses and accidents of Spanish occupation. In the meantime, livestock introduced by the Spanish to these islands in the first voyages of exploration, including cattle, horses, hogs, and dogs, had flourished in the absence of predators, human or otherwise. The multinational "marooners" of Hispaniola and nearby Tortuga who came to be known as buccaneers were thus hunters in a "wild country" that was not wild at all; its natural state was a far cry from pristine and far from the crowds of indigenous agriculturalists that had populated the region in 1492.

The early "brethren of the coast," or *frères de la côte*, of northern Hispaniola, as described by the French Jesuit historians Charlevoix, du Tertre, and Labat, were an odd lot indeed. They lived the Crusoe life, but in pairs, a custom called *matelotage* with legal implications suggesting a kind of same-sex marriage. Accompanied by domesticated dogs, protection against the multitudes of wild ones, the "mates" spent six months or so each year hunting cattle in the interior, tanning hides to trade and curing meat on their boucans. They wore coarse clothing, apparently consisting of a rough pair of cotton or linen trousers topped by a loose-fitting shirt, and slept under makeshift mosquito nets. Their caps, belts, and shoes were of rawhide, their dwellings simple stilted shacks thatched with palm-fronds, called by the Taíno word *barbacoas* (or *ajoupas*). Contemporary descriptions suggest that the early buccaneer "camper-hunters" were fond of tobacco and drink, and these commodities, along with muskets, powder, and shot, were what they sought at trading fairs on Tortuga. Here the buccaneers arrived after their half-year hunt, all so soaked in slaughter that contemporaries claimed they appeared to have been tarred.[1] It was here also that the jerky-makers became sea-predators. Gaining frequency in accordance to their growing numbers, they put together quasi-expeditions in long dugout canoes, traveling in groups of twenty or so, and sneaked up on Spanish coastal traders. The captive crew was typically thrown overboard or given the canoe, depending on the mood of the buccaneer captors,

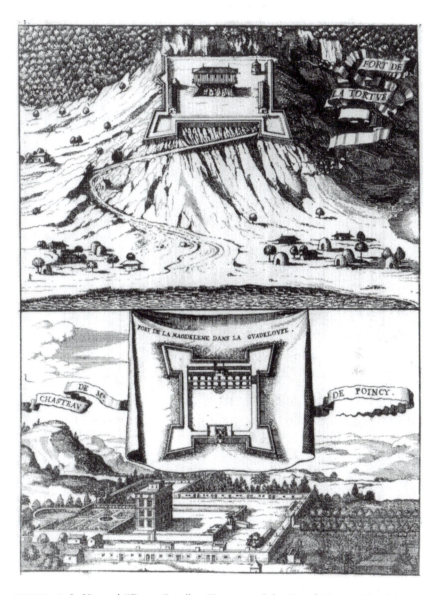

FIGURE 4.1 Le Vasseur's "Dove-Cote" on Tortuga and the French Fort on Guadeloupe

Source: Jean-Baptiste Dutertre, *Histoire des Antilles*, Paris: 1667 (courtesy of the James Ford Bell Library, University of Minnesota).

the prize taken back to Tortuga, the loot distributed democratically, and all participants left to spend freely before returning to the cow hunt on Hispaniola. It was an adventurous if barbaric life.

Tortuga, a tiny island with little to recommend it other than its natural, rocky defenses, was an early subject of contention between English and French colonialists. The Spanish, for their part, tried time and again to dislodge both interloping nations from the island, but with little lasting effect. The first legal claimants of Tortuga (besides the Spanish, who never had any use for the island anyway) were English members of the Providence Company, an organization more interested in establishing a colony on Providence Island (Colombia's Providencia, off the east coast of Nicaragua). The company members grew a small amount of tobacco here, but a Spanish punitive force, aided by an Irish dissenter called by the Spanish "Juan Morf," drove the settlers out in 1634. They were soon back, now with more African slaves than white planters (or cow killers, as the case may be), in 1636. As the company's optimistic name suggests, the more distant Providence Island was the primary English objective for colonization and fortification at this time (the 1630s), although the Spanish retook it in 1641. Before its fall, English refugees from French raids on Tortuga made their way to Providence and plotted their return—though many were subsequently annihilated by the Spanish at Providence. All this English focus on Providence (and Spanish resolve to drive them out) helped a French Huguenot named le Vasseur establish a firm foothold on Tortuga after 1640. He built himself a fort and residence atop a rocky promontory overlooking the harbor on the southeast end of the island and called it his "dove-cote." A violent encounter with some 500–600 Spanish soldiers sent out from Santo Domingo in 1643 proved the utility of this post, and le Vasseur faced no further challenges until the early 1650s.[2]

As a French Protestant, le Vasseur proved as vehemently anti-Catholic as any Englishman, and captured Spaniards were likely to find themselves subjected to an Inquisition-like torture in one of his dungeons or cages (one of which he called "Purgatory"). le Vasseur's primary interests were not religious, however, but rather pecuniary, and he built a fortune by collecting a variety of local taxes and fees, mostly on the buccaneer hide and tobacco trades. This Huguenot fiefdom was not approved of by the French governor on St. Kitts, de Poincy, and a ruse was dreamed up to dislodge the petty tyrant. De Poincy sent a nephew to Tortuga to invite le Vasseur to St. Kitts for a celebration of his recent victory over the Spanish, ostensibly with the plan that the nephew would take control of the island as soon as le Vasseur was out of sight. le Vasseur was too intelligent for this flattery and deception, however, preferring to celebrate in his "dove-cote." Nevertheless, a quarrel with two mates, a pair called Martin and Thibault, led to le Vasseur's murder in 1653. A relieved de Poincy immediately sent a seasoned fighting gentleman, the Chevalier de Fontenay, as the first official governor of Tortuga and the Coast of St. Domingue. Fontenay's colony, according to Spanish intelligence sources, was made up of some 700 French, and probably other European residents, along with some 450 slaves, 200 of African origin and 250 Native Americans, apparently Maya-speakers taken from the Yucatán Peninsula.[3]

Members of the nearby Audiencia of Santo Domingo were outraged by this flagrant colonizing and claiming of parts of their district's own periphery, and the president, Juan Francisco Montemayor, sent out a punitive force in November of

FIGURE 4.2 A Hispaniola Buccaneer

Source: Alexander Exquemelin, *Histoire des Avanturiers*, Paris: 1678 (courtesy of the James Ford Bell Library, University of Minnesota).

1653. Three of the five ships dispatched were lost or broken up in a storm, but the two leading vessels arrived off Tortuga on 10 January 1654. The ships were fired upon by guns mounted on le Vasseur's old platform, so Montemayor and his infantry commander, Gabriel Roxas del Valle Figueroa, decided to attempt a landing about a league (5.6 km) to the west. After nine days' fighting—which apparently included a brilliant Spanish move, the setting up of eight or ten big guns on a hill across from the platform—Fontenay surrendered the island. Some Dutch vessels aided the evacuation of spoils and merchandise in the midst of all the fighting and confusion, and Montemayor and Roxas found little of value to reward their efforts. Fontenay's brother was taken hostage to Santo Domingo and the remaining residents were evacuated (by the French themselves) to Port Margot, on the Hispaniola coast.

The Spanish were intent on keeping their enemies off Tortuga, and a garrison of 150 men was stationed there following the defeat of Fontenay. The veteran chevalier did return following the release of his brother, but his small force of 130 French and a few Dutch soldiers failed to dislodge the Spanish even after twenty days of hard fighting. Tortuga might have become another *presidio*, or permanent dependency, like San Agustín, in Florida, but instead the Spanish abandoned the island after eighteen months' occupation. These were tough times for the Spanish treasury and fiscal pressures forced the audiencia to back off. Into the void stepped Elias Watts, an English merchant recently active in Jamaica, and he and his family set about remaking Tortuga into a popular trading post and buccaneering base. Watts acted under authority of Jamaica's new governor, General Brayne, and began planning raids on the Spanish of northeastern Hispaniola, aided by some French survivors of the 1653 Fontenay disaster. A mostly buccaneer party of 400 landed at Puerto de la Plata on Palm Sunday 1659. They made their way to the town of Santiago de la Vega, some 35 km inland, and surprised its governor and inhabitants, holding the former hostage and pillaging at will. On returning to the seaside the buccaneers were met by an ambush of local militiamen, but after threatening to slit the governor's throat they were allowed to pass. The hostages were released on the coast and the raiders returned to Tortuga to divide their booty, which amounted to over 300 pesos each.[1] Tortuga itself would fall into French hands by 1660, primarily due to the diplomatic wiles of one Jeremie Deschamps, a former resident, but it continued to serve as a base for buccaneers and merchants of all nationalities. Meanwhile Jamaica was developing its own reputation as a buccaneer entrepôt.

Port Royal, Jamaica: Pirate Haven

Spain never had a great deal of interest in the island the indigenous Taínos called Jamaica, though it is arguably the most strikingly beautiful of the Greater Antilles, and possibly the most ecologically diverse. There were provisional settlements on the north coast, such as Sevilla la Nueva (attacked by French corsairs in the 1540s), and eventually a sort of capital was established on the south end, called Santiago

de la Vega (present-day Spanish Town—near Kingston), but Jamaica's lush mountains and clear streams carried no gold. Perhaps blessed in that sense, its indigenous
inhabitants were nevertheless enslaved and later "entrusted" to Spanish masters
in the peculiar tributary institution of the *encomienda*, and were said to be nearly
extinct by 1520. By the early seventeenth century the island was as moribund in
terms of human activity as it was alive with natural splendor. Only the feral cattle
and other domestic animals introduced early after the conquest upset the balance,
as on Hispaniola, Cuba, and Puerto Rico—until, that is, the arrival of the English.

In 1642, at the height of Spain's fight with England over the establishment of
permanent colonies in the western Caribbean (including Providence), a Captain
William Jackson set out to punish the enemy and offer a good old-fashioned
English show of force—quite consciously in the spirit of Drake. Against the protests of the Spanish ambassador, Alonso de Cárdenas, Jackson was backed by the
admiral of the English fleet, the Earl of Warwick, and carried a full royal commission condoning whatever exploits he might undertake. The expedition picked up
700–800 volunteers at St. Kitts and Barbados, bringing total forces to some 1,100,
and several port towns of Tierra Firme and Central America, including Maracaibo
and Trujillo (Honduras), were sacked. The Jackson expedition was notable for
little else beyond these raids except a brief skirmish, killing forty English, and a
ransoming of Santiago de la Vega, in Jamaica. The disappointing booty consisted
of 200 head of cattle, 10,000 pounds of manioc-flour bread, and only 7,000 silver
pesos, but the natural beauty of the island inspired twenty-three adventurers to
voluntarily maroon themselves and live among the Spanish and their livestock.[5]

Inspired by similar dreams of an English tropical paradise in the Indies, Oliver
Cromwell followed the advice of the famous "English-American," Thomas Gage
(whose description of the "Dutch" Diego el Mulato was noted earlier), and set
about organizing his own imperialist mission. Gage's report suggested that an
armed removal of the Spanish from much of the Caribbean would be no great
feat, and Cromwell took this questionable advice literally. A large expedition made
up of some 2,500 fighting men, with sea forces under Admiral William Penn and
land forces under General Robert Venables, left England in December of 1654.
The fleet reached Barbados in January of 1655, picked up almost 4,000 recruits
and several more vessels, then stopped at St. Kitts and Nevis for another 1,200.
Such a large and hastily organized marine turned out to be more liability than
asset, and Penn and Venables soon set to bickering over tactics and targets. An
attempt on Santo Domingo, which began on 13 April 1655, was repulsed easily
by the Spanish in two waves, first on the 17th and then on the 25th of the same
month. As in other cases of successful local defense initiatives mentioned earlier,
the elite defenders of Santo Domingo were amply rewarded with titles from
the Spanish Crown.[6] All was not lost for the English, however, as an angry Venables pulled out his forces and sailed for Jamaica, where he easily took Santiago
de la Vega. The Spanish on Jamaica accepted Venables's terms, which included
abandonment of the island within ten days and forfeiture of all property (the
same conditions offered to the defeated English on Providence in 1641). The

13 November 1655: Twenty-two English "Calvinists" are captured at Tampico by mulatto cowhands and brought to the capital.

8 September 1658: The loss of Jamaica is confirmed. Of the 400 men sent to its relief, 300 have been hanged from balconies, or have had their throats cut.

13 July 1659: Cromwell is dead! Thanksgiving services at the cathedral.[8]

Although the loss of Jamaica was hardly as important as the defense of Santo Domingo, from these select entries one can see how seriously the affair was taken in the colonial capital of New Spain; the English heretics were getting to be dangerously near neighbors. Also visible in these entries, unlike those recorded by the English, is the prominence of black and mulatto defenders, both at Santo Domingo and on the Mexican mainland. Though Guijo does not elaborate, his entries suggest both contempt for captured invaders and praise for the courage of Spain's most unsung colonial heroes.

Port Royal, situated on a thin spit of sand across from what would later become Kingston, was now, as Tortuga had been, a buccaneer base. As with Tortuga also, and recalling the *beys* of the Barbary Coast as well, its governors would issue all manner of commissions allowing violent seizure of Spanish vessels and towns. They authorized anything, really, as long as a tithe was paid to the issuing official upon return to port. Port Royal, with its south-facing backside covered by Fort Cromwell (later renamed Fort Charles), also became, in no time at all, a bustling port town complete with strumpets and wine, gaming tables and ale houses, and even a church or two. Colonists were recruited from Scotland and Ireland, from London's jails and streets, and from the other English settlements in the Indies; Jamaica, it was hoped, was to be permanent, impregnable, and profitable. By 1658 the island counted some 4,500 residents of European heritage and approximately 1,500 African slaves, most of them clustered around what would later be called Kingston Harbor. Thirsty buccaneers could choose from among the following drinking establishments in short order:

TABLE 4.1 Seventeenth-Century Taverns of Port Royal, Jamaica (with date of registry in parentheses)[9]

The Black Dogg (1682)	The Blue Anchor (1679)
The Catt & Fiddle (1676)	The Cheshire Cheese (1684)
The Feathers (1681)	The Green Dragon (1674)
The Jamaica Arms (1677)	The King's Arms (No.1, 1677)
The King's Arms (No.2, 1682)	The Salutacon (1680)
The Shipp (1674)	The Sign of Bacchus (1673)
The Sign of the Mermaid (1685)	The Sign of the George (1682)
The Sugar Loaf (1667)	The Three Crowns (1673)
The Three Mariners (1677)	The Three Tunns (1665)
The Windmill (1684)	

English Jamaica, or rather, Port Royal, was soon the site of numerous buccaneer rendezvous. Some of the first raiding missions were carried out on the Tierra Firme coast, notably at Santa Marta and Riohacha, by former officers of Venables and Penn. Certain official participants displayed some ambivalence about these raids, and a few, such as the short-lived governor Robert Sedgwick, even denounced them as dishonorable. Jamaica under Edward D'Oyley was unabashedly pro-buccaneer, however, and D'Oyley participated in or sponsored a number of raiding missions until his removal in August of 1661. He led raids on Panama and Cartagena in the later 1650s, but success came instead to an expedition he sponsored under command of Christopher Myngs. In early 1659 Myngs pulled off what might be regarded as the heist of the century (after Piet Heyn, of course) while looting Spanish settlements along the coast of Venezuela. He and his followers raided Cumaná and Puerto Cabello, then found at the small town of Coro treasure valued at some £200,000 to £300,000.[10] According to witnesses, Spaniards fleeing the raiders left behind twenty-two chests containing 400 pounds of silver each, along with assorted jewelry and worked silver items (and some cacao beans). It is difficult to know why so much silver was being stored at Coro, as it was hardly located along the usual treasure route, but the presence of cacao suggests the money had been diverted while en route to Caracas. Caracas was the principal growing region for raw chocolate in this period, and a thriving trade with New Spain was threatened by the buccaneers. In any case, the Coro raid stung deeply.

This incredible booty, which reached Port Royal on 23 April 1659, was cause for major celebration—and hot dispute. Myngs, although officially sanctioned, acted more like a pirate than a naval officer. He and his closest associates plundered the prizes before their required inspection at Port Royal and for this and related infractions the now unlucky captain was sent to England to face trial. There he discovered that Governor D'Oyley and other Jamaica officials had taken part in similar pre-inspection despoiling, and that they had helped themselves to goodly portions of "his" silver besides. Myngs filed suit in order to enforce some degree of honor among his fellow thieves, a difficult task in average times, but impossible in the midst of the Restoration. Charles II acceded to the throne in May of 1660, and peace with Spain was openly proclaimed, if not universally respected. For his part, Captain Myngs would have other opportunities to make up for this loss.

Meanwhile, Governor D'Oyley found it necessary to return to England to sort out his financial and legal affairs with Myngs and others in 1661, and was replaced by Lord Windsor. Windsor immediately set about rationalizing the armed forces of Jamaica, formed an Admiralty Court (later bane of buccaneers), established proper legal procedures with regard to property rights, and called in all older privateering commissions. These he promptly replaced with his own commissions, ensuring his cut of pirate proceeds—again reminiscent of the Algerian *beys*. The so-called peace with Spain was fragile enough in Europe, weakened substantially by Charles's marriage to the Portuguese Catherine in 1662, but "beyond the line," in the West Indies particularly, it was already broken. The veteran Myngs returned to Jamaica in September of 1662 to lead an expedition, manned by some 1,300 volunteers (many of them buccaneers), against Santiago de Cuba. Here the English met again with their old Spanish-Jamaican foe, Arnoldo Ysassi, successfully taking the town and fort in early October after a night-march over rocky terrain. The raid hurt Spanish morale and strained diplomatic relations in Europe, but the buccaneers met with surprisingly little booty considering their troubles.

Again flouting the official peace, Myngs led a large expedition backed by the Jamaica Council against the western Yucatán port of Campeche in December of 1662. As with the October raid on Cuba, Myngs and his followers, again mostly buccaneers, ran into trouble with storms and contrary winds, but still managed to reach their objective. Now, early on the morning of 9 February 1663, the English landed over 1,000 men above the town and by ten o'clock that morning held Campeche hostage. Accounts of booty seized in this raid vary widely (on the order of 150,000 pesos' worth of merchandise, probably), but compared with his great success at Coro in 1659, which had yielded over a ton of silver, Myngs would always find himself disappointed.[11] He returned to Port Royal on 13 April in the *Centurion* and his free-spending crew was gladly received by tavern-keepers, merchants, and bawds.

Whatever the take at Campeche, the Myngs attack did great damage to English–Spanish relations in Europe. In Madrid funds were raised to refit the Caribbean patrol fleet, the Armada de Barlovento y Seno Mexicano (Gulf of Mexico and Windward Island Navy), but this effort soon fizzled due to Spain's enormous and worsening financial crisis. It was precisely in these years, the end of Philip IV's reign (1621–65), that Spain hit bottom in terms of both debt and bullion production. The king seemed oblivious, and the arts flourished at court—this was the era of the great painter Diego de Velázquez, for example—but Spain's bankers were demanding interest payments with increasing shrillness. The precise depth of the so-called Seventeenth-Century Depression remains unclear, but certainly Spain's financial obligations on the Continent ballooned just as Potosí and other mining centers in the Americas faltered. Add to this imperial cash-flow crisis pirates and their continual harassment of the treasure fleets, and shipping in general, and it becomes clear how desperate Philip IV's situation had become. Furthermore, smuggling was now the rule rather than the exception throughout the empire, creating a drastic drop in customs duties and other imposts.

Spain sued for an end to hostilities after the Campeche raid and the restored Charles II of England obliged. The truce meant little, however, as the semi-official ventures of the Myngs variety were soon replaced by expeditions born purely of alehouse conspiracies. Although peace had been secured by an exchange of

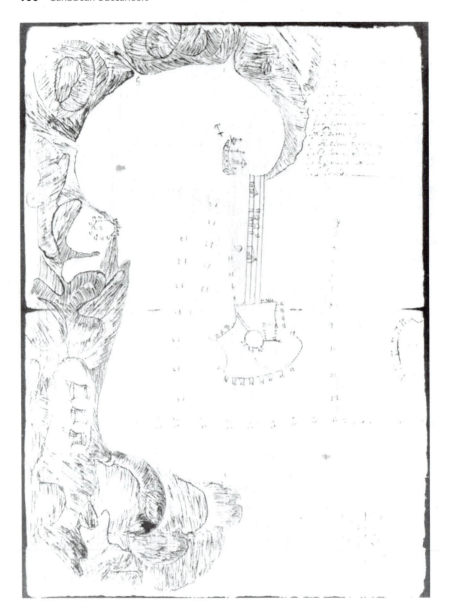

FIGURE 4.3 A Spanish Spy's Map of Port Royal, Jamaica

Source: Frank Cundall and Joseph Pietersz, *Jamaica Under the Spaniards*, Kingston: 1919 (from Archivo General de Indias [Seville], Mapas y Planos Santo Domingo).

prisoners taken at Campeche and Santiago de Cuba—several of the English had been held for a time in Seville and Cádiz—in Jamaica the agreement translated into little more than a hushed condoning of buccaneer raids. Outlaws who had been operating out of Tortuga and northwest Hispaniola were still welcomed at

TABLE 4.2 English Buccaneer Captains of Jamaica and Tortuga, c. 1663[12]

Captain	Ship	Crew	Guns
Sir Thomas Whetstone	a Spanish prize	60	7
Captain Smart	Griffon, frigate	100	14
Captain Guy	James, frigate	90	14
Captain James	American, frigate	70	6
Captain Cooper	his frigate	80	10
Captain Morris	a brigantine	60	7
Captain Brenningham	his frigate	70	6
Captain Mansfield	a brigantine	60	4
Captain Goodly	a pink	60	6
Captain Blewfield	a barque	50	3
Captain Herdue	a frigate	40	4

Note: Four more privateers were said to be at Jamaica at this time, but no details are known.

Port Royal, drawn by its great stores of merchandise and notorious nightlife as much as by its ambivalent stance toward Spain. In June of 1663 a Captain Barnard outfitted an ad hoc expedition and left Port Royal for San Tomé, on the Orinoco River. He and his mates plundered the town and returned soon after to recount their adventures and spend the spoils. In October of the same year a Captain Cooper arrived in Port Royal with two Spanish prize ships, the galleon *María* of Seville and a smaller bark. The *María* carried a cargo of wine, olives, and oil, but most importantly it carried 1,000 *quintales* (c. 46,000 kg) of mercury from Almadén (Spain), destined for the silver-processing *patios* of New Spain.[13] Some of the cargo, presumably including the mercury—which in this period and atmosphere of debauchery would have been handy in treating syphilis—was sent to England, and, as his job required, Spain's ambassador, don Patricio Moledi, loudly protested the whole affair. The English all but shrugged off his complaints, however, and the deputy governor of Jamaica, Lyttleton, claimed that the peace had only banned attacks on land targets, exempting ships at sea. Thus, in this atmosphere of unresolved tension, Port Royal harbored and entertained the likes of the above buccaneer captains.

Henry Morgan and the Treaty of Madrid

Jamaica and Tortuga continued to serve as buccaneer bases throughout the 1660s, and it was in this period that the greatest chronicler of buccaneer life, the apparently French-born barber-surgeon who sailed with the Dutch, Alexander Olivier Exquemelin, made his first appearance in the West Indies. In 1666, Exquemelin (anglicized as Esquemeling) arrived in Tortuga as an *engagé* for an agent of the newly formed French West India Company, or Compagnie des Indes. He was eventually removed from servitude by the governor, D'Ogeron, and went on to accompany numerous buccaneering expeditions, of which he left a fine account in 1674 (translated from the Dutch and published in 1684 as *The Buccaneers of America*). Exquemelin's most memorable stories, really eyewitness accounts, regard Henry Morgan's raids on Portobelo and Panama, to be treated in short order, but some context for these raids is necessary to understanding their broader implications.

In 1664 Sir Thomas Modyford was appointed governor of Jamaica, and as soon as he arrived at Port Royal he began sending reassuring letters to Spanish officials at Santo Domingo and Cartagena. Modyford was desirous of following a peaceful course, even of opening up free commerce between Jamaica and the settlements of the Spanish Caribbean; Spanish contrabandists had already shown themselves quite willing to buy English-held slaves at Port Royal, after all. The Spanish were understandably suspicious of this offering of an olive branch, especially when buccaneers carrying Jamaican commissions continued to ravage their ships and ports. After zealously punishing several unsuspecting buccaneers at Port Royal, however, Modyford was quickly made to understand the error of his ways. The buccaneers did not attack him, they simply deserted the port and made for the friendlier waters of French-held Tortuga and Hispaniola. This shift led to such a precipitous decline in commerce at Port Royal that Modyford changed his mind and began to tolerate and then openly support "peacetime privateering," or piracy, within a few months of his arrival.

More important than Modyford's personal opinions were changes taking place in Europe. England was entering into hostilities with the Dutch, and their temporary allies the French, by the mid-1660s. The impending war took the focus off Spain's colonies and opened up new possibilities for plunder among the interloping northern Europeans themselves. Soon the English were organizing expeditions against the Dutch at Curaçao, Saba, St. Eustatius, and Tobago, and against the French at Tortuga. Equally quick to move against former friends, the Dutch under Admiral de Ruyter attacked Barbados, Montserrat, and Nevis. As for the French, had Modyford not gone back on his early promises and courted the buccaneers, an expedition from Tortuga and St. Domingue might have been sent against Jamaica. There Governor D'Ogeron had established a new post at Petit Goâve, on the southwest peninsula of Hispaniola, and commissions for notably vicious raiders like Captain l'Olonnais and Michel le Basque flew freely. D'Ogeron had tried to domesticate some of his company's subjects by financing fledgling plantations and "importing" a number of French women to Hispaniola, but most buccaneers preferred the unattached life of the sea-rover.

Some of these restless individuals joined an expedition put together by Governor Modyford under Edward Morgan (not to be confused with Henry Morgan) in April 1665. Overoptimistic perhaps, Modyford planned on the raiders driving both the Dutch from Curaçao and the French from Tortuga. The buccaneers recruited for this expedition immediately mutinied, as it turned out, and left Jamaica only after being guaranteed an equal distribution of spoils (as per their tradition). Constant quarreling and bad weather left a somewhat reduced force to attack the Dutch outpost on St. Eustatius on 23 July. The buccaneers, outnumbered and outgunned by the Dutch, nevertheless took the island and its fort with little effort (the Dutch officers in charge were thought to have been "drunk or mad" for giving up so easily).[14] The nearby island of Saba followed suit, and the business of dividing booty, mostly consisting of African slaves, who numbered over 900, among officers and buccaneers soon led to new quarrels, and the provisional fleet dispersed.

A number of less grandiose privateering missions against Dutch targets met with better success during this period, including the seizure of Tobago by the buccaneers Searles and Stedman in 1666. In January of that year a more official operation was put together under a well-known buccaneer captain named Mansfield (Exquemelin's "Mansvelt") to go against the Dutch again at Curaçao. The buccaneers met up at Bluefields Bay (southwest Jamaica) in November of 1665 and sailed for southern Cuba to buy or steal provisions. They seem to have quickly fallen to the latter method, and even went so far as to sack the town of Sancti Spiritus, which lay some 70 km inland. The buccaneers took to looting and ransoming, mistreating citizens of both sexes, and generally causing mayhem to such an extent that they forgot their original objective. No one went to Curaçao and only Mansfield, apparently feeling somewhat guilty, headed off with a small force to make an attempt on Santa Catalina Island (formerly English Providence). A rather stealthy plan of attack paid off, and the island was taken with minimal fighting and left with a small garrison. Mansfield then proceeded to lead his men on a series of raids on the Central American coast, sacking a number of small settlements from Nicaragua to Panama before returning to Port Royal.

Several other English buccaneer captains seem to have been active along the Central American coast during this time as well, including a Morris, Jackman, and Morgan (probably the soon-to-be-famous Henry). This group of buccaneers and their followers raided the Tabasco River region, south of Campeche, in early 1665, sacking a Spanish settlement called Santa Marta de la Victoria.[15] After overcoming an ambush on their way back to the Gulf coast the buccaneers cruised around the Yucatán Peninsula to the Gulf of Honduras, where they raided Trujillo and other smaller settlements. Continuing southward along the Mosquito Coast of Nicaragua, they decided at last to attempt an attack on Granada, a remote city on Lake Nicaragua that promised some genuine booty. With great stealth they anchored their vessels somehow out of sight in Monkey Bay, paddled up the San Juan River in canoes, and sneaked up on the practically undefended town of Granada, at the northwest end of the lake. According to their own accounts, the buccaneers simply walked into the *plaza mayor*, or city center, took charge of whatever guns were mounted around town, and proceeded to terrorize the inhabitants for approximately sixteen hours. If this sounds too easy, it probably was—apparently the buccaneers had made the acquaintance of some 1,000 disgruntled indigenous auxiliaries along the way.[16]

When Morris, Jackman, Morgan, and their followers returned to Port Royal, their tales of easy pickings in Central America fired the imaginations of many would-be English conquistadors. In spite of their repeated losses in this time of supposed peace, the Spanish did not wait helplessly for aid from the crown. Don Juan Pérez de Guzman, president of the Audiencia of Panama, quickly organized an expedition to retake the symbolic but also strategic island of Providence, or Santa Catalina. An English slaver, the *Concord*, was captured at Portobelo—possibly there trading slaves legally—and put into Spanish service under José Sánchez Jiménez. Sánchez Jiménez reached Providence on 10 August 1666 and quickly made it Spanish Santa Catalina again. The sixty- or seventy-odd buccaneers that had been left to guard the island after Mansfield's raid, including Captains Smith, Whetstone, and Stanley, surrendered after three days of hard fighting on 15 August. As they understood it, they would be allowed to return to Port Royal upon giving up the island to the Spanish, but apparently something had been lost in the translation; they soon found themselves transported to dungeons and hard labor in Panama instead. Several of the buccaneers in fact died from overwork, mostly in repairing fortifications at Portobelo, and disease, but several lived to seek their revenge in the company of Henry Morgan.

Captain Henry Morgan, whose reputation was on the rise among the buccaneers, had also paid his dues. By one account he was kidnapped as a youth in Bristol, and had served a full sentence of indenture on Barbados before making his way to Port Royal. With the death of Captain Mansfield, the notorious but popular "privateer" whom he had accompanied in the sack of Sancti Spiritus and subsequent raids, Morgan, in his early thirties, moved in to fill the leadership void. The situation in Port Royal was as uneasy as ever—Governor Modyford was receiving strong signals for peace in the colonies from London while animosity toward the Spanish among his subjects in Jamaica was on the rise. In trade negotiations Spain clung to its monopolies and offered little more to the English than the terms of trade granted the Dutch at the Treaty of Münster: they could do no more than bring a few previously licensed cargoes, mostly of African slaves, to a few official ports of entry. By the time these terms were being made public in late 1667, Modyford was preparing for a Spanish attack on Jamaica. Though probably exaggerating Spanish resolve on this score, he was right to expect hostilities rather than peace.

With Modyford's blessing, Henry Morgan set out for Cuba on what he described as a preemptive strike on Spanish invading forces (which were largely hypothetical) in early 1668. The town of Puerto Príncipe was sacked, its governor killed, and as usual its citizens robbed, tortured, and generally terrorized. There was no apparent plot afoot to take Jamaica, but the persistent rumor served to justify further attacks of this kind. Next on the list of land targets was Portobelo (northern Panama), site of recent aggressions and supposed outrages against English Jamaicans, and Morgan set out to take it with an accompaniment of some 400 men in June of 1668. The narrative of this mission may be found in numerous texts, including that of Exquemelin, but in summary it consisted of the following stages: (1) using a former English prisoner who knew the terrain, Morgan and his men approached the fort in canoes and took a sentinel hostage; (2) the sentinel was made to ask the Spanish garrison commander for a surrender, which request was answered with gunfire; (3) the pirates took the fort, blew up a number of soldiers in a powder magazine, and moved on to the Spanish town; (4) the governor of the place holed up in another castle and beat back the pirates, so Morgan forced a number of captive nuns and friars to approach the castle as a human shield; (5) the governor chose to kill his own people rather than give access to the castle, but still enough ladders were placed to allow the pirates entry; and (6) with fireballs and powder-pot explosives in hand, Morgan's forces took the castle, killed the governor and a number of others, and proceeded to plunder the town.

Although by no means as important as Cartagena or Panama City, Portobelo was a grave loss for the Spanish. The person whom Exquemelin calls the governor of Panama (probably the president of the audiencia) had sent a relief force to the town, but too late to effect a capture of the buccaneers, who were already preparing to sail back to Jamaica. A company of Spanish soldiers was cut off by the buccaneers at a choke point on the mule path into town, and the pirates continued their attempts to ransom Portobelo for cash before leaving. The president balked, leaving the poor citizens to come up with 100,000 pesos in silver on their own, and further asked Morgan to reveal the means by which he had taken such a fortified town with so few men. Exquemelin gives us a perhaps embellished account of this exchange, but it makes for a good story nonetheless: Morgan was said to have sent the "governor" a pistol and a few bullets, with a note requesting that he accept these gifts and keep them for a year, after which time he (Morgan) would "come to Panama and fetch them away." The "governor" was said to have returned the weapon to Morgan, accompanied by a gold ring and a message saying this was a symbol of his promise not to allow such a visit.[17] As history, or perhaps rather legend, would have it, it was Morgan's prediction that came true.

As was customary among the buccaneers by this time, the booty of Portobelo was not taken straightaway to Port Royal—it was all too notorious how avaricious governors could be when pirate ships arrived. Instead Morgan and his men sailed for the coast of Cuba, where they found themselves in possession of some 250,000 pieces of eight and a fair quantity of silks and other merchandise. As per another buccaneer custom, injured pirates were remunerated in the manner of modern workman's compensation claims before shares were distributed (a lost right arm could be worth 500 pesos, for instance, or five slaves). On returning to Jamaica in mid-August, Morgan filed a report of his actions, making it appear as if he had only stopped at Portobelo for reconnaissance purposes. No mention was made of the tortures applied to the Spaniards, or of the human shield incident; less still was made of the booty taken. Modyford saw Morgan's raid for what it was, an act of war, and thus openly pressed for similar attacks elsewhere; having started the hostilities, the English could not afford to lose momentum. With this sort

Towne of Puerto del Principe taken & sackt

Part 2: Chap: 5.

FIGURE 4.4 Buccaneers Capturing Puerto Príncipe, Cuba, 1668

Source: Alexander Exquemelin, *The Buccaneers of America,* London: 1699 (courtesy of the Swem Library Special Collections, College of William & Mary).

of backing, Morgan and other buccaneer captains led a series of punishing raids on the coasts of Venezuela, Cuba, Campeche, and other Caribbean targets, and a rendezvous at a favorite spot, a small island off the southwest coast of Hispaniola called Ile-à-vache (Cow Island), led to the hatching of a plot to take Cartagena.

Heavy drinking and a serious explosion on one of the principal ships of the expedition led to a more modest course, however. Again in the midst of serious talk of peace with Spain, Morgan, one of the few captains to survive the shipboard inferno, led an expedition against Maracaibo, which was still recovering from attacks by French buccaneers under l'Olonnais and Michel le Basque. The sort of outrages committed at Portobelo were repeated in March of 1669 at Maracaibo, and similar booty seems to have resulted (much of it taken off a relief ship that had been set afire in the harbor, according to Exquemelin).

After this second audacious but successful attack, again on a Spanish city of only third rank, Morgan set about planning a more serious undertaking at Ile-à-vache, namely a massive attack on the geographically protected city of Panama. Morgan and a substantial buccaneer fleet, including a number of French ships recruited (or coerced) from Hispaniola and Tortuga, set out in December of 1670 for the Chagres River. It seems not to have bothered Morgan in the least that he had received a direct order from the Jamaican governor not to engage in hostilities against the Spanish on land at this time. As it was, however, the Spanish were engaging in petty raids of their own on the north coast of Jamaica, mostly under a Captain Manuel Rivero Pardal. The so-called "English" buccaneers under Morgan and many others were doing a good deal more damage at Santa Marta, Riohacha, Campeche, and so on, but Rivero Pardal's attacks (repaid with death by Captain Morris, who captured him off the east end of Cuba) were amplified to a shrill war cry. Morgan's 1,800-man expedition, which had originally aimed to hit

FIGURE 4.5 Henry Morgan's Attack on Spanish Ships near Maracaibo

Source: Alexander Exquemelin, *The Buccaneers of America*, London: 1699 (courtesy of the Swem Library Special Collections, College of William & Mary).

Santiago de Cuba along the way, sailed through storms off Hispaniola and nearly broke up, but shortly regrouped before stopping at Santa Catalina Island to make it (English) Providence Island once again. A few renegade guides familiar with the trails to Panama were picked up here, and the fleet sailed on, arriving at the mouth of the Chagres River on 19 December 1670.

The Spanish had had word of Morgan's coming, and the Panamanians were already evacuating goods and citizens onto ships anchored in the Pacific by the time his forces landed at Chagres. Panama was a merchant city of great importance to the empire, namely in the transshipment of Peruvian silver from the Pacific to the Atlantic where it was exchanged for African slaves, European cloth, paper, wine, iron, olives, and other goods. In short, the Spanish were not about to give Panama over to foreign adventurers without a struggle. The audiencia had sent troops to reinforce the forts at Chagres and Portobelo, and the president himself headed a militia unit sent to block the several mule-paths to Panama from Venta Cruz and Portobelo. The first buccaneers, under a Lieutenant-Colonel Bradley, thus met with fierce resistance from the castle of San Lorenzo on the Chagres, site of the first serious engagement of the Panama adventure, and suffered some 150 casualties. As Exquemelin tells it, here as an eyewitness, a strange event turned the tide in favor of the invaders: apparently in the heat of battle a buccaneer was shot through with an arrow, which he then pulled out and wound with cotton, stuck in his musket, and fired back at the castle. By chance, as the incredible story goes, the cotton wrapping caught fire in the muzzle and landed flaming in a thatch roof, sending up a building or two in short order before setting fire to an ill-placed powder keg. The confusion caused by the fire and explosion were apparently sufficient distraction to allow the pirates to begin burning the wooden palisades that protected the Spaniards, and the fort soon broke. Bradley the buccaneer and the local governor both died in the siege, but Chagres Castle was now in the hands of the pirates.

Conveniently tardy, Morgan arrived from Providence Island days later and set his men to refurbishing the fort for their own defenses. On 9 January 1671 he set off up the Chagres River with 1,400 men in thirty-six large canoes and several other types of river-going craft. After four days on the water the pirates, led by guides familiar with the region, were dying of hunger. Apparently they had had little but pipe-tobacco to satisfy them all this time, and when they came upon an abandoned Spanish camp, some were so hungry they boiled some leather bags found there and ate them like meat. As Exquemelin tells it:

> Some persons who never were out of their mothers' kitchens may ask how these Pirates could eat, swallow and digest those pieces of leather, so hard and dry. Unto whom I only answer: That could they once experiment what hunger, or rather famine, is, they would certainly find the manner, by their own necessity, as the Pirates did. For these first took the leather, and sliced it into pieces. Then did they beat it between two stones and rub it, often

dipping it in the river, to render it by these means supple and tender. Lastly they scraped off the hair, and roasted or broiled it upon the fire. And being thus cooked they cut it into small morsels, and eat it, helping it down with frequent gulps of water, which by good fortune they had nigh at hand.[18]

Given the hunger of the buccaneers, and the heat and hard work of the passage, it is a wonder they did not mutiny and force a retreat. Fortunately, for them at least, on the fifth day they found a small store of wine, flour, and plantains hidden in a hollow away from the river and Morgan ordered it distributed equally and served up immediately. Farther upriver the pirates came across more hidden provisions, but also encountered a company of indigenous allies of the Spaniards who harassed them with arrows before disappearing into the forest. The buccaneers, feeling pinned down, camped and cleaned their arms, still complaining of hunger, and reached Venta Cruz on the following day, a week after having set out from the fort at Chagres. The Spanish had continued their scorched-earth tactics, retreating toward Panama and leaving the town of Venta Cruz burned and free of food or animals. A small stash of bread and wine quickly made all who partook violently ill. From here the journey to Panama was some eight leagues (c. 45 km), no doubt laid with ambushes at every turn, but Morgan nevertheless struggled to keep up spirits among his followers as he devised a plan of attack.

Morgan wasted little time in moving onward, sending out 200 men to blaze trail and leaving a smaller contingent behind to guard the canoes. The pirates encountered more warriors and arrows at a choke point in the trail called Quebrada Oscura, or Dark Ravine, and several were wounded. The buccaneers passed through just the same, encountering and killing several indigenous defenders in a wood at the far end of the *quebrada*. Every time the pirates saw a group of Native Americans they attempted to capture and interrogate them, but every time their quarry disappeared, sometimes taunting them in Spanish from some high point off the trail. In the evening of the eighth day the pirates were caught in a heavy rain and struggled to keep their guns covered and dry; they had found no dwellings left unburnt and had to make shelter with their clothes and what leaves they could find. On the ninth day some Spanish troops were seen at a distance, but Morgan's men could not catch up to them. A hill was discovered and climbed and for the first time the buccaneers saw their objective, the city of Panama, and just beyond it the placid South Sea. More important at this stage, they spied a herd of cattle and *burros* in a valley below and quickly set about capturing and slaughtering as many of these beasts as they could lay hands on. In true buccaneer fashion, according to Exquemelin, they ate chunks of roasted ass-meat half raw, "For such was their hunger that they more resembled cannibals than Europeans at this banquet, the blood many times running down from their beards to the middle of their bodies."[19]

With bloody beards and full bellies, and dreams of Panama and pillage, Morgan and his pirate army now set out to take their prize. Without encountering any resistance, again only catching sight of retreating Spaniards as they marched, the pirates came within sight of the steeples of Panama's churches on the evening of the ninth day. They were so overjoyed to have come this far that they made as much noise as possible with drums, fifes, trumpets, and yells. The Spanish sent out a unit of cavalry to inspect the enemy and blow trumpets in response, and a number of big guns were fired from the city (the pirates wisely camped just out of range). According to Exquemelin, the buccaneers were not disheartened in the least by this show of resistance. On the contrary, they could hardly sleep with all the excitement of the impending battle.

On the morning of the tenth day Morgan took the advice of one of his guides and bypassed the direct route into the city, instead following a narrow passage through a thicket. This turned out to be a wise choice, as it forced the Spanish to abandon several recently constructed stockades, but by the time the pirates got a good look at Panama's defenses, even at this angle, they lost much of their cheer. It was decided at this point, largely due to the perceived impossibility of retreat without heavy losses, to go ahead, fighting to the death against what appeared to be suicidal odds. Morgan divided the men into three "battalions," sending one of true buccaneers, the sharpshooting cow-slayers of Hispaniola, against the town first. The buccaneers were faced with the best trained of the Spanish forces, the cavalry, but because the savannah that lay before Panama was boggy and soft the horses had trouble maneuvering. The buccaneers knelt and fired on the riders, bringing down quite a few, and likewise did damage to a unit of infantry sent to back them. Another Spanish stratagem, the driving of bulls around to the rear of the buccaneer sharpshooters, likewise yielded poor results. Most of the bulls were spooked by the gunfire, but those that were not did little harm; the buccaneers were accustomed to such animals, after all, and thus shot them at leisure.

This first engagement ended badly for the defenders of Panama, and greatly encouraged Morgan and the buccaneers. Spanish foot soldiers, upon seeing the cavalry fall to pieces, fired their guns and ran, and a captain was captured and made to reveal the strength and manner of the remaining defenses. He claimed that local forces consisted of at least 2,400 foot soldiers (including those just met), not counting slaves and indigenous auxiliaries, and 400 horsemen. The city itself was guarded by many temporary ramparts fitted with large guns. The buccaneers had lost many of their own number in the first engagement, but on seeing that they had killed or disabled more than 600 enemy soldiers they regained hope and began planning the next charge. After a brief rest, Morgan led the pirates against the city's outskirts, where the Spanish met them with continual cannonades of musket balls and shrapnel (called dice shot), along with small arms fire. A large number of the invaders were felled by this method, but the buccaneers neverthe-less overwhelmed the town's principal defenses within three hours. According to Morgan, those Spanish subjects charged with manning the guns and barricades inside the city deserted their posts and burned them, making the pirates' entry all the easier.

Once in charge of Panama, Morgan wisely prohibited the drinking of wine, claiming it was poisoned but probably more mindful of the sobriety needed to hold such a remote city and make an escape besides. Almost immediately a great fire broke out, according to Exquemelin set by Morgan's followers but by other accounts set by Spanish homeowners and their servants—in any case it left much of the city in ashes within hours of the pirates' victory. The occupation lasted twenty-eight days, during which time the buccaneers raided the countryside and nearby islands of Taboga and Taboguilla, desperately searching for hidden booty and torturing inhabitants. A galleon loaded with most of Panama's liquid wealth had gotten away into the Pacific, and some of the fine altars and retables of the city's churches escaped seizure by the wiles of nuns and friars—one sixteenth-century altar was apparently tarred to cover its goldwork and hence spared. A bark loaded with biscuit and a small amount of silver from Paita was easily captured as it put in unsuspectingly at Taboga, but the treasure galleon remained elusive. Exquemelin gives several examples of how the increasingly desperate pirates tortured the unlucky citizens of Panama, sparing no one if it was believed they knew the hiding place of some cache of valuables. A servant caught with a key dangling from a pair of trousers (which he himself had taken from his master's belongings) was interrogated in the following manner:

> Not being able to extort any other confession out of him, they first put him on the rack, wherewith they inhumanly disjointed his arms. After this they twisted a cord about his forehead, which they wrung so hard, that his eyes appeared as big as eggs, and were ready to fall out of his skull. But neither with these torments could they obtain any positive answer to their demands. Wherewith they soon after hung him up by the testicles, giving him infinite blows and stripes, while he was under that intolerable pain and posture of body. Afterwards they cut off his nose and ears, and singed his face with burning straw, till he could speak nor lament his misery no longer.[20]

The unfortunate servant was finally ordered killed by a slave with a merciful lance thrust. Such was the means by which the buccaneers found their "purchase" and hence their pay. If we can believe such writers as Exquemelin, and there is no reason why we should not, there existed among the buccaneers more than a few sadists.

Morgan realized now, after three weeks of pillaging, that little more booty would be discovered in the vicinity of Panama. A group of pirates had planned to outfit a ship and raid the Spanish South Sea before returning to England by way of Asia, but Morgan discovered the plan and ordered the ship scuttled in the harbor. All the mules available were loaded with booty and some 600 wretched and starving Spanish prisoners were rounded up and marched off northward across the isthmus on 24 February 1671. The prisoners were assured that they would be taken to Jamaica and sold if they did not somehow come up with sufficient monies to ransom themselves, a clear impossibility at this juncture and the cause for great sorrow and despair among the captives. At Venta Cruz the buccaneers, including Morgan, submitted themselves to a thorough search by fellow pirates prior to setting off downriver to Chagres Castle. This act of conspicuous honesty was considered unusual by many of the buccaneers present, and indeed they would later find themselves cheated by Morgan and other of the expedition's leaders before leaving for Jamaica. From Chagres Morgan sent a demand for ransom money to the Spanish at Portobelo, but a negative reply hurried his return, in semi-secrecy, to Port Royal. The Panamanian prisoners were not taken along but rather abandoned in haste, and the average participant in this historic raid found himself with only 200 silver pesos to show for his troubles and crimes.

If the buccaneers themselves, save Morgan, of course, came away from the sack of Panama with little in the way of valuables, the Spanish suffered enormous losses in terms of ships, buildings, mules, merchandise, fortifications, guns, labor, and so on. They estimated these losses in terms of millions of pesos, human lives excluded except in reference to slaves. Meanwhile the English had concluded a peace treaty in Madrid before this event took place: Spain had agreed in July of 1670 to recognize English holdings in the Caribbean, including Jamaica, as sovereign territory in exchange for an end to hostilities. Needless to say, news of Morgan's raid on Panama, while celebrated in Port Royal and discreetly applauded in London, was seen as a flagrant act of deception by the Spanish. In Madrid there was talk of a conspiracy to slow the publication of the treaty's terms in Jamaica in order to help Morgan along. England replied by arresting Governor Modyford and transporting him back to London to spend time in the Tower. It was a symbolic gesture that would mean even less to the Spanish once they saw Morgan rewarded for his illegal actions with a deputy governorship soon afterward. Clearly English authorities and even merchants wanted it both ways; piracy was good for showing the Spanish what the English were capable of (without taxes and royal expenditures), yet piracy was already recognized as a long-term danger to the colonies England was settling and developing in the Caribbean. Given this recognition of future security needs, the time of reckoning was at hand for the buccaneers.

Years of ambivalence toward the buccaneers meant the problem would not easily disappear, however. Still, England now entered into a new phase in overseas policy led by the new acting governor of Jamaica, Thomas Lynch. The buccaneers, or privateers, as they were euphemistically called, were to be offered an amnesty. Ships and other property taken from this point on were to be restored to their rightful owners, commissions from previous officials were to be handed over, and thus by this plan, piracy was to be ended voluntarily by the buccaneers themselves. Of course the buccaneers were not so willing to give up their lucrative profession, especially considering the alternatives. The straight life of the plantation attracted but few, and already in 1671 the Spanish were complaining of continued buccaneer raids—often headed by Englishmen—off the coasts of

Cuba, Central America, and Tierra Firme. The English authorities at Port Royal claimed to be keeping to the treaty and loudly denounced any such sea-robbers as renegades, but little cooperation was had from Tortuga and other pirate bases. A Captain Thurston and Diego el Mulato (a.k.a. Diego Grillo, another renegade from Havana, not the one who had pirated with the Dutch after 1629) continued to harass Spanish shipping using French Tortuga as a base. Thurston and Grillo were captured and executed by the Spanish in 1673.[21] In this case it was the Spanish who dealt harshly with pirates, but the English at Jamaica also tried and executed a buccaneer named Johnson in 1672—a case that sharply divided residents of the island. Since most private citizens of Port Royal still made their living dealing in stolen merchandise and providing the buccaneers with services, Johnson's hanging seemed rather extreme.

Another example of continued English buccaneering after the Treaty of Madrid comes from a series of eyewitness accounts given by ex-captives in Cartagena. In this case a number of mariners testified as to the ethnic makeup and intentions of the pirate crew that captured their frigate, the *San Antonio y las Ánimas*, near Cabo de la Abuja (between Santa Marta and Riohacha, Tierra Firme) in July of 1674. Asked what happened, a twenty-eight-year-old sailor named Simón Rodríguez claimed that while sailing to Riohacha the *San Antonio* was overtaken by thirty men in a brigantine (*bergantín*), outfitted with thirty oars and carrying two large and four small mounted guns. The captain was an Englishman named "Juan de Emprená" (or Juan de Prenas), and the crew, which carried a commission (*patente*) from Tortuga, consisted of "different nations, mixed English, Spanish, Portuguese, and French"; one pirate was even identified as a "Portuguese mulatto." Two leagues windward (southwest) of Riohacha the prisoners were put ashore and robbed of some 6,000 pesos, and the pirates sailed away in their frigate. Asked what the buccaneers' intentions were, Rodríguez claimed the captain, who spoke Spanish, had told him that they awaited a fleet, to be dispatched at any moment by the English Parliament, "with 4,000 men to join and incorporate with the pirates of the island of Jamaica and other places and islands where they reside" in order to seize Cartagena and "go up the Magdalena River to sack the Villa of Mompóx." The sailor went on to claim that this expedition against Cartagena was to be led by "General Henrique Morgan, who also has been commissioned Perpetual Governor of Jamaica and General of all the Coasts of the Indies."[22] This was clearly a case of rumor-mongering on the part of the buccaneers, but its effect was no joke for the Spanish; the captives' testimonies created such a panic in Cartagena that copies of these claims were sent to distant parts of the Viceroyalty of Peru in order to raise defense funds. When testimonies such as these were read aloud in Quito and Lima, the Treaty of Madrid seemed moot.

The English did not in fact have any such plans, and continued to make amends to the injured Spanish, at least in theory, in the wake of Morgan's raid on Panama. Morgan himself was sent to England in April of 1672 to be tried for his crimes, but he was already legendary both in the Caribbean (as these testimonies suggest) and in Europe, and no one expected a harsh sentence. None came. In fact, Morgan's arrest led only to greater fame in London and the court of Charles II, and though never named as "General of the Indies," or "Perpetual Governor of Jamaica," he did receive an appointment as deputy governor in January of 1674, under Lord Carlisle. Morgan returned to his old haunts in early 1675, under the interim governor, Lord Vaughan (whom he preceded in arriving at Port Royal), and quickly re-established his reputation as the hard-drinking friend of the buccaneers he had always been. There was no army of 4,000 Englishmen and no design to sack Cartagena, as the Tortuga pirates had claimed, but Morgan's convivial attitude with the buccaneers kept everyone, including his English superiors, off guard. Political shifts in Jamaica itself would cause Morgan to change his tune soon after, but in the meantime he gave the sea-robbers a wink and a nod behind the scenes when the actual governor was loudly threatening all pirates with the gallows.

As noted before, the English were following a double course: on the one hand they claimed to be actively suppressing the buccaneers, and on the other they encouraged the illegal activities of at least some of them. The English were, like the Dutch and French before them, greatly interested in opening up Spanish American ports to trade, by force if need be. The Spanish, following their usual monopoly policies, wanted none of this trade and continually captured and harassed English smugglers, most of them carrying cargoes of African slaves (a Port Royal specialty). The other thorn in Spain's side during this period was the continued English practice of cutting dyewood along the Yucatán and Honduran coasts. The Spanish had only formally recognized the English island settlements of Jamaica, St. Kitts, and Barbados and treated this practice of guerrilla forestry on the mainland for what it was, a direct affront on their sovereignty. Diplomatic pressure nevertheless seemed useless to stop it, and Spanish naval forces in newly dispatched patrol vessels, including a number of locally constructed quasi-galleys called *piraguas* (French and English "pirogues"), tried unsuccessfully to root out the practice. A Dutch buccaneer captain named Yallahs was even briefly employed to chase and capture English log-cutters after 1671, and he took at least a dozen ships. That these attempts to control the English buccaneer-woodcutters were ultimately ineffectual, however, was evidenced by the subsequent development of British Honduras (now Belize).

Meanwhile Deputy Governor Morgan (now Sir Henry, upon his return from England) continued to upset his superior, Lord Vaughan, for all but flagrantly supporting the buccaneers. Vaughan charged, and it was proved true, that Morgan had issued letters to buccaneers operating out of Tortuga and Hispaniola encouraging them to bring their stolen wares to Port Royal for pre-approved sale. This business of dealing with buccaneers under the table was brought to a head in the case of a pirate captain named John Deane, who was detained in early 1676 for carrying stolen goods and sailing without commission under various national colors (none English). Morgan supported Deane just as Vaughan prosecuted him, and the case led to the home government issuing the first standing commission to an overseas colonial court of "oyer and terminer" (i.e., granting the Jamaica Admiralty the right to issue death sentences without chance of appeal). Though some rogues had been executed before in Jamaica, for murder and other violent crimes, only after 1677 could pirates be executed simply for being pirates. It was a significant innovation.

The problem of English pirates operating with commissions from Tortuga and elsewhere was partially resolved by an act of April 1677 making it a felony to sail under foreign colors without permission from the home government. The law had some positive effect, and a number of buccaneers relinquished their French commissions as a result. Still, pirates like James Browne, a Scottish captain active in the late 1670s, continued to plunder Spanish and even licensed Dutch ships under commissions from the governor of Tortuga, D'Ogeron (succeeded by de Pouançay in 1675).[23] The English on Jamaica under Lord Vaughan would not tolerate such violations, however, and after Browne was captured with a cargo of stolen African slaves in a remote Jamaican bay, he was tried and summarily hanged in Port Royal. It was now clear that English policy had shifted, and buccaneers of all nationalities began to steer clear of Jamaica for fear of similar reprisals.

Buccaneers as Loggers and Privateers

English buccaneers continued to sail alongside French *flibustiers*, or "filibusters," out of Tortuga and Petit Goâve in spite of the law, and as Louis XIV's European policies drifted toward war these pirates even joined official expeditions against the Dutch at Curaçao and elsewhere. Some of these joint wartime raids detoured to Spanish settlements—perhaps unsurprisingly—and in early 1677 English buccaneers under a Captain Barnes captured Santa Marta and kidnapped its governor and bishop. A buccaneer-aided French raid on Curaçao in early 1678, under command of the French vice-admiral, Compte d'Estrees, became a fiasco when most of the fleet ran aground off the nearby Ile d'Aves. The Count gave up the fight after this mishap and returned to France, but French buccaneers led by a Captain Grammont made the best of a bad situation by camping out on the island and salvaging the wrecks from the reef. The English buccaneer chronicler William Dampier claims they lived quite well for three weeks from these goods, which the waves themselves carried to them, "in all which Time they were never without two or three Hogsheads of Wine and Brandy in their Tents, and Barrels of Beef and Pork."[24] Thus the government's misfortune was transformed into a beachcomber's feast. Other French filibusters active in the Caribbean during these years may not have lived so well, but they managed to sack Margarita, Trinidad, San Tomé, Maracaibo, Trujillo (Honduras), Campeche, and parts of Cuba.

The largely anti-buccaneer policies of Jamaica's Lord Vaughan were all but forgotten under Lord Carlisle, his successor as governor (Morgan remained as deputy). Carlisle arrived in Port Royal in July of 1678 and immediately courted the pirates, claiming they were needed for the island's defense against the marauding French. Several buccaneer captains, whose subsequent exploits in the Pacific will be treated in the next chapter, such as John Coxon and Bartholomew Sharp, carefully exploited this newly relaxed official stance. In one instance they unladed at Port Royal a large quantity of stolen merchandise, including several tons of indigo taken near Honduras, in late 1679. Carlisle and Morgan welcomed the thieves, and with such encouragement they soon organized an expedition to Portobelo. The group left Port Morant, on the southeast coast of Jamaica, accompanied by four other English buccaneer captains, Essex, Row, Allison, and Maggott, and several hundred men, in January of 1680. Two other captains and their crews, under Cooke and the Frenchman Lessone, joined in along the way, and Portobelo was taken on 17 February 1680. Spanish land and sea forces just missed them as they left, and the pirates regrouped and distributed booty at the nearby site of Boca del Toro. Two more buccaneer captains based in Jamaica, Sawkins and Harris, joined the group and together they sailed for Golden Island, off Darien (eastern Panama). From this base they headed overland with 334 men to the Pacific Ocean. Only the wary Frenchmen stayed behind during this episode, but within a few years a number of French pirate bands, one of them including the filibuster-journalist Raveneau de Lussan, would try their luck in the Pacific as well.

It would be partly true to say that the buccaneers raided the South Sea in response to changing policies in the Caribbean. The political problem of piracy was still unsettled in both the English and French colonies—Jamaica's Carlisle was hardly an enemy and St. Domingue's D'Ogeron was an open ally—but the tide was turning. Those buccaneers who stayed behind to continue their raids in the Caribbean would face ever harsher penalties after 1680, and those known to have participated in the most recent raid on Portobelo, including Captain Coxon, were actively pursued. Coxon had crossed the Panamanian Isthmus but found his South Sea crewmates wanting in experience and fractious in temperament and thus returned; he was back in Jamaica by mid-1680. In what was perhaps a last-ditch effort to show his anti-pirate fervor, Carlisle personally chased Coxon away from Jamaica while on his way to England in May 1680. Even more strange was the about-face of Henry Morgan. With Carlisle's departure Morgan was now acting governor of Jamaica and he used this position to prove that he too was reformed, a true pirate-hater. Morgan was now under pressure from both the home government and from the emerging class of planters and merchants on Jamaica, Barbados, and elsewhere in the English West Indies. The passage of anti-pirate legislation by Jamaica's council in 1681 and the subsequent Jamaica Act of 1683 at last cemented England's policy toward buccaneering in the Caribbean. The legislation was enacted, and under the terms of the former several members of Bartholomew Sharp's South Sea band (treated in the next chapter) were tried in Port Royal after returning from a long voyage around Cape Horn to Barbados in early 1682. For the unsuspecting buccaneers, Henry Morgan must have seemed the sellout of the century.

The buccaneers clearly resented this change of policy and further exacerbated tensions with the English in the Caribbean by raiding ships and ports belonging to persons of their own nationality. In the midst of this situation Thomas Lynch, the old activist governor of Jamaica, returned to office in late May 1682. His first task was to catch up to a buccaneering vessel under command of a Frenchman named Jean Hamlin. Hamlin's flagship, *La Trompeuse* (the Trickster), had been stolen from English logwood cutters, who had rented it from a Frenchman resident in Santiago de la Vega (Spanish Town), Jamaica. The ship seems to have had a history of falling into the wrong hands, as it turned out that its so-called owner, an ex-buccaneer and devout Protestant named Peter Pain (or Peter Pan), had stolen it in Cayenne, port town of French Guiana. The French government wanted both Peter Pain of Cayenne and *La Trompeuse* back, but the ship was now in the hands of pirates. Pain was eventually sent in chains to Petit Goâve in 1684, but meanwhile Hamlin and his followers took between sixteen and eighteen Jamaican trading vessels before being chased off by a frigate sent out by Governor Lynch in October of 1682. This effort did not lead to capture, and Lynch sent out another frigate in December, the *Guernsey*, but with similarly disappointing results. Old buccaneers like Captain Coxon were now hired to search for *La Trompeuse*, but Hamlin moved quickly, leaving Ile-à-vache for the haven of Danish St. Thomas, in the Virgin Islands.[25]

St. Thomas, under the rogue Danish governor Adolf Esmit, himself a former pirate, would serve as a new buccaneer haven until October of 1684. After paying due respects to Esmit, Hamlin refitted his ships and soon made for the Guinea Coast of Africa. Here, off Sierra Leone, Hamlin and his followers spent the month of May 1683 capturing seventeen English and Dutch slavers and gold traders. From a modern perspective Hamlin may have been simply robbing the robbers, but he made no friends. Even his crew was unhappy, it seems, mostly over the division of spoils, and as in the case of so many buccaneer bands, Hamlin's soon split into several smaller groups. One group followed a Captain Morgan (apparently no relation to the deputy governor) while still in Africa, another split away at Dominica, in the Windward Islands, and *La Trompeuse* arrived in St. Thomas with Hamlin and a crew of thirty-eight, three-fifths of whom were Africans.[26] Within days of landing, *La Trompeuse* was burned in St. Thomas harbor by an English naval officer, a Captain Carlile of the HMS *Francis*, an action that drew an official letter of protest from Governor Esmit. After a narrow escape from the burning ship, the notorious but suddenly generous Hamlin found shelter with Esmit, and by mid-1684 there was talk of new depredations carried out by the same French pirate and sixty recruits sailing defiantly in a ship they called *La Nouvelle Trompeuse*. Esmit was ousted from St. Thomas in October of 1684 with English help, but filibusters like Hamlin now found refuge at Morgan's old haunt, the Ile-à-vache, off Hispaniola. Hamlin was one of the last of the successful pirates of his generation, but his resiliency only proved the difficulty of suppressing Caribbean buccaneers.

As will be seen in the final chapter, buccaneering in its more or less classical form did not end until about the turn of the eighteenth century, with most historians agreeing on 1697, the year Cartagena was sacked by a French combined naval and buccaneer expedition. In essence, however, the sea change had begun in the early 1680s when the first colonial anti-buccaneering laws were passed in Jamaica and French Hispaniola and the first English and French anti-pirate expeditions were launched. The raids of buccaneers such as l'Ollonais, Myngs, Mansfield, Morgan, and others would be followed by nearly two decades of raiding in the Spanish Pacific, or South Sea, however, and some buccaneers would even make their way to the Indian Ocean as a result of official intolerance in the Caribbean—making the so-called Pirate Round. (The problem of the Barbary Coast corsairs was ongoing, by the way, and a large proportion of the ransoms paid by Spanish regulars in the Mediterranean consisted of funds raised in Spanish American churches.) The Caribbean by this time was no longer simply Spanish, and the golden pirate opportunities of the 1660s were quickly disappearing with the rise of home-government intolerance. The less guarded and still thoroughly Spanish South Sea, on the other hand, seemed to offer just such opportunities to buccaneers in the 1680s, though not without recognizable risks to life and limb. That buccaneers flowed into this geographically isolated region in substantial numbers after 1680 proves how willing or perhaps desperate they were to take such risks.

For the Spanish seaborne empire the second half of the seventeenth century was a period of crippling military, financial, and political blows in the Indies and in Europe. Only one among many scourges to afflict the empire was the rise of buccaneering in American waters, but the depredations of these multinational and occasionally renegade Hispanic pirates were no small matter after about 1660. As it turned out, by the time Spain finally recovered from the various disasters of the seventeenth century, including a noticeable decline in bullion production and a massive reduction in the volume of trade, piracy in the Americas was no longer a problem of such gravity. The most significant intervening event was the War of the Grand Alliance, or King William's War (1689–97), which saw many buccaneers and filibusters absorbed into privateering and naval operations, mostly French against English, Dutch, and Spanish. The Spanish were by no means out of the picture as sovereignty conflicts with the interlopers continued in places like Florida, the Bahamas, Campeche, Honduras, and Darien (in 1699, for example, the Scots Darien Company attempted to settle the region romanticized by the buccaneer Lionel Wafer and his companions).[27] Buccaneers were active in all of these regions through the 1690s but most of the English subjects among them, like the infamous William Kidd, whose story will be related in the final chapter, joined the crown in the fight against the French. As it happened, some of Kidd's pirate associates in the years following King William's War were veterans of the South Sea buccaneer raids treated in the following chapter. Though increasingly spread over more and more distant parts of the globe, the early modern pirate's world, it would seem, was a small world after all.

BOX 4 GAMBLING IN THE SEVENTEENTH CENTURY

Next to larceny and murder (and perhaps drinking, rape, and torture), the pirates of the Caribbean are remembered for their prodigious gambling. Games of chance were not restricted to pirates, however, and were hugely popular throughout Europe and the Americas in the seventeenth century. Only in England during the Interregnum (1649–60) was gambling prohibited, and even then it probably flourished in secret. The subsequent Restoration unleashed a torrent of gaming pastimes then popular on the Continent, including cards, dice, cockfights, billiards, board games, horse racing, and so on. Many of the games played and wagered upon swept through Europe much like clothing fashions and some, like the omnipresent three-player card game "Hombre," originated in Spain. The pirate journals of the period refer to games of cards and dice rather often, and from other sources it is possible to understand how some of these games were played. Charles Cotton's *Compleat Gamester* (published in 1674), for example, is a treasure-trove of gaming rules—and methods of cheating—relevant to the era of the buccaneers. A sample dice game, called "Inn and Inn," is described as follows:

> "*Inn and Inn* is a game very much used in an ordinary, and may be play'd by two or three, each having a box in his hand. It is play'd with four dice. You may drop what you will, six-pences, shillings, or guinneys. Every Inn you drop, and every Inn and Inn you sweep all; but if you throw out, if but two plays, your adversary wins all; if three play, that *Out* is a Bye between the two other gamesters, which they may either divide or throw out for it. Here you are to observe that Out is when you have thrown no Dubblets on the four dice; Inn is when you have thrown two Dubblets of any sort, as two Aces, two Deuces, two Kings, &c. Inn and Inn is, when you throw all Dubblets, whether all of a sort or otherwise, viz. four Aces, four Deuces, or four Cinques, or two Aces, two Deuces, two Treys, two Quarters, or two Cinques, two Sixes, and so forth. . . . Your Battail [kitty] may be as much and as little as you will, from twenty shillings to twenty pounds, and so onward to a thousand, which Battail is not ended till every penny of that money agreed upon for the Battail be won; and it is but requisite, for it is frequently

seen that in a Battail of ten pound a gentleman hath been reduced to five shillings, and yet hath won at last the Battail.

For a gamester that would win without hazarding much his money, dice that will run very seldom otherwise but Sixes, Cinques, Quarters, &c., are very necessary. If those instruments are not to be had, a Taper-box will not be amiss, that as the Dice are thrown in many stick by the way, and so thrown to advantage.

Source: Charles Cotton, *The Compleat Gamester* (London: R. Cutler, 1674), 80–81.

Notes

1 Labat quoted in Clarence H. Haring, *Buccaneers in the West Indies in the Seventeenth Century* (London: Methuen, 1910), 68.

2 Ibid., 65. For this section see also Philip P. Boucher, *France and the American Tropics to 1700: Tropics of Discontent?* (Baltimore: Johns Hopkins University Press, 2008). On Providence, see Karen Ordahl Kupperman, *Providence Island, 1630–1641: The Other Puritan Colony* (New York: Cambridge University Press, 1995).

3 Haring, *Buccaneers*, 82.

4 Ibid., 114–15.

5 Ibid., 50. Spanish documents on the Jackson raid not cited by Haring may be found in Colombia's Archivo General de la Nación, Bogotá, Section Historia Civil 6:21. These documents concern the pillage of Maracaibo and Gibraltar.

6 Translations of relevant documents may be found in Irene A. Wright, ed., *Spanish Narratives of the English Attack on Santo Domingo, 1655* (London: Royal Historical Society, 1926). As shown in Appendix A, numerous Spanish elites received encomiendas in distant Venezuela as remuneration for their service in defense of the crown. A festival was also to be celebrated annually in the capital, and 500 pesos distributed among the poor (p. 68).

7 Haring, *Buccaneers*, 89.

8 Quoted in Lesley B. Simpson, *Many Mexicos*, 4th ed. (Berkeley: University of California Press, 1966), 145–46.

9 David Pawson and Michael Buisseret, *Port Royal, Jamaica* (Oxford: Clarendon Press, 1975), 194, appendix 12.

10 Haring, *Buccaneers*, 98.

11 Juan Juárez Moreno, *Corsarios y piratas en Veracruz y Campeche* (Seville: EEHA/CSIC, 1972), 20–26. Juárez Moreno refers to Myngs by the name given in Spanish documents, "Cristóbal Innus."

12 Haring, *Buccaneers*, 111.

13 Ibid., 273, appendix.

14 Ibid., 130.

15 Ibid., 139, fn.

16 Ibid., 139.

17 [A.O. Exquemelin], *The Buccaneers of America* (Glorieta, NM: Rio Grande Press, 1992 [1684]), 142.

18 Ibid., 196. A more detailed account of this and later raids by Morgan is in Peter Earle's *The Sack of Panamá: Sir Henry Morgan's Adventures on the Spanish Main* (New York:

Viking Press, 1981). Earle believes Morgan to have been of gentle birth, introduced to the Indies in the Penn-Venables expedition of 1655.

19 Ibid., 203.

20 Ibid., 215. Haring, *Bucccaneers*, cites the same passage (p. 188) but omits mention of the testicles.

21 Haring, *Buccaneers*, 201.

22 A copy of this remarkable series of testimonies was found in the Archivo Nacional de Historia in Quito, Ecuador, in the series "Popayán," caja 5 (1674). Rodríguez's declaration is in folios 2v–3v. The Portuguese mulatto was identified by the *San Antonio*'s pilot, twenty-four-year-old Pedro Daniel; Daniel also claimed to know one of the pirates as a renegade Spanish sailor from Sanlúcar de Barrameda "named Juan but [I] cannot remember his last name (*apellido*)" (ff. 7–7v).

23 Haring, *Buccaneers*, 217.

24 Quoted in ibid., 221. See also the superb study by Jesse Cromwell, "Life on the Margins: (Ex)Pirates and Spanish Subjects on the Campeche Logwood Frontier, 1660–1716." *Itinerario* 33:3 (2009): 43–71.

25 Haring, *Buccaneers*, 234.

26 Ibid., 235.

27 Ignacio Gallup-Díaz, *The Door of the Seas and Key to the Universe: Indian Politics and Imperial Rivalry in the Darien, 1640–1750* (New York: Columbia University Press, 2004).

5

BUCCANEERS IN THE SOUTH SEA

In spite of significant geographical barriers, the spilling over of buccaneering from Caribbean into Pacific waters was a logical development. As has been seen, emergent North European nation-states with colonial holdings and shipping interests in the Caribbean were coming to view buccaneering as a potential danger; it was a monster they had helped create, but its criminal energies were becoming more and more difficult to direct solely at enemies. Thus the governments of England, France, and the Netherlands, following Spanish and Portuguese policy only after being stung by piracy themselves, finally began to actively pursue and punish the buccaneers. For a time their policies were uncertain and even contradictory, but by the 1680s it became clear to the famed pirates of the Caribbean that their days were numbered. Some would go "straight," though with great reluctance, under French and English amnesty offers, others would find their fate on the gibbet or in fetid jails, and still others would continue to rove the sea beyond the reach of colonial governors and naval patrols, some in the Pacific and others in the more distant Indian Ocean.

John Narborough and the Charlatan

Bartholomew Sharp and his band of buccaneers (introduced in the previous chapter) were not the first Englishmen to visit the South Sea in the seventeenth century. As Peter Bradley has shown, at least one English expedition entered Peruvian waters between the time of Richard Hawkins, captured in 1594, and Sharp's entry in 1680. This expedition, under command of John (later Admiral Sir) Narborough in the 300-ton, thirty-six-gun *Sweepstakes*, was not apparently aimed at piracy but rather reconnaissance and smuggling. Whereas the Dutch Chilean venture under Hendrick Brouwer in 1642 had attempted to plant a settlement at Valdivia, the Narborough voyage of 1669–70 attempted to trade knives, axes, needles, pins, tobacco pipes, and other petty merchandise for Chilean gold.[1] Also unlike the Dutch, Narborough and his men tried to contact the Spanish settlers directly, ignoring the notoriously warlike Native Americans of the region as potential allies or trading partners. In fact, Narborough's instructions, born originally of Cromwell's failed "Western Design" but now revived by Charles II in the era of Anglo-Dutch rivalry, were explicit in prohibiting conflict, or "meddling" with Spanish settlers and traders. This standing order must have been difficult for Narborough to follow, especially given his past as a companion of the famed Caribbean buccaneer captain Christopher Myngs.

As an incident of foreign maritime intrusion into the Spanish Pacific, Narborough's voyage was virtually inconsequential—but not quite so. The expedition yielded much information for the English regarding both the east and west coasts of Patagonia, as well as a detailed chart of the Strait of Magellan, but perhaps more interestingly it produced a mysterious figure, a sort of agent-provocateur captured by the Spanish and known to us only as "Don Carlos." Apparently Captain Narborough had put this individual ashore with a small quantity of merchandise just south of Valdivia's harbor on 15 December 1669. Don Carlos soon disappeared, and some of his English crewmates went ashore at Valdivia to ask if the Spaniards living at the garrison had encountered their friend and his trade goods. An exchange of pleasantries and mutual feasting led to no information regarding don Carlos's whereabouts, but both sides took pains to note the strength of the other. The English misread this incident as a welcome, and the four English subjects who put ashore to trade some days later on 18 December—Lt. Thomas Armiger, John Fortescue, Hugh Coe, and Thomas Highway—were immediately captured and imprisoned. Narborough, completely taken by surprise, could negotiate their release only by entering the harbor and anchoring within range of Valdivia's guns—these were the only terms the Spanish would allow. With a rather weak reference to Francis Drake and John Hawkins's supposed betrayal at San Juan de Ulúa under similar circumstances in 1568, Narborough declared this option unacceptable and set sail for England via the Strait of Magellan on 22 December.

Narborough's unfortunate colleagues, including the mysterious don Carlos, were left to their fates. According to Bradley, who studied their testimonies before the Spanish war tribunal in Lima, all of the *Sweepstakes'* losers had interesting life histories. Highway was in fact a thirty-four-year-old mulatto from North Africa who had been baptized at Sanlúcar de Barrameda (Spain) at the age of fourteen, and had served don Carlos for some years. Of Armiger, we know only that he was a forty-seven-year-old lieutenant; of Coe that he was a twenty-eight-year-old trumpeter from Wapping; and of Fortescue that he was likewise twenty-eight, a soldier and mapmaker from the Downs.[2] Don Carlos may have actually been named Carlos Henríquez Clerque, as his Spanish interrogators first recorded; variations on this name appear elsewhere.

Apparently a charlatan and perhaps a pathological liar, don Carlos continued to offer conflicting testimonies to his captors for over a decade. He claimed to be the true "director" of the Narborough expedition, an Alsatian Catholic in the service of the English crown, and a friend of various Peruvian officials. Adding to all this intriguing testimony, don Carlos alleged that he was an unrecognized, illegitimate son of Prince Rupert, Count Palatinate of the Rhine. He also claimed to be connected to the court of Catherine of Bragança, recently married to England's Charles II. The Peruvian viceroy believed don Carlos to be Portuguese, and it is quite possible that he was a Portuguese Jew resettled in London after the marriage of Catherine and Charles in 1662. Bradley even suggests that don Carlos was concocting stories to cover his connections with London-based merchants and foreign agents, among them Diego de Peñalosa y Briceño and Simón de Cáceres, who had long sought foreign aid in undermining Spanish trade monopolies in the Americas.[3]

News of the entry of Bartholomew Sharp and his companions into more northerly Pacific waters around 1680 led to a hardline policy against supposed pirates, and don Carlos's new story, that he was a Franciscan priest from Cuzco acting in disguise, apparently as a double agent, was not sufficiently convincing to save him from torture and execution. Ever inventive, under a final torment the mysterious don Carlos claimed that he was in fact Olivier Belin of St. Malo (France), but neither this revelation nor his apparent lack of violent or seditious intentions saved him from a hideous end by garrote around 8 May 1682. The fate of his fellow prisoners is not well known, but those not executed seem to have died in prison. What then are students of pirate history to make of this bizarre series of incidents regarding abandoned English spies in Chile? Clearly the overall effect of the Narborough expedition on the Spanish Pacific was minimal in that no ships were taken and no settlements attacked, but given don Carlos's verbal excesses, the whole viceroyalty was in fact put into a panic over possible spying connections among internationally mobile Spanish officials. This was a mere prelude, however. Compared to these insinuations and allegations of the 1670s, the attacks of Sharp and those who followed him into the South Sea after 1680 constituted a genuine invasion.

Bartholomew Sharp: Pirate Captain of Last Resort

Having experienced a relative calm in the South Sea in the years following the Dutch intrusions of the early 1640s, the Viceroyalty of Peru had allowed its defenses to wither. The fleet assembled to face Hendrick Brouwer's supposed returnees was considered largely unnecessary following the Dutch peace in 1648, and Valdivia reverted to its earlier function as a fortress against rebellious Mapuches. In spite of faltering silver production, the third quarter of the seventeenth century was a time of relative economic expansion in the Pacific region and this shift was evident in the growing tonnage of shipping, much of it illegal, linking Peru with New Spain.[4] Intercolonial commercial shipping, which carried a wide variety of bulk goods, including wines, fruits, flour, timber, cheap cloth, indigo, cacao, and so on, boomed as local defense spending declined. The much resented *donativos* and *situados* (what might be called "pirate-war taxes") were still present, and highlanders from Santafé de Bogotá to Santiago de Chile paid dearly in the form of these imposts to defend the more vulnerable Caribbean ports of Portobelo, Cartagena, and Santa Marta. In the meantime the Pacific squadron, or Armada del Mar del Sur, fell into disuse, its ships and crews proving more expensive to maintain than they were worth. Likewise, port fortifications from California to Tierra del Fuego fell to ruins. No attempt had been made to keep up the walls around Callao, for example, since their construction during the decades-past Dutch threat. Substantial debts to contractors were still outstanding in Lima in 1656, and between the action of the waves and inaction of the authorities, the walls of Callao were full of breaches by the 1670s.[5] Officials all along the west coast knew their defenses were weak, and thus responded with panic when rumors such as those started by the mysterious don Carlos hinted at international intrigue and pending invasions.

Though Spanish officials in Lima thought these international conspiracies were in some way linked to the buccaneers, Bartholomew Sharp and his compatriots entered the South Sea in April of 1680 in total ignorance. The buccaneers were split into a half-dozen factions, under as many captains (none apparently with any experience in the Pacific) and their actions reflect disagreement and disarray rather than rational organization and clear objectives. Oddly, however, it was this very unpredictability, the fluid dynamic, as it were, of the first South Sea "pirate cycle," that kept the Spanish off guard. Since it was clear that not even the pirates knew where they were going, how could the Spanish know? Throwing caution to the wind, this mostly English-born, self-described "pack of merry boys" set out across the Darien wilds with one common objective: South Sea booty. To put it bluntly, the pirates were driven, according to one participant, by nothing more than "the sacred hunger of gold."[6]

Sharp and the buccaneers had left Golden Isle—which had no gold, it seems—on the northeast coast of Panama (or Darien) on 5 April 1680, and arrived in the Gulf of San Miguel around 20 April. They had been led by a group of autonomous Native Americans, possibly Cuna Cunas, and during their overland trek the buccaneers managed to temporarily satisfy their "sacred hunger" by sacking a small gold placering settlement called Santa María (presumably Caná, in Panama's eastern mountains). Once in the gulf, the pirates used canoes borrowed from their indigenous friends and stolen from the Spanish and set out to face a makeshift armadilla near Perico. With their usual boldness and audacity the pirates took the day, killing seventy-five Spanish subjects and wounding twenty, but losing several of their own leaders to wounds and dissent in the process. A 400-ton ship, the *Santíssima Trinidad*, was also captured during this engagement, and the pirates began planning their South Sea cruise. Captain Coxon, the supposed leader of the expedition at this juncture, opted to return to the Caribbean with fifty or so followers, and though his exploits in those familiar seas in the following years were memorable (see Chapter 4), the men he left behind in the Gulf of San Miguel did not forgive him this desertion.

Now under a Captain Sawkins's command, the South Sea buccaneers took a trading bark off Taboga Island loaded with wine, brandy, powder, and silver pesos, some 50,000 of them, all intended for the Panama garrison (this was a *situado* payment, apparently). A bout of drinking and gambling ensued, parting the majority of fools from their hard-won 240-peso shares. A flour vessel was taken shortly thereafter, and while searching for yet more provisions the pirates attacked Pueblo Nuevo, on the southwest coast of Panama. Captain Sawkins was cut down in what was variously described as a brave or reckless frontal charge on the town, leaving Bartholomew Sharp in command of the pirates. Such was his lack of charisma, however, that seventy more companions deserted to return to the Caribbean. Of the 146 men that remained, three would go on to write some of the best of the English buccaneer journals, namely those of Basil Ringrose, Lionel Wafer, and William Dampier. Sharp left a journal also, but his literary skills were more on a par with his abilities as a leader. The group set out from Coiba Island, west of Panama, on 6 June in the *Trinidad* (anglicized *Trinity*) and a smaller vessel, accompanied by a captured Spanish pilot, and reached Gorgona Island, off the Barbacoas coast (southwest Colombia) for careening and victualing on 17 July. Gorgona, a stopping point for Pizarro over a century and a half before, was uninhabited except by poisonous snakes and capuchin monkeys—the latter of which greatly amused Wafer—and the island became a favorite pirate haunt for years to come.

The buccaneers continued southward on 25 July, putting in at another uninhabited island, called Isla de la Plata by the Spanish and Drake's Isle by Ringrose. Another buccaneer journalist recalled: "Here it is reported Sir *Francis Drake* shared his mony. And here a great many of our Men plaid theirs away, and were fit for new adventures." Tortoises and feral goats provided the pirates with more meat, and on continuing south and entering the Gulf of Guayaquil a small vessel was sighted and soon overtaken. The same anonymous pirate quoted above (apparently John Cox) described the captives as "a parcel of merry blades, gentlemen, who drinking in a tavern made a vow to come to sea with that vessel and thirty men, and take us."[7] Led by Captain Tomás de Argandoña, the "merry blades" revealed to the buccaneers the sort of welcome they might receive in Guayaquil and Callao; though underfunded and poorly trained as usual, the ad hoc defenses of both cities were sufficient to face a band of only 146 pirates. A buccaneer attempt on either, now that word of their presence was out, would have been suicidal, and Sharp and his followers kept to a strategy of attack by sea and plunder of only small and relatively defenseless coastal settlements. In frustration, perhaps, Sharp's men shot a friar who had been captured along with Argandoña's "gentlemen." Regarded simply as one more mouth to feed, the priest was jettisoned while still alive.

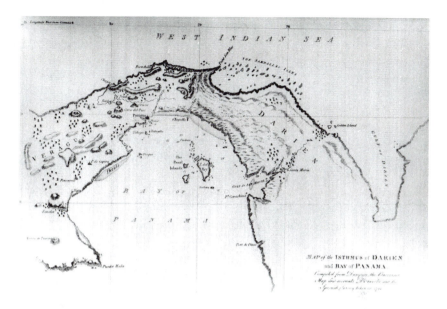

FIGURE 5.1 Map of the Isthmus of Darien and Panama

Source: James Burney, *Chronological History of Voyages and Discoveries in the South Seas,* London: 1803.

As has been seen in the case of Morgan's raid on Panama, the buccaneers, for the most part, were not romantic characters in the classical sense, and the Spanish were not far wrong in describing at least some of them as monsters, sustained by raw flesh. Still, some individual pirates seem to have felt twinges of conscience from time to time, and most of those who kept journals made clear distinctions between valor in battle and sadism in extracting information from prisoners. It should also be noted that these were cruel times for anyone falling into "enemy hands," be he or she pirate, renegade, or common criminal. With this in mind, one can better understand the tendency among pirates to push the boundaries of conventional warfare, usually with terror, and to ignore accepted limits on courageous behavior in battle; the buccaneers may have been motivated by treasure, but they were *always* fighting for their lives. Torture was standard practice among all European nations at this time, both at home and abroad, and executions by hanging, beheading, and garrote were common. Throughout the colonial world, besides, the significant body parts of all executed individuals were exhibited publicly for maximum deterrent effect—a practice revived in the early eighteenth-century pirate trials of British North America, as noted in the final chapter. Thus the numerous disincentives of getting caught, on either side, were at least partly responsible for these outrageous extremes of behavior.

Sadistic tendencies satiated for the time being, Sharp and his band continued southward, passing the important Peruvian port of Paita and capturing a

Guayaquil bark headed for Callao with a cargo of cacao, cheap textiles, and timber. A few prisoners were taken in this incident of 4 September but they were soon sent off in their crippled vessel so that the buccaneers could preserve rations. The pirates were getting desperate for food and water by the time they attempted landings at Ilo and Arica, well south of Lima, in late October. High seas prevented their initial efforts, but on 27 October they landed forty-eight men at Ilo. The town was taken easily, despite a mounted militia's resistance, and a sugar mill was ransomed for cattle. The residents of Ilo tricked the invaders, however, rounding up 300 defenders instead of a much hoped-for herd of buccaneer-style "meat on the hoof." Rather than face such forces directly, Sharp's hungry men withdrew, burning the sugar mill to spite their enemies. Somewhat more successful attacks were launched at Coquimbo in early December, followed by a landing at the nearby town of La Serena. The fruits of the pirates' endeavors consisted, aside from several tens of thousands of pesos in ransoms, of actual and much-needed supplies of fruits, namely apples, pears, strawberries, peaches, and cherries.[8] To this scurvy-fighting bounty (which would have been better if it had included citrus fruits) was added the much-loved fruit of the vine, mostly in the form of wines and brandies. By the time the drunken pirates were driven out of La Serena they had also accumulated some 500 pounds of ornamental silver and jewelry, most of it church-related.

For their shortcomings the inhabitants of La Serena received a sharp reproof from the Peruvian viceroy, Liñán y Cisneros, and it appears that there were in fact a number of cowardly or at least foolish defensive moves. Only one act of courage, which Bradley notes, seems to have been attempted: in the dark of night a Native American "navy commando" of sorts was sent out to the pirates' ship to attach an incendiary device to its rudder. The unnamed swimmer floated out to the *Trinity* on two seal skins and managed to light his tar-and-brimstone device on the stern post, but the pirates discovered the fire quickly enough to prevent significant damage. Seeing that they had worn out their welcome on the Chilean coast, the buccaneers sailed west to the Juan Fernández Islands, former haunt of Dutch pirates and future home of marooners such as Alexander Selkirk, partial inspiration for the novel *Robinson Crusoe* (1719). Here the ship was repaired and booty was redistributed; Sharp himself was said to have gained so much loot by this time, either by wile or by gambling, that he suggested returning to the Caribbean. The less lucky among the crew rebelled, however, putting a John Watling in Sharp's place as captain; they agreed that the Spanish South Sea was not yet exhausted of possibilities.

The band left Juan Fernández on 12 January 1681 with a strong desire to take Arica, outlet for Potosí's famed silver. The pirates, now under Watling's command, landed on 30 January after having outsailed a squadron of Spanish ships sent to capture them. Members of this fleet, under command of Santiago Pontejos and Pedro Zorilla, could only console themselves with the fact that the South Sea was large. Also, the buccaneers were skilled sailors; it would be no easy task to overhaul them using large and unwieldy military vessels. The buccaneers' luck ran thin at Arica, however, and of ninety men sent ashore to take the town, only forty-seven were left able to fight at the end of the day. Sharp, ever lucky in such situations, got away from this engagement with both his life and the captaincy of the expedition. Watling had been killed along with twenty-eight others, and another score were wounded or captured. Spanish forces, mostly local citizens with minimal training and second-rate weapons, had at last held off a serious buccaneer incursion. Still, as Bradley notes, the pirates had given them quite a scare by "fighting recklessly with an unnatural disdain for all risks and making light of death."[9] Perhaps the buccaneers simply preferred a musket ball in the head now to a rope around the throat later.

Sharp, who might have said "I told you so," did not feel so compelled to return to the Caribbean after all. The diminished band now cruised unhindered up and down the Peruvian coast before being further diminished by the hiving off of some forty-five dissenters (and three Darien natives) at Isla de la Plata. This party, which included the journalists Lionel Wafer and William Dampier, left for the Panamanian Isthmus in a longboat and two canoes on 16 April 1681. Most of these buccaneers made the crossing and met up with French companions on the Caribbean coast in late May; Wafer would spend some time as a "captive" guest of Cuna Cuna in Darien, and would detail his experiences among them in a remarkable memoir. Sharp and his now tiny band of seventy—a fine number when distributing booty, but short for engaging the enemy—stuck to offshore sneak-attacks. The *San Pedro*, a prize taken off the Quito coast on 10 July, yielded a welcome booty of 40,000 silver pesos, along with the usual cacao beans and cloth. Before the sailors could lose their 234-peso shares to Sharp's cards, another two prizes fell into buccaneer hands almost without struggle. A packet boat was taken off Cabo Pasado on 27 July, yielding little, but a merchantman called the *Santo Rosario* (or "Holy Rosary") was taken nearby on the 29th. This second prize added ninety-four pesos to the average seaman's chest (a large quantity of silver bars were mistaken for tin and ignored), but the merchant ship also yielded a trump card worth its weight in gold.

The *Santo Rosario* carried a *derrotero*, or book of South Sea nautical charts, and their loss to the buccaneers was considered a significant breach of security. It was Basil Ringrose who first realized the value of this sailing rutter, wrested as it was from the hands of a wailingly reluctant pilot who tried to cast it overboard. The sea charts were in fact of little direct use to the buccaneers—they were too vague to be of value to such experienced seamen, and where they were helpful only a larger landing force could have benefited.

Even though Sharp had left the Caribbean in a period of relative laxity toward buccaneering, he and his companions would be hard-pressed to excuse their actions upon returning to English ports; their occupation was quick becoming a capital crime from Massachusetts Bay to Barbados. Furthermore, the acting gover- nor of Jamaica was the ex-pirate captain Henry Morgan, and he seemed strangely

FIGURE 5.2 Basil Ringrose's Map of Gorgona Island

Source: Alexander Exquemelin, *The Buccaneers of America*, London: 1699 (courtesy of the Swem Library Special Collections, College of William & Mary).

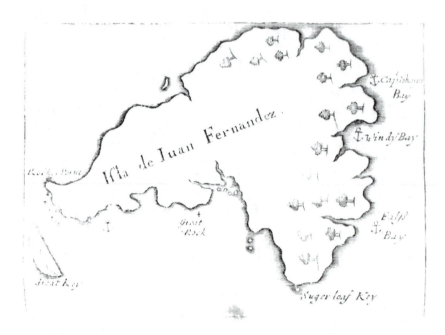

FIGURE 5.3 Basil Ringrose's Map of Juan Fernández Island

Source: Alexander Exquemelin, *The Buccaneers of America*, London: 1699 (courtesy of the Swem Library Special Collections, College of William & Mary).

intent on making an example of Bartholomew Sharp. The old buccaneer perhaps felt he could win favor at court by issuing a warrant for this upstart pirate's arrest, but Sharp was not the easy prey that he appeared. To claim to have gathered useful military intelligence could cast an entirely different light on otherwise unjustifiable acts of piracy against the Spanish, and the derrotero, renamed the "South Sea Waggoner" and repackaged by the expert mapmaker William Hack in London, would in fact get Sharp, Ringrose, and several of their companions off the hook, and off the gibbet, in a later series of trials.

Sharp's band left the *Rosario*, and the Pacific, shortly after capturing the maps, though not without attempting a brief and unrewarding excursion on land at Paita. Rough seas and storms slowed the pirates on their way south and caused them to miss the opening of the Strait of Magellan. Still, in what must be considered one of the more remarkable feats of long-distance sailing and navigation of the time, the *Trinity* rounded Cape Horn just before Christmas and reached Barbados by running down its latitude (i.e., maintaining a constant course along its latitude) on 28 January 1682. Having sailed wide of the Atlantic coast of South America in order to find favorable winds, Sharp and his men had not seen land since Tierra del Fuego and were extremely anxious to put in at Barbados for provisions, and to begin spending their shares of booty. A cool reception there and then at Antigua convinced the now-desperate band of pirates to split up and seek their fortunes individually; Sharp, Ringrose, and several others sailed for England while the rest made for Jamaica, Barbados, Virginia, and New England. Those unfortunate enough to land at Port Royal were imprisoned by acting governor Morgan, and one of them was even executed for being a "bloody and notorious villain."[10] The buccaneers' trusty Spanish vessel, the *Trinity*, was destroyed by fire while riding at anchor off St. Thomas, victim of the same English Navy men who fired Jean Hamlin's *Trompeuse*.

The arrival of Bartholomew Sharp, Basil Ringrose, John Cox, William Dick, and several other members of the South Sea crew at Dartmouth on 26 March 1682 was not celebrated, but the outlaws had a number of interesting stories to tell, and, more importantly, a book of maps to sell. Spain's ambassador in London, Pedro Ronquillo, pushed hard for punishment of the intruders, providing an eyewitness testimony from a captive taken on the *Rosario*, Simón Calderón, but the High Court of Admiralty acquitted all. For the Spanish this was a slap in the face, an outrage, further proof of the insincerity of the English in controlling their own subjects abroad during peacetime. Sharp and his band had caused the destruction of some twenty-five ships, stolen at least three, killed some 200 Spanish subjects, and plundered several towns. Furthermore, outfitting a squadron to chase the pirates from Peru had cost the treasury over 200,000 pesos.[11] For the English, ignoring all this, the arrival of the buccaneers offered an opportunity to learn of Spanish strength in the Pacific; Charles II could hardly condone the punishment, much less execution of such adventurous, self-financed, and willing spies. Indeed, considering all the bickering and splitting up of Sharp's band during a year-and-a-half of pillaging, it was amazing that the buccaneers had survived at all. Instead, their tales of wealth unguarded were soon transformed into new expeditions with the united aim of South Sea trade and plunder.

A Second Pirate Cycle in the South Sea

The Spanish were not unprepared for further hostilities in the Pacific. As Bradley and Clayton have shown, local initiative counted for a great deal, especially in important port towns like Guayaquil and Arica, and local militias were made larger and better armed than ever. Lima could claim combined units totaling just over 8,000 men in 1680, consisting of companies segregated by "caste" (*casta*) or status (*calidad*, i.e., Spaniards, mestizos, mulattoes, blacks, and Native Americans). Naval forces, on the other hand, remained insufficient, and declined further during this period. The unreliable armada consisted of two hulking Guayaquil-built galleons, 825 tons burden each and virtually unmaneuverable, and a small dispatch vessel. Merchant ships could on occasion be drafted for war purposes (their owners were required by law to arm them), but a firmly entrenched patrimonial political system was only made more corrupt by these new crossovers between public and private defense initiatives. In order to spend the extra money required to outfit their ships for war, merchants had to be rewarded with favors, usually choice political positions that offered a modicum of legitimacy and a stipend. Indeed, as will be seen, the entry of the buccaneers into the Spanish Pacific did much to stir the political waters of the region. Not only merchants used the heightened threat to their advantage, so did local *caudillos*, or political strongmen, gold miners, plantation owners, and even semi-autonomous groups of Native Americans and runaway slaves. In some ways the threat of a foreign enemy helped galvanize the various factions that vied for local power along the Pacific rim of Spanish America.

What Bradley calls the "second wave" of South Sea buccaneers consisted of a large number of loosely organized bands of French and English subjects (with the usual complement of Dutch pilots, renegade mulattoes, and so on), most of them inspired by Sharp's successes and by increasing hostility toward their type in the Caribbean colonies. By 1684 even the French governor at Petit Goâve, de Cussy, was forced to stop granting privateering commissions. Among the first to plot a Pacific raid, unsurprisingly, were the recently returned buccaneers—and Sharp deserters—William Dampier, Lionel Wafer, and John Cook. These adventurers met up in Virginia, were joined by Edward Davis and William Cowley, and set out from the Chesapeake in the *Revenge* with eighteen guns and a crew of seventy on 23 August 1683. They intended to reach the South Sea by way of the Strait of Magellan, but a preliminary trip to the Cape Verde Islands convinced them of the need to "purchase" (i.e., steal) a better vessel. Off the Guinea Coast the buccaneers captured a Danish slaver and traded the *Revenge* for sixty African women and girls, whom they put aboard their new flagship, re-christened as the *Bachelor's Delight*. Humorous as it may sound today, it is doubtful that the captives shared this joke, especially when they began to die from cold, disease, and hunger during the long southern passage to the Pacific.[12]

After rounding Cape Horn (rather than negotiating the Strait), Cook and his band sailed for Valdivia, on the south coast of Chile. Here they came across, to the astonishment of all, an English ship. As it turned out, Basil Ringrose and other survivors of Sharp's expedition in England had managed to round up sufficient financial backing—mostly from London speculators, apparently—for a return to their old haunts. Thomas Eaton commanded the *Nicholas*, which met Cook, and Charles Swan, a veteran of Morgan's Panama expedition, commanded the *Cygnet*, on board which Ringrose traveled. These English ships were outfitted for smuggling, but their intentions would soon be negated by the Spanish, who had no interest in opening their markets to buccaneer merchants. The ships had been fitted with big guns for just such a contingency, and arms of all kinds would in fact come in quite handy. Having lost track of the *Cygnet* while passing through the Strait, Eaton joined Cook and set off for the Juan Fernández Islands for repairs and recovery. While there, some of the pirates received treatment for scurvy and other ailments, and a most interesting encounter occurred. As it turned out, Sharp's band (then under the soon-to-be-killed Captain Watling) had abandoned an indigenous Nicaraguan, a Miskito Indian fellow named William, on the islands back in January of 1681. William had survived quite nicely at Juan Fernández, living from the milk and meat of feral goats, from fish, shellfish, and various wild herbs, and no doubt from the absence of violent encounters with foreign criminals and Spaniards. The original Robinson Crusoe (before Alexander Selkirk), William had wisely chopped the metal parts of his musket into a variety of tools, including a knife, harpoon, saw, and fish hooks.[13]

While Swan ran into troubles at Valdivia, Cook and Eaton sailed northward in search of a treasure ship presumably heading from Callao to Panama. Arica was passed up, partly because of the shortage of manpower (just over 100 total), and only a few flour vessels were captured north of the outer Lobos Islands on 18 May. The buccaneers realized they had lost the element of surprise in the Spanish Pacific due to Swan's talkative behavior while trying to negotiate a release of prisoners farther south, and soon they retired to the Galápagos Islands to store provisions. Here the disheartened buccaneers spent several weeks careening and reconnoitering the somewhat otherworldly archipelago, and Cowley and Dampier filled notebooks with their quasi-scientific observations of the islands' very original-looking species. In mid-June the pirates left for New Spain to try their luck with Manila galleons and the like, but while stealing cattle at Nicoya (western Costa Rica) it was discovered that their arrival in these seas, too, had been anticipated. To compound matters, Captain Cook died, creating some friction between the two ships' crews, friction that would soon lead to schism. Davis, meanwhile, took over command of the *Bachelor's Delight* and sights were set on the port of Realejo.

Realejo, off the northwest coast of Nicaragua, proved well guarded, so the pirates cruised northward to Amapala Island. After a month of careening, victualing, and menacing what few Native Americans came within view, Eaton left for Cocos Island and eventually the East Indies (c. November 1684, reaching England by October 1686). Davis and his followers returned to Peruvian waters in hopes of meeting up with other buccaneers, and possibly Swan and the *Cygnet*. Swan had sailed north to the Gulf of Panama and had run across a number of straggling buccaneers in piraguas. These turned out to be members of a party under Peter Harris, nephew of the Captain Harris killed in Sharp's expedition, which had just crossed to the Pacific via Darien and repeated the 1680 raid on the Santa María gold camp.[14] The marchers had come away with some 120 pounds of gold in this raid, and perhaps used a portion of it to persuade Swan to give them a bark. From here the combined crews sailed south to Isla de la Plata (Drake's Isle) to rendezvous with Davis and his "bachelors."

Davis and his crew had meanwhile attempted to land at Manta and Santa Elena, on the central coast of the Audiencia of Quito, but a new scorched-earth policy promoted by the Peruvian viceroy allowed for little booty, and no captives made themselves available for torture and interrogation. Again, Dampier busied himself with descriptions of everything in sight, perhaps keeping in mind the value of "intelligence" in case of a piracy prosecution back home, or in the English-American courts. His accounts of tar pits and wrecked treasure ships off Punta Santa Elena—the former already exploited, since pre-Columbian times, and the latter already salvaged by slave divers from Guayaquil—would inspire future English incursions.

After joining up with Swan and Harris in early October of 1684, Davis and his unlucky buccaneers, now some 200 strong, attempted to sack Paita and then Guayaquil. Paita yielded little of value, but was burned to spite the inhabitants; Guayaquil was spared by the timely advice of a Native American guide-turned-Spanish spy. Now short of provisions and desperate for a prize, the buccaneers took several vessels plying the waters between Guayaquil and Lima. One carried Quito cloth and three others carried slaves, almost 1,000 of them, presumably en route from Panama to the coastal plantations of Peru. Several slaves were made to join the crew, though apparently as slaves rather than free partners. It is again Dampier, in his journal, who reveals the limits of "buccaneer democracy" in this regard. He envisioned a pirate-run gold camp at Santa María (Darien) staffed with such African slaves as could be stolen from the Spanish in the South Sea. With typical hyperbole he states, "we might have been Masters not only of those Mines . . . but of all the Coast as high as Quito."[15] In the meantime, captured slaves would do the ships' drudgery. Later, most likely, they would be sold as contraband to unscrupulous Spanish buyers.

Davis, Dampier, and the gang headed north to the Gulf of Panama toward the end of 1684, capturing a packet boat near Isla del Gallo (southwestern Colombia) in December. A piece of intercepted correspondence revealed that the Tierra Firme Fleet was waiting at Portobelo for the annual Peruvian treasure shipment, news that obviously delighted the hard-luck "bachelors" of the pirate crew; they sailed for Panama immediately. While waiting for the treasure ships from Arica and Callao near the Pearl Islands, another modest prize, a ninety-ton ship carrying little of value, was taken in early January. The silver fleet was slow in coming, but new buccaneers from the Caribbean were not. In mid-February the English were joined by a group of mostly French filibusters (200 French, 80 English) led by François Grogniet and a Captain Lescuyer. Davis and Swan realized the benefit of greater numbers in their planned endeavor and the newcomers were given the most recent prize, called the *Santa Rosa*, and invited to join the hunt. In return, Grogniet gave the English pirates blank and essentially expired commissions from the French governor at Petit Goâve—flimsy but presentable legal justification for their pillaging. Only Swan turned down the offer of a commission, worried about the legal implications for his sponsors back in England. Unlike the others, he had been sent on a smuggling mission, and would try to maintain the merchant facade to the end. On 3 March another group of Caribbean buccaneers entered the Pacific via the Gulf of San Miguel, this time a band of 180, mostly English, under a Captain Townley. Word had clearly gotten out that the South Sea was the place to be, for in early April yet another group of some 264 pirates appeared, now mostly French, and under command of Captains Rose, le Picard, and Desmarais. The swelling pirate forces, now over 900 strong in three large vessels and five or six small ones, were further augmented by a small party of English under Captain William Knight, who joined the mass from the west coast of New Spain.

For their part the Spanish were troubled by the simultaneous tasks of sending the treasure fleet to Panama and clearing the South Sea of buccaneers. As has been seen, the so-called Armada del Mar del Sur was in sad shape in the 1680s, and it was small besides, consisting only of the unwieldy galleons *San José* and *Nuestra Señora de Guadalupe*, along with a small, eighty-ton patax, the *San Lorenzo*. The larger ships had been laid up for major repairs during the cruisings of Swan and Davis and were only fit to sail in early 1685. Due as much to merchant reluctance as actual availability, it seems, only two armed merchant ships were offered to accompany the armadilla when it left Callao for Panama on 7 May 1685: these were the *Pópulo* and the *Rosario*.[16] Also due to merchant hemming and hawing, most of the privately owned silver shipments for the year were retained and only a small amount accompanied the half-million or so pesos belonging to the crown.[17] If ships were wanting, men were not—1,431 salaried individuals accompanied the five-ship armadilla, under the astute triple command of Tomás Palavicino, Antonio de Vea, and Santiago Pontejos.

The Spanish were ably led and the buccaneers missed a great opportunity. Apparently overcome by boredom or drink, the 960-odd pirates guarding the usual entryway of the galleons only spied the Spanish fleet when it was bearing down upon them, its treasure already safely unladed and new men and supplies taken on. The buccaneers met the Spanish off Pacheca Island on 28 May, and although the multinational intruders had outlined a strict plan of attack, it fell to pieces in short order. That night, Palavicino and his men tricked the pirates into thinking their galleons were repositioning by snuffing and relighting stern lanterns; in the morning they found the buccaneers in disarray and chased them easily from the bay. Bitter and disappointed (mostly with one another), the pirates fled to Coiba Island, to the west of Panama. Grogniet was called a coward by the English and "cashiered," and a later joint raid on nearby Pueblo Nuevo increased English–French tensions; the Protestant English had apparently offended their Catholic allies by chopping the limbs off of religious statuary. The Spanish victory was a pyrrhic one, at best, but at least the treasure had been landed safely. Celebrations in Lima and elsewhere were quickly calmed, however, with news that the galleon *San José* had blown up in an accident off Paita during the return voyage, killing 241 crewmembers.

As they were wont to do, the pirates hived off into several bands after the Panama disappointment. Swan and Townley cruised the coast of New Spain in hopes of taking a Manila galleon, and Davis headed south (after an unsuccessful attack on Realejo, with the others) to raid the South American coast once again. Grogniet and the other Frenchmen, some 340 of them, spent most of the following year engaging in small-scale raids up and down the Central American coast before heading well south, to Guayaquil, in early 1687. Bad luck befell a number of the English buccaneers during a sojourn in Amapala Bay, off northwest Nicaragua, and many died from a sort of tropical fever which the surgeon Lionel Wafer did his best to treat (the buccaneers, like earlier pirates and privateers, almost always counted a surgeon among their numbers). Swan and Townley made their way toward Acapulco, sailing behind an advance force in piraguas and spending most of October engaging in petty foraging and hunting raids around Tehuantepec and the deserted port of Guatulco. In late November Townley backed away from an attempt to take a prize in the harbor of Acapulco, protected as it was by the guns of the new castle of San Diego. The pirates cruised northward to Petatlán and Ixtapa, raiding for provisions but hoping to intercept a Manila galleon instead. Their timing was right, as the *Santa Rosa* arrived off Cabo San Lucas from the Philippines toward the end of November 1685. To the buccaneers' chagrin, however, the China ship was "miraculously" guided past them by a pearling vessel, unseen, to Acapulco.[18]

Swan and Townley vainly tried to find the galleon in the ensuing weeks, but hard-pressed for provisions they broke apart and raided several coastal settlements, including Santiago de Salagua and parts of the Banderas Valley, near the opening of the Gulf of California. Finally realizing they had missed their Acapulco-bound quarry, Swan and Townley split up, the former sailing north and the latter south. Swan's band, now busy victualing for a Pacific crossing in the *Cygnet*, made the mistake of attempting a raid on an inland town called Sentispac on 26 February 1686. The Spanish had followed their old course of defense by "scorching" the coast, and the now desperate pirates, said to be reduced to eating dogs, cats, and horses by this time, were all too open for suggestions. They took the town, located some 25 km upriver from the coast, with little difficulty. A well-prepared ambush by local residents, however, took the wind from their sails; as they returned to the coast, fifty buccaneers, including the famous hydrographer Basil Ringrose, were killed. Swan, his forces reduced from 140 to about 90, spent the next month and a half victualing and careening along the coast and among the Tres Marías Islands before setting sail for the East Indies on 10 April 1686. Swan would die in suspicious circumstances on Mindanao (Philippines), but the *Cygnet* eventually reached Madagascar, a new pirate haunt in the Indian Ocean. The great buccaneer journalist William Dampier and other survivors of the Swan expedition reached England in September of 1691.

Townley and his band, meanwhile, had made few stops along the coast of New Spain on their way back to the Gulf of Panama. They were sighted by the Spanish off Zacatula (near Ixtapa) in February 1686, and they freed prisoners near Acapulco shortly afterward. The band lost four crewmembers to Spanish captors sometime before April, however, when they appeared before the courts in Mexico City. Nicoya, on the Costa Rica coast, was reached by March of 1686.[19] In July of the same year Townley took his crew to the Gulf of Panama, watering and victualing on the Pearl Islands and capturing several small barks in the vicinity. The Panamanians once again felt besieged, but not so much as to agree to Townley's terms of prisoner exchange in early August. Instead they replied with a punitive expedition that met the pirates off Taboga Island on 22 August. The engagement went well for the buccaneers, but not for Townley, who died from his wounds on 9 September. The remaining pirates, who now consisted of more Frenchmen than Englishmen, tried to bargain with the audiencia and archbishop of Panama once again, but without effect. To add urgency to their principal demand that five imprisoned buccaneers be released, the pirates sent twenty severed captives' heads to the Spanish president, promising to do the same to the remaining ninety if rebuffed. Somewhat shaken by this act of terror, the president complied, but the buccaneers added a further extortion, demanding a money ransom for the last of the captives in their custody. In an exchange reminiscent of Barbary Coast rescate, the pirates were given as much cash as could be mustered in Panama, a sum of only 10,000 pesos.[20]

The buccaneers, now under command of the French captain, le Picard, spent the next six months or so engaging in petty raids up and down the Panamanian coast, sacking also the Costa Rican town of Nicoya in early January of 1687. The 250-odd pirates, who had fallen out by nationality among themselves by this time, were faced with continued Spanish hostilities and dwindling chances at booty. Better equipped than in the past, the Spanish now guarded Panama City with two triple-decker warships, boasting eighteen guns each, and a fifty-two-oar galley fitted with five cannon and four swivel guns. The buccaneers had only a handful of barks, piraguas, canoes, and a galiot (a small galley-like vessel), and only four cannon of any size among them.[21] A sort of peace agreement had been reached between the Spanish and some of the native peoples of Darien by this time, as well, making an overland return to the Caribbean more dangerous than ever. All things considered, then, a cruise south to Peru sounded comparatively inviting

to le Picard and his men when Grogniet entreated them in late January. As will
be seen later, the buccaneers of the "second wave" would have their day at last at
Guayaquil in mid-April of 1687.

In the meantime, the third buccaneer party of note after the Panama breakup,
under Davis in the now decidedly less pleasant *Bachelor's Delight*, was causing
mayhem all up and down the Peruvian coast. The crew, which included a number
of Frenchmen, along with the English captains Harris and Knight, had first put in
for water and food at Cocos Island. Harris apparently left from here to make his
way to the East Indies, but the remaining pirates sailed south for the Galápagos
Islands, hoping to dig up their old stores of flour. Davis and his followers were first
sighted by Spanish subjects off Huanchaco, just north of Trujillo (Peru), in February of 1686, but not until an attack on the small desert town of Saña, farther north,
were they able to take anything of value. A local militia force of 130 men, some
mounted, was quickly overwhelmed by the 200-odd buccaneers who landed at
Chérrepe in early March. A surprising 300,000 pesos-worth of coin, tableware,
and jewelry was extracted from the townspeople, along with some indigo dye and
400 much-appreciated jars of wine. A subsequent incident of rape and pillage at
Paita was bested by the capture of two prizes, a Panamanian frigate carrying 350
slaves and the *Nuestra Señora de Aranzazú*, carrying sugar and guns. The pirates
took on thirty-nine of the slaves as crewmembers, again most likely as slaves rather
than equals, and retired to the nearby hamlet of Colán for a respite. They apparently needed the rest, as the next few months would find them engaged in almost
non-stop robberies, both at sea and on land.

Attacks on the small coastal settlements of Huacho and Huaura in May of
1686 yielded little booty, but gave ample opportunity for the crueler sort among
the pirates to practice their specialty. At Huaura a priest was shot for protecting
his church and a local magistrate's throat slit when his ransom failed to material-
ize. Two other captives were beheaded at Chancay for similar infractions and a
priest beaten to death at Casma in June. As Bradley notes, these incidents created
a sense of terror all along the Peruvian coast, and many towns were temporarily abandoned as a result of the apparently escalating pirate threat.[22] Towns of
medium size were no less vulnerable, as the citizens of Pisco were to find out on
11 July. On this day the buccaneers landed 123 men at nearby Paracas and took
the town with ease, aided, apparently, by incompetence and an accident involving
gunpowder among the locals. Lima could not be relied upon for aid, and indeed
the Viceroy Palata had tried to recall Pisco's only artillery pieces for ship service
against the buccaneers. Though in the end it did them no good, the citizens of
Pisco and Ica, most notably 500 women, had forcibly prevented the removal of
the guns by rioting in the town square.[23] Ignorant of all this, the buccaneers took
Pisco and its prominent personages hostage and killed thirty-two defenders, half
of them from the companies of *españoles* and half from those of the *negros libres*,
or free blacks, and mulattoes. A ransom of 20,000 pesos and twenty jars of wine, a
regional specialty, left the hapless citizens of Pisco sour.

Again filled with the delights (and depravities) of bachelorhood, Davis and his crew made for the coast of Chile, but only after first cruising boldly into the harbor of Callao, taking four small prizes and taunting the seemingly impotent citizens and officials of Lima. The improved Peruvian armadilla had been sent to Panama in early July, and by the time it returned south Davis was already out of reach and threatening Coquimbo. In cruising the Chilean coast, the pirates' heads were always filled with "golden dreams," as Bradley notes, but Coquimbo was not to be another Pisco—its gold mines were not so rich as the pirates believed, anyway. The buccaneers pulled back, put in for timber (for ship repairs) at Ilo, and left the coast for the Juan Fernández Islands to careen and victual. A small group headed by Captain Knight decided to return to the Caribbean via the Strait in the prize-ship *Asunción*, but the others, having gambled away much of their loot, presumably to Knight's men, were in favor of continued depredations in the South Sea. Although reduced to fewer than 100 pirates, Davis's band enjoyed several successes in journeying northward beginning in early 1687, partly since the Spanish had assumed their departure from the Pacific along with Knight. A raid on Arica in early February yielded 40,000 pesos, and Ilo gave up welcome supplies of sugar, oil, and fruit. A predawn attack on Cañete produced a 5,000-peso ransom, happily paid by the town's residents for the safe release of the corregidor and his family, who had been captured in their beds.[24]

A series of half-hearted or at best minimally rewarding landings and prize-takings north of Paracas ended on 23 April off Huarmey, where a straggling member of the armadilla finally met the buccaneers. The ship, which had separated from the fleet and was putting in for water at Huarmey, was the *Santa Catalina*, with six guns and 145 men, under command of Captain Gaspar Bernabeu de Mansilla. The pirates quickly got the upper hand in a firefight and the *Santa Catalina* was run aground, drowning some fifty crewmembers.[25] Davis and his crew made little of this engagement, but for the Spanish it was a bruising defeat, leaving them as it did with only one other galleon, the twelve-gun *San Francisco de Paula*, and a patax to defend the entire Pacific South American coast. Davis's attacks on the towns of Santa and Colán in early May yielded little in the way of booty, but news was gathered from dispatches that Grogniet and his followers were busily pillaging Guayaquil. Not wanting to miss out, Davis and his followers quickly sailed north to join the Frenchmen.

Grogniet and Guayaquil, 1687

After sailing south from Nicoya in February, Grogniet, le Picard, and an English captain, George Hout (or Hutt, or Huff, depending on the source) arrived off Puná Island in mid-April of 1687 with about 300 followers. The buccaneers and filibusters had been seen by sentinels at Manta and Punta Santa Elena, and it was really no surprise when a report arrived in Guayaquil that unfamiliar lights had been seen on the island on 18 April. For some unknown reason the most senior local official, the corregidor, Fernando Ponce de León, did nothing more than put his 200-man defense force on alert, waiting for the pirates to make the first move. This turned out to be a grave error and Ponce de León would never live it down. In the early hours of 20 April, a rainy Sunday, Grogniet, le Picard, and Hout, guided by an indigenous river pilot and a fugitive mulatto named Manuel Boso, led three prongs of an attack that delivered the town to them before noon. The newly outfitted wooden fort of San Carlos gave way last, but without much struggle since its guns were pointed the wrong way. In the fighting only nine buccaneers were killed and twelve wounded, while the Spanish suffered three or four times as many total casualties. The residents of Guayaquil had not been too careless in sequestering valuables, however, as the pirates found only 10,000 pesos in cash, along with the odd pearls and plate. Under the circumstances, a prolonged period of haggling over ransoms, Mediterranean style, was inevitable.

According to the pirate journalist Raveneau de Lussan, Grogniet and his followers demanded one million pesos in gold and 400 sacks of flour for the release of over 600 captives and several ships and barks. If paid, for good measure the town would not be burned, a reminder of Morgan's 1671 visit to Panama. Spanish sources, according to Bradley and Donoso, put the ransom at a more easily imaginable 300,000 pesos, but still this was an incredible sum of cash, and would have to come from Quito or Lima, if it came from anywhere. Quito, the seat of the audiencia, was located some weeks away over rough trails and was in such dire financial straits at the time that the local government would be hard-pressed to ransom its principal port.[26] The ransom money was indeed slow in coming, and the pirates pulled back with their prizes and captives to Puná Island by 26 April, a wise move considering the dual possibilities of attack from land and sea. Other reasons for leaving Guayaquil included the common consensus that it was a pest-pot, followed by an apparent buccaneer cooking mishap that burnt half the town.

In the meantime the pirates entertained themselves with the wine, women, and song (and food) of Guayaquil. The town's musicians were captives, as were most of the principal ladies, and de Lussan claims that: "The women of the city were of extraordinary beauty" and though at first they "conceive[d] a keen horror and aversion for us . . . when they came to know us . . . if I may say so, they felt very differently toward us, giving indications of a passion bordering on folly."[27] The good life on Puná Island did not satisfy everyone, apparently, as four severed heads were delivered to Spanish officials on 9 May to express the buccaneers' impatience regarding the ransom (de Lussan claims the victims had been made to throw dice to decide their own fate). Grogniet had died of his wounds on 2 May, to be replaced by le Picard, and it was in the midst of this strange atmosphere of dissolution and apprehension that Davis and his Anglo-American "bachelors" arrived on 16 May, bearing bad news. It seems that the Spanish negotiators, according to a captured dispatch, did not intend to pay the ransom. They claimed instead, in a letter to the viceroy, to be holding out for the arrival of the armadilla: "And when they must needs send me yet fifty heads," a Spanish negotiator asserted in the dispatch, "I judge that that loss is less detrimental to us than if we were to allow to live persons of such evil intentions."[28] The news enraged the buccaneers, who immediately demanded money and flour, threatening to decapitate the remaining captives. Soon they exhausted the stores of the negotiators, however, which amounted to only 42,000 pesos and 100-odd sacks of flour, and the pirates were forced to turn their attentions to a Spanish sea attack by 27 May.

The three Spanish vessels the buccaneers now faced were not part of the armadilla per se, but belonged rather to a private defense contractor called the Compañía de Nuestra Señora de la Guía, or the Our Lady of the Guide Company. That this company existed at all was strong evidence that the merchant communities of Pacific Spanish America were fed up with the weakness of royal defenses. The buccaneers had been given virtually a free hand in these seas since 1680, and commerce, both legal and illicit, had suffered considerably. The company thus managed to raise substantial funds from both coastal merchants and highland industrialists (the mercury mine owners of Huancavelica contributed some 250,000 pesos, for example), and outfitted two warships and a patax.[29] The larger ships were commanded by experienced Biscayan sea captains, the *San Nicolás* under Nicolás de Igarza and *San José* under Dionisio de Artunduaga, but their brief encounter with le Picard and the buccaneers ended in a stalemate, and both sides scattered with relatively minimal losses by 2 June.[30]

The company's efforts would pay off more directly in a later engagement with filibusters along the coast of New Spain, but for now the pirates maintained the upper hand, or at least their freedom to roam. They regrouped shortly after the battle on the nearby Isla de la Plata, then stopped at Punta Santa Elena to release the remaining prisoners and divide their loot, which yielded a substantial 400 pesos per man. The French buccaneer journalist Raveneau de Lussan claims that many members of his band had won so much silver in gambling that they feared they could not carry it home; thus gold and gems, being more compact, became disproportionately valuable among the filibusters. They would pay a substantial premium to gold-rich mates to convert their pieces of eight.[31] Meanwhile, the despoiled and angry citizens of Guayaquil—many pointing the finger of blame at the corregidor, Ponce de León—struggled to rebuild, now at a new and presumably more defensible site a few kilometers downstream from the old one.

After Guayaquil, the loosely organized forces of le Picard, Hout, and Davis split again, Davis and his followers choosing to return to the Caribbean by way of the Strait of Magellan (only the *Bachelor's Delight* was fit for such a journey), and le Picard choosing to cruise northward for an eventual land passage across Central America. le Picard and his men reached as far north as Realejo by mid-July of 1687, putting in at Tigre Island, in Amapala Bay, on the 23rd.[32] The French buccaneers then continued northward in search of lost mates (a French band that had not joined them at Guayaquil), sacking what few settlements they could find along the way between Tehuantepec and Acapulco. Not finding their companions, le Picard and his 280-odd followers returned to Amapala Bay in late December, scuttled their ships, and began the long (c. 600 km) overland trek to the Caribbean via the Segovia River. They arrived two months later at the aptly named Cape Gracias a Diós, on the Mosquito Shore, and dispersed, most, like de Lussan, finding their way back to Hispaniola and Tortuga to tell their tale within a year.

The return of Davis and his crew was no less adventurous, as they experienced what turned out to be a tsunami on 20 October off the Peruvian coast near Lima, and made possibly the first European sighting of Easter Island shortly thereafter.[33] Davis and his crew stopped for water and victuals at the normally pleasant and refreshing Juan Fernández Islands only to find them overrun with dogs let loose by the Spaniards. Part of the low-cost "earth-scorching" policy common throughout the West Indies, these dogs were left on the island to kill off the feral goats that sustained the buccaneers and marooners. Nevertheless, five crewmembers stayed behind, surviving for three years (presumably on dog flesh) until they were recovered by the John Strong expedition in late 1690. The rest of the crew, after putting in briefly at Mocha and Santa María on the south Chilean coast, made the long passage around Cape Horn (storms had forced them past the Strait), arriving in the North Atlantic in the spring of 1688. An English buccaneer amnesty had been proclaimed in May of 1687, but unfortunately for the South Sea adventurers, a final clause specifically excluded them. Members of the Davis band, including the famous journalist and surgeon Lionel Wafer, were thus captured in the lower Chesapeake in 1688 and taken to Jamestown, Virginia, to be tried for the crime of piracy. After several years of litigation the pirates were freed to sail for London, but £300 worth of their booty was retained by the local government to found the future College of William and Mary.

Captain Franco, Shipwrecks, and Contraband

The 1680s, arguably the most damaging decade of piracy in the Spanish South Sea, were to slowly fade into history and legend following the exit of le Picard and Davis. What followed, after a short interval of small-scale raiding by forty or so French buccaneers, was a long-term trend toward smuggling. The French buccaneers who remained after 1687 consisted of two groups, one of them made up of about fifty of Grogniet's lost mates along the New Spain coast, and the other, with just over forty, entering the Pacific via the Strait of Magellan just as Davis and his crew were leaving. As Gerhard and Bradley have shown, these straggling bands of filibusters, apparently led by a "Captain Franco," (a.k.a. Franz Rools, a Zeelander), managed to terrorize both the New Spain and Peruvian coasts all out of proportion with their numbers for about half a decade. The first band watered, victualed, and careened for some time among the Tres Marías Islands at the opening of the Gulf of California before being joined by their companions from the south. Now over ninety strong, they attacked coastal settlements from Navidad to Mazatlán, devastating the towns of Sentispac, Acaponeta, and Rosario between late 1687 and mid-1689. They failed to sight any Manila galleons despite their regular cruising to Baja California from Cape Corrientes, but it is highly unlikely that such poorly armed pirates could have captured one of these massive ships, anyway. The Spanish were up in arms nevertheless, and a warship under Antonio de Mendoza sailed out of Acapulco in December of 1688, engaging the pirates north of Matanchel (southeast of Mazatlán) in late January. Mendoza succeeded only in scattering the filibusters, preferring to escort the incoming Manila ships to Acapulco rather than pursue the enemy.

The buccaneers stayed on the Tres Marías Islands for some months more, trying their best to extort ransoms from the few remaining Spanish subjects on the coast. They revealed their criminal origins by terrorizing several hostages, including a priest named Águilar, who had his ears and nose cut off in order to speed the delivery of coin and tobacco.[34] Several other prisoners escaped to Chametla, on the coast near Mazatlán, after laying hands on a canoe. These escapees claimed that the pirates numbered ninety-two, and were only equipped with a small, eight-gun ship and a twenty-four-oar piragua. Their plan was now to raid the coast of Peru and then set sail for the East Indies. The viceroy of New Spain outfitted a much larger reconnaissance force at Acapulco by July of 1689, but the pirates appear to have left for Peruvian waters by mid-May, when they dropped off the last of their bedraggled prisoners at Acaponeta. As usual, the crown's help came too late to be of use to persecuted coastal settlers. The final filibusters were next discovered off Isla de la Plata, near the Audiencia of Quito, in June of 1689. On 15 October of that year they took the storeship *San Francisco Javier* off Cabo Blanco and made for the Galápagos Islands with prisoners in tow.

Amazingly, a number of the Spanish subjects taken prisoner by Captain Franco and his filibusters from the *San Francisco Javier* lived to tell their tale. After spending some time on the Galápagos, forty-three of the captives were set adrift in a bark with a small store of rations. Though the pirates had made certain that none of the castaways were sailors (kept as informants and deckhands), the entire group managed to arrive off the Barbacoas coast near Gorgona Island eighteen days later. As was customary in such situations, a local crown official took testimonies from a number of the parched and hungry survivors on Christmas Day 1689 in order to ascertain the pirates' motives and assess their strength. One witness, Pedro de la Milla, claimed that Franco's crew consisted of about 110 men, "less twenty blacks who serve for everything and twenty Indian sailors who were taken from [our] ship and from a flour bark." Milla also claimed that the filibusters had captured a dispatch vessel sailing from Panama to Paita, and that, "this witness heard the pirates say that they found some loose letters advising [them] that the King of France was at war with Our Lord, the King, and [the King] of Portugal and the Genoese Emperor [sic] and Holland, and [I] heard them say that five English ships were coming through the Strait [of Magellan] to raid [*corsar*] in this South Sea."[35] Given the new state of war and the possibility of English reinforcements, the buccaneers, according to Milla, decided to cruise for a while longer in the region;

their earlier plan had been to sail home straightaway to France. Local officials, always interested in advancing their careers—and certain of a slow response from the viceroy—quickly organized reconnaissance missions to seek out the Franco band. The buccaneers, however, had already refitted the *Javier* for battle on the Galápagos, replacing their worn-out ship, *Urqueta*, and sailed northward.

The next year was spent cruising the coast from southern New Spain to Valdivia (Chile), apparently with little profit; furthermore the English ships, which probably would have attacked them anyway, failed to appear. The remaining buccaneers were few in number and Spanish shipping had been so severely disrupted by the pirate attacks of the previous decade that few prizes now hove into view. What little booty the buccaneers did manage to seize consisted mostly of much-needed food and wine, along with less desirable items, such as common cloth, some rope, sails, timber, and a few slaves. Still under command of the mysterious Captain Franco, the filibusters roved about almost randomly from their bases on the Galápagos and Juan Fernández Islands before finally breaking into two bands in December of 1692. Franco's group spent another full year raiding shipping from Iquique to Pisco, taking at least one useful prize, the *Nuestra Señora del Rosario*, which was fitted for the return voyage to the Atlantic on the Galápagos Islands in late 1693. This tiny band of pirates passed the Strait of Magellan in December and after putting in at Cayenne (French Guiana) reached La Rochelle in early September of 1694. The other group of filibusters, the last to raid Pacific waters, managed to take two important prize ships and gather some 17,000 pesos in ransom monies. To their chagrin, however, their best prize, the *Santiaguillo*, broke up at the mouth of the Strait in early 1694. Four crewmembers returned to Valdivia in canoes, where they were captured, but the remaining survivors managed to build a seaworthy craft from the wreck and make the passage to Cayenne and finally France by 1695.⁶⁰ In true buccaneer fashion, they had casually sailed—in a makeshift vessel, no less—through seas considered positively deadly by contemporaries.

As noted above, war broke out in Europe before the last of the French filibusters had cleared the Spanish Pacific. Contrary to what the buccaneers believed, however, this conflict pitted England and virtually everyone else in Europe (including Spain) against France. King William's War, or the War of the Grand Alliance, as it came to be known, began in 1689, and commissions against French-owned ships flew freely. One such English commission landed in the hands of a Captain John Strong, commander of the ship *Welfare* and a would-be privateer anxious to cruise Peruvian waters. Like Narborough and Swan a decade before, he hoped to open some sort of regular trade with the Spanish in the South Sea as well. To this end he carried a stock of dry goods, including cloth, stockings, arms, and tools. With a 270-ton, forty-gun ship manned by a crew of ninety, Strong left Plymouth for Madeira and the Cape Verdes on 1 November 1689. The island stops were relatively short and uneventful, but while trying to put in for water along the Atlantic Patagonia coast of South America at Puerto Deseado the ship was blown southeastward, landing on a chain of islands which Strong called the Falklands (after the English Navy treasurer) on 27 January 1690. With little reason to tarry here, an attempt was quickly made to pass the Strait of Magellan and the crew arrived after some difficulties in Pacific waters by 21 May. Strong headed north along the Chilean coast, landing at the deserted island of Mocha and attempting to land at Valdivia. The Spanish, still very much afflicted by the buccaneers and not knowing Strong's intentions, treated him to a cannonade.[37]

After a brief but similar incident in Herradura Bay on 8 July 1690, Strong sailed northward looking for a place to water. More than half of Strong's crew had fallen ill during the passage of the Strait, and nine had died. Also, an interpreter sent ashore at Herradura to show the Spanish the *Welfare*'s commission from the newly installed English monarchs, William and Mary, had apparently deserted, and Copiapó, a likely watering spot, was bypassed in a fog. In short, things were not faring well. Strong held out hope, however, and continued sailing north all the way to Paita. As it turned out he had read Dampier's account of sunken silver ships near Guayaquil and had serious intentions of attempting a salvage. Strong hoped to follow in the footsteps of Sir William Phips, governor of Massachusetts Bay Colony, who had recovered £300,000 worth of booty from a Spanish shipwreck north of Hispaniola in 1687.[38] After failing to land at Paita the *Welfare* at last found relief at Túmbez, just south of Guayaquil, on 12 August, where a small but illegal exchange of food and merchandise took place.

A coastal trader carrying timber to Paita from Guayaquil, under Captain Alejandro de la Madrid, was taken soon after, though not robbed. Strong instead treated Madrid's crew to a feast and showed them his commission to hunt French pirates. Goods were cordially exchanged and Strong found that some Frenchmen had indeed been raiding in these waters six weeks prior (most likely Franco's band); he was also told that gold could be found in the Túmbez River—no surprise since it lay downstream from the famed mines of Zaruma. But Strong had not come to mine gold; the Englishman was instead interested in hearing news of the shipwrecks that littered the nearby coast, and he politely inquired as to their whereabouts. His hosts claimed to know only of a small cloth carrier like their own that had sunk a few years prior off Punta Santa Elena and had already been salvaged. Strong's men searched the area in a longboat, but found nothing. The ship they must have been looking for was a 1,000-ton galleon sunk in the Bay of Chanduy in October of 1654, the *Jesús María de la Limpia Concepción*, but even that wreck had been almost entirely salvaged already.[39]

Disappointed with their searches in the Gulf of Guayaquil, and with their welcome by local citizens wearing thin, Strong decided at last to return to England. The *Welfare* landed on the Juan Fernández Islands on 12 October in search of water and victuals, but found also four crewmembers left behind three years earlier by Davis. The marooners seemed happy enough at the rescue, but two of them were not to enjoy it for long; they would find themselves in Spanish clutches less than a month later when Strong attempted a last trading mission near Concepción. In this final incident in the Spanish South Sea, a longboat was sent ashore with twelve men and a copy of Strong's commission. Only one man returned, and he was badly wounded. The Davis refugees who were captured in this landing had the misfortune of being sentenced to death for their earlier acts of piracy, while the others were apparently sent inland to the presidios of central Chile. Though it confounded Strong, all of this Spanish hostility was in keeping with the Viceroy Monclova's general attitude toward foreign ships in the Pacific: they might be enemy French or currently "friendly" English, but according to the treaty terms issued by the Junta de Guerra, or War Tribunal, in Madrid, they were not welcome here, even if blown ashore by storm. An angry Strong passed the Strait of Magellan and reached Barbados in mid-February 1691, where he picked up a cargo of sugar. The *Welfare* ultimately managed to take two prizes off Ireland, one Dutch and one Norwegian, before returning to a disappointed group of London shareholders in June. Dampier's South Sea treasure wrecks, like the possibility of open markets, had proved illusory.

The English would be back to harass Spanish shipping and force a trade in contraband goods soon enough, but for now it was the French who considered large-scale ventures to the South Sea. A six-ship expedition was organized at La Rochelle in mid-1695 under Jean-Baptiste de Gennes, but after a number of setbacks on the coast of Africa and at the opening of the Strait of Magellan the voyage was abandoned. De Gennes and his crew returned to France disappointed via Ilha Grande (Brazil) and the West Indies, and Monclova, the Peruvian viceroy, breathed a sigh of relief. As in other cases he had heard news of the French expedition's reversal of fortune from letters brought overland from Río de la Plata.

With the Peace of Ryswick in 1697 and the founding of the French Compagnie Royale de la Mer Pacifique a new trading venture was soon under way. Piloted by an ex-buccaneer and commanded by Jacques Gouin de Beauchesne, a 700-man, seven-ship fleet left La Rochelle 17 December 1698. Beauchesne did not enter the South Sea until late January 1700, and his smuggling efforts along the Peruvian coast were less than rewarding. Local residents were reluctant to engage in trade even though they needed the goods and the peace meant that the French were no longer enemies. A single denunciation for contrabanding could still destroy a family's fortune, and fortunes were increasingly hard to build in this era of "skinny cows." Beauchesne managed to trade some goods at Ilo, Pisco, and Callao, however, before sailing to the Galápagos Islands to water and victual. His return south led to rejection at Guayaquil, Paita, and Yerbabuena, so he forced a final trade at Ilo in October before returning to France. The entire voyage was undertaken at a loss of 100,000 *livres*, but still the French were encouraged, and, like the English, they intended to return.[11]

The era of buccaneers in the South Sea was clearly over, but the era of smuggling was just beginning. Shift or no shift in type of intruders, the Spanish did not much alter their policy. Merchants had raised some 300,000 pesos to outfit two new warships by 1695, the 700-to-800-ton galleons *Santísimo Sacramento* and *Nuestra Señora de la Concepción*, and a patax, the 250-ton *Santa Cruz*.[41] This was a significant improvement, but really only entailed a replacement of ships originally commissioned in the 1650s and 1660s. In New Spain a pair of small galleys was built in 1690, expressly for hunting buccaneers and escorting Manila galleons.[42] Militias were continuously trained all up and down the Pacific coast, but little royal money was spent to outfit them. As with many other aspects of defense, local initiative was far more important than crown or viceregal policy or aid. In some places, such as the gold-camps of Barbacoas, in the northwestern Audiencia of Quito, local officials advanced their careers by offering to privately outfit pirate-hunting expeditions. They thus added titles such as "Maestre de Campo" and "Sargento Mayor" to their names, enriching themselves now in politics as they had previously in mining and commerce. Lima's defensive walls, as has been seen, were largely financed by private donations, mostly from the city's own residents, and lesser cities like Trujillo soon followed. Here a resident Italian engineer named Giuseppe Formento designed what later critics derided as a largely ornamental perimeter.[43] Useful or not, the "pirate wall" of Trujillo was a source of local pride.

The crown and viceroys such as Monclova quickly realized that the Pacific coast was simply too extensive to wall off, the waters offshore too vast to patrol adequately. As had proved true in the Caribbean, the Spanish Empire in the Pacific was simply too large to be actively defended. As a result, small settlements would have to defend themselves when intruders showed up, and small trading vessels, if they refused to travel in convoys or arm themselves, would have to be sacrificed from time to time. The consequences of seventeenth-century buccaneering in the Spanish South Sea may be summarized as follows: (1) the volume of trade (legal and otherwise) was reduced for nearly two decades, killing merchant profits and causing a shortage of customs and sales tax revenues; (2) cities and towns along the coast became more isolated from one another and regionalist animosities (as, for example, between Guayaquil and Lima) were exacerbated by a growing sense of crown abandonment; and (3) as in the Dutch era, crucial bullion shipments were diverted from Spain's ever-emptying coffers to local defense needs, including unnecessary fortifications and a largely useless navy.

In spite of their shortcomings Spanish authorities in the Pacific region cannot be blamed for most of these results, especially given the financial and political misfortunes the empire suffered during this period. Still, it is difficult to deny that had Spanish authorities managed to control the offshore islands, such as the Tres Marías, Coiba, Cocos, Gorgona, Isla de la Plata, the Galápagos, and Juan Fernández, the buccaneers might have had a much harder time surviving in these seas. No such control was established, even after the buccaneers and filibusters had gone, and this continued neglect allowed the next wave, mostly of French and English smugglers and privateers, to exploit the multiple offshore islands of the Spanish Pacific once again. The pirates always found hideaways to careen and water, in these seas and elsewhere, but like all social types they still dreamed of genuine home bases, places that welcomed and even sponsored them like Tortuga and Jamaica's Port Royal once had. In the next wave those bases would be as far-flung as Madagascar and New York City, but none would last for long.

BOX 5 EARLY MODERN SHIPWRECK SALVAGE

Recent discoveries of sunken Spanish treasure galleons off the Florida Keys and elsewhere in the Caribbean may lead one to believe that modern technology is prerequisite in the business of underwater salvage. Late twentieth-century developments, including high-tech sonar, radar, and satellite positioning systems, and of course scuba gear and various mechanical lifters and blowers, have indeed improved the process, but diving for lost treasure is nothing new. In fact both the Spanish and their European enemies, including, as we have seen in Chapters 5 and 6, a number of pirates, were accomplished "wreckers" in the early modern era. As many modern salvagers will attest, most locatable wrecks were all but picked clean within a few years of sinking. How could this have been so given the technology of the day?

First, shipwrecks were not as random as might be imagined, nor were sinkings instantaneous. Ships lost in deep water were indeed lost for good, but these were the minority—most wrecks occurred within a dozen kilometers of shore, often on coral reefs or sandbars. Aside from accidents occurring in frequented harbors such as Veracruz, Santo Domingo, San Juan, Cartagena, and Havana, ships tended to pile up along the edges of natural choke points such as the Florida Strait. With fewer hurricanes and fewer reefs, wrecks along the Pacific coast were less frequent and were more often the result of grounding in estuarine shoals and sandbars. Wrecks of both kinds often allowed some survivors to reach safety, either in ships' boats or by swimming among the flotsam, and given the flota system, news of a missing ship or two was quickly followed by a search and recovery mission. Cities such as Havana and Guayaquil supplied these missions with boats, barges, rafts (see Figure 3.2), food, equipment, and, most importantly, divers.

As Peter Earle has shown, early modern salvage diving was generally low-tech to the point of being crude, but human endurance and skill were surprisingly effective in compensating for most technical shortcomings. Free divers in this era were almost universally slaves, most of African origin, though some were Native American. Their methods were simple: Grab a stone, take a deep breath, and dive for treasure (though not for the diver to keep, but rather the master). Ropes or chains were attached to sunken cannon, chests, salvageable timbers, and so on, to be raised by windlasses attached to a ship's yardarm or a barge-based derrick. Gold and silver were of course the first things sought out and recovered, and many salvagers preferred not to spend costly days working to recover less valuable (and often heavier) items.

Many slave divers in seventeenth-century Guayaquil, for instance, were professional pearl divers rented to salvagers by the day, along with their rafts, and could thus become quite expensive after just a week or two of diving. Success rates were remarkable nonetheless, and salvage specialists, often contracted by merchant shippers or the crown, could live quite well—that is, as long as they could defend themselves against marauding foreign pirates.

Inventors did apply their efforts to the problems of breath-holding and underwater labors in the early modern era, and although most of their contraptions appear to have been useless, or at least only occasionally adopted, they presage later developments. Among these were the diving bell, a very heavy bronze or cast iron church bell, more or less, lowered to some point just above the sea floor, where a diver could periodically respire; a Spanish design from 1583, submitted to Philip II by a Sicilian named José Bono, is representative (see Figure 5.4). As Earle notes, several modified versions of the diving bell were employed by English salvagers in the seventeenth and eighteenth centuries, especially in reef-filled Bermuda, but due to natural air compression they had a lower limit of eleven fathoms (c. 22m). Other devices were more scuba-like in their intentions but were rendered largely impractical due to the same problems that plagued diving bells: compression and flotation. Some early seventeenth-century Spanish designs attributed to Jerónimo de Ayanz included inflated pig's bladders with breathing valves and lead weights, portable bellows apparatus, and various snorkel-like breathing

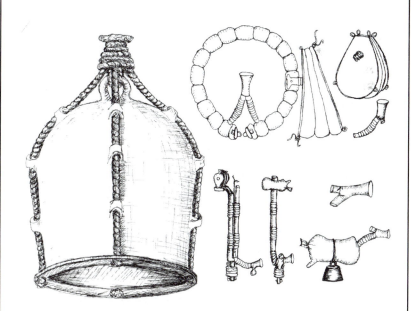

FIGURE 5.4 Sixteenth- and Seventeenth-Century Spanish Diving Equipment

Source: Adapted from manuscripts in the Archivo General de Indias, Ingeniería y Muestras.

tubes (see Figure 5.4). As far as the pirates were concerned, it was far easier to leave this kind of imaginative, dangerous, and expensive hard work to the Spaniards, then "recover lost treasure" by force of arms on shore.

For more details, see Peter Earle, *The Treasure of the Concepción: The Wreck of the Almiranta* (New York: Viking Press, 1980); and Javier de Castro, *La recuperación de pecios en la Carrera de Indias* (Barcelona: Espai/Temps, 1990). On the famous wreck of the *Nuestra Señora de la Atocha*, a gold carrier from Tierra Firme lost near Key West in a hurricane, see R. Duncan Mathewson, *Treasure of the Atocha* (New York: Dutton, 1986). This was one of few wrecks not located and salvaged by the Spanish or their enemies in colonial times.

Notes

1 Peter Bradley, *The Lure of Peru: Maritime Intrusion into the South Sea, 1598–1701* (New York: St. Martin's, 1989), 90. See also the facsimile edition of John Narborough's *Account of Several Late Voyages and Discoveries to the North and South* (New York: Da Capo, 1969 [1694]).

2 Bradley, *Lure of Peru*, 216 fn 19. Narborough's men reached Lima just as reports of Morgan's activities in the vicinity of Panama arrived; see Robert R. Miller, ed. and trans., *Chronicle of Colonial Lima: The Diary of Josephe and Francisco Mugaburu, 1640–97* (Norman: University of Oklahoma Press, 1975), 168–69.

3 Bradley, *Lure of Peru*, 98. Bradley treats the story of Don Carlos in greater detail in his article "Narborough's Don Carlos," *Mariner's Mirror* 72:4 (1986): 465–75. Narborough himself revealed his suspicions about Don Carlos's experience in the South Sea early in his journal; see *Account of Several Late Voyages*, 19–20. See also Clayton McCarl, "Carlos Enriques Clerque as Crypto-Jewish Confidence Man in Francisco de Seyxas y Lovera's Piratas y contrabandistas (1693)," *Colonial Latin American Review* 24.3 (Aug. 2015).

4 Bradley, *Lure of Peru*, essentially agrees with the thesis of Lawrence A. Clayton, who described the situation in "Local Initiative and Finance in Defense of the Viceroyalty of Peru: The Development of Self-Reliance," *Hispanic American Historical Review* 54:2 (May 1974): 284–304.

5 Bradley, *Lure of Peru*, 100.

6 Philip Ayres, ed., *The Voyages and Adventures of Captain Bartholomew Sharp and Others in the South Sea* (London: Philip Ayres, Esq., 1684), 1.

7 Ayres (Cox), *Voyages and Adventures*, 22, 24.

8 Bradley, *Lure of Peru*, 114.

9 Quoted in ibid., 118.

10 Bradley quoting Morgan, in ibid., 121.

11 Ibid., 126–27.

12 Cowley hardly mentions the African women in his journal but notes that upon reaching Cape Horn about 14 February, "where we chusing of Valentines, and discoursing of the Intrigues of Women, there arose a prodigious Storm" (in William Hack, ed., *A Collection of Original Voyages* [London: James Knapton, 1699], 6). Several sailors blamed the storm on the presence of the women, many of whom expired from hypothermia shortly thereafter.

13 Bradley, *Lure of Peru*, 131.

14 Peter Gerhard, *Pirates on the West Coast of New Spain, 1575–1742* (Cleveland: Arthur H. Clark, 1960), 158.

15 Quoted in Bradley, *Lure of Peru*, 135.

16 Lawrence A. Clayton, in "Trade and Navigation in the Seventeenth-Century Viceroyalty of Peru," *Journal of Latin American Studies* 7:1 (May 1975): 1–21, describes earlier voyages of the *Pópulo* (1677–78), when it carried Huancavelica mercury to New Spain in exchange for Chinese wax, pepper, and other contraband.

17 Bradley, *Lure of Peru*, 139.

18 Gerhard, *Pirates on the West Coast of New Spain*, 171.

19 Ibid., 174.

20 Ibid., 182.

21 Ibid., 183.

22 Bradley, *Lure of Peru*, 144.

23 Ibid., 145.

24 Ibid., 147.

25 Ibid., 148.

26 Ibid., 151.

27 Raveneau de Lussan (trans. Wilbur), *Voyage to the South Seas*, 211.

28 Bradley, *Lure of Peru*, 152.

29 Clayton, "Local Initiative and Finance," 297–302.

30 Raveneau de Lussan gives a good account of the engagement, in which he was wounded. The translation can be found in Marguerite Eyer Wilbur, *Raveneau de Lussan: Buccaneer of the Spanish Main and Early French Filibuster of the Pacific* (Cleveland: Arthur H. Clark, 1930), 221–26. See also María del Pilar Bernal Ruiz, *La toma del puerto de Guayaquil en 1687* (Seville: EEHA, 1979) and Sebastian I. Donoso, Piratas en Guayaquil: Historia del asalto de 1687 (Guayaquil: El Universo, 2006).

31 Raveneau de Lussan, in ibid., 227. An ounce of gold was said to be valued at 80–100 pieces of eight among the buccaneers, or five to six times the ratio current in Peru (c. 16 pesos per ounce of fine gold).

32 Gerhard, *Pirates on the West Coast of New Spain*, 186.

33 Bradley, *Lure of Peru*, 154.

34 Gerhard, *Pirates on the West Coast of New Spain*, 191.

35 Milla's testimony was found in the document "Autos de Don Bartolomé Estupiñán sobre la fuerza del enemigo pirata," Archivo Nacional de Historia, Quito (Ecuador), "Popayán" series, caja 10 (1689), ff. 3–5 [author translation]. See also Kris Lane, "Buccaneers and Coastal Defense in Late Seventeenth-Century Quito: The Case of Barbacoas," *Colonial Latin American Historical Review* 6:2 (Spring 1997): 143–73; and E. Ducéré, ed., *Journal de bord d'un flibustier (1686–1693)* (Bayonne: A. Lamaignère, 1894), 58–60.

36 Bradley, *Lure of Peru*, 169.

37 Ibid., 172.

38 A salvage effort on this same site is discussed by Tracy Bowden in "Treasure from the Silver Bank," *National Geographic* 190:1 (July 1996): 90–105. The Phips salvage is described in detail in Peter Earle, *The Treasure of the Concepción: The Wreck of the Almiranta* (New York: Viking Press, 1980).

39 Bradley, *Lure of Peru*, 173–74. See also Bradley's "The Loss of the Flagship of the Armada del Mar del Sur (1654) and Related Aspects of Viceregal Administration," *Americas* 45 (1989): 383–403. Salvagers have apparently returned to this wreck as well; see the *New York Times* (14 April 1997), A6.

40 Bradley, *Lure of Peru*, 182.

41 Ibid., 180.

42 Gerhard, *Pirates on the West Coast of New Spain*, 198.

43 Bradley, *Lure of Peru*, 164.

6

PIRATES, MERCHANTS, AND CONQUISTADORS IN THE INDIAN OCEAN AND CHINA SEAS

It is said that the cousin of our late Emperor has re-conquered the province of Kwangtung from the Manchus. He requires all the support he can get in order to wreak even more havoc on the Manchus, who to our great sorrow have captured our illustrious country . . . I have decided to support him with well-equipped troops and junks. We are short of money to pay the many expenses, hence I must levy an annual tax for the Emperor. The inhabitants of the Pescadores [Islands] are counted the same as other subjects . . . Therefore I have sent my men to the Pescadores to collect the annual tax . . . All junks departing from here bound for that destination must carry a pass issued by me and pay a certain tax. Those who do so are exempt from any further taxes and will not be harassed. All these junks will not be required to pay any other tax, not even as much as a single straw. I have forbidden my inferiors to demand any such on pain of death; I shall never allow such abuses to occur.[1]

Thus did Cheng Lien, naval commander at Amoy, on China's southeast coast just west of Taiwan, describe his efforts to tax seaborne trade to raise funds for the dying Ming Dynasty. It was mid-1650 and already too late: the Manchu or Qing invaders were firmly in power on the mainland and soon they would expand offshore. Taiwan would serve as a last holdout once the Dutch were defeated in 1661, but the struggle for the fringes amid the Ming fall enabled the rise of numerous sea raiders, including the famous Koxinga, Cheng Lien's cousin, to pillage and extort, but also to trade, at will. The exploits of these pirates, corsairs, and merchant-conquistadors remain only partly understood, still cloaked in the fog of eastern and western imperial rivalries.

This chapter offers a brief overview of early modern piracy in eastern seas, primarily in the Indian Ocean and western Pacific. Maritime pillage in this vast and interconnected region resembled that of the Mediterranean and Atlantic, but as will be seen there were many local variations and considerable change over time. In general, the volume and value of sea traffic in these waters exceeded that of the Atlantic before 1750, and political disunity meant that there was much booty to be had as well as competing sponsors and fences for sea marauders to choose from. Although reliable monsoon wind patterns created a self-contained trading sphere, the Indian Ocean and western Pacific became increasingly connected to the wider world after 1500. The pirates of the eastern seas, in turn, became increasingly global actors. Suppressing them, too, would be part of a global endeavor.

In the first decades of the sixteenth century, just as Spanish conquistadors sacked the gold- and silver-rich empires of what they called the Western Indies, Portuguese conquistadors set about doing the same in the fabled East Indies. Their task was not easy and their numbers small, but waves of Portuguese adventurers seeking royal favor and wealth used their state-of-the-art ships and guns to stunning effect, toppling local, mostly seaside kingdoms throughout the Indian Ocean basin. Those unwilling to negotiate were made offers they could not refuse.

Seeking trade with the Spice Islands, China, and Japan, the Portuguese pushed on into the western Pacific as well, establishing a trading post near Nagasaki by 1542. By 1556, having gained Macao, at the mouth of China's Pearl River, the Portuguese were the dominant seaborne players in this vast region. Despite their small numbers, they remained the sea power to beat for almost a century. Eventually, Dutch, English, and French interlopers displaced them, often with the help of local lords and other regional allies. The Portuguese conquered no great empires in the East Indies, but they succeeded where Columbus had failed in realizing the east–west mercantile dreams of Marco Polo.

Were the Portuguese pirates? Certainly they did not think so, and like their Spanish contemporaries they justified their violent overseas expansion and appropriation of others' goods with a papal grant that required them to propagate their Roman Catholic faith in exchange. As we have seen in Chapter 1, a papal bull led Portugal and Spain to divide the world into two hemispheres of influence in 1494. Portuguese mercantile and military endeavors in the East were thus justified by universalist claims of far-flung, overseas dominion. Spanish and Portuguese claims abutted one another in Brazil on one side of the world, and on the other in the Philippines.

Although Portuguese pecuniary aims won out, religious concerns were genuine. Whereas the Spanish found no evidence of Judaism or Islam as they toppled states and spread Christianity in the Americas, the equally militant Catholic Portuguese encountered both Muslims and Jews almost everywhere they went. Christians were much rarer, and the Portuguese were initially unsure what to make of

Brahmanic peoples and Buddhists other than to consider them idolaters. Island tribal groups whose religious practices were even more inscrutable sometimes attacked at sea, and the Portuguese were quick to label them not only pirates but also godless cannibals and headhunters. In this they echoed the Spanish.

Not only the Indian Ocean basin, but much of the western Pacific monsoon circuit had long been the province of Muslim seaborne traders, and in some cases local princes converted to Islam partly in response to Portuguese militancy. Jewish and other ethnic merchant groups, including Armenians, Jains, and others, moved freely as well. The Portuguese aim was to tax trade in these Eurasian seas, and also to monopolize certain commodities such as pepper, cinnamon, cotton textiles, and cloves. For many longtime residents of the Indian Ocean basin this new regime of seaborne dominion by a single outside interloper looked and felt like extortion, and sometimes piracy—especially when merchants had their goods confiscated.

Again, the Portuguese did not see it that way; many in the first generation described themselves as pious conquistadors. Most of the major East African and Asian trade nodes, from Mogadishu to Melaka, were Muslim principalities, and this enabled the Portuguese to cast their violent takeover of a more or less peaceful trading zone as an extension of the crusade. In doing so they sometimes provoked jihad in response, but political divisions among Muslim and non-Muslim princes prevented concerted resistance. Only the Ottomans offered a counterweight to the Portuguese at sea in the sixteenth century, but as described later, even their efforts were thwarted, mostly as a result of internecine struggles.

Some defiant local traders and fishermen resorted to piracy despite Portuguese threats and reprisals, and corsairing in the name of certain Muslim princes also grew. Whether or not the Portuguese and other Europeans "introduced" piracy to the Indian Ocean basin or simply made it metastasize by ratcheting up tensions and competition with unfamiliar trade restrictions remains hotly debated among historians. Acts of seaborne pillage, here as elsewhere in the early modern world, were often cloaked in religious language, making "true" motivations almost impossible to determine. Sources, furthermore, tended to be richest in detail on the European side, further distorting the picture. Only from the victims' perspective did it all feel like piracy.

Pirates of the Indian Ocean

Despite a string of spectacular early successes, the Portuguese were never unopposed in eastern seas. They faced organized opposition in the northern Indian Ocean from the Egyptian Mamluk Empire along with Indian allies by 1508. Yet even after defeating the Portuguese at Chaul, in northwest India, the Cairo-based Mamluks proved unable to keep up the pressure and local merchant enclaves were too divided to hold their own. In 1517 the Mamluks fell to the mighty Ottomans, who at the time of the Spanish conquests of Mexico and Peru were annexing portions of Eastern Europe, the Middle East, and North Africa. They were also becoming a formidable sea power, first in the Black Sea and Mediterranean, then in the Indian Ocean. To match the kings of Portugal, the Ottoman sultans after defeating the Mamluks were dreaming of their own pepper empire extending all the way to Indonesia.

Under Selim I, the Ottomans sought to outflank the Portuguese, starting in the Red Sea. With the fall of the Mamluks, the Ottomans gained control of the holy cities of Mecca and Medina, and they also now taxed Cairo's highly lucrative spice trade that linked many Indian Ocean producers to Mediterranean and northern European consumers (other routes went through Iraq and Iran).

As historian Giancarlo Casale has convincingly shown, the Ottomans, driven by a universalist, messianic message to match that of the Portuguese and Spanish, proved highly capable of assembling large and well-armed fleets in the Red Sea and Persian Gulf, and finally in the Indian Ocean proper.[2] Many expeditions against the Portuguese were led by famous Mediterranean corsairs working on behalf of the sultan or his governors in Egypt, Iraq, and Arabia. From bases such as Jiddah, port of Mecca, the Ottomans sent fleets to recapture forts and ports taken by the Portuguese in East Africa, the Arabian Peninsula, and South Asia. They even allied with the Muslim principality of Aceh, on the northwest coast of Sumatra, a link that survived into the seventeenth century.

Were the Ottomans pirates? Certainly they did not think so, despite Portuguese claims to the contrary. The first Ottoman mission to set out was to be led by a corsair who had been named governor of Jiddah, Hussein al-Rumi. On his way to Yemen he was forced to turn back upon hearing of Selim I's death in 1520. Despite the false start, Ottoman policy under Selim's successor, Suleiman the Magnificent (1520–56), renewed the aggressive response to growing Portuguese sea power. Meanwhile, in the Mediterranean, Suleiman's forces captured the Christian corsairing base of Rhodes, home of the Knights of St. John; this 1522 seizure was a major turning point in seaborne power on that side of the Suez.

After suppressing a rebellion in Egypt, grand vizier Ibrahim Pasha, Suleiman's right-hand man, set out to remove the Portuguese from major forts in the northern Indian Ocean. In 1527 Ottoman forces led by corsairs Selman Reis and Hayreddin al-Rumi captured Yemen and established control over the entrance to the Red Sea. This drew numerous Muslim merchants from as far away as Malaysia to seek Ottoman protection from Portuguese aggression and demands. Unfortunately for them, a fight between the two corsair commanders undid Ottoman gains, at least temporarily. Selman Reis was murdered in 1528 at Hayreddin al-Rumi's request, and he in turn was murdered on orders of Selman's nephew, Mustafa Bayram.[3]

The Portuguese took advantage of the power vacuum to win back control of the Red Sea entrance in 1529, but the Ottomans soon regrouped. Mustafa Bayram established ties with merchants in textile-rich Gujarat (in northwest India) who considered the Portuguese pirates, and Mustafa helped them defend against a Portuguese attack on the city of Diu in 1531. The Ottomans then seized Iraq from their Shiite neighbors, the Safavids, which gave them control of Basra and the western terminus of the Persian Gulf. The Portuguese held out at the gulf's mouth with their fort at Hormuz, which gave them access to Iran, and a long standoff ensued, breached occasionally by merchants willing to ignore the religious and imperial enmity that stood in the way of commerce. By 1536 the Ottomans had rebuilt their navy in the Red Sea, and they had made alliances with the famous Malabar pirates of southwest India, discussed in more detail later. Meanwhile, Diu was essentially handed to the Portuguese by its ruler in exchange for help against the rising Mughals.

From 1538 through the 1550s the Ottomans pursued an aggressive strategy in the Indian Ocean, trying but ultimately failing to oust the Portuguese from several of their most heavily defended bases. An attempt to retake Diu failed in 1538, as did a second try in 1546. But there were also significant Ottoman victories: the Portuguese failed to capture Suez in 1541 and lost again at Basra in 1546. The Portuguese also stumbled while trying to prop up the isolated Christian Kingdom of Ethiopia. Through it all, Ottoman spice routes remained open despite constant Portuguese pressure. As Casale and other historians have noted, the Ottomans may not have been winning all the battles, but throughout the sixteenth century they were giving the Portuguese a run for their money in the maritime trade war.[1]

The Corsair Sefer Reis

The 1550s were a difficult decade for the Ottomans in the Indian Ocean, starting with major defeats at Hormuz in 1552 and Muscat in 1553. These were simply the endpoints of major naval showdowns that resulted in considerable losses for both the Ottomans and the Portuguese. In short, the Ottomans hoped to extend their control of the Red Sea to include the Persian Gulf and all of the Arabian Peninsula. Fortunately for the Iberians, the Ottoman admirals they faced, despite long experience and great successes in the Mediterranean and Black Seas, were not ready for the rigors of Indian Ocean seafaring, and their mistakes tipped the scales in favor of the Portuguese.

A corsair countercurrent, as Casale has shown, was offered by Sefer Reis, a maverick seaman to match the likes of the later Francis Drake.[5] Sefer (Reis means "Captain") developed a keen strategy to raid Portuguese merchant shipping by hiding out in shallow coves with nothing more than a few oared galleots. He laid ambushes, attacked swiftly, and then fled against the wind, rowing close to shore, leaving the sail-dependent Portuguese in their deep-water vessels unable to follow. Thus, as official Ottoman naval expeditions faltered throughout the 1550s, Sefer Reis triumphed.

Sefer's successes eventually caught the attention of Ottoman authorities, and in 1554 he was sent to escort vessels under Black Sea veteran Seydi Ali from the Persian Gulf around the Arabian Peninsula and up to Suez. Upon finding out that the

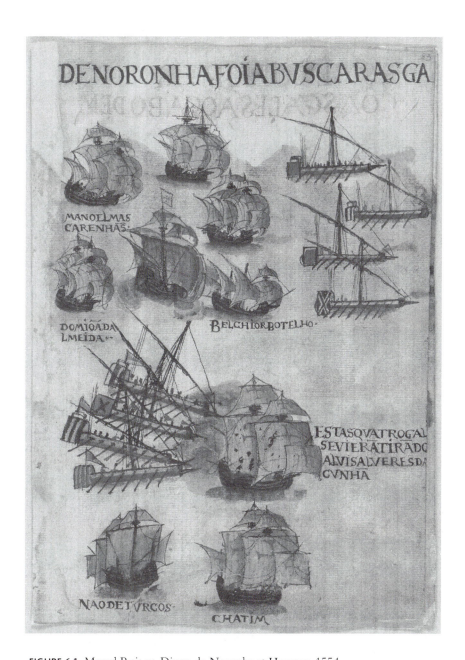

FIGURE 6.1 Murad Reis vs. Diogo de Noronha at Hormuz, 1554

Source: Lisuarte de Abreu, *Livro de Lisuarte de Abreu*. Pierpoint Morgan Library, New York, M. 525.

Ottoman fleet had been defeated at Muscat, Sefer followed the Portuguese victors to India, where he set up an ambush and captured four ships and 160,000 *cruzados* in gold. Despite a Portuguese counterattack that nearly reversed his fortunes, Sefer triumphed in the end and returned to Suez a hero, or at least a fabulously rich corsair. His efforts to win the Indian Ocean admiralship with gifts of gold to the sultan and the governor of Egypt were rebuffed, and it seems that again palace intrigues scuttled Ottoman Indian Ocean policy.

Undaunted, Sefer returned to corsairing from his base at Mocha, capturing Portuguese vessels off the coast of India beginning in 1556, and culminating in a bold entrapment of a relief force to Ethiopia near the mouth of the Red Sea in 1560. This last victory led the Ottoman governor of Egypt to secure Sefer Reis's promotion to supreme commander of the Indian Ocean fleet. After several small-scale ventures Sefer set out to raid the Portuguese-controlled Swahili coast of Africa in 1564. The plunder promised to be huge, but in December of 1565 the great corsair died of a sudden illness, leaving no successors of such skill in his wake.

The Ottomans in no way gave up on the Indian Ocean following the death of Sefer Reis, and in fact they launched a major initiative to strengthen ties with distant Aceh immediately after, in 1566. Ottoman gunners aided in Acehnese attacks on the Portuguese at Melaka in 1568 and 1570, and again in the 1580s, during the reign of Ottoman Sultan Murad III. Other Ottoman subjects participated in corsair raids launched from Ceylon, the Maldives, and the Indian subcontinent. Merchants under Portuguese protection suffered badly, and high-ranking officials were captured and ransomed by the pirates of Malabar. Despite new challenges from the Mughal emperor Akbar after 1576, plus ongoing war with the Safavids in Iran, Ottoman overseas momentum rolled on into the 1580s. Key were new diplomatic missions to the Swahili Coast, led by the corsair Mir Ali Beg in the 1580s, spurred in part by the death of Portugal's King Sebastian in Morocco in 1578 and Philip II of Spain's subsequent takeover of the Portuguese empire in 1580.

Mir Ali Beg was in some ways the natural successor of the great corsair Sefer Reis, and his bold capture of numerous Portuguese vessels off the coast of East Africa in 1586 made him famous and rich. Perhaps a better Ottoman analogue of England's Francis Drake than Sefer, Mir Ali did everything he could to "singe the king of Spain's beard" in eastern waters now that Philip II of Spain was also Philip I of Portugal. In addition to considerable plunder, Mir Ali's first East African foray brought dozens of Swahili Coast ambassadors anxious to win protection from the sultan at Istanbul.

Ottoman desire to develop a properly fortified empire in the Indian Ocean was strong but material support was weak, and although Mir Ali's second East African expedition in 1589 started well, it ended badly. After fortifying Mombasa, a city whose support he had won on his previous voyage, Mir Ali was captured by the Portuguese under Tomé de Sousa Coutinho. From Africa he was taken to Goa, where he died in prison sometime in the early seventeenth century, allegedly a convert to Christianity. Mir Ali's great misfortune—totally unexpected—had been to be pinched between the Portuguese arriving by sea from India and Zimba warriors attacking from the African interior.[7]

Ottoman fights with the Portuguese continued through the end of the sixteenth century, but on a lower level and much smaller scale than in the era of Suleiman the Magnificent. As Casale notes, Ottoman overseas expansion proved enormously costly, just as it had for the Portuguese and Spanish. As everyone got tired and went broke, diplomacy won out over naval confrontation. Talk of pulling back in the Indian Ocean had long been in the air, and more so after the Ottoman loss to the Christian Holy League at Lepanto in 1571, in the eastern Mediterranean. The Ottomans continued to court friends in distant Aceh and beyond, but the prospect of direct military aid faded quickly after 1590. Into the void stepped Dutch corsairs, along with homegrown pirates like those of India's Malabar Coast.

The Malabar Pirates

As Sebastian Prange has argued, piracy in the Indian Ocean predated the arrival of the Portuguese and Ottomans.[8] The most famous pirates of the region, mentioned by Marco Polo, Ibn Battutah, and other medieval travelers, occupied a few ports on India's southwest coast, major source of the world's pepper. There is evidence to suggest that the Malabar pirates were Hindus, or at least non-Muslims, although many appear to have converted to Islam in the sixteenth century. The Malabaris were said to raid in sizeable fleets that set out during the agricultural off-season, and some sources suggest they belonged to a caste of fisher-folk, the Mukkuvar. In any case, the Malabar pirates' relations with local princes who controlled the pepper trade were ambivalent, and evidently included protection rackets and shared spoils.

The Portuguese considered the Malabaris the most incorrigible pirates of the entire Indian Ocean, yet they consistently failed to suppress them. As far as Hindu, Muslim, and other merchants were concerned, the Portuguese were no better; they had arrived in the Indian Ocean uninvited, seeking to control the pepper trade and tax everything else, partly in the guise of protection *against* pirates like the Malabaris. Ships that failed to carry the costly Portuguese pass, or *cartaz*, were considered fair game for plunder. Prange suggests antecedents for this safe-conduct pass system in medieval times, but it appears to have been highly localized. The Portuguese enforced it everywhere (or rather, they tried).

Anthony Disney has argued that Portuguese actions in the Indian Ocean, particularly in the first decades of the sixteenth century, can hardly be characterized as anything other than piracy, or at least state-sponsored corsairing.[9] Most conquest enterprises were privately funded, and the crown got portions of seized booty, whether taken on land or at sea. Plus there were many occasions in which local Portuguese governors sponsored expeditions with no other aim than to plunder rich ports and kingdoms, Hindu, Muslim, or Buddhist. This sort of licensing of pillage carried on into the early seventeenth century, although the Portuguese never matched the great inland conquests of the Spanish in the Americas. Booty taken at sea was subject to a twenty percent royal duty.

But it is the Malabaris who are remembered as pirates. Relying on the early seventeenth-century account of French traveler François Pyrard of Laval, Prange suggests that the Malabar pirates, now identified as Mappila Muslims, developed increasingly close relations with local Nair lords, who paid tribute to the kings of Calicut, the major port in the region. Charges of piracy, contraband trade, and fencing of stolen goods eventually led the Portuguese at Goa and the Zamorin lords of Calicut to join forces and attack what they regarded as the main Malabari pirate base at the mouth of the Kotta River, called Putupattanam, in 1599. After a failed attempt on the fort, the Portuguese eventually toppled the Malabar "pirate king," Kunjali IV, in 1600. The Frenchman Pyrard arrived shortly after to find the pirates and their land-based merchant fences regrouping.

Pyrard describes the Malabar pirates' market activities and redistributions of booty as follows:

> All the merchants of the coast, when they hear that the galleots of the pirates are about to come in, hold themselves in readiness to buy their goods cheap, and then they have the assurance to go and sell them in the markets of the very merchants of whom they were taken. These latter frequently buy them back a second time; and though they recognize their own goods, that matters not, so long as they have the Portuguese passport. The priests of their religion, too, and the poor are on the lookout, and come distances of thirty leagues to get their share; for they well know that these Malabars have made vows, in case they make a good prize, to give so much to the poor, and never fail to acquit themselves therein.[10]

Although we do not learn from Pyrard how booty was redistributed among the pirates themselves, this short passage suggests a firmly rooted pirate culture shot through with religious customs and reciprocal ties. Despite the fear they struck in the hearts of the Portuguese and myriad unsuspecting merchants, the Malabaris' generosity with friends appears to have been institutionalized. Pyrard claimed they were the best hosts he had ever met.

Local Indian Ocean sea raiders continued to plunder commercial vessels throughout the seventeenth century, but their activities were overshadowed by new European interlopers, primarily the Dutch, but also the English and French. At first these were company men: part merchant, part corsair. They engaged in plunder, but they wanted trading posts. As in the Atlantic, company-sponsored Dutch corsairs proved virtually unstoppable after 1621, striving to displace the Portuguese from every one of their enclaves. Success came swiftly, and thanks largely to the Dutch East India Company (VOC), by the time Portugal parted ways with Spain in 1640 its once mighty merchant empire was a shambles—not dead, but badly beaten. The Dutch, like the Ottomans before them, readily allied with locals who hated the Portuguese, promising not to interfere in matters of faith. Dutch relations with Aceh were a case in point.

The English were early rivals of the Dutch, with their own East India Company and a string of far-flung trading forts. The French and other Europeans, including (unsuccessfully) the Genoese, followed later in the seventeenth century. Everyone complained of the Malabar pirates along with corsairing under false pretenses by fellow Europeans, but it was only after 1680 or so that freelance piracy reemerged as a major concern in these seas. This time it was mostly Anglo-American bucca-neers who upset the balance of power, making use of Madagascar and neighbor-ing islands as rendezvous points and even permanent bases.

It was these Anglo-American buccaneers' increasingly bold attacks on Muslim pilgrim vessels on their way from India to Jiddah after 1690 that got everyone's attention. Soon known as "Red Sea men," these former Caribbean plunderers upset English East India Company relations with the mighty Mughals and lesser allies. Interfering with fellow Englishmen's lucrative and hard-won trade arrange-ments would not be tolerated, and soon the "Red Sea" pirates were the objects of a global manhunt. As will be seen in Chapter 7, the most successful Indian Ocean pirate of the Golden Age was Henry Avery, and the most famous was "pirate hunter" turned pirate William Kidd. The actions of both would help bring on the anti-pirate forces of the British Royal Navy following the 1702–13 War of the Spanish Succession. What has since been called the War against the Pirates would be fought here, too, in eastern seas. Malabari and other local pirates in the Persian Gulf would suffer alongside European buccaneers.

Sea Raiders of East and Southeast Asia

"I learned in these islands that this city [of Manila] had been burned by a pirate and that there had been a war." Thus did Dr. Francisco de Sande, one of the first Spanish governors of the Philippines, begin his account of the 1574 siege of Manila by "the pirate Limahon."[11] Known in Chinese as Lin Feng, Limahon was only one of the most famous corsairs to cruise East Asian waters in early modern times. Others included Wang Zhih and the great Zheng Chenggong, known in the West as Koxinga. The Spanish, as we have seen, were by no means the only targets of pirate aggression in eastern seas, and indeed they were seen by some locals as "long-nosed" pirates themselves. But it may be useful in the context of this book to use Spanish Manila as a point of reference from which to view the several East and Southeast Asian piracy cycles that raged between the sixteenth and eighteenth centuries. They were often of much greater magnitude than any-thing going on in the Americas or even in the Indian Ocean. Perhaps only Medi-terranean piracy vied with China Seas piracy in terms of scale.

For Western pirates going back to the time of Francis Drake (who sailed through these waters without doing much damage shortly after Limahon's great siege of Manila) the Spanish and Portuguese East Indies were attractive if less

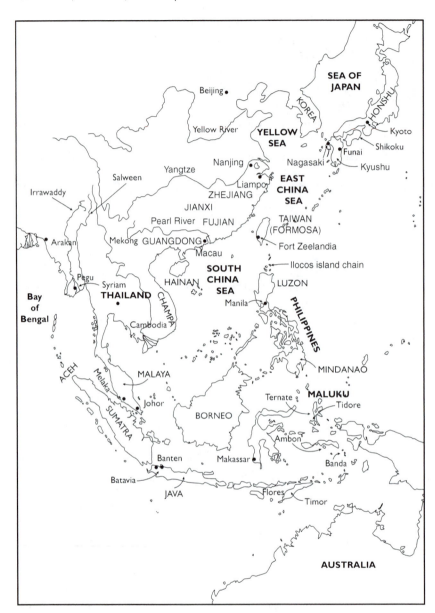

MAP 6 Greater Southeast Asia in the Age of Piracy

frequently reached hunting grounds. Dutch corsairs were the great exception, but as in the Indian Ocean most of their land raids and high seas interventions were company-sponsored even when their acts felt like ordinary piracy to their victims. Most of what the Spanish and other European interlopers in these waters called piracy was carried out by local residents, whether Japanese, Chinese, Korean, or Southeast Asian. Historians of the region are quick to point out that Europeans unfairly branded many groups as pirates, but as in the Mediterranean and Atlantic, piracy was often in the eye of the beholder. Chinese government authorities, for example, tended to share this victim's perspective.

As in the Indian Ocean, piracy in the Greater China Seas long predated the arrival of European maritime colonizers. Europeans simply introduced a new dynamic to the business by establishing commercial footholds like Manila and importing American silver, along with new weapons. With the rise of the Ming Empire after the mid-fourteenth century CE, whole sections of China's central Zhejiang coast, plus much of southern Japan, served as bases for sea raiders who paid no attention to central authorities. The early Ming rulers responded by developing naval patrols and building forts, and even by deploying substantial army units to protect coastal cities. Contemporary chroniclers suggest that they suppressed piracy quite effectively by the time of the great exploratory voyages of Admiral Zheng He between 1405 and 1433, which reached East Africa. In subsequent years the Ming pulled back from the sea and the pirates again flourished.

The first great cycle appears to have started in the early 1540s, just as the Portuguese were establishing their first base in Japan. The cycle ended around 1567, when the Spanish were completing the conquest of the northern Philippines. But this piracy cycle had little to do with either of these Iberian interlopers. As in the late fourteenth century, the principal victims of this wave of raids were Chinese and Korean shippers and coastal residents, and the main perpetrators were a mix of seafaring folk whom the Chinese claimed were Japanese, the famous *wako* or "dwarf pirates." Many *wako*, or *kaizoku*, as they were known in Japan, used small islands off Kyushu as bases, and some were sponsored by *daimyo*, or local lords. Most historians agree that the pirates of this cycle were multiethnic and not easily assigned a proto-national identity. Limahon, for example, appears to have been of mixed Chinese-Japanese ancestry.

Several factors contributed to this new piracy cycle. As Ming protection in the early sixteenth century decreased, trade in compact valuables such as gold, silver, copper, spices, fragrant woods, and silks increased. Trade volume swelled all over the region, but especially between China and Japan. The increasingly inward-looking Chinese state essentially withdrew from naval affairs and this enabled the rise of extensive clans of competitive contraband traders who inevitably resorted to violent theft and paramilitarization as they rejected Ming trade bans and competed with one another.

Formal relations with Japan also grew sour, and when the Ming again attempted suppression of contraband trade after 1522, piracy soared. Rising poverty among China's huge coastal population, according even to contemporary historians, served as a key "push" factor. Few options looked better than piracy for many, and so began several decades of raiding by mostly Chinese and Japanese *wako* based in either southern Japan or on islands just east of Huangzhou or west of Taiwan. The raiders ranged all the way from northeastern Korea to southwestern China, sacking towns and ransoming captives on an unprecedented scale. After peaking in the early 1550s, the *wako/kaizoku*/"pirates of the China Seas" were again suppressed by a series of Ming offensives, mostly launched in the 1560s.

One of the most famous pirates from this period and persistent bane of Ming authorities was Wang Zhi, a former Chinese salt merchant. As historian Maria Grazia Petrucci has shown, Wang Zhi's strange career demonstrates how some individuals embraced piracy as an adaptation to the complex and shifting political economy of coastal East Asia in the mid-sixteenth century.[12] Wang Zhi resisted Ming attempts to tax and limit his trade in the 1530s, so he moved just offshore to Shuangyu Island to expand ties with Japan. After his vessels suffered attacks by Chinese pirates, Wang Zhi hired Japanese pirates as guards, and soon a cycle of attack and retaliation led to the creation of a new order. Wang Zhi's victory as a kind of regional mob boss drew many Chinese followers and he became a local hero for creating jobs and spreading wealth. However, his high profile drew renewed Ming attention, so much so that the pirate lord chose to shove off and resettle in southwest Japan by 1545.

In Hirado, on northwest Kyushu, Wang Zhi won the sponsorship of a local *daimyo* and entered the gun and gunpowder business. It turns out that Wang Zhi was the first East Asian conduit for new European firearms technology, introduced by the Portuguese in 1542. Wang Zhi was soon supplying Japanese and Chinese buyers with copies of Portuguese handguns and cannons, along with the necessary gunpowder—which the Chinese had of course invented and therefore knew how to make. New demand for gunpowder's basic ingredients encouraged smugglers like Wang Zhi to send Japanese sulfur to the mainland in exchange for saltpeter.

It was an explosive mix, especially in the hands of pirates. To this the Portuguese added Christianity. In exchange for gun making tips offered by Portuguese Jesuits, many prominent Japanese contraband traders and pirates converted to the western faith. These Japanese Christian pirates, in command of large, well-armed vessels called *atakabune*, became major allies of the Portuguese until their expulsion decades later during the Tokugawa crackdown on the foreign faith. But before all this, Ming authorities caught up with and executed Wang Zhi in 1559. With the waning of the great mid-century pirate cycle, many Japanese *kaizoku* settled into the business of coastal protection rackets, discussed in further detail later.

One of the survivors of Ming efforts at pirate suppression in the 1560s was Lin Feng, or Limahon, who shifted south and turned his energies on the Spanish and their native and Chinese allies at Manila in 1574. As Igawa Kenji has shown, the Philippines were a major Asian trading crossroads long before the Spanish arrived, exporting gold, beeswax, and foodstuffs in exchange for cloth, porcelain, drugs, and metal ware. What the Spanish brought to this already abundant trading sphere after establishing their base at Manila in 1571 was American silver, both from Peru and Mexico. Silver attracted merchants and pirates. Asian merchants interested in American silver included not only Chinese and Southeast Asians from Borneo and the Spice Islands, but also Japanese. Some of these Japanese merchants, like the mixed-heritage Limahon, were also pirates, switching hats as need arose.[13]

Limahon first appears in the records in 1571, when he attacked the city of Shenquan on China's southern Guangdong coast. An attack the next year on the neighboring city of Chenghai was repulsed, sending Limahon to the Philippine island of Luzon, where he built a base on the north coast. Chinese naval forces pursued him, and he fled to Taiwan, then to Hainan Island far to the southwest. In September 1574 Limahon and his followers gave up on increasingly risky Chinese mainland targets in favor of Spanish Manila. Spanish sources say he was drawn to the city after capturing a Chinese junk on the way home from Manila loaded with Mexican half-pesos. Dr. Francisco de Sande, who arrived soon after Limahon's raid and collected testimonies, described his forces at their landing outside the city of Manila as follows:

> The corsair continued his journey, and, intending to make an attack at dawn, anchored outside the bay, and sent all his small boats ashore in charge of some captains, in the early part of St Andrew's Eve. They say that the corsair remained with the ships, but that in the boats there were 700 men, among whom were a few arquebusiers, and many pikemen, besides men armed with battle axes. They were clad in corselets which are coats lined with exceedingly thick cotton. They had durable bamboo hats, which served as helmets; they carried cutlasses and several daggers in their belts, and all were barefoot. Their manner of warfare or of fighting was to form a squadron composed of men with battle-axes, among whom were placed some arquebusiers, a few of the latter going ahead as skirmishers. One of every ten men carried a banner, fastened to his shoulders and reaching two palms above his head. There were other and larger banners also, so that it appeared as if some important personage was coming who served in the capacity of master of camp. These, then, were the people who made the first attack.[14]

The Spanish barely survived Limahon's marine-style invasion, which was said to have involved several thousand pirates and hundreds of Japanese mercenary auxiliaries. This was not all: Sande claimed that Limahon had almost as many women on board his fleet as men, suggesting a fully mobile pirate society and possibly a plan to colonize Manila. Significant portions of the Spanish capital were burned to the ground, but poor planning by the attackers and solid gun handling by the Spanish seem to have combined to force Limahon to back off. He may not have had enough trained arquebusiers or cannons, although Sande claimed that his forces had captured a huge bronze gun called "Vigilante" from a Spanish ship offshore.[15]

In any case, Spanish naval relief forces under Juan de Saucedo arrived just in time to prevent a second sortie from neighboring Cavite, and Limahon retreated from there to Ilocos, some forty miles away. Chinese allies subsequently helped the Spanish drive the pirates out of the Philippines altogether, but Limahon continued raiding in the South China Sea until the late 1580s. Other *wako* bands attacked smaller targets claimed by the Spanish, but the successful defense of Manila encouraged many, including several of Japan's pirate-sponsoring *daimyo*, to seek peaceful trade. Yet the situation remained extremely tense, and Spanish officials throughout the colonial period worried about their vulnerability. One thing that greatly disturbed Sande and other officials was the willingness in the midst of Limahon's attack of thousands of seafaring Moros to join the *wako* in pillaging Christian Manila.

By the time of Limahon's attack on Manila in 1574 the Spanish and Portuguese were still struggling to define each other's spheres of influence in East Asian waters. On the one hand this was the far side of the Line of Tordesillas, but as with the division of the Canary and Madeira Islands in the East Atlantic, here the Portuguese ceded control of an archipelago they might have claimed due to precedent, in this case Ferdinand Magellan's stop and "martyrdom" on Mactan Island in 1520. Magellan was Portuguese, but he had sailed for Spain. So as long as Mexico-based Spaniards took the initiative and firmed up that earlier claim, Portugal would agree to leave the Philippines alone and concentrate on the Spice Islands and trade enclaves at Macao, Nagasaki, Melaka, and elsewhere. The Spanish–Portuguese union allowed for more cooperation against various alleged corsairs between 1580 and 1640, but even then tensions over jurisdiction and defense costs festered. Still, the Iberians remained a tiny presence in the western Pacific's crowded waters, and their grand political and religious claims and designs, for example a Spanish proposal to invade and conquer China as if it were Inca Peru or the Aztec Empire, struck regional authorities as quixotic.

As historian Peter Shapinsky has shown, in Japan on the eve of Tokugawa unification several powerful pirate clans and their land-based sponsors shifted away from the long-distance attacks typical of men such as Limahon toward creation of coastal protection rackets. Shapinsky traces one band, the Noshima Murakami, that operated in the inland Seto Sea between the islands of Shikoku and Honshu. By at least the 1560s the band moved from violently extorting money to selling pass flags. The purpose of these banners was unambiguous, as made clear from local correspondence from 1585: "Regarding the flag pass, we send it according to your petition. It is to be used to ensure that nothing untoward occurs as you travel to and fro on the seas...."[10] In establishing an organized protection racket of this kind, the Noshima Murakami were paralleling the contemporary shift from piratical raiding to "taxing" of sea lanes witnessed in the Mediterranean. Unlike the Barbary corsairs, however, the Japanese pirate-racketeers seem not to have established a long-running kidnapping and ransoming business as well.

With Ming assertion and Japanese unification South China Sea piracy seems to have waned by the turn of the seventeenth century, but for the Spanish a chronic religious war that spawned piracy around the edges much as in the Mediterranean developed in the southern Philippines. As noted earlier in the story of Limahon's attack on Manila, the *moros* or "Moors" of Mindanao and neighboring islands were anxious to maintain their religious and personal freedom despite Spanish claims to their territory and their souls, and as a result they took every opportunity to sack and pillage Spanish and Spanish-allied ships and towns. Occasionally they took hostages, but the tendency was to give no quarter. Moros captured by the Spanish were frequently enslaved and sold, not ransomed or "redeemed" as a means of gaining rents. Moro piracy was thus a chronic menace throughout the early modern period, and it proved persistent until Philippine independence and beyond.

Although they were generally less pushy than the Spanish, Portuguese religious and commercial claims angered many local sovereigns as well, particularly in China, Japan, and what is today Indonesia. As with the Spanish and Filipino Moros, in places like western Sumatra or southern Sulawesi this chronic animosity gave rise to piratical attacks under the guise of either crusade or jihad, and as in the Mediterranean the infusion of "confessional" mistrust rendered judgment of these acts' prime motives difficult. Sources from seventeenth-century Makassar suggest potent religious motivations, but these tended to be closely intertwined with commercial ones.[17] What is clear is that the Spanish and Portuguese were quick to label merchants and recalcitrant local lords as pirates when it suited their interests. Offering protection from such folks would be a favorite tactic of other European interlopers, including the Dutch, English, and French. They tended to suppress their missionary impulses in favor of commercial ones, often siding with local authorities in opposition to the Spanish and Portuguese. They introduced their own protection rackets, which could serve as seedbeds of empire.

As in the Americas, it was not long after the Spanish–Portuguese union of 1580 that Dutch corsairs made their way to East Asian waters. This was the world trading region the Dutch coveted most, far more than the Caribbean or South Atlantic, and it was here, primarily in Indonesia, that their longest-lasting and most profitable colonial projects took root. An attack by Dutch corsair Olivier van Noort near Manila in December 1600, described in Chapter 3, left both sides bruised, but the heaviest losses were suffered by the Spanish, commanded by the future President of Quito, Antonio de Morga. The remnants of the wreck of Morga's flagship, excavated by marine archaeologists in the 1990s, remain on permanent display in Spain's Naval Museum in Madrid. This Dutch corsair attack on Iberian claims in the Far East was just the beginning.

With the foundation of the VOC in 1602, the monopolistic Spanish and Portuguese claims on East Asian sea trade proved moot. To boot, the Dutch seizure and looting of the *Santa Catarina*, a treasure-laden Portuguese carrack, taken in 1603 near Singapore in reprisal for various alleged misdeeds, provided the case needed by Dutch jurist Hugo Grotius to argue his new theory of *Mare Liberum* or the Freedom of the Seas, first published in 1609. As legal historian Lauren Benton has shown, what for the Iberians was an act of sheer piracy was for the Dutch an expression of the right of all to carry on as they pleased in open waters. As a result of this case, Grotius also wrote at length on "justified predation."[18]

The law of the sea, as in medieval times, was "catch as catch can," with the axiom: "Good luck defending yourself." Papal grants of jurisdiction or dominion would do you no good in open seas. In quick succession, VOC-sponsored expeditions ousted the Portuguese from Melaka, the Spice Islands, Taiwan, Makassar, Japan, and many other prize posts. English merchants, too, felt as though they had been attacked by pirates on the Banda Islands, the world's only source of nutmeg, but VOC company man Jan Pieterszoon Coen would claim only to be following orders and respecting the demands of shareholders. As Charles Boxer put it, Coen was no pirate, he was an "empire builder."[19] The Spanish held out at Manila, but they were on notice, and they doubled down in trying to protect their treasure galleons, the annual *naos de la china* that crossed the Pacific each year heavy laden with silk for Mexico and Spain and American silver for China.

As we have seen, Dutch corsairs were not freelance criminals but rather company employees who were charged with extending what were at once commercial and state claims. But Dutch acts of pillage with the aim of taking over trade monopolies were certainly perceived and suffered as acts of piracy by their primarily Spanish and Portuguese victims. Much like their brethren in arms in the Americas, Spanish and Portuguese residents and officials in the East Indies spent considerable effort and money organizing expeditions and attempting defense against what they called pirates or corsairs, be they Dutch, Chinese, Japanese, "Moorish," or otherwise.

Also as in the Americas, the allies of these and other Europeans won concessions for their aid in fighting the "pirate enemy" as well. Fighting the "pirate enemy," especially a "heretical" one, was a great way to win a title or sinecure. Among those who probably suffered most in all of this confusion and fighting were the countless Chinese merchants who had long plied these warm but tempestuous seas in search of safe havens in which to trade their silks and porcelain for sandalwood, spices, metals, and other primary goods.

Koxinga and the Struggle for Taiwan

The Chinese would have their revenge with the emergence of one of the greatest East Asian sea raiders of all time. Called by the Dutch Koxinga, Zheng Chenggong emerged after 1661 as the most feared pirate since Limahon. Koxinga was in fact the son of another pirate and merchant named Zheng Zhilong, whose raiding and trading activities from the 1620s to his surrender to Qing authorities in 1646 were legendary. As Paolo Calanca has shown, continued Ming bans on foreign trade into the late 1630s encouraged continuation of the earlier pattern of smuggling and piracy. This policy gave rise to piratical clans such as the Zheng.[20]

Zheng Zhilong engaged in various acts of pillage, but he also took a page from the Japanese *kaizoku* and established a widespread protection racket, complete

FIGURE 6.2 A Chinese Sand-boat, Early Seventeenth Century

Source: The Original is Held by the Harvard-Yenching Library of the Harvard College Library, Harvard University.

with pass flags. Beyond this, he won over poor coastal residents by offering them a portion of his take from pirate raids and extortion. Ming military authorities were demoralized amid budget cuts and contradictory decrees. The whole empire was in distress; pirates like Zheng only made things worse. Palanca cites the laments of a contemporary observer, Zhu Yifeng: "The Fujian commanders fear [sea] bandits more than they do the law, [while] the people follow bandits more willingly than they do the officials."[21]

South China's seaborne Robin Hood could not go on forever as an outlaw, and indeed he offered to "go legit," as historian Tonio Andrade memorably put it, and serve the Ming as regional commander after 1628.[22] He appears to have retained considerable autonomy through the next decade, but Zheng Zhilong was not treated so well by the Qing after his surrender to them in 1646. They held him prisoner until 1661, when he was executed. Well before this time his son, Zheng Chenggong, or Koxinga, whose mother was Japanese, had taken the helm. Koxinga became not only a pirate but also a militant proponent of Ming restoration.

Koxinga's raids in the 1640s and 1650s spread terror all up and down the coast of China, and he even threatened the major city of Nanking in 1658. Like his predecessors the *wako* he moved freely between South China, Southeast Asia, and Japan. He also continued to secure income from protection in the manner of the Barbary corsairs, much to the chagrin of European and Chinese shippers.

In Tonio Andrade's gripping account, Koxinga's 1661 defeat of the Dutch on Taiwan marks a watershed in global history. The Dutch, who had driven the Spanish and Portuguese from Taiwan in 1624, had long been accused of piracy by Chinese and other shippers who resisted their monopolistic claims. The Dutch had also introduced the most current European guns, ships, and fort-building techniques. Andrade follows Chinese historians who claim that the so-called Military Revolution began in China in the twelfth century CE and spread to the rest of the world, but he accepts that European improvements in gun making and fort building were significant. What he finds in the case of Koxinga's seizure of Taiwan is a near-even showdown; documents suggest the battle between these great China Seas corsairs could have gone either way. However this may be, Koxinga's victory established a base for the southern Ming exiles, and although he died in 1662 his son, Zheng Qing, carried on the struggle until the Qing invasion of Taiwan in 1683. After this date piracy in the Greater China Seas was significantly reduced. It was not until the late eighteenth century that major new piracy cycles irrupted.[23]

A curious incidence of East Asian piracy from the age of buccaneers may serve to tie this section back to the Americas. In 1690 the Mexican polymath Carlos de Sigüenza y Góngora published what some have called the first Latin American novel. Titled *The Misfortunes of Alonso Ramírez*, this short work chronicled the capture by pirates in the Philippines of a young carpenter from Puerto Rico, his crossing of the Indian and Atlantic Oceans after winning freedom from the rogues, and his ultimate shipwreck on the coast of Yucatan. Thanks to the detective work of historian Fabio López Lázaro we now know that Ramírez was not only a real person, but that his account of capture by buccaneers northwest of Manila in the spring of 1687 is corroborated by one of his captors, none other than the great "pirate hydrographer" and compulsive journalist William Dampier.[24]

Ramírez's story is perhaps a minor one in the annals of pirate history, but through the ghost writing of Sigüenza y Góngora we learn many interesting details from a captive's perspective. Young Ramírez had migrated to Mexico in search of work after learning his trade and serving as a sailor in the Caribbean. Hard times and instant widowhood apparently drove him to commit some criminal act for which he was punished by exile to the Philippines. From 1682, Ramírez served as a sailor on supply ships bringing food to Cavite for the Manila galleons. It was on one of these supply runs that Ramírez was captured by Dampier's buccaneers aboard the *Cygnet*, which had just arrived in eastern seas from a disappointing string of South Sea raids (see Chapter 5). The mostly English buccaneers' disappointments continued despite capture of some vessels near Cambodia and Thailand, but Ramírez gives us, albeit through the filter of Sigüenza y Góngora, a damning account of the captive's life on a pirate ship.

Aside from the terrors of interrogation that followed Ramírez's initial capture, he describes incessant labor demands throughout the text. He and the other captives were required to clean guns, swab decks, braid cables, hull rice, and perform countless other shipboard chores and kitchen drudgery almost non-stop. The pirates had also captured some slaves, but pretty much every captive had to do this kind of work. Ramírez describes several buccaneers as raving drunks, and on one occasion he claims they forced a sick captive to eat excrement for failing in his duties. Despite all this, Ramírez appears to have won the buccaneers' favor in the course of the voyage into the Indian Ocean toward Madagascar, as they not only released him but also gave him a slave of his own, a young boy from Mozambique, and apparently also his own prize vessel, complete with a cargo of copper and tin ingots and other potentially valuable items. All this was a little difficult to explain when Ramírez washed up on the shores of Yucatan on 11 September 1689, just north of the buccaneer logwood-cutting territory of Belize. Was he a pirate or a captive? Or was he a petty smuggler hoping to avoid prosecution by claiming to have valuable intelligence on the pirate enemy in the Pacific? As López Lázaro demonstrates, it is quite possible that he was all three.

In sum, Indian Ocean and East Asian piracy in the early modern period resembled counterparts in the Americas, the greater Atlantic, and the Mediterranean, but with some twists. First, sea raiding in these seas appears to have occurred in cycles of tremendous scale, with thousands of raiders and countless vessels putting to sea in such turbulent decades as the 1550s and 1650s. Only in the Mediterranean could we find mobilizations approaching this scale, and these were usually formal armadas.

As in the West as well, there emerged great Indian Ocean and East Asian corsair leaders or pirate lords, depending on how one wished to define them, and some grew so powerful that they challenged Portuguese and Chinese royal authorities and even won legitimacy. The best, or most wily of them, like Wang Zhi and Zheng Zhilong, were masters at playing off regional political rivalries and exploiting loopholes, making their money betwixt and between. Others, like Sefer Reis and Mir Ali Beg, simply took corsair daring to the end of its tether, much like Francis Drake.

Also as in the West, Indian Ocean and East Asian sea raiding was both an aspect of and a response to new European overseas political claims, either of control of trade routes or of ports and landmasses. The great difference here was that Western claims on Eastern Seas in the early modern period remained overshadowed by local power plays, even in weak moments such as the fall of the Ming Dynasty or the stumbling of the Ottomans. Times would change, but Koxinga's expulsion of the Dutch from Taiwan in 1661, like Limahon's near-seizure of Manila back in 1574, was a salutary reminder of the Europeans' precarious positions throughout East and Southeast Asia. The persistent Malabaris played a similar role in the Indian Ocean. Around the edges, too, there lurked the occasional wide-eyed buccaneer, never a long-term threat but often the source of the most exotic pirate yarns yet heard in the taverns of London, Amsterdam, Boston, and Port Royal.

BOX 6 MONSOON SAILING

Columbus's greatest discovery was arguably the north Atlantic wind and current system that allowed for timely round-trip travel between Western Europe and the Americas north of the equator. In truth the system had been discovered by Portuguese predecessors, but they had not followed it nearly as far south and west. North Atlantic trade winds were generally predictable despite the seasonal threat of hurricanes, and the Gulf Stream always flowed. The Portuguese faced a much harder task in their East and South Atlantic endeavors. They spent decades figuring out the far more complex winds and currents of Africa's west coast, and also the broader circulatory patterns in the South Atlantic. Pedro Alvares Cabral's great fleet bumped into Brazil by chance in 1500 on its way to India while following the prevailing winds discovered by Cabral's predecessors. Pirates, as we have seen, followed fast in the wake of these seaborne pioneers. Many of the earliest ones, attacking both Spanish and Portuguese targets in the Atlantic, were French.

When the Portuguese entered the Indian Ocean in 1498, they were aided by local pilots who helped them understand yet another wind system, the seasonal monsoon. Whether for peaceful or violent purposes, sailing in the Arabian Sea, the Bay of Bengal, and the South China Sea had always relied on monsoon winds. These very ancient, predictable, and often intense winds are the product of seasonal heating and cooling of the Eurasian continent and neighboring seas.

For sailors in the Arabian Sea, high summer temperatures on the Indian subcontinent create low pressure, sucking in moist air from the warm Indian Ocean to the south. This summer monsoon blows strongest from about June to September, allowing sailors a quick trip from East Africa's many ports to the west coast of India. During the fall the monsoon fades, and in winter the wind flow reverses, as cool high pressure on the Eurasian continent pushes south. What this seasonal flip meant for early modern sailors was that one could catch the winter monsoon from India's west coast to the east coast of Africa—or to the Persian Gulf or Red Sea—but the return trip would have to wait until summer, when the flow reversed. There was no fighting the monsoon in the Indian Ocean unless, as the Dutch later discovered, one sailed far to the south to catch prevailing westerlies to Australia, a route that presented its own dangers.

Another monsoon cycle in the South China Sea ties into seasonal temperature cycles in Australia, along with Siberian high pressure in the northern hemisphere winter. This complex interaction affects sailing in two major ways: wind patterns shift direction seasonally and massive storms can form between October and January. As in the Indian Ocean proper, Europeans relied on native sailors of many ethnicities to introduce them to these complex wind systems, along with a range of large and small currents that could be caught or were best avoided, depending on their flows and strength. An exception was the Manila Galleon route across the north Pacific, a true Spanish discovery.

In sum, Europeans in eastern seas mostly slotted themselves into existing monsoon travel patterns, which encouraged more interaction, more competition, and, by extension, more piracy. So-called Red Sea men like William Kidd followed the paths of others, catching pilgrim ships and straggling vessels as they plied known waters according to the monsoon schedule. Despite their learning of major Indian Ocean and South China Sea monsoon systems, Europeans fell victim to shipwreck more often than piracy. This was especially true of the long-haul voyages to the East Indies and back to Europe via the Cape of Good Hope. The Dutch lost several ships on Australia's rugged west coast, and the Portuguese lost many more among the treacherous reefs of southeast Africa. A whole genre of literature known as the "Tragic History of the Sea" emerged to recount these baleful episodes of maritime disaster. It seems there were worse things than being attacked by pirates.

Boxer, Charles R. *The Tragic History of the Sea*. Foreword by Josiah Blackmore. Minneapolis: University of Minnesota Press, 2001.

Wey-Gómez, Nicolás. *The Tropics of Empire: Why Columbus Sailed South to the Indies*. Cambridge, MA: MIT Press, 2008.

Notes

1 Cheng Lien's letter to the Dutch governor of Taiwan, 2 July 1650, quoted in Cheng Wei-Chung, *War, Trade and Piracy in the China Seas, 1622–1683* (Leiden: Brill, 2013), 150.

2 Giancarlo Casale, *The Ottoman Age of Exploration* (New York: Oxford University Press, 2010), chapter 1. This section relies very heavily on Casale's extraordinary revision of Indian Ocean history in the sixteenth century.

3 Ibid., 47.

4 Ibid., 74–75.

5 Ibid., 93–114.

6 Ibid., 164–66.

7 Ibid., 173–76.

8 Sebastian Prange, "A Trade of No Dishonor: Piracy, Commerce, and Community in the Western Indian Ocean, Twelfth to Sixteenth Century," *American Historical Review* 116:5 (Dec. 2011): 1269–93.

9 Anthony Disney, *A History of Portugal and the Portuguese Empire, vol. 2: The Portuguese Empire* (New York: Cambridge University Press, 2009), 154.

10 Pyrard of Laval, François. *The Voyage of François Pyrard of Laval to the East Indies, the Maldives, the Moluccas, and Brazil.* 2 vols., Albert Gray, trans. (New York: Burt Franklin, 1964–71, orig. publ. 1619, reprint of 1887–90 ed.), 1: 342.

11 Francisco de Sande in Filibiniana Book Guild, *The Colonization and Conquest of the Philippines by Spain: Some Contemporary Source Documents, 1559–1577*, Rafael Bernal, intr. (Manila: FBG, 1965), 294–303.

12 Maria Grazia Petrucci, "Pirates, Gunpowder, and Christianity in Late Sixteenth-Century Japan," in Robert J. Antony, ed., *Elusive Pirates, Pervasive Smugglers: Violence and Clandestine Trade in the Greater China Seas*, pp. 59–71 (Hong Kong: University of Hong Kong Press, 2010).

13 Igawa Kenji, "At the Crossroads: Limahon and Wako in the Sixteenth-Century Philippines," in Robert J. Antony, ed., *Elusive Pirates, Pervasive Smugglers: Violence and Clandestine Trade in the Greater China Seas*, pp. 73–84 (Hong Kong: University of Hong Kong Press, 2010).

14 Sande in Filibiniana Book Guild, *The Colonization and Conquest*, 301.

15 Ibid., 296.

16 Peter D. Shapinsky, "With the Sea as their Domain: Pirates and Maritime Lordship in Medieval Japan," in Jerry Bentley, Renate Bridenthal, and Kären Wigen, eds., *Seascapes: Maritime Histories, Littoral Exchanges, and Transoceanic Exchanges*, pp. 221–38 (Honolulu: University of Hawai'i Press, 2007), 233.

17 See William P. Cummins, ed. and trans., *A Chain of Kings: The Makassarese Chronicles of Gowa and Talloq* (Leiden: KITLV Press, 2007), 87–91.

18 Lauren Benton, *A Search for Sovereignty: Law and Geography in European Empires, 1400–1900* (New York: Cambridge University Press, 2010), 124–37.

19 Charles R. Boxer, *The Dutch Seaborne Empire, 1600–1800* (New York: Penguin, 1990), 210–21.

20 Paolo Calanca, "Piracy and Coastal Security in Southeastern China, 1600–1780," in Robert J. Antony, ed., *Elusive Pirates, Pervasive Smugglers: Violence and Clandestine Trade in the Greater China Seas*, pp.85–98 (Hong Kong: University of Hong Kong Press, 2010).

21 Ibid., 88.

22 Tonio Andrade, *Lost Colony: The Untold Story of China's First Great Victory over the West* (Princeton: Princeton University Press, 2011), 30. Compare with Cheng Wei-Chung, *War, Trade and Piracy*. See also José Eugenio Borao Mateo, *The Spanish Experience in Taiwan, 1626–1642: The Baroque Ending of a Renaissance Endeavor* (Hong Kong: Hong Kong University Press, 2009); and the sources in *Spaniards in Taiwan*, 2 vols. (Taipei: SMC, 2002).

23 Robert J. Antony, "Piracy and the Shadow Economy in the South China Sea, 1780–1810," in Robert J. Antony, ed., *Elusive Pirates, Pervasive Smugglers: Violence and Clandestine Trade in the Greater China Seas*, pp. 99–114 (Hong Kong: University of Hong Kong Press, 2010). See also Antony's book *Like Froth Floating on the Sea: The World of Pirates and Seafarers in Late Imperial South China* (Berkeley: University of California Press, 2003); and Dian Murray, *Pirates of the South China Coast, 1750–1850* (Stanford: Stanford University Press, 1987).

24 Fabio López Lázaro, *The Misfortunes of Alonso Ramírez: The True Adventures of a Spanish-American with 17th-Century Pirates* (Austin: University of Texas Press, 2012). The book includes a fine annotated translation of Sigüenza y Góngora's text.

7
THE LAST BUCCANEERS AND PIRATE SUPPRESSION

Individuals properly described as buccaneers continued to be active in the Caribbean in the years following the South Sea raids, but for the most part this type of free-association piracy was in decline. Concerted efforts to root out the multinational sea-robbers, as has been seen, began in earnest in the 1680s, but a series of international wars intervened, stalling the eradication plans of England, France, and Spain. This chapter treats the last significant buccaneer episodes in the Caribbean before turning to the rise of a group of pirates known commonly as "freebooters." These were the last pirates of the early modern Americas, and some of them were in fact simply veteran seventeenth-century buccaneers in eighteenth-century disguise. What most distinguished the freebooters from their predecessors, however, was their almost universal rejection of national and religious authorities, their predominantly lower-class maritime origins, and their overwhelmingly Anglo-American heritage. Among the most notable of these outlaws were William Kidd, Henry Avery, Edward Teach, Bartholomew Roberts, and two of history's few known female pirates, Ann Bonny and Mary Read. The last pirate cycle, which occurred in the wake of the War of the Spanish Succession (1702–13), would witness more raids than ever before on English, French, Dutch, Danish, Portuguese, and even Mughal Indian trading vessels. The Spanish were not exempted from these depredations, but their problems with the Anglo-American freebooters tended to concentrate more around shipwrecked treasure vessels than buccaneer-style land raids. Indeed, the freebooters' principal enemies were their own former masters, not the Iberian "papists" of centuries past, and in what might be considered an historical irony, at least in the long view, it was primarily English property law rather than Spanish defensive resolve that finally wiped out the pirates.

The Buccaneer Denouement

With the change in official policy in Jamaica, French Hispaniola, and even Danish St. Thomas, emerging pirate bases included the Bahama Islands, particularly the English company-colony of New Providence. The Bahamian governor in the early 1680s, Robert Clarke, had recently issued letters of marque against Spanish vessels in retaliation for local disputes in the Strait of Florida. These commissions were technically illegal, but apparently upset colonists of New Providence had demanded some means of legitimate retaliation. As it turned out, they made their living in part by salvaging Spanish shipwrecks in these notoriously dangerous, reef-filled waters and their work naturally conflicted with the desires of the ships' owners. Soon open hostilities erupted with the Spanish, based mostly at San Agustín (Florida) and Havana, and some English pirates found themselves with legal cover once again. One such buccaneer who had little interest in shipwreck salvage but much in piracy was Captain Coxon, the same man who had so recently been across the Isthmus of Panama. Coxon revealed his Bahamian commission to Jamaica's Governor Lynch, who promptly sent it to England in hopes of having Governor Clarke censured.

Clarke was removed from the Bahamian governorship by late July of 1682, but his successor, Robert Lilburne, was ill equipped to stop the illegal activities of the buccaneers. A group of salvagers, led by a Thomas Pain (supposedly acting as a pirate hunter commissioned by Lynch), attempted an attack on the Spanish fortress at San Agustín in March of 1683, but managed only to raid a few neighboring hamlets. The buccaneer-salvagers had flown French colors during the attack, but they retired to English New Providence, where Lilburne was powerless to deal with them. The Spanish, from their base at Havana, retaliated by sacking New Providence twice, first in January of 1684, then later in the same year. The settlement was burned to the ground, several men killed, a number of settlers and slaves taken prisoner to Havana, and the remainder left to find their way to Jamaica or the Carolinas as refugees. In defending their shipwrecks the Spanish meant business, and these attacks were so thorough that the English Bahamian colony was temporarily abandoned.

If the Bahamas offered but little market for the buccaneers' services in these years, French Hispaniola continued to welcome them. The official French policy, like that of England, favored buccaneer suppression, but the political reality, especially given the weak governorships of D'Ogeron and de Pouançay, was otherwise. As it so happened, the French, and more specifically the planters of the Compagnie des Indes, had no other protection against their enemies in these seas besides mercenaries; the filibusters were entertained, albeit reluctantly, for this contingency. Haring notes that St. Domingue harbored between 2,000 and 3,000 buccaneers in 1684, and they commanded at least seventeen armed vessels.[1] Using Petit Goâve as a base, and carrying often blank and outdated commissions, pirates such as Captain de Grammont continued to harass the Spanish at sea and on land. De Grammont and a force of 180 filibusters attacked La Guaira, the port of Caracas, in mid-1680, but the pirate came away with only a little booty and a serious wound in the neck.

De Grammont's revenge would come soon enough in the form of a massive raid on Veracruz, New Spain's principal port, in May of 1683. In this surprisingly successful attack de Grammont was joined by the veteran Dutch pirate captains Nikolaas van Hoorn and Laurens de Graaf, along with one other Dutchman, one Frenchman, and two Englishmen. With forces totaling about 1,000, these multinational pirates met at Roatan Island (off Honduras) to lay their plan. Somehow they had discovered that the citizens of Veracruz were expecting two ships from Caracas, so the pirates entered the port at midnight on 17 May in the prescribed number of vessels (keeping the others anchored out of sight) and flying Spanish colors. The ruse worked and the sleeping town was in the hands of the invaders within hours. After four days of plundering and ransoming prominent captives, including the governor, don Luis de Córdova, and an old Irish merchant, John Murphy, the buccaneers retired to a nearby island to divide the spoils. The raid yielded the remarkable dividend of 800 pesos per average participant, a substantial return on four days' work. Unsurprisingly, the captains fought over their shares, and van Hoorn later died of a wound sustained in such a dispute with Laurens de Graaf. Ever attentive, de Grammont was there to help relieve van Hoorn of his duties (and perhaps of a portion of his treasure) before the ships returned to Petit Goâve.[2]

Governor de Pouançay was succeeded by de Cussy, who arrived at Petit Goâve in April of 1684 to replace the unpopular interim governor, de Franquesnay. On orders of the king, de Cussy was to actively prosecute the buccaneers, but the local situation and a lack of judicial tools made this task impossible. Again the problem of defense was considered too pressing to risk alienating the pirates, and booty-laden men such as those recently returned from Veracruz did little to bother local merchants. Still, it was clear to the buccaneers that even on French Hispaniola things were changing; the king had sent two more crown officials to aid in suppressing the pirates in August of 1684. De Grammont and Laurens de Graaf, seemingly unbothered by de Cussy's reproach, set out with some 1,100 men from Ile-à-vache in mid-1685 for Yucatán. The capital city of Mérida was spared by careful defense planning (and its location, some 25 km from the coast), but the port of Campeche fell to the invaders. The pirates plundered the town for six weeks, burning everything in sight before sailing to Hispaniola.

The Spanish retaliated with attacks on French shipping in the Caribbean and de Grammont, who was apparently a former navy officer anyway, was commissioned by de Cussy as "King's Lieutenant" of the Santo Domingo coast. A prodigious gambler, de Grammont seems to have lost his last bet by attempting a final pirate raid on some unknown Spanish American port before accepting his new honorary title and its legal obligations. He and a crew of 180 mysteriously disappeared in early 1686. Laurens de Graaf had better luck, apparently, as he accepted the title of "Major" from de Cussy and went on to fight the English after war broke out in 1689. He married Marie-Anne Dieu-le-veult of Tortuga in March of 1693 after she threatened to shoot him for insulting her, evidence that women also drove hard bargains in the buccaneer era. Fond of adventure to the end, de Graaf died in May of 1704 after taking part in the founding of French Louisiana.[3]

Lynch and other English officials in the West Indies found none of this French-sponsored marauding amusing. French, Dutch, and English buccaneers, all sailing with blank commissions from Petit Goâve, were now setting their sights on English merchant shipping and vulnerable coastal settlements. Spain had also applied diplomatic pressure on the English to help suppress the pirates, but it was the threat of domestic losses that drove the English to act. In fact, by the time Governor Lynch died in office in late August of 1684 it was English merchants and planters in Jamaica and Barbados who were demanding an end to the buccaneer era. Local Spanish officials were highly skeptical of English resolve in this regard, and some even got their revenge for past wrongs by outfitting pirate-hunting pirogues that occasionally raided English merchantmen and even fishing boats. Lynch and his followers protested loudly to officials in Havana and elsewhere, but in a sense the English were simply getting a taste of their own medicine. Meanwhile Lynch had had to contend with internal division in the form of the disgruntled Henry Morgan and his now-out-of-office faction. Very much in the buccaneer tradition, Morgan and several of his friends and relatives had been dismissed from the local government in Port Royal for drunkenness and disorderly conduct, but they were not exiled from Jamaica. Even Morgan knew that although a hard stance against buccaneering was good for Jamaica in the long run, in the short run it only made the island vulnerable. In the absence of a navy to hunt them down, Anglo-American buccaneers simply shoved off, setting up shop elsewhere.

Elsewhere, besides French Hispaniola or Danish St. Thomas, was New England, or more broadly, several towns and cities located along the eastern seaboard of British North America. Merchants based in these colonies ignored a series of shrill new proclamations that echoed the Jamaica Act of 1683, and traded openly with notorious pirates in Boston, New York, Philadelphia, and elsewhere. Michel Landresson (a.k.a. Breha) and Thomas Pain were two examples, the former trading in stolen goods in Boston and the latter in Rhode Island during the 1680s.[4] Charleston, South Carolina, actually became a pirate haven of sorts in spite of repeated proclamations and royal investigations of local officials. The Spanish at San Agustín responded to the nearby threat in South Carolina with a damaging raid on the plantations below Charleston in late 1686. A French-English counterattack was planned, but interrupted by the incoming governor, James Colleton. The anger stirred up by these actions even outlived the coming of an anti-buccaneer squadron commissioned in August of 1687 by James II and commanded by Sir Robert Holmes. Haring went so far as to call the Carolina shores a "second Jamaica," and the existence of a Scottish settlement called Port Royal (originally French) added to the association.[5] The Holmes fleet helped drive the

heard one in the street cry, "An earthquake!" Immediately we ran out of the house, where we saw all people with lifted up hands begging God's assistance. We continued running up the street whilst on either side of us we saw the houses, some swallowed up, others thrown on heaps; the sand in the streets rise like the waves of the sea, lifting up all persons that stood upon it and immediately dropping down into pits; and at the same instant a flood of water breaking in and rolling those poor souls over and over; some catching hold of beams and rafters of houses, others were found in the sand that appeared when the water was drained away, with their arms and legs out. The small piece of ground whereon sixteen or eighteen of us stood (thanks be to God) did not sink.[8]

Seeing the English in distress at Port Royal, French filibusters under Governor Ducasse raided settlements along the normally protected south coast of Jamaica. A large expedition sent out in June of 1693 even aimed to capture the island altogether, but Ducasse and his 1,500 followers succeeded only in damaging the sugar economy and harrying shipping. Most of the destruction took place in the southeast, near Port Morant, but Carlisle Bay was also invaded and sacked. Local militia forces, totaling only about 700 men, managed to hold the French off, barely sparing Spanish Town and the crippled settlement and forts of Port Royal. The French filibuster attacks wrecked the local economy nevertheless, leaving 50 sugar mills in ruins, over 200 houses burned, about 100 soldiers killed, and some 1,300 African slaves missing, presumed stolen.[9] A retaliatory attack of sorts was launched from England in early 1695 under Commodore Wilmot, and in a rare joint venture with the Spanish Barlovento Fleet took Cap François and Port de Paix on St. Domingue. The old buccaneer captain Laurens de Graaf was apparently put to shame by the invaders at Cap François, but due to illness among the English and Spanish crews, the more important settlements of Petit Goâve and Leogane were spared. The French did not suffer near the damage sustained by the English in Jamaica, but they were slow to respond with new hostilities.

The war was winding down and so were the buccaneers, at least in their seventeenth-century form, and perhaps the capstone of the era was a French attack on Cartagena in April of 1697. Governor Ducasse had received orders to round up the buccaneers of Hispaniola to join with a fleet arriving from France under the Sieur de Pointis. De Pointis, who commanded almost 4,000 men, was not pleased by the free-spirited ways of the 650-odd buccaneers who came along, and he seems not to have gotten along well with Ducasse, besides. The fleet, now with nine frigates, seven large buccaneer vessels, and a number of smaller craft, was the largest assembled in the Caribbean in recent years, and the Spanish and English were duly alarmed. Jamaica, now under Governor Beeston, braced for an attack, but the French had other plans. The governor sent words of caution to the Spanish at Portobelo and Havana, and meanwhile an English naval squadron under Admiral Nevill was dispatched to protect the Caribbean colonies and

Spanish treasure ships. As luck would have it, de Pointis and his men were already busily attacking Cartagena when Nevill reached Barbados on 17 April.

The soldiers and citizens of Cartagena de Indias, often called the "Key to the Indies" and perhaps the most heavily fortified city in Spanish America by this time, did their best to hold off the French attack. The city's defenses were woefully undermanned, however, and many big guns poorly mounted. Two weeks of steady fighting and cannonades led eventually to the loss of the forts at Boca Chica and Santa Cruz toward the end of April, followed on 6 May by the garrison guarding the city. The arrival of de Pointis and Ducasse was no surprise, but only a portion of the city's treasures had been removed inland, to the town of Mompóx. The Spanish yielded the city to the invaders and paid a ransom of several million pesos, hoping that with this the French would leave them alone. The buccaneers found themselves cheated by de Pointis, however, and after much bickering over the redistribution of the ransom monies returned to sack Cartagena once again. They took another several millions worth of booty, mostly from previously spared churches and monasteries, before retiring to Ile-à-vache. De Pointis, meanwhile, had quickly returned to France by way of Cuba and Newfoundland, barely escaping the Nevill fleet near Jamaica. The buccaneers were less fortunate, and on their return to Hispaniola they lost their two largest treasure-carriers to the English.[10]

King William's War ended in 1697, and the buccaneers, English, French, and otherwise, once again found themselves unwelcome in American waters. As north European merchant interests grew to control not only the supply of manufactured goods to their own colonial possessions but also those of the Spanish, the buccaneers appeared more like mere thieves and less like potential allies. They would have one more chance, however. The following quarter-century would witness the outbreak of another war, the War of the Spanish Succession, and the buccaneers would again be absorbed temporarily into privateering missions. The later 1710s and the 1720s would witness the last gasp of piracy in the Caribbean, this time in the form of the quasi-anarchistic Anglo-American freebooters.

Although the buccaneer era ended with the French sack of Cartagena in 1697, the threat of piracy in the Caribbean, and in the Americas more generally, was hardly past. World events around the turn of the eighteenth century allowed for one more pirate cycle, one that would end with an unprecedented multilateral extermination campaign. Some key figures in the first half of this period, such as Henry Avery and William Kidd, took the pirate threat abroad, terrorizing shipping and trading ports in the Indian Ocean and African Atlantic for a time, but they always returned to American waters to sell their booty and recruit followers. Avery would disappear as the Americas' most wanted fugitive by 1700 and Kidd would meet a bad end in London in the following year after a bitter trial, but other sea-robbers soon took their places in the rogues' gallery of early modern piracy.

The interval between the era of Kidd and the likes of Blackbeard was significant, however, and the War of the Spanish Succession (called Queen Anne's War by Anglo-American colonists, after the current English monarch) pitted the

French and Spanish against the Dutch and English on land and at sea in order to decide the future of Spain's monarchy. The *casus belli*, in short, was that the sickly and disabled Spanish king, the Hapsburg Carlos II (1665–1700), had died without an heir. After the death of a favored Bavarian relative in 1699 he had named the Bourbon Philip of Anjou, grandson of the French Sun King, Louis XIV, as successor. As a result the English and Dutch, fearful of French domination in Europe and the Americas, joined forces to prevent Philip's accession to the Spanish throne.

For the remnants of the buccaneers in the Americas, the War of the Spanish Succession presented an opportunity to return to semi-legitimacy as privateers, much as they had done during King William's War, and many did so. In this capacity, and as common seamen in the service of the English Royal Navy, they helped defeat the Franco-Spanish alliance by 1713. Changes in the Austrian House of Hapsburg forced the victors to recognize the Bourbon Philip as king after all, but he was made to renounce his claim to the French throne. In addition, the English won control of Gibraltar and the Balearic Island of Minorca, along with the exclusive right to supply slaves (the coveted *asiento*) to Spanish America. When the war ended, however, so many seamen were thrown out of work by privateers and royal navies that a new piracy cycle seemed inevitable. The pirates returned in force, producing such memorable characters as Edward Teach (a.k.a. Blackbeard) and Stede Bonnet, Ann Bonny and Mary Read, Bartholomew "Black Bart" Roberts and John "Calico Jack" Rackham; indeed the most notorious of Anglo-American pirates were products of this particular cycle. The last pirates' fluorescence was to be short-lived, however, as a concerted campaign of pirate suppression, led mostly by the English Royal Navy but also by privately financed individuals, would soon push the pirates of the early modern era off the world stage and into the realm of legend and history.

Henry Avery and Captain Kidd

The 1690s were transitional years in world history and they gave rise to two transitional pirate figures of note, Henry Avery (a.k.a. John Every), immortalized as the "King of Pyrates" by Daniel Defoe, and William Kidd, best remembered for the legend of his buried treasure. In truth, Avery died a pauper and Kidd buried no loot, but the careers of these two individuals are notable in that their trajectories reveal the harsh consequences of Europe's, and particularly England's, sudden shift from collusion to intolerance of pirates and their wild escapades. The deaths of both men foreshadowed the events of the last pirate cycle, particularly the post-war extermination campaign of the 1710s and 1720s, but their lives also demonstrated the increasingly rebellious, anti-government sentiment developing among pirates of all nationalities. As anti-piracy campaigns grew in scope and intensity, so declined the pirates' sense of national ties and religious loyalty.

Avery and Kidd were also significant for other reasons, however, one of them being their early run-ins with agents of the growing English East India Company.

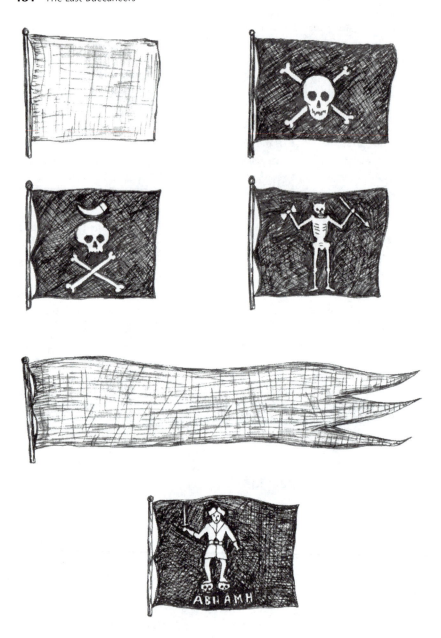

FIGURE 7.1 Early Eighteenth-Century Pirate Flags

Henry Avery's crimes against subjects of Mughal India in the mid-1690s so incensed the administrators of the company that the war on piracy itself became a worldwide business for the first time. As with many overseas ventures of the early modern era, the war on sea-criminals was a business in the literal sense, and

William Kidd, himself a former Caribbean buccaneer, joined the crusade against the likes of Avery as a freelance pirate hunter. Political difficulties in London and the temptation of easy prey in foreign seas changed Kidd's mind, and in a twist of fate worthy of Greek tragedy Kidd ended his life a victim of the same forces he had initially joined.

Avery's story was less tragic, but it had elements of a moral fable that attracted the likes of Daniel Defoe and other contemporary writers. As with most of the pirates of the period, Avery's story was embellished and misconstrued during his own lifetime, but the basic elements of Defoe's narrative have been corroborated by sworn depositions and other sources. Avery appears to have cruised the Spanish Pacific with buccaneers such as Bartholomew Sharp and others in the early 1680s, but his most notable exploits occurred while a mate on an English privateering mission, a mission aimed at plundering the riches of Spanish America but which soon turned mutinous when its crew was left unpaid.

In 1694 Avery took charge of the ship *Charles II* off La Coruña (northwest Spain), renamed it the *Fancy*, and with a crew of men described as "true Cocks of the game" made his way to West Africa.[11] Avery and his "gamecocks" began their cruise by terrorizing a number of coastal African settlements, enslaving and robbing local peoples who mistook them for merchants. Soon after, a pair of Danish slave ships were taken and destroyed, and parts of their crews absorbed. The pirates sailed southward around the Cape of Good Hope and into the Indian Ocean, hoping to find supplies and water at Madagascar, a large island off the Mozambique coast whose unguarded southern and eastern perimeters were fast becoming pirate havens. Madagascar had initially interested French and English merchants searching for new sources of slaves in the 1660s and 1670s, and this trade was continued by the pirates, who began to arrive in the Indian Ocean from the Caribbean—on the so-called Pirate Round—during the anti-buccaneering raids of the 1680s. Avery and his crew found the supplies they needed on the southern tip of Madagascar and sailed northward to the island of Johanna (modern Anjouan), in the Comoros chain, to rest and careen. Their objective was to capture one of the richly laden Muslim pilgrim ships that passed between Surat, in India, and Mocha, on the southwest Arabian coast.

Avery soon managed to upset the agents of the English East India Company in two respects. First, he issued a letter proclaiming his intentions to attack only non-English ships; according to his instructions there was to be a signal given to prevent accidental capture of English East Indiamen. This letter would not appear to be problematic at first glance, but it led the already suspicious trading partners of the company, particularly the Muslim Gujaratis of India, to believe that the English were all conspiring at piracy against them. Second, Avery and his followers, who now included a number of Anglo-American buccaneers just met near the Persian Gulf, captured two pilgrim vessels in early 1695, a feat which netted some £1,000 per man (mostly in the form of Spanish-minted coin, incidentally). The capture and plunder of these ships, the *Fath Mahmadi* and *Ganj-i-Sawai*, only seemed to prove the Gujaratis' and the Mughals' suspicions. Having thus done much to upset Anglo–Muslim relations in the Indian Ocean in these two respects, Avery returned to Johanna to careen the treasure-laden *Fancy* before sailing to the Caribbean island of Providence, where he bribed a local governor with purloined gold and "elephants' teeth" (ivory).[12]

Avery's end is legendary, and though accounts conflict, the best story has the pirate going underground in southern England and losing his entire treasure to duplicitous Bristol merchants. Be this as it may, a number of Avery's crewmembers were even less fortunate than he; six were hanged in London after a difficult trial in 1696. What made the trial difficult was the jury's reluctance to convict English subjects for alleged crimes against Muslims sailing in distant seas—in the first round, which verdict was soon thrown out, the pirates were acquitted. Apparently the East India Company's idea of protecting the greater commercial good of the nation had not yet sunk in for the average Englishman. Still, since the English justice system was a more flexible instrument in those days, the men were quickly retried, the jurors properly threatened, and the men duly served with a guilty verdict and the hangman's noose. Thus the company directors could persuade their Mughal allies that in spite of Henry Avery's escape, not all Englishmen were rogues.

William Kidd would make his mark in the East India business as well, but he enters the historical record as a petty Caribbean buccaneer hired to cruise against the French in King William's War (or the War of the Grand Alliance). The year was 1689, and if later testimony can be trusted, Kidd must have been about forty-four years of age. A native of Greenock, Scotland, and son of a Presbyterian minister, he endeared himself to English officials by leading a successful privateering raid on the tiny French island of Mariegalante (near Guadeloupe) at the very beginning of the war. Apparently his crew was less fond of him, and most deserted with their shares of booty soon after the raid. Kidd sailed to New York, in part to search for his former mates, but quickly found himself in the midst of a local rebellion. By chance he chose the winning side, lent his ship to carry arms and supplies, and was subsequently rewarded by the incoming governor with money and favors. Though New York City at this time was a notorious pirate haven and home to numerous merchant "fences" (i.e., receivers of stolen goods), Kidd's connections were, by the standards of the day, perfectly legitimate. On 16 May 1691 he married a two-time widow named Sarah Bradley Cox Oort and within a few years purchased a house on Pearl Street.[13] In the most unpiratical fashion, Mr. and Mrs. Kidd had two daughters, went to church regularly, and essentially lived the life of prosperous city folk. Or so it was until the adventure bug bit William Kidd once again. In early 1695 he sailed for England to seek a privateering commission.

Pirates were the talk of the town by the time Kidd reached London, and through a series of fortuitous connections with newly powerful Whig lords he found himself in command of a pirate-hunting vessel called the *Adventure Galley* by early 1696. As the name suggests, the 287-ton *Adventure Galley* was a hybrid, a sort of oared galleon meant to be useful in close combat and when winds failed.

Kidd and his small crew of seventy men, all bankrolled by London speculators and sanctioned by the king himself (who, in the manner of an Algerian *bey*, was to receive 10 percent of any booty recovered), sailed first for the New England colonies, where they found another ninety crewmembers (some of the first group dropped out, leaving 152 total), and then for the Indian Ocean. After brief stops at Madeira for wine and the Cape Verde Islands for salt, the *Adventure Galley* sailed southward to round the Cape of Good Hope. Just before reaching the Cape, however, Kidd and his crew fell in by chance with an English navy squadron, an encounter the privateer would rather have missed and which would cause him later trouble in court. Before the ailing navy men could press Kidd for half his crew (their right in wartime), the *Adventure Galley* sneaked away, making wise use of its oars in a calm.[14] They reached Tulear, Madagascar, on 27 January 1697 without incident, but English authorities were already suspicious of Kidd and his crew's intentions.

The scurvied privateers resupplied with fresh food and water at Tulear before sailing north to the Comoro Islands to careen and refit the *Adventure Galley*. Along the way Kidd and his crew came across several East Indiamen, large, well-armed company ships that wanted nothing to do with predators—Kidd still claimed to be a pirate-hunter but already no one in the entire Indian Ocean believed him. The company men's suspicions would be confirmed soon enough, but for now the privateers were simply trying to survive a host of tropical fevers. Over thirty men died by the time the *Adventure Galley* left the tiny island of Mohilla, and Kidd spent several weeks searching for replacement crewmembers among the islands. As Robert Ritchie has shown, it was at this juncture that Kidd seems to have first demonstrated his change of mind; had he sincerely wanted to capture pirates, he would have sailed for Ile St. Marie, on the east coast of Madagascar. Here was a true pirate base known to every New Englander, and nearly everyone else, which at the time was home to nearly 200 pirates under the colorfully named Captains Hoar and Shivers. Instead, Kidd's crew followed the April monsoon winds northward to the Red Sea, hoping, it seems, to repeat the success of that infamous "king of pyrates," Henry Avery.

Kidd would not be so lucky, however, as the East India Company now escorted the pilgrim fleets from Mocha to Surat. One of the ships that evaded Kidd and the crew of the *Adventure Galley* in the Strait of Bab-al-Mandeb, at the mouth of the Red Sea, was the *Ganj-i-sawai*, the same vessel robbed by Avery some three years earlier. Avery's luck was not with Kidd, and the pilgrim ships, guarded by capable Anglo-Dutch escorts, made their escape. Short of supplies, particularly water (a commodity of great value in this region during the month of August), Kidd and his men sailed for India. After capturing a small trader off the Malabar coast in late August and imprisoning its English captain and pilot and a Portuguese-speaking sailor, Kidd put in at last at Carwar for water and supplies. Here agents of the East India Company discovered his secret intentions; he was a pirate to be hunted, not the pirate hunter he claimed to be. Some crewmembers were dissatisfied with this shift in affairs, and with Kidd's supposedly tyrannical captaincy (said to be most un-pirate-like), and they managed to desert. One such crewman was Benjamin Franks, a Jewish gem merchant who had been ruined by the Port Royal earthquake of 1692. Ever resourceful, Franks had joined Kidd in New York in hopes of reaching gem-rich India; there he might serve as a factor for relatives in London, which, before being displaced by Antwerp, was the diamond capital of the world.[15]

In early September the *Adventure Galley* was chased by two vessels sent from Goa, Portugal's viceregal capital on the central Indian coast, with specific orders to capture Kidd. Portugal was no longer the principal European player in the region, but it was not so weak as to suffer losses to meddlesome pirates without a struggle. Unfortunately for the chasers, Kidd's guns were still operational and he badly damaged the smaller of the two Portuguese ships when it became separated from its companion. Having escaped this first punitive strike, Kidd sailed south again, stopping at Calicut and bumping into more English East India Company representatives than he would have liked. The inevitable showdown came in Tellicherry on 3 November, where Kidd barely escaped his multiplying English foes; the crew was near mutiny and Kidd lashed out at one grumbler, named William Moore, killing him with a wooden bucket. Moore's last sigh was said to have included the following words: "Farewell, farewell, Captain Kidd has given me my last."[16] The incident was also immortalized in "The Ballad of Captain Kidd," a song sung by nineteenth-century U.S. sailors but clearly of greater vintage:

> *I murdered William Moore,*
> *As I sailed, as I sailed,*
> *I murdered William Moore,*
> *As I sailed.*
> *I murdered William Moore*
> *And left him in his gore,*
> *Not many leagues from shore,*
> *As I sailed, as I sailed,*
> *Not many leagues from shore, as I sailed.*[17]

Soon after this unfortunate incident, which like his run-ins with navy and company vessels would come back to haunt Kidd at his trial, the *Adventure Galley* came in with a small, Dutch-owned trading vessel called the *Rupparell*. Kidd flew French colors, a ruse that led the *Rupparell's* captain to produce French papers after coming aboard the *Adventure Galley* (and speaking with a French crewmember posing as captain). By claiming to be French, the prize, a local dry goods carrier, was thus legal prey under Kidd's commission. The booty was small, but this act of piracy was important; like William Moore's murder, the capture of the *Rupparell* would loom large years later in London. A few similar trading vessels were taken in the following months along the Malabar Coast, but the prize that made Kidd famous did not appear until 30 January 1698. On this day the 400-ton *Quedah Merchant*, a spice and cloth ship based at Surat but captained by an Englishman, John Wright, hove into view. The same French color scheme used on the *Rupparell*'s captain was tried, with similar results. Attempts by an Armenian merchant named Coji Babba to alter Kidd's robbing mood with a gift of 20,000 rupees were rebuffed, and the bulk of captured merchandise taken to the port of Caliquilon to be sold. After a few more small acts of piracy on the coast, Kidd and his much richer and happier men sailed for Madagascar.[18] The *Adventure Galley* was barely seaworthy, but fortunately for the pirates its pumps, which required eight hands at all times, could now be manned by captives rather than themselves.

Kidd's principal objective was to return to New York, to his wife and daughters and, presumably, to a richer, more settled life. After a brief sojourn on Ile St. Marie, where he met with Robert Culliford, a former mate (one of the deserters after the 1689 incident on Mariegalante and now notorious East Indies pirate), Kidd and a much-reduced crew sailed for home in the *Quedah Merchant*, renamed *Adventure Prize*. The *Adventure Galley* had been scuttled in the harbor of Ile St. Marie and salvaged for hardware. Kidd arrived at the Caribbean island of Anguilla, near the Virgin chain, in April of 1699, and soon discovered that a warrant was out for his arrest on charges of piracy. In light of this development he sailed for Danish St. Thomas, where his requests for protection from English naval vessels were denied; no friend of pirates like his predecessor, the current governor was willing to let the strange East India ship come to port but would promise no protection.[19] Kidd's crew sailed the *Quedah Merchant* to Mona Island, just west of Puerto Rico, and then shoved off for a remote spot on Hispaniola, on the banks of the Higuey River. In the meantime Kidd had met up with Henry Bolton, a West Indies publican and sometime smuggler who agreed to help the pirate unload his merchandise. The next month or so was spent trading booty with Bolton and his associates, who resold the fabrics and other items at Curaçao, St. Thomas, and other Caribbean market nodes known to accept "non-traditional" goods. Kidd finally sailed northward in late May in a new sloop, the *St. Antonio*, with hopes of negotiating an agreement with his old London sponsor, Lord Bellomont, now governor of Massachusetts and New York.

Given the politics of piracy then current in England and its colonies, it was a dicey situation for both Kidd and Bellomont: Kidd wanted an official pardon and Bellomont wanted his money. But the Whig governor had sense enough to take the moral, or at least judicial high ground, and it was almost inevitable that he should end up getting the better of his buccaneer associate. Though he could easily have sailed away, Kidd chose to put his fate in Bellomont's hands in Boston, a decision that would cost him his life. Kidd was imprisoned in New England through most of the winter of 1699–1700, shipped to the Court of Admiralty (in England) in February of 1700, interrogated rigorously in mid-April, and sent to the notoriously vile Newgate Prison shortly thereafter; throughout he was said to be despondent, near suicidal. The now famous pirate captain, a man whose name already conjured up images of vast treasure and exotic seas, would spend a year in solitary confinement before being hanged on 23 May 1701.

As Robert Ritchie has shown, William Kidd was in effect sacrificed to politics. Since no one had managed to capture Henry Avery, and given the escapes and acquittals of other pirates in recent years, Kidd's execution became a sort of peace offering intended to placate the directors of the East India Company—the Armenian merchant Coji Babba was even brought to London to testify against Kidd and witness the brutal effectiveness of English justice. Kidd's death was less useful, however, as a means of vindicating his Whig associates, such as Bellomont, and the prominent investors found themselves unable to backpedal their way out of the scandal.[20] In short, Kidd died a symbol of piracy more than a genuine villain. His only consolation, perhaps, was that he had managed to unlade (not bury) some treasure off Long Island for his wife before sailing north to Boston. Sarah Kidd, who remarried yet again, lived until 1744. She did not enjoy great wealth, however, a fact that inadvertently contributed to the legend of her famous husband's lost treasure.

Henry Avery and William Kidd were remarkable in being truly global rather than simply "American" or Atlantic pirates. It should be remembered, however, that their market connections and hideouts (and families) were located primarily in the Caribbean and North Atlantic colonies no matter where they robbed. Madagascar was a partial exception, but few pirates, including these two, thought of this remote haven as home. Though the island did become a base for some noteworthy sea-robbers in subsequent decades, the notion of a "pirate republic" on Madagascar was a figment of the popular imagination. The buccaneers had simply been forced, as in the case of the South Sea pirates of the 1680s, to temporarily exploit unguarded islands. In fact, some of Kidd's associates, such as James Kelley and Edward Davis, were veterans of the *Bachelor's Delight* South Sea adventure of 1683–85; they knew both the hardships and payoffs of long-distance pirating voyages. A pirate's duty, after all, was to locate, steal, and carry off booty wherever it lay. By this time, however, the law, and the English Royal Navy, followed close behind. The English Act of Piracy of 1699 was significant for allowing more colonial courts to try and execute sea-robbers—even if prominent they would not have to be tried in England like Kidd. The navy, which had counted only twenty-five ships in pay in 1685, had also expanded dramatically during King William's War (1689–97), with 234 ships (and over 45,000 men) by mid-1696.[21] By chance, the death of Kidd occurred just as the peace of 1697 was wearing thin, but by 1702 the Royal Navy swelled again, this time absorbing even the most recalcitrant pirates.

The Sack of Rio de Janeiro

What attracted career pirates to Brazil at the turn of the eighteenth century was the discovery of prodigious amounts of gold, most of it excavated in the highlands north of Rio de Janeiro. Rio, given its relative proximity to the main mining districts of the interior and the presumed security of its bay, was deemed the natural, official outlet for Brazilian gold. A mint was soon added to the king's treasury offices. The coast around Rio is rugged and forested, however, and gold is compact and therefore easily smuggled. Other nearby coastal towns such as Parati became attractive targets for pirates and contraband traders who feared getting caught in Rio. Offshore islands such as Ilha Grande also served as temporary bases.

Freelance pirate-smugglers were a new menace, but the greatest raid on Rio in the age of piracy occurred during the War of the Spanish Succession, with two back-to-back French attacks in 1710 and 1711. The city's inhabitants defended themselves ably in the first instance, but not in the second; the city was shamefully evacuated and ransomed at enormous cost. Was the sack and ransoming of Rio in 1711 a pirate attack? Not exactly, but neither it nor the 1710 attack were strictly naval affairs, either. Both expeditions were headed by privateers, and their principal aim was to win the sort of treasure taken at Cartagena de Indias by De Pointis and his buccaneer auxiliaries in 1697.[22]

French merchants and crown officials knew all about the Brazilian gold rush, and once Portugal declared against them, they pooled capital to go after their share. The Portuguese king Pedro II had initially sided with France's Louis XIV at the start of the War of the Spanish Succession, but he soon backed out and joined the English and their many allies with the Methuen Treaty of 1703. French privateers immediately responded by plundering dozens of Portuguese outposts in the Atlantic, Pacific, and Indian Oceans. Having just recovered from similar beatings by the Dutch, this was a lot to bear.

In 1710 an expedition headed by Jean-François le Clerc, a native of the Caribbean island of Guadeloupe, left Brest for Rio with six ships and about 1,500 men. The expedition reached Guanabara Bay in mid-August, and after reconnoitering for several days, le Clerc landed with most of his troops about forty miles south of Rio on 11 September. He had been aided by runaway slaves. A long march through dense forest ensued, and although Rio's governor proved inept at nearly every juncture, the French forces were eventually beaten in street battles by armed locals, among them Jesuit high-school students and numerous slaves. Holed up in a sugar warehouse, le Clerc and a few hundred survivors eventually surrendered, and although some were sent home, le Clerc himself was murdered in shadowy circumstances.

When word of le Clerc's death reached France, a new privateering mission was quickly organized to avenge him—and hopefully to make a fortune besides. The new venture was backed by prominent investors, including France's admiral, the Count of Toulouse, and it was also openly approved by the king. Even with royal blessing, the mission was aimed at plunder, not permanent seizure of territory or even destruction of forts or fighting vessels. As such, most investors were merchants from St. Malo, hometown of the expedition's leader, René Duguay-Trouin. A true corporate raider, Duguay-Trouin swore not to let his shareholders down.

The 1711 expedition barely escaped an English attempt to intercept it near Brest, and despite the call for secrecy word reached Rio from Lisbon that a second French attack was imminent. As historian Charles Boxer argued, Rio would be lost not so much due to the genius of Duguay-Trouin, although he made some brilliant moves, but rather due to the dismal quality of Portuguese military leadership. The governor, Francisco de Castro Morais, was completely inept, and he consistently failed to coordinate land actions with those of naval commander Gaspar da Costa Ataide. Duguay-Trouin sailed straight into the bay almost exactly a year after the landing of his predecessor, le Clerc, and although many men were swept from the decks by gun and cannon fire from forts on either side, the penetration was complete.

Over 3,000 Frenchmen landed on one of Rio's splendid beaches on 14 September 1711, but with no time to rest. Duguay-Trouin and his men soon set up and fortified positions all around and above the city and began blasting away at its heart. After some heroic but fruitless attempts by low-level officers to dislodge Duguay-Trouin from his post in the bishop's country house, Governor Castro was presented with an offer on 19 September: pay a generous ransom or see his city bombed and burnt to the ground. Castro Morais refused to surrender or pay, only to order a nighttime evacuation of the city two days later, surprising everyone. A stunned Duguay-Trouin and his followers awoke to find themselves in total control of a deserted Rio de Janeiro. Not wanting to give up on the needed ransom, the French privateer then pursued Castro Morais to his hideout. This time the weak and embattled governor gave in. Royal and private treasure worth more than 610,000 *cruzados* in gold was handed over in short order.

Known widely as "a perfect gentleman," Duguay-Trouin returned the city of Rio to its chagrined inhabitants and sailed home to pay out shares to stockholders and accept thanks from his king. The corsair's luck nearly ran out when two of his ships went down in a storm near the Azores, one with considerable treasure aboard, but in France Duguay-Trouin received a hero's welcome in early 1712 and a side-venture in contraband trade he had sent to Peru paid considerable dividends to help offset the shipwreck. The next year, the Treaty of Utrecht ended the War of the Spanish Succession, relieving Portugal but flushing thousands of out-of-work soldiers and sailors into the Atlantic, where many joined the last wave of freebooters, most of them Anglo-Americans. One who sought Brazilian treasure was Bartholomew "Black Bart" Roberts, who died with a diamond-studded gold cross.

Treasure Wrecks and the Anglo-American Freebooters

The War of the Spanish Succession absorbed nearly all available European and colonial American seamen, either as navy recruits or as privateers, and little piracy per se was noted between the years 1702 and 1713. From the Spanish point of view, however, this was again a mere technicality, and in Spain's American colonies the

scourge of privateers could feel about the same as that of pirates. When the privateers were not raiding coastal shipping or plundering vulnerable settlements they
were hovering around shipwrecked Spanish treasure galleons. As seen in previous
chapters, the English in particular were fond of fishing for treasure in Spanish
waters, at times with great success. These operations, like the earlier ones headed
by William Phips off the north coast of Hispaniola (1687) and John Strong off
the coast of present-day Ecuador (1690), were mostly joint-stock salvage ventures
with secondary smuggling aims. Former buccaneers were recruited for these ventures from the Bahamas, Bermuda, Jamaica, and the Carolinas, but sometimes they
simply organized themselves and preyed independently on Spanish salvagers. After
the war the situation worsened, as when the entire Spanish treasure fleet was lost
in a hurricane off Cape Canaveral, Florida, in 1715. Partly as a result of this disaster
a new pirate cycle began; desperate individuals who had met while searching for
sunken treasure or while raiding the Spanish divers' camps rendezvoused at the
Bahamas and planned new raids, mostly on French and English shipping. It was
another privately financed English venture, however, that would attempt to drive
these emerging freebooters from the Bahamas and end their marauding altogether.
This for-profit anti-pirate mission was led by Governor Woodes Rogers, himself
a veteran of privateering raids in the Spanish South Sea and elsewhere in the first
decade of the eighteenth century. Rogers's and other related privateering voyages
will be discussed briefly before turning to the Caribbean freebooters.

An early privateering voyage during the War of the Spanish Succession was
captained by the ex-buccaneer William Dampier, and was organized in 1702 with
the aim of plundering Spanish shipping either in the vicinity of Buenos Aires or in
the South Sea. The majority of participants in this expedition seem to have been
rogues, and the voyage was even delayed to await Dampier's old friend and South
Sea veteran Edward Morgan's release from jail.[23] Morgan was at least an *experienced* rogue, as he had also sailed to the Pacific with Captain Swan in the *Cygnet*
in the early 1680s. The expedition barely held together at all, however, perhaps
due to Dampier's lack of leadership skills, and the whole voyage was strangely
reminiscent of Bartholomew Sharp's fractious endeavors in the region more than
two decades earlier. By the time Dampier and his weakened crew approached a
Manila galleon off the northwest coast of Mexico in late 1704 there was little
hope of success. The massive galleon, called *Nuestra Señora del Rosario y San Vicente
Ferrer*, simply blasted away at Dampier's tiny *St. George*, leaving the privateers
barely able to escape with their lives. Dampier and a few remaining crewmembers eventually managed to capture a small prize off the Peruvian coast before
sailing to the East Indies, but they returned to England with little booty to show
their subscribers in 1707. Meanwhile Spain's ally, France, sent numerous trading
missions to the Pacific, including the first recorded foreign (i.e., non-Spanish)
voyage to cross the Pacific from west to east. This expedition, headed by Nicolas
de Frondat in the *St. Antoine*, traded several million livres-worth of merchandise
along the Peruvian and Chilean coasts in 1709.[24]

Back in England, William Dampier was again recruited, this time as a pilot and advisor to the more successful South Sea voyage of Woodes Rogers (1708–11). Backed by investors in Bristol, Rogers hoped to capture both French ships such as Frondat's and whatever Spanish bullion carriers might come his way. Rogers, in the 320-ton *Duke*, was joined by Stephen Courtney, commander of the 260-ton *Duchess*. Though the structure of command was unusual, enacted entirely by committee, the voyage managed to remain cohesive and mostly successful. In an interesting sidelight of the Rogers expedition, Alexander Selkirk, an independent-minded Scotsman who had been marooned by members of Dampier's 1703–05 voyage, was rescued from the Juan Fernández Islands. His story, along with those of earlier marooners noted in Chapter 5, such as the Miskito Indian William, later served to inspire Daniel Defoe's *Robinson Crusoe* (1719).

The privateers found success at Guayaquil, where Rogers and his men repeated the 1687 depredations of Grogniet and his followers (though with greater civility, Rogers claimed). A variety of prizes were subsequently taken off the northwest coast of South America, and Rogers was unopposed in occupying offshore islands; for example, the crew spent considerable time careening and victualing on Gorgona Island, well within sight of the Barbacoas coast of the Audiencia of Quito. Partly as a result of this casual treatment by the Spanish, whose South Sea armada had again fallen into disrepair, Rogers was able to execute the feat of feats, the capture of a Manila galleon on 2 January 1710 off Cabo San Lucas. The estimated value of the cargo of the galleon, the 400-ton *Nuestra Señora de la Encarnación*, was some two million pesos.[25] Unlike Dampier's earlier debacle, Rogers's voyage produced a substantial dividend, and his success helped fuel the ruinous English stock market crash of 1720 known as the South Sea Bubble.[26] As noted above, Rogers himself would return to American waters in short order, not as a pirate, but rather as a pirate-hunter. In this regard, he was far more scrupulous than William Kidd.

As the war ended in July of 1713, the Spanish South Sea again became a target of genuine pirates. The Treaty of Utrecht gave the English the slave asiento and the right to import one shipload of merchandise per year to Spanish America, but for English merchant-adventurers, this was far too small a concession, and numerous smugglers and pirates followed in Rogers's wake. An Englishman identified by Spanish sources as "Captain Charpes" was active in the South Sea with forty-eight Irish and twenty black crewmembers just as the war was ending, but few prizes were taken. In 1715 a veteran of Dampier's failed 1703–5 mission, John Clipperton, entered the Spanish Pacific in the *Prince Eugene*. Clipperton's pirates seized goods worth some 400,000 pesos off the Peruvian coast near Paita, but were captured by a Spanish war vessel off New Spain in 1716.[27]

Clipperton was soon released and by early 1719, in the midst of renewed hostilities with Spain (Philip V wanted the French throne after all), he set out from Plymouth on a South Sea privateering expedition. Clipperton commanded 180 men on the thirty-six-gun *Success* and George Shelvocke 106 men on the twenty-four-gun *Speedwell*. Clipperton was apparently an incorrigible alcoholic and neither he nor Shelvocke was considered an able leader. Both ships entered the Spanish Pacific during the southern hemisphere spring of 1719 and cruised separately for the next year-and-a-half. As in the case of Woodes Rogers and the earlier buccaneers, Clipperton and Shelvocke careened and victualed, entirely unmolested, on the various offshore islands of Juan Fernández, Gorgona, the Galápagos, Cocos, and Coiba. Their cruisings yielded little booty, but Clipperton managed to recapture his old ship, the *Prince Eugene*, in early 1720 somewhere north of the Galápagos chain. Eleven of Clipperton's men, eight African and three English, either deserted or were marooned on Cocos Island in January of 1721. Shelvocke had his own island difficulties at Juan Fernández, where the *Speedwell* ran aground and had to be dismantled in order to build an escape pinnace. The privateers sailed off in this vessel in mid-October of 1720 and soon after captured the 200-ton *Jesús María* near Pisco.

Sailing northward along the coast in this new vessel, and stopping only to terrorize the town of Paita for a day, Shelvocke eventually met up with Clipperton on Coiba Island on 5 February 1721. The two ships' crews had become so reduced by scurvy and desertion that only 120 men remained between them. Even this small number of sea-raiders could not hold together, however, apparently due to some unnamed personal animosity between the two captains. The quarrel led to a rapid split, Clipperton choosing to sail to the East Indies, where he lost his vessel, and Shelvocke remaining off the Pacific coast of North America in hopes of a lucky catch. None came his way and the war ended, so Shelvocke decided to sail to the East Indies in late August of 1721. When he at last returned to England the following year he was tried for piracy and embezzlement (Shelvocke had sold his ship in Macao and sailed home as a passenger), but apparently managed to evade his pursuers by sneaking off to the Netherlands.[28]

A few other pirating and smuggling missions found their way to the Spanish South Sea in the decades following the Clipperton–Shelvocke raids, but none, except that of George Anson (1741–44), which netted a silver-laden Manila galleon, found much success. Much more important in the years following the Treaty of Utrecht was the problem of piracy in the Caribbean Sea and along the Atlantic coast of North America. Unlike the semi-official privateers of the South Sea, these, the pirates of the last great cycle, were admittedly the most common of criminals, many of them anti-social bandits who scorned authority in general. To call them "anarchistic marauders," as authors like Robert Ritchie have, is perhaps unfair to anarchists, but the term does reflect their disdain for hierarchical government and for authority in general. These pirates were not simply parasites on Spanish settlements and shipping, but also on those of England, France, the Netherlands, and virtually everyone else after 1713. As a result of this generalized and growing predation on colonial holdings and commerce by aging buccaneers and out-of-work seamen, the increasingly powerful states of Europe declared unilateral war on piracy. The sea-rogues, it was agreed, were to be exterminated like so many cockroaches.

Although the Spanish state declined in political importance in Europe and slowly lost its monopoly grip on its American colonies, it was still Spanish America that supplied much of the world's bullion. By the early eighteenth century the treasure fleets of New Spain and Tierra Firme were too large and well armed for all but the most concerted of pirate efforts, yet they were still vulnerable in other ways. On 31 July 1715 the entire combined Spanish treasure fleet was smashed by a hurricane off Cape Canaveral, Florida, sinking seven million pesos' worth of bullion and coin along with great amounts of dyestuffs, tobacco, hides, and other raw materials. Over half of the 2,500 crewmembers and passengers unlucky enough to have boarded at Havana perished in the storm and its aftermath. Within days surviving Spanish officials began organizing salvage operations and by late October some five million pesos had been recovered by divers. Spain's English neighbors in the Carolinas, Jamaica, and elsewhere learned of this tragedy, and in spite of official peace they moved quickly to seek a share. The first outsiders to despoil the wrecks were not pirates, but rather "pirate-hunters" commissioned by the English governor of Jamaica, still based at Port Royal. These raiders, under command of Captains Jennings and Wills, attacked a coastal Spanish salvaging encampment and stole recovered treasure, including some 120,000 pesos in coin, in January of 1716.[29] Related acts of this kind included the capture of a small Spanish vessel off the south coast of Cuba by a black sea captain named Fernando Hernández, apparently a renegade Spanish subject commissioned by the governor of Jamaica. Hernández's actions, which netted some 250,000 pesos in cash and sumptuary goods, were viewed in the same light as Wills and Jennings's attacks on the treasure salvors by the Spanish: no matter what English authorities claimed, these were acts of piracy.

Spanish officials based in Havana protested and the English responded favorably; the Jamaican governor, Hamilton, was recalled, and the thieves, Jennings, Wills, and Hernández, were ordered arrested and sent to England. The fates of Wills and Hernández are not known, but Jennings escaped to the ramshackle settlement of New Providence, in the Bahamas, a site that was fast becoming the Anglo-American pirate base of choice. Partly in response to the 1715 wreck of the Spanish treasure fleet, the Bahamas attracted hundreds, perhaps even thousands of pirates between 1716 and 1718. Marcus Rediker has estimated that some 5,000 pirates cruised American waters between 1716 and 1726, with some 1,000 to 2,000 active at any given time.[30] Many, if not all, of the Anglo-Americans among these sea-rovers stopped at the Bahamas to careen, carouse, sell stolen goods, and plan new exploits. Since their exploits were not limited to raiding Spanish salvage operations and short-run trading vessels, the pirates were soon denounced in the court of the English king, George I (1714–27). Though the king did not allocate navy vessels or personnel for the operation, he approved a commission for a privately financed anti-pirate expedition to the Bahamas. The commission was granted to the former South Sea privateer Woodes Rogers in 1718, and despite some resistance he had a number of alleged sea-robbers hanged, leaving the Bahamas largely pirate-free by 1720. As if to show that fighting crime did *not* pay, Rogers died in Nassau a poor man in 1732.

In the meantime, however, pirate captains such as Edward Teach, John Rackam, Benjamin Hornigold, and others frequented Nassau and other Bahamian villages. While these individuals deserve special attention, it should be noted that something is known also of "the average pirate" during this period. Based on several samples of pirate crews active in the 1710s and 1720s, Rediker has shown that the common Anglo-American pirate was an unmarried, low-status male with experience in the merchant marine, privateering missions, or the Royal Navy, and was of an average age of twenty-seven years. In short, the pirate was much like any other seaman except for the fact that he chose to make his living "on account" rather than by the meager wages of legal employ.[31] Indeed, several observers remarked that when pirates overtook merchant vessels, the lowly and abused seamen who manned them were often all too willing to join their captors. The advantages of the pirate life were several for a common laborer with no better than a 50 percent chance of reaching the age of thirty.

Early eighteenth-century pirate command structures were, in the tradition of the buccaneers, far more democratic than those of the above-named institutions, and likewise these later freebooters compensated injured members before dividing booty into shares. Pirate captains and quartermasters, the two most elevated officers on board, were only slightly better compensated than the lowest sailor, thus reducing envy and other forms of "class" discontent. This, as Rediker rightly observes, was a reflection of how the pirates viewed themselves, as "risk-sharing partners," like joint-stock investors, rather than common "wage-laborers."[32] Although Rediker's argument that the eighteenth-century pirates were "social bandits" is rather strained considering the undeniable presence of sadistic tendencies, not to mention undisguised avarice among more than a few, it is clear that the average seaman in this era faced only grim alternatives in straight society.

That pirate society was unlike any found on land in the period is demonstrated by the examples of Ann Bonny and Mary Read, among only four or five female pirates on record for the early modern period. Read and Bonny sailed together in the crew of John Rackam, an experienced pirate known for his flamboyant dress. "Calico Jack," as Rackam was known, had taken over command of a pirate crew formerly led by Charles Vane, a notorious freebooter captain chased for two years by Woodes Rogers and eventually captured and hanged at Port Royal in March of 1720. Since pirate ships, like those of the privateers, merchant marine, and navy at this time, were generally same-sex outfits, Bonny and Read were forced to dress as men most of the time. Women on board ship were considered bad luck by some superstitious sailors, but more concrete was the possibility of sexual conflict, usually in the form of jealous infighting. In a story reminiscent of the life of the Basque nun-turned-lieutenant, Catalina de Erauso, whose martial exploits against the Dutch were noted in Chapter 3, Read and Bonny were cross-dressers before they became seaborne fighters. Their remarkable stories first appeared in

FIGURE 7.2 Ann Bonny and Mary Read

Source: Charles Johnson, *History of the Pyrates*, London: 1724 (courtesy of the James Ford Bell Library, University of Minnesota).

print in Charles Johnson's *General History of the Pyrates* (1724), and they captured the imaginations of thousands of readers when Johnson's work was translated into Dutch, French, and German.[55]

According to the story, Mary Read was born in London and Ann Bonny in some part of Ireland. Both were illegitimate and both were raised dressed as boys, Read because her mother sought support of relatives and Bonny because, apparently, she wanted to. Read followed a career much like Catalina Erauso's, enlisting in the army and fighting in Flanders and Holland. During this time she is said to have revealed her identity to a soldier whom she loved, but when he died she sailed to the West Indies to seek her fortune in a Dutch vessel. The ship was captured by pirates, whom Read joined, again fighting with the sort of courage she had shown in Europe. Bonny's life was different in that she was taken as a youth to South Carolina by her father, who established himself in Charleston as a planter and merchant. Bonny made a name for herself in the colonies by beating a would-be rapist within an inch of his life, and then by running off to join the pirates. Somewhere along the way she joined the crew of John Rackam, whom she courted, and made the acquaintance of her fellow cross-dresser, Mary Read. After numerous robberies both proved their courage one last time when their ship was finally captured by an English patrol vessel in 1720. According to Johnson's account, when their ship was boarded only the two women pirates "and one more" stood to face their attackers, pistols in hand. Read was so upset at the spinelessness of the crew that she shot and killed one of her companions. Read and Bonny escaped the gallows by "pleading their bellies" (i.e., claiming pregnancy, which was subsequently proved), but "Calico Jack" was not so lucky. Seeing her former lover at the gallows Ann Bonny is said to have remarked in disgust, "if he had fought like a Man, he need not have been hang'd like a Dog."[34]

Like many pirates who managed to escape the gibbet, the ends of the lives of Mary Read and Ann Bonny are less well known than their beginnings (Read was said to have died from fever in jail, Bonny to have escaped). Better known by far was the death of Edward Teach, a notoriously cruel and unusual pirate captain commonly called Blackbeard. Teach was a native either of Bristol or Jamaica (he had relatives in Spanish Town), where he signed on as a privateer during the War of the Spanish Succession. When the war ended Teach followed the somewhat predictable path to piracy, finding his way to the Bahamas in the company of the renowned pirate captain Benjamin Hornigold by 1717. His career was to be short but memorable, largely due to his theatrical tendencies, which included the habit of wearing slow-burning fuses in his twisted, dreadlockish hair. Leaving Spanish shipping and settlements alone for the most part, the two pirates, Teach now in command of his own sloop, cruised for Anglo-American ships along the Carolina and Virginia coasts. Sometime before 1718 they sailed back to the Caribbean, where Teach captured a Martinique-bound French vessel. This ship became the *Queen Anne's Revenge*, and it served as Blackbeard's floating fiefdom until his death in late November 1718. Using this vessel Teach led his band of pirates on numerous attacks in the West Indies and the Gulf of Honduras, still targeting English and French rather than Spanish ships. A much quoted snippet of Blackbeard's logbook deserves repeating as it evokes an atmosphere of on-board dissent blunted only by drink: "such a day, rum all out—our company somewhat sober—a damn'd confusion amongst us! Rogues a-plotting—great talk of separation—so I look'd sharp for a prize—such a day, took one, with a great deal of liquor on board, so kept the company hot, damned hot, then all things went well again."[35]

Hot or cold, Blackbeard's crew was generally successful, and by January 1718 he was terrorizing English ships around the Leeward Islands, particularly St. Christopher (St. Kitts). From here he sailed to the North Carolina coast, where he hoped to take advantage of an official amnesty for pirates who surrendered themselves. Rather than expose the pirate who had come his way, the local governor, Charles Eden, became Blackbeard's accessory, receiving a portion of booty (again, rather like an Algerian bey) in exchange for judicial immunity. Given this convenient arrangement, Blackbeard was allowed to terrorize the southeast coast of North America virtually at will until merchants complained to the governor of neighboring Virginia. Blackbeard was also said to be fond of terrorizing his own men, however, and in one instance apparently locked them in the ship's hold with him, forcing them to endure a fire and brimstone smoke-out. The test was meant to simulate hell, and perhaps unsurprisingly the last man out was Blackbeard, a smoking, hirsute vision of excess whom his crewmembers believed to be truly demonic. Blackbeard's pyrotechnics did not render him invincible, however, and an attack by two vessels sponsored by the Virginia governor, Spotswood,

FIGURE 7.3 Blackbeard the Pirate

Source: Charles Johnson, *History of the Pyrates*, London: 1724 (courtesy of the James Ford Bell Library, University of Minnesota).

overwhelmed him and a reduced crew near Ocracoke Inlet, North Carolina, on 22 November 1718. The battle was a close one, but Blackbeard fell at last, having sustained by one account some twenty pistol and cutlass wounds. Led by Lieutenant Robert Maynard of the Royal Navy, the pirate's killers sailed to the town of Bath, then on to Jamestown, all the while eliciting cheers as they glided by with Blackbeard's gruesome-looking severed head hanging from the bowsprit of their sloop.[36] Such baroque displays of criminal body parts were slow to die in the early modern Americas, and according to legend Blackbeard's skull was made into a base for a punchbowl in a Williamsburg tavern.

In this era of bizarre and notable pirate captains, Bartholomew Roberts, a.k.a. "Black Bart," stands out as a paradoxical figure. Roberts, a Welshman, began his career as a slaver and only turned pirate after being captured by freebooters off the Guinea Coast in 1719. Similarly intriguing perhaps was Stede Bonnet, an associate of Blackbeard who was said to have abandoned a prosperous sugar plantation on Barbados to become a pirate simply to escape his overbearing wife. But Roberts was unusual for other reasons, most importantly for his ability to balance discipline with criminal audacity; indeed, he was arguably the most organized, and consequently the most successful, sea criminal of his day. Whereas pirate crews like Blackbeard's seemed helpless, or rather mutinous, without rum, Roberts was a sober man and did not allow his followers to drink aboard ship. Likewise, Roberts forbade women and boys to travel in his company, a departure from the ways of the unfortunate Calico Jack Rackam, captain and sometime lover to Ann Bonny. Indeed, Black Bart resembled more the authoritarianism of the Royal Navy (and the puritanism of the English middle class) than the quasi-anarchism of the pirate tradition. Roberts's departure from the straight path was clear-cut nevertheless, and he quickly established himself as a bold and unforgiving sea predator.

Black Bart's first notable act of piracy was not committed in the Spanish Caribbean or along the coasts of North America but rather in Brazil, where several ships of a merchant fleet were pillaged off Bahia. The attack yielded some 40,000 moidores (gold coins, Portuguese *moedas*) and a diamond-studded cross, which Roberts took to wearing around his neck from this time onward—it was a fine complement to his damask suit and feathered cap.[37] From Brazil Roberts and his crew ranged widely in American waters, attacking ships from Barbados to Jamaica, then, in a wide detour, off the Newfoundland Banks, many leagues to the north. As in the case of Edward Teach, Roberts seems to have preyed mostly upon English and French rather than Spanish or Dutch shipping, and apparently as a result of some injustices received at the hands of officials based at Barbados and Martinique, Black Bart flew a flag depicting himself standing on two human skulls, the letters "A.B.H." and "A.M.H." beneath them. The initials were symbols of Roberts's thirst for vengeance and stood for "A Barbadian's Head" and "A Martinican's Head" (see Figure 7.1). How many Barbadians and Martinicans actually lost their heads to Black Bart and his men is unknown, but the symbolism of the flag follows Marcus Rediker's suggestion that many pirates in this period were deeply antagonistic toward familiar authorities.[38] Symbols of class antagonism such as these were certainly genuine, but they should not be taken at face value. Pirates since the time of Drake (if not before) had used the notion of vengeance as a pretext for robbing innocent parties; past insults and humiliations need not be classist to serve as an excuse to plunder. To draw a modern analogy, it is no accident that thieves often bear intense personal hatreds toward the police, but it is the appropriation of property belonging to others that motivates them first, not these "class" or anti-authoritarian hatreds.

That Black Bart was as materialistic as he was idealistic is further evidenced by his unmatched record of 400 ships captured by 1721. Fortune's wheel was turning for the successful pirate and the crew of the *Royal Fortune*, however, and the end came near Parrot Island off the Guinea Coast on 10 February 1722. Roberts was killed by a single shot to the throat in a firefight with an English man-of-war, the *Swallow*, under command of the colorfully named Captain Chaloner Ogle, and his body was thrown overboard in full regalia (as per his instructions) before the battle ended. The remaining crewmembers had what might be called the royal misfortune of surviving only to be hanged soon after at Cape Coast Castle, a slaving post on the central coast of present-day Ghana.[9] In this, their final act, Black Bart's men joined the 400–500-odd pirates (of all nationalities) hanged by English colonial authorities between 1716 and 1726.[10] Though public fascination with pirates and their audacious exploits grew enormously in precisely these years—the crueler and more outlandish their deeds the better—official policy had turned sharply against them. For merchants and other victims of such men as Bartholomew Roberts and Edward Teach, pirates were vermin, not heroes. Like Kidd and Avery in the days before the War of the Spanish Succession, they were to be hunted down and exterminated as soon as possible. The campaign was so successful that by 1730 almost no one expected pirate attacks in the Americas, including the captains of Spain's beleaguered but still bullion-rich flotas. War at sea was to be endemic in the eighteenth century, but the era of the freebooters was over.

BOX 7 SEA FOOD, OR THE PIRATE DIET

The average seaman did not eat well in the early eighteenth century and judging from journals and other writings the average pirate fared little better, at least most of the time. Rations consisted of salt meat, usually pork or beef, or salt fish, four or more times a week, along with some cheese, butter, peas, and rock-hard sea biscuit. Another favorite source of carbohydrates and protein among northern European pirates was boiled dumplings, called "dough-boys," often cooked in seawater to conserve precious stores of fresh water, especially on long voyages. Fresh foods, particularly vegetables and anti-scorbutic fruits (lemons and limes were best, oranges and grapefruits good), but also meats, were highly prized, and pirates could be said to have raided coastal settlements for fresh victuals at least as often as for booty (recall the rawhide-eating pirates of Morgan's day). Scurvy, a debilitating condition of generalized tissue breakdown caused by a chronic lack of ascorbic acid (or vitamin C) in the diet, was not well understood in early modern times, but by the early eighteenth century most sailors knew that citrus fruits and juices helped prevent it. Only the pirates who made extended (i.e., over six-week-long) voyages to the Pacific and Indian Oceans needed to worry about this disease, but even so it seems to have been much more common among Dutch and English rather than French and Iberian crews. English merchant and navy captains and supercargos were in fact much hated for shorting seamen their due rations, which by this time included a critical juice allowance (Rediker, *Between the Devil and the Deep Blue Sea*, 40).

At sea the catch of the day, usually trapped, but also netted and hooked, included modern-day restaurant favorites such as snapper, shark, catfish, grouper, albacore, and many others. William Dampier mentions pickling shark flesh with pepper and vinegar off the west coast of Africa during an early 1680s pirate cruise (Dampier, *New Voyage Round the World*, 107). By contrast, Spanish sailors usually ate salt cod (*bacallao*) from the North Atlantic and sardines, along with rice, beans, and the inevitable biscuit. According to Carla Rahn Phillips, the average Spanish seaman's diet was, contrary to popular belief, well rounded and highly caloric in the early seventeenth century (and probably later, as well; see Phillips, *Six Galleons*, 164). It is unlikely that the pirates of the next century lived so well, but generalizations about how poor their diet was should be approached with caution. One pirate favorite not to be found in most restaurants today was sea turtle, a meat considered among the most delicate in the world and certainly the best to be found in the West Indies.

Though North Atlantic sailors probably preferred to baste their catch with butter rather than olive oil, the taste for sea tortoise was most likely borrowed from the Spanish—who in turn probably learned of it from Native Americans. As Phillips notes, tortoise was a popular ship-board meat on the early seventeenth-century American treasure fleets, usually laded at Havana (Phillips, *Six Galleons*, 164). As in the days of the buccaneers, the early eighteenth-century pirates prepared turtle and other fresh flesh in myriad ways aboard ship, always careful not to set fire to planks and rigging. On land, of course, the barbecue method was always preferred. In some regions, such as the Spanish Pacific, sea lions and seals were butchered, but feral goats, when available, were considered far more edible; an anonymous pirate of the 1680–81 Sharp voyage to the South Sea notes in one journal entry, for example: "Our men feasted on shoar with Barbakude, Goats and Fish &c" (Philip Ayres, ed., *Voyages and Adventures of Captain Bartholomew Sharp and Others in the South Sea*, 22). In the Caribbean and Gulf coast regions of the Americas, manatees, which some imaginative (or drunk) sailors mistook for mermaids, provided at least a healthy dose of fat. Another Caribbean favorite was "salamagundi," a spicy, pickled fish plate that Black Bart was said to have enjoyed just before his death off the coast of Africa (see recipe below). In extreme southern latitudes pirates ate penguins, but no one seems to have sung their praises.

Salamagundi (Jamaican-style)

4 large pickled herrings	salt and pepper
1 breast of cold chicken, cooked and minced	lettuce
	radishes
3 apples, minced	tomatoes
3 onions, cooked and minced	1 hard-boiled egg

Slit each herring along the side, being careful not to take the cut right to the head or tail, keeping the fish intact. Carefully scrape out the flesh and remove the bones. Clean the fish skin, pound the flesh with chicken, apples, and onions, season with pepper and salt. Pack the mixture inside the fish skins till they look full and plump. (Old Jamaican recipes tell you to garnish with barberries and samphire, but failing these, a bed of lettuce and a garnish of sliced radishes, tomatoes, and egg are very good indeed.) Serves four (In Mary Slater, *Cooking the Caribbean Way* [London: Spring Books, 1965], 51; similar recipes for salamagundi [or "salmagundi"] can be found in numerous eighteenth- and nineteenth-century North American cookbooks. The word also came to refer to any miscellany, as in Washington Irving's early nineteenth-century literary journal, *Salmagundi*.).

All of these interesting if not always nourishing "sea foods" had to be washed down with something, and it is in the realm of drink that the pirates excelled as connoisseurs. Water was necessary even for the most incorrigible alcoholics, but it was often in short supply and was difficult to preserve given the sealing technology of the time. In its stead North European pirates drank beer whenever possible, though never "small beer" (i.e., light beer with little alcohol), which they derided as an unmanly beverage fit only for women and children. Brandy was a favorite in the seventeenth century, and William Cowley noted in his journal that the crewmembers of the *Bachelor's Delight* found themselves able to hold three quarts of the stuff per day without noticeable effect in the extreme cold of Cape Horn (in William Hack, ed., *A Collection of Original Voyages* [London: James Knapton, 1699], 7). Around the turn of the eighteenth century, Woodes Rogers, the privateer captain and later pirate-hunting governor of the Bahamas, noted in his journal that common sailors drank deeply of a concoction known as "flip," apparently consisting of beer, rum, and sugar, warmed and served in a tin can (Rogers, *A Cruising Voyage Round the World*, 5) (for a more eggnog-like and less nauseating modern flip recipe, see below). Another spiced and sweetened favorite was "bumboe" (or "bombo"), a sort of rum punch common since medieval times. What the English called "rum" (the term originated in Barbados in the 1620s, apparently) was essentially hard alcohol distilled from molasses in the Spanish (*aguardiente*) or Portuguese (*cachaça*) fashion. Straight rum was issued with rations even on navy ships, but pirates seem to have been far more generous in their portions, as evidenced by Blackbeard's suggestion of binge drinking aboard the *Queen Anne's Revenge*. "Grog" was a later invention, and referred simply to a watered-down rum ration. Spanish and Portuguese ships were especially prized by pirates since they often carried substantial quantities of wines and brandies—much of this was for trade, presumably, but the average Spanish sailor's ration included a liter or so of wine per day, at least in Hapsburg times. Portuguese and Madeira wines, along with Spanish and Canarian sack (or sherry) were hugely popular in England in both war and peacetime, but distant parts of the Spanish Pacific also produced fine grape spirits, especially along the Chilean and Peruvian coasts. The town of Pisco, in particular, was justly famous for its clear, *quebranta* grape brandies. Raveneau de Lussan relates that Captain Davis's crew, possibly after having savored Pisco's finest, was so incredibly drunk in an encounter with Spanish vessels near Lima that they failed in *twenty* attempts to come alongside their prey (Lussan, *Voyage to the South Seas*, Wilbur trans., 215). Hard liquor was generally stored in bottles and jugs, wine and beer more often in wooden casks of varying sizes. Seventeenth-century pirates such as Esquemeling and Ringrose often spoke of opening "pipes" of Spanish or Portuguese wine, a reference to a very large cask, or *pipa*, weighing about 345 kg. As might be expected, it was customary to keep drinking steadily until either the pipe ran dry or one's consciousness slipped away, whichever occurred first.

Egg and Rum Flip

1 egg	1 teaspoon rum
1 teaspoon sugar	1/4 pint milk

Separate the egg. Cream yolk thoroughly with sugar. Add rum and milk. Whip white stiffly and fold in. Serve chilled. (It is hard to imagine the pirates taking such care to "fold" their egg whites when concocting flip, but the general idea survives.) (Recipe in Slater, *Cooking the Caribbean Way*, 235).

Perhaps the most common vice among pirates and other early modern seamen was tobacco smoking, and supplying this habit was considered, like the standard issue of rum, an aspect of victualing. As in Henry Morgan's time, the pirates often smoked to stave off hunger and thirst—it was not unusual, after all, to sail for a week or more surviving on nothing but a handful of maize kernels, a gulp of water, and several pipes of tobacco per day. The long-distance tobacco trade was growing rapidly in the early eighteenth century, and Anglo-American seamen were commonly employed by Scottish merchants, who shipped thousands of hogsheads (barrels weighing over 200 kg) of the leaf to European markets, much of it contraband. Tobacco was produced throughout the Caribbean and in Brazil by this time, but Virginia's product was generally considered superior among Anglo-Americans. Wherever it originated, tobacco was normally smoked by pirates and others in long-stemmed clay pipes, and occasionally in cigars; in whatever form, the vice was loudly decried as a kind of drunkenness by Puritans and other moralists. As an indication of the approximate popularity of pipe smoking in this period, the archaeologist Robert Marx discovered more than 500 clay pipes, most of them pre-smoked and bearing a wide variety of maker's marks, in the vicinity of a single tavern destroyed by the Port Royal earthquake of 1692—more amazingly, perhaps, Marx recovered some 12,000 pipes from the site in all (Marx, *Pirate Port*, 126). Indeed, when common seamen broke into their ships' stores, they most often stole tobacco and rum, suggesting that when they became pirates their first desire was access to unlimited quantities of both (Rediker, *Between the Devil and the Deep Blue Sea*, 129). Though these vices of excessive drinking and heavy tobacco use no doubt led to death by cancer and liver damage in some cases, the average pirate more often died by violence or infectious disease before the effects of toxic habits could manifest themselves. To be sure, only a few pirates might have lived long enough to die in the *delirium tremens* of Robert Louis Stevenson's paranoid buccaneer character, Billy Bones. The true "black spot," perhaps, was on this old pirate's liver.

Notes

1 Clarence H. Haring, *Buccaneers in the West Indies in the Seventeenth Century* (London: Methuen, 1910), 240.

2 Ibid., 242–43. This episode is beautifully recounted in David Marley's *Sack of Veracruz: The Great Pirate Raid of 1683* (Windsor, Ontario: Netherlandic Press, 1993). The remarkable story of John Murphy, aka "Juan Morf" is told on pp. 18 and 47–48. See also the account and partial document transcriptions in Juan Juárez Moreno, *Corsarios y piratas en Veracruz y Campeche* (Seville: EEHA/CSIC, 1972).

3 Haring, *Buccaneers*, 246.

4 Ibid., 251. Landresson headed the last French buccaneers in the Pacific before being replaced by "Captain Franco."

5 Ibid., 251. See also Mark Hanna, *Pirate Nests and the Rise of the British Empire, 1570–1740* (Chapel Hill: University of North Carolina Press, 2015); and the classic account by George F. Dow and John H. Edmonds, *The Pirates of the New England Coast, 1630–1730* (Salem, MA: Marine Research Society, 1923).

6 Haring, *Buccaneers*, 254.

7 Ibid., 258.

8 A merchant, quoted in Robert Marx, *Pirate Port: The Story of the Sunken City of Port Royal* (Cleveland: World, 1967), 16.

9 Haring, *Buccaneers*, 261. Jean-Pierre Moreau, in his wide-ranging *Pirates: flibuste et piraterie dans la Caraïbe et les mers du sud, 1522–1725*. (Paris: Tallandier, 2006), chapter 7, calls this the era of "bourgeois filibusters."

10 Ibid., 265–66.

11 Avery and Kidd's stories are drawn largely from Robert C. Ritchie, *Captain Kidd and the War against the Pirates* (Cambridge: Harvard University Press, 1986); Avery is quoted on p. 86. For documents relating to Kidd and Avery, see J. Franklin Jameson, ed., *Privateering and Piracy in the Colonial Period: Illustrative Documents* (New York: Macmillan, 1923), 153–257.

12 Ritchie, *Captain Kidd*, 87–89. See also Peter Earle's brisk account of Avery and the other "Red Sea Men" in *Pirate Wars* (London: Methuen, 2003), chapter 7.

13 Mrs. Kidd owned another house on Wall Street, future home of the New York Stock Exchange.

14 Ritchie, *Captain Kidd*, 75–78.

15 Ibid., 65–66, 102.

16 Ibid., 106.

17 With musical notation in Philip Gosse, *The History of Piracy* (London: Longman, Green, 1932), 183. For an earlier version of this ballad, see Jameson, *Privateering and Piracy*, 253–57.

18 Ritchie, *Captain Kidd*, 108.

19 Ibid., 165.

20 Ibid., 209.

21 Ibid., 155, 161. The rise of the English Navy in response to piracy at this time is thrust of Peter Earle's *Pirate Wars*.

22 I am drawing here from the excellent narrative of these attacks by Charles R. Boxer, *The Golden Age of Brazil, 1695–1750: Growing Pains of a Colonial Society* (Berkeley: University of California Press, 1962).

23 Peter Kemp and Christopher Lloyd, *Brethren of the Coast: The British and French Buccaneers in the South Seas* (London: Heinemann, 1960), 140.

24 Peter Gerhard, *Pirates on the West Coast of New Spain, 1575–1742* (Cleveland: Arthur H. Clark, 1960), 205–9.

25 Ibid., 214.

26 Peter T. Bradley, *The Lure of Peru: Maritime Intrusion into the South Sea, 1598–1701* (New York: St. Martin's Press, 1989), 189.

27 Gerhard, *Pirates on the West Coast of New Spain*, 218–19.

28 Ibid., 220–26. For a full account, see Kenneth Poolman, *The* Speedwell *Voyage: A Tale of Piracy and Mutiny in the Eighteenth Century* (Annapolis: Naval Institute Press, 1999).

29 Mendel Peterson, *The Funnel of Gold* (Boston: Little, Brown, 1975), 365, 371.

30 Marcus Rediker, *Between the Devil and the Deep Blue Sea: Merchant Seamen, Pirates, and the Anglo-American Maritime World, 1700–1750* (Cambridge: Cambridge University Press, 1987), 256.

31 Ibid., 260.

32 Ibid., 264. The argument is expanded in Rediker's *Villains of All Nations: Atlantic Pirates in the Golden Age* (Boston: Beacon Press, 2004).

33 Marcus Rediker, "Liberty Beneath the Jolly Roger," in Margaret S. Creighton and Lisa Norling, eds., *Iron Men, Wooden Women: Gender and Seafaring in the Atlantic World, 1700–1920* (Baltimore: Johns Hopkins University Press, 1996), 3. This essay is also expanded in Rediker's *Villains of All Nations*, chapter 6. See also Jo Stanley, *Bold in Her Breeches: Women Pirates across the Ages* (London: Pandora, 1995), chapters 9–11.

34 Ibid., 5.

35 Quoted in Peterson, *Funnel of Gold*, 430 (also in Gosse, *History of Piracy*, 194).

36 Peterson, *Funnel of Gold*, 437. Remains of Blackbeard's flagship, the *Queen Anne's Revenge*, have apparently been located near Beaufort, North Carolina (*New York Times*, 4 March 1997, A8). Similar recovery efforts have been under way for some years on Samuel Bellamy's ship *Whidah*, wrecked 27 April 1717 off Cape Cod (the wreck is described in Peterson, *Funnel of Gold*, 446–47). Bellamy, by the way, had himself salvaged the 1715 Florida treasure wrecks.

37 Gosse, *History of Piracy*, 188.

38 Rediker, *Between the Devil and the Deep Blue Sea*, 269.

39 Gosse, *History of Piracy*, 189.

40 Rediker, *Between the Devil and the Deep Blue Sea*, 283.

CONCLUSION

The violent deaths of Bartholomew Roberts, Edward Teach, and other such prominent pirates in the 1710s and 1720s marked the end of an era. A brief reprise of piracy in the Caribbean would occur a century later, during the various Spanish American independence struggles, but for the most part piracy, at least in its quasi-anarchistic and endemic seventeenth-century form, was already the stuff of legend in Blackbeard's day. What is one to make of this extended episode of sea predation and its principals? This study has attempted to treat the early modern pirates in their broader world historical context, to de-mythologize the actors and their activities while still acknowledging their individual audacity and cunning. As shown earlier in various examples, the pirates' stories are compelling enough without embellishment. Indeed, as with other topics in early modern history, such as long-distance trade, witchcraft, and slavery, the truth about piracy was often stranger than anything imagined by writers of fiction. Likewise, the early modern sea-rovers when viewed from more than simply post hoc nationalist perspectives were not the two-dimensional heroes or villains their contemporaries made them out to be. As was true of Christopher Columbus, Francis Drake was neither a saint nor a "dragon," but rather an unnervingly complex figure who made the most of his circumstances. The same could be said of Sefer Reis, Limahon, or Koxinga. Though motivated by the possibilities of easy wealth in distant seas—much like the early discoverers and conquistadors, perhaps—the pirates were not simply greedy men with fast ships and big guns. (Or, at least not *all* of them were greedy men with fast ships and big guns.)

The age of piracy also coincided with the beginnings of European political and religious expansion, and in these struggles' very competitive overseas aspects the pirates often played important roles. In the case of the Barbary Coast and early French corsairs, the complexities of the Iberian Reconquest and the Protestant Reformation meant that acts of violence against Spanish and Portuguese shippers and colonists took on broader implications besides the simple pecuniary. Ottoman-sponsored corsairing in the Indian Ocean was similarly charged with the fervor of faith. Likewise, the acts of most Elizabethan and Dutch raiders entailed some kind of political or religious subtext—always subordinate to plunder, of course, but still present in the form of charred corpses and smashed altars. Indeed, in spite of long distances and relative isolation, no one, neither pirate, colonist, nor merchant, acted unaware of newly globalized political, economic, and religious rivalries. With this in mind, it becomes clear that what the Spanish and Portuguese almost universally called piracy was in this earlier stage more often privateering. Home governments, however weak, usually condoned rather than decried the predatory acts of their subjects abroad, especially those against "hypocrites" and "papists" thought to be living too well "beyond the line." By the sixteenth century Spain and Portugal, in the envious eyes of Dutch, French, and English burghers and monarchs, had become too big, too strong, and too rich. In the absence of deep coffers and professional navies, self-sponsored pirates could be a handy weapon in the struggle to break the Iberians' Catholic grip on the wealth of the world. Arguably it was the Ottomans who responded most forcefully to Iberian overseas expansion.

The age of piracy also coincided with the rise of merchant empires, and the pirates of the sixteenth and seventeenth centuries were often accomplished contrabandists, commercial interlopers in regions claimed or settled by Spain and Portugal. Portuguese assertions of maritime dominion in the Indian Ocean turned peaceful merchants unwilling to buy passes into pirates while also encouraging the growth of traditional pirate cultures such as that of the Malabar Coast. Others copied the Portuguese by establishing regional extortion rackets. That contraband traders were often turned away violently, as in the cases of John Hawkins on the coast of Mexico and the Dutch salt-miners of northeastern Venezuela, led to acts of vengeance, acts that were often out of proportion with the original, perceived insult. Such painful reprisals against contrabandists served as pretext rather than motive for plunder, however. Given the prevailing mercantilist conceptions of wealth throughout the early modern era, it was expected that monopolies would be guarded like sovereign territories and only breached by force of arms, like city walls. Thus English, French, and Dutch trader-pirates in the first half of this era could expect to return home to a welcome reception in their respective European capitals—no matter what their crimes "beyond the line." In London, Paris, and Amsterdam they sold their booty, told tales of unprotected wealth, sought financing for further ventures, received titles for their alleged bravery, and so forth. Only in the later seventeenth century, with the simultaneous appearance of Caribbean island-based buccaneers and more open markets, can one talk of pirates as universally criminal, randomly acting sea-robbers. They might be church-desecrating English Protestants or reverent French Catholics, but when silver, spices, silks, and liquors were to be had, the seventeenth-century buccaneers knew no gods but Mammon and Bacchus—and no laws but their own.

These pirates were unlike many of their predecessors socially, as well. The French corsairs had been led by petty nobles and rebellious Huguenots in the sixteenth century, and the booty they took does not seem to have been distributed democratically. The Elizabethan pirates and corsairs seem to have been similarly hierarchical, though the distribution of loot among crews like Drake's appears to have been considered generous for its time. Malabari pirates were famous for their potlatch-like generosity to the poor and for giving tribute to their land-based protectors, but we do not know how they rewarded themselves. Perhaps the worst off among common pirate-sailors were the Dutch *varendvolk*, or common company seamen, who seem never to have been content with their rations, wages, shares, or instructions. To say that the seventeenth-century buccaneers and later pirates were a departure from Baroque hierarchies would be an understatement. They had leaders and certainly bickered over the distribution of shares, but in essence the buccaneers and freebooters were self-governing, near-egalitarian, conscientious of the welfare of their fellows, and more interested in great times than great titles. In short, they actively rejected the rigid class biases then entrenched in Europe and self-consciously mimicked in the colonies. Many, such as Henry Morgan and Alexander Exquemelin, had experienced personal hardships as servants or soldiers in the West Indies and chose the buccaneer life for the almost unbelievable freedom it offered them. In turning pirate, the buccaneers and others mocked European conventions of estate, sexuality, religious authority, and judicial process, and on occasion even disregarded, as in the cases of Diego el Mulato (both of them), Mary Read, and Ann Bonny, the color and gender prejudices of their day. From this perspective the seventeenth- and early eighteenth-century pirates seem almost to have been true revolutionaries, quasi-anarchists in the age of absolutism. Yet from the perspective of their Spanish, Portuguese, and increasingly northern European (and finally Mughal) victims as well, the pirates, male or female, low-born or high, were heartless criminals, vicious individuals who had rejected civilized society in favor of barbarism, greed, and bloodlust. From this perspective the sea-robbers were not social bandits at all but rather incorrigible thieves, murderers, rapists, heretics, renegades, and foreigners, always "evil" and always "other" (yet somehow strangely familiar).

In this last sense the pirates were destined to be almost mythical figures in the European and colonial American imaginations, even in their own day. Towering "self-made" figures like Koxinga seem to have been similarly mythologized in parts of East Asia; uncertainty and imperial rivalries made their rags-to-riches stories possible. In an age of royal excesses and heightened dramatic awareness, particularly in Restoration England, but also in Louis XIV's France and Carlos II's Spain, the very idea that an unremarkable pickpocket could transform himself into the "King of Pyrates"—or an orphan-girl into their queen—after a brief career in the distant Caribbean or Indian Ocean had great appeal. It was the age-old story of the little beggar making good, snubbing and even bettering, and finally buying the authorities, those pompous enemies of the people. The tale of the successful pirate served as high drama for the lower classes, stark testimony of the unpredictable fortunes of the ambitious and unethical.

Still, the growth of piracy, whatever its social causes, was becoming a significant economic threat to the same nations that spawned it. For the stockholders of the various European overseas trading firms multiplying in this era, pirate stories were not for contemplating and laughing about—as far as they were concerned there was no moral lesson to be learned from true tales of larceny on the high seas. Whereas in the late seventeenth century buccaneers such as William Dampier, Basil Ringrose, and Raveneau de Lussan were rewarded for the information they gathered, like freelance heroes in the age of reconnaissance, by the early 1700s a pirate without a bounty on his head was a rare figure, bundles of maps and notes under his arm notwithstanding.

In sum, the pirates of the early modern era have been subjected to perhaps more revisionism—and blatant invention—than any other single identifiable group active in the period, this in spite of their marginality. Also, like other inter-stitial or "liminal" actors in the unscripted drama of world history, the pirates of the "Great Age" have been both over- and underrated as agents of change. Their actions were often irrational, even in the short run, and it was not uncommon for them to miss enormous payoffs due to drunkenness, infighting, or ignorance. In the long run, however, the pirates appear to have followed a generally rational pattern; they identified and clustered around "choke points," singled out straggling ships, repeatedly attacked known bullion storage ports, and so on. To paraphrase "Slick Willie" Sutton's famous reference to bank-robbers' affinity for banks, the pirates robbed Spanish ships and ports because "that's where the money was."

Pirate attacks and pirate threats notwithstanding, Spain continued to build its colonial empire—part export enclave, part articulated regional economy—and in the overall scheme of things the pirate raids were not as significant as some historians have believed. For example, defense costs, when weighed against the overall volume of Spanish trade in the early modern period, were not outrageous. Spain and Portugal spent far more of their treasure defending regional land claims (including their own borders up to 1668), and shipwrecks were so frequent they generated a whole genre of baleful literature. Yet the pirates were a significant nuisance, it can be argued, since it was in the attempt, mostly after the turn of the seventeenth century, to defend distant ports and seas that Spain and Portugal were first forced to shoulder substantial economic burdens that yielded no income. The pirates may not have reaped the treasures they were after, but they certainly sowed their share of fear; direct hits like Piet Heyn's or Henry Morgan's were rare, but indirect losses in unused armaments, soldiers' salaries, and unnecessary fortifications grew to be substantial, if not staggering. Only three years after its founding, Limahon revealed the vulnerability and hence the cost of defending Manila. Exactly how costly overseas colonies were cannot be known with precision, but the Iberian empires would most certainly have been happier and more prosperous without them. Instead, whether in the Mediterranean, Indian Ocean, or East Atlantic, the Caribbean or great Pacific, pirates were simply a fact of early modern life. Successful or unlucky, deviants or high-born courtiers, Muslims, Hindus, Jews, or Christians, the pirates have continued to fascinate, and evade, modern researchers. They remain as enigmatic and elusive, perhaps, as Stevenson's memorable pirate and cook, Long John Silver. The present study is nothing more than an essay, an attempt to plumb the depths of meaning of Silver's parrot's cry, the unforgettable: "Pieces of eight! Pieces of eight!"

AFTERWORD TO THE SECOND EDITION

Piracy is among the world's oldest professions, and it shows no signs of disappearing. The post-Cold War world of permeable borders, instant communications, untraceable investments, and sparse regulation has proved amenable to sea robbers. With the explosive growth of global trade in recent decades, cycles of piracy have irrupted in the South China Sea, the Malacca Strait, and the Gulf of Aden, to name only a few hot spots. Pirate attacks have been costly for global shippers and terrifying for victims, but the cost of suppressing them remains daunting. As of this writing, no nation, corporation, or international coalition seems willing to police the seas.

Today's pirates have been aided by weak and so-called failed states, both products in part of post-Cold War neglect, as well as by the growth of international crime organizations engaged in drug smuggling, human trafficking, wire fraud, and many other schemes. Incidents of maritime theft, kidnapping, and extortion have been reported along the coasts of Africa, in ports and waters off Central and South America, and even on the Amazon River. Pirates have also returned to their fabled haunts in the Caribbean and Mediterranean. Are today's pirates fundamentally different from those of yesteryear?

Contemporary observers have been loath to describe post-Cold War pirates as romantic mavericks or loveable rogues. From the perspective of victims, whether ship owners, crews, investors, or tourists, today's pirates are faceless, stateless, "global" criminals. Some East African and Southeast Asian pirates have been demonized by the West's so-called War on Terror since September 11, 2001, yet pirates' links to militant Islam and other ideological movements remain tenuous.[1] Terror has always been a favorite pirate tactic, but not much more so than for terrestrial bank robbers. On the other side, for pirates to proclaim themselves jihadists would seem suicidal, especially in the age of drones, although it would certainly add fear. Perhaps in the literature of the world's poorest and most marginalized countries we will see the appearance of a Somalian Jack Sparrow or a Filipino Mary Read. Such figures no doubt already exist in story and song.

Has the definition of piracy changed? I do not think so. Pirates today, like those of history, survive as parasites on global seaborne trade and transport. Although pirates have long claimed to be motivated by social injustice or political oppression, they are by definition opportunists seeking pecuniary gain. Their aim is to profit by skimming from capital and human movements in unpatrolled waters. Some recent observers have argued that the frequent taking and ransoming of hostages makes today's pirates different, presumably more contemptible than their forebears, but this unsavory method of securing booty is as old as piracy itself.[2]

Defining piracy and identifying pirates' practices are necessary exercises, but framing contemporary sea raiding as nothing more than armed robbery with speedboats, automatic rifles, and cellphones still rests on a range of assumptions. Most of these derive from, on the one hand, the legacy of several centuries of European overseas imperialism, and on the other, the global human rights movement that emerged after World War II. Are today's pirates anti-imperialists whose crimes constitute protest against neo-colonialism? Most observers would say "no" given today's map of nation-states, but scholars should probably listen closely to modern pirate rationales to understand variations. From a human rights perspective, are today's pirates crueler than the many outsiders who, after the death of economic nationalism, have relentlessly extracted their countries' fish, timber, petroleum, fresh water, and minerals? Again, we might resist the "high-low" comparison, but even St. Augustine pondered the pirate's claim of relative innocence against the land-based pillager Alexander the Great. Both Alexander and his pirate captive might today be charged with crimes against humanity.

Scholars tend to take sides, depicting today's pirates—like those in the past—as either obstacles to global peace and prosperity or as local freedom fighters or anarchists holding out against evil empires. The rise of "anti-imperialist," communist China would seem to throw a monkey wrench into these old, bipolar equations, but China's thoroughly capitalist thirst for resources and vast shipping capacity have put it firmly on the side of the West when it comes to contemporary piracy. China's global commercial empire, like so many before it, has already taken on the roles of both pillager and pillaged. Pirates are given no quarter as "social bandits."

It is my hope that readers of this new edition of *Pillaging the Empire* will contemplate this age-old tension between the formal global political economy and its informal or criminal challengers. As argued in the first edition, understanding piracy as a dynamic rather than a static social or economic phenomenon requires taking into account change over time as well as different perspectives even within the same global context, down to the same moment or incident. We have to ask whenever possible what perpetrators, victims, and enforcers or "suppressors" saw and what they thought they were doing in any given instance, *Rashomon*-style. The pirate historian's central conundrum may not concern scale, as in the question of "the pirate and the emperor" cited by St. Augustine, but rather perspective. Can piracy be in the eye of the beholder while also being an objective fact?

In the world of entertainment, the Disney Corporation's *Pirates of the Caribbean* franchise, led through the 2000s by the inimitable Johnny Depp, inspired millions of enthusiasts and took pirate fantasy into the realm of the undead. "Pirated" copies of the Disney films have no doubt far outsold authorized ones, with profits trickling down to the street hawkers of Dhaka, Manila, and Port-au-Prince. This leads to another post-Cold War issue: an Internet search today using the word "piracy" skips the high seas in favor of the murky cyber-world of copyright infringement, as well as counterfeit merchandise branding. Cyberspace may in fact be a new kind of lawless ocean, with phishers, hackers, identity thieves, and "wiki-leakers" as new kinds of pirates. But "real" Somalian pirates, along with their victims and heavily armed opponents, have also been depicted on the silver screen.

Scholars of piracy have been busy in recent years as well, and in many fields. Literary critics, economists, political scientists, anthropologists, archaeologists, and sociologists have all examined piracy, applying new models and methodologies. Piracy has also drawn new interest from historians of science and art, and more conventional historians of piracy have been swept along by the rise of Atlantic history, world history, and—for the era of emerging nation-states—transnational history.[3]

Legal historians have explored the importance of piracy in the rise of international law and the so-called Law of the Sea. Lauren Benton, for example, has traced changing Western European conceptions of overseas "jurisdiction" versus "dominion" as they grew out of conflicts over pillage and reprisal.[4] Others have linked piracy to cycles of empire building and contraction, with pirates and privateers serving as essential if unwashed subcontractors of state violence. Still others have explored the activities of women pirates along with women who sponsored or harbored them. Historians and literary specialists have also awakened us to pirate sexuality, race and enslavement, and even pirate cuisine.[5]

The study of piracy, like that of commodity movements, empire building, or mass human migration, links continents, seas, and islands, yet we remain for the most part stuck in Cold War spatial models and culturally rigid if not fundamentalist modes of thought. Piracy is by nature fluid and transitory. It defies both national and area studies models of history, although for many years it tended to be seen through nationalist, ethnic, or regional lenses. Sorting out the combinations and contradictions generated by global piracy—yesterday's and today's—will likely occupy scholars for many years to come. Rarely recording their actions, much less their motives, hopes, or fears, the pirates themselves remain as elusive as ever.

Atlantic Piracy

Scholarship on Atlantic piracy has grown considerably in the last two decades. Numerous studies have linked corsairs, buccaneers, and freebooters to larger trends in political economy. Others have stressed identity, sexuality, and other more individualistic concerns." Harry Kelsey has led the charge in taking "heroic" Elizabethan corsairs such as Francis Drake and John Hawkins down a peg, reminding readers of their deep involvement in the early slave trade.[7] For the seventeenth and early eighteenth centuries, the maritime working-class arguments made by Marcus Rediker, Peter Linebaugh, and others have remained popular, reinforced by marine archaeologists such as Barry Clifford.[8] Challengers to these utopian claims include historian Arne Bialuschewski, whose growing body of work reflects wide knowledge of published and manuscript sources in many languages. As Bialuschewski has shown, much of the surviving evidence does not support the romantic image of the "classic" Atlantic pirate as color-blind social bandit.[9]

Most recent work on the so-called Golden Age of piracy has focused less on class formation and conflict in favor of pirate links to commercial networks—the means by which pirates and privateers fenced or disposed of stolen loot, and how certain communities came to depend on piracy for survival. The work of Mark Hanna, for example, has emphasized the importance of official collusion at the local level in colonial cities such as Newport, Rhode Island, and Charleston, South Carolina. Jesse Cromwell has traced pirate/smuggler networks in Venezuela as well as the mix of violent and non-violent exchanges in buccaneer-era Campeche. Linda Rupert's book on Curaçao also fills a gap in our knowledge of such networks, first treated in the Dutch Atlantic case by Wim Klooster.[10] Blanket anti-piracy laws were not enforced in such places, allowing them to serve as havens of tolerance and occasional recruiting grounds. Capital gains were reinvested in new pillaging enterprises. Other scholars are applying currently fashionable models such as Social Network Analysis and Game Theory to help explain how piracy became embedded in certain societies at one time or another.

Historian Carla Gardina Pestana has recently argued that our image of early English Jamaica as an "instant" pirate haven is mistaken. Pestana notes that Jamaican governor Edward Doyley invited "buccaneers" from Tortuga and Hispaniola in 1657 to shoot feral cattle rather than to defend the new colony. He was not, in other words, intentionally seeking pirates. According to Pestana, he would have been hard pressed to find them. Historians like myself have long assumed that there existed a reservoir of seasonal if not full-time pirates on or near Hispaniola dating to the 1630s or earlier, but Pestana sharply challenges this assumption. She finds that Port Royal, Jamaica's infamous pirate nest, took a while to build—and Cromwell's "Western Design" took a while to die. Buccaneers like Henry Morgan represented novelty rather than continuity.[11] Pestana's revision of the record on locally rooted pirates in early Jamaica and in the greater Caribbean is essential reading, although the almost exclusively English and "official" perspective provided by the key documents cited leaves room for new distortions.

The lack of Spanish documentation aside from a tract on Tortuga suggests a static view of "piratas," when expert witnesses took note of ambiguities and gray areas amid much hype and misinformation. Contraband trade was an ancient fact of life by the 1650s, and not every Spanish subject was a terrorized fool, stuck on a word. Like the term "terrorist," the term "pirate" was widely used to defame or discredit one's foes, and even former trading partners. Perhaps Pestana's main contribution is to remind us of the importance of England's incipient navy, which was in fact of far greater concern to the Spanish than freelance buccaneers (whom authorities usually suspected were not "freelance" actors at all but rather spies and provocateurs). Many early raids that historians (including myself) have glossed as piratical were formal, or at least "paramilitary" in character, and men like Henry Morgan were treated by both the English and Spanish as spearheads if not quite sanctioned leaders of formal invasions backed by Parliament. "Privateers" (another term to watch) had real commissions, and yet at times they also committed real acts of piracy. Pestana is correct in saying that historians must examine each case to make the distinction, and to question claims of continuity. Not everyone who raped and pillaged was a pirate, yet piracy cycles often accompanied or closely followed cycles of war. We need multiple perspectives, sensitivity to change over time, and a close attention to language.

Most historians of piracy continue to focus on the North Atlantic and Caribbean regions, as it was here that most treasure flowed. But new work on Portuguese, French, Dutch, and English traders and marauders has built a case for South Atlantic piracy as a story in its own right. Most recent work has concentrated on Dutch raiding, which was increasingly formalized under the auspices of the West India Company after 1621. As argued in Chapter 3 of this book, the West India Company's seizure of Pernambuco and northern Brazil by 1630 was viewed by the unified Portuguese and Spanish crowns, not to mention local inhabitants, as a grand pirate enterprise. For the Dutch it was no such thing, and under the governorship of Maurice of Nassau (1637–45), a degree of religious tolerance and pre-Enlightenment interest in scientific exploration impressed even some Brazilians.[12] Pernambuco nevertheless served as a base for Dutch corsair raids in the South Atlantic, and even into the South Pacific. After the Dutch were driven from Brazil in 1654, new waves of corsairing (or privateering) and outright piracy overlapped with contraband trade, much of it aimed at obtaining silver via the contested Río de la Plata estuary. It was Argentine historian Zacarias Moutoukias who pioneered the systematic study of Dutch "corsair connections" here and others have followed in his wake.[13]

Historians of the slave trade have become increasingly keen to note connections between African coast slave raiding, bartering, and commercial poaching with patterns of piracy found elsewhere. Much of the new scholarship, such as that of James Walvin, has focused on English slaving ports near the Niger Delta, but historians are now taking a closer look at piratical connections in Portuguese West Central Africa, namely Congo and Angola.[14] The Portuguese had always claimed to be "rescuing" African captives via local intermediaries, and this kind of moral cynicism drew fire as early as the 1560s. Slave raiding was certainly piratical, but was trading for captives through middlemen piracy, too?

The British would eventually argue that it was, but only after outdoing all other European interlopers in buying and sending millions of Africans to the Americas to labor in plantations, mines, and households.[15] Most importantly, perhaps, historians of the slave trade have begun to emphasize the links between slave raiding, contraband trading, capital accumulation, and land-based imperial expansion. Piracy, like the slave trade, like plantation agriculture, like mining, was a business—a nasty one that most participants were anxious to wash their hands of as soon as possible. Were the pirates universally hated for their misdeeds in their own time? Apparently not, as literary scholars Nina Gerassi-Navarro, Claire Jowitt, and Richard Frohock have shown.[16] Even as Atlantic pirates raped, murdered, and pillaged, their audacious acts became the stuff of romance and legend—at times even among their mostly Iberian victims. Such was the wrath of God.

Mediterranean Piracy

It may be too much to claim that piracy originated in the Mediterranean Sea, but its history there is the oldest on record. The word pirate is of Greek origin, although we know that ancient Egyptians also feared marauding "sea peoples." Recent studies of piracy in Greek and Roman times have proved essential for understanding the shifting relationships between freelance raiders, merchant colonies, city-states, and full-blown empires.[17] Also, the use of antipiracy campaigns as a political tool—a kind of ancient "war on terror" headed up by the likes of Pompey the Great—has drawn renewed attention from historians and political scientists. Piracy's relative importance in ancient economies remains less clear due to the nature of surviving sources, but the record does tell us that sea robbery was both a career and a cost.

Studies of medieval piracy in the Mediterranean have also flourished, although the later part of this long period is best documented. For the early stretch, the importance of sea raiders after Rome's decline continues to be hotly debated.[18] Even those great Norse pirates the Vikings managed to raid Mediterranean shores, but gauging their impact is no simple exercise. The later medieval period begins to look more familiar to historians of early modern times, in part because confessional differences emerged as new pretexts for sea raiding.

Cycles of seaborne crusade and jihad, along with heightened commercial competition, yielded many new accusations of piracy and new means of piratical gain. Historians have begun to pay more attention to the rising significance of captive taking and ransoming in this period, along with practices of extortion or the promise not to raid or kidnap in exchange for tribute. These were not new practices in the global history of piracy, but they gained a level of formalization not seen elsewhere due to the Mediterranean's compact geography, the absence of a standing imperial navy, and long years of commercial and in some cases religious interconnection.

For the early modern period (c.1450–1750), historians have for many years emphasized the depredations and extortions practiced by North African pirates, most but not all of them Muslims. It is often forgotten that Christians also engaged in piracy, slave-trading, and gangster-style extortion. New work on the Knights of St. John of Malta shows them to have been as predatory as the so-called Barbary corsairs, especially in the seventeenth century, and as Molly Greene has shown, one of their easiest targets was Greek Christian shipping, which operated under Ottoman license.[19] More information is also coming to light regarding the Knights of St. Stephen, raiders who operated from Livorno as well as Malta, Genoa, and other Christian bases. Jewish corsairs and "merchant fences" could be found on both sides of the Muslim–Christian divide.[20]

Studies of piracy in the modern Mediterranean have perhaps thrived more than for any other period. Specifically, the U.S. and Western European war on the Barbary corsairs that spanned the first decades of the nineteenth century has drawn considerable attention since the attacks on New York and Washington in 2001.[21] Were the Barbary corsairs jihadists, primarily, or had piracy and extortion become essentially business ventures by the time the U.S. entered the global scene at the end of the eighteenth century? Put another way: Was Thomas Jefferson's project for a coalition to suppress the Barbary pirates in the era of Napoleon a kind of war on Islamist terrorism or a sign of new economic times—a call to arms in the name of free trade? Most of the evidence points to the latter.

Piracy in Asian and East African Seas

Scholarship on Asian piracy has also surged dramatically. Asian piracy flourished, and continues to flourish, in two main regions: the Indian Ocean proper and the westernmost Pacific, with some occasional extensions and overlaps. Much recent scholarship on Asian piracy—east and west—has expended considerable energy defining piracy itself and relating it to European and later U.S. imperialism. A main question has been: Was piracy a Western invention, or did it have bona fide cognates in Asian and East African cultures? The work of historian Giancarlo Casale on Ottoman naval and corsair operations in the Indian Ocean—largely in competition with the Portuguese—challenges this and other claims.[22]

Sebastian Prange has revised the history of piracy in the Indian Ocean during the medieval and early modern eras.[23] Prange challenges the longstanding claim that the Portuguese introduced the phenomenon soon after 1500 by creating a monopoly trade and pass (*cartaz*) system. Before Prange, many historians argued that peaceful trade had for centuries been the norm along the monsoon circuit, with religious, ethnic, and political differences counting for little in the face of reliable profits. Prange argues that competition over trade networks extended further back in time in this region, particularly in what some historians have called the Afrasian Seas, and he suggests that India's famous Malabar Coast pirates of the sixteenth and seventeenth centuries were not new on the scene. They had long been a menace to merchants and had also enjoyed ties to landed groups in the interior.

Although the Malabar pirates may have had deep roots, they and other Asian sea predators seem to have found more to steal with the arrival of European shippers anxious to tap the region's enormous wealth. European overseas expansion did generate new piracy cycles, even if not everyone agreed that what they were doing was piracy. As Charles Davies points out in a later context in the Persian Gulf, Westerners were quick to demonize as pirates those free-roving sea peoples they disliked, justifying their violent suppression.[24]

East Asian piracy has also spawned a huge outpouring of scholarship in the last fifteen years or so, ranging from studies of the Japanese Wako, or "dwarf pirates," of the sixteenth century to the Sea Dayaks and other raiders of the Indonesian, Philippine, and other tropical archipelagos.[25] As in the case of the medieval to modern Indian Ocean, scholars of this region remain for the most part attached to the notion that piracy was a Western European invention. That is, many argue that sea raiding was not a major problem prior to European maritime expansion into the waters off East and Southeast Asia, on the one hand, and on the other, that European attempts to control shipping lanes and monopolize ports created the backlash they conveniently labeled "piracy" so as to justify suppression. Once this philological problem of defining piracy against local terms such as *kaizoku* is resolved we may expect deeper insights.

The work of Tonio Andrade on early modern Taiwan adds clarity to raiding language for the seventeenth-century China Sea, balancing European and Asian claims of piracy.[26] Here locals faced Portuguese, Spanish, and Dutch interlopers, along with colonists and raiders representing or fighting against China's Ming and Qing dynasties. Mainland China's strongest claims to Taiwan date to the turbulent and piratical years of the seventeenth century, when the island was an imperial gaming chit. As Andrade shows, the battle for Taiwan was as symbolic as it was strategic, and the decisive Chinese victory over Dutch sea raiders and would-be colonists stands as a reminder that mainland resources need only be turned outward to rearrange the imperial game board. Subsequent Qing withdrawal from maritime endeavors permitted European interlopers considerable room to operate, with disastrous consequences for China in the longer term.

On the American side of the Spanish Pacific, new work has also appeared. Glyndwr Williams has continued to open new vistas on British raiding and trading in the Big Blue, which also included substantial scientific exploration and occasional efforts at shipwreck salvage.[27] Scholars have also revisited the British privateering expeditions led by John Narborough, Woodes Rogers, George Anson, George Shelvocke, and others. Other scholars such as Benjamin Schmidt have re-examined earlier Dutch raiders in the Spanish "South Sea," and still others are taking a new look at the wave of French buccaneers that plagued Spanish towns and shippers from 1680 to 1695. Ignacio Gallup-Díaz and Arne Bialuschewski are highlighting the significance of pirate ties to indigenous peoples in Panama and elsewhere.[28]

All told, global piracy studies are alive and well. As scholars turn to neglected world regions and ask new questions of their sources or come upon new evidence in the archives or at the bottom of the sea, we may expect more growth in the field and no doubt a fuller understanding of this age-old seaborne criminal phenomenon. It is difficult to imagine today's cash-strapped universities opening whole programs in Pirate Studies, but new generations of historians and other specialists will no doubt battle successfully for scarce resources, identify new points of attack, and deploy new weapons as they upend our most cherished beliefs, set fire to our temples, and smash our idols. To each I say, "Yarrr!"

Notes

1 Peter Leeson, in *The Invisible Hook: The Economics of Pirates* (Princeton: Princeton University Press, 2009), considers today's pirates to be something quite different from those of the so-called Golden Age. Other views include Martin Murphy, *Small Boats, Weak States, Dirty Money: Piracy and Maritime Terrorism in the Modern World* (New York: Columbia University Press, 2010); Andrew Palmer, *The New Pirates: Modern Global Piracy from Somalia to the South China Sea* (London: I.B. Tauris, 2013); Jay Bahadur, *The Pirates of Somalia: Inside Their Hidden World* (New York: Pantheon, 2011). Bahadur's is the most ethnographic account.

2 Leeson, *The Invisible Hook*, 203–5.

3 Of special value is an essay collection edited by C.R. Pennell, *Bandits at Sea: A Pirates Reader* (New York: New York University Press, 2001). See also the many works of Angus Konstam, including *The World Atlas of Pirates* (New York: Lyons Press, 2009). On archaeology, see Russell K. Skowronek and Charles R. Ewen, eds., *X Marks the Spot: The Archaeology of Piracy* (Gainesville: University Press of Florida, 2006).

4 Lauren Benton, *A Search for Sovereignty: Law and Geography in European Empires, 1400–1900* (New York: Cambridge University Press, 2010). See also Hans W. Blom, ed., *Property, Piracy and Punishment: Hugo Grotius on War and Booty in De Iure Praedae— Concepts and Contexts* (Leiden: Brill, 2009); and Michael Kempe, "Even the Remotest Corners of the World: Globalized Piracy and International Law, 1500–1900," *Journal of Global History* 5:3 (2010): 353–72.

5 On pirates and empires, see especially James Pritchard, *In Search of Empire: The French in the Americas, 1670–1730* (New York: Cambridge University Press, 2004); Peter Earle, *The Pirate Wars* (London: Methuen, 2003); Jon Latimer, *Buccaneers of the Caribbean: How Piracy Forged an Empire* (Cambridge: Harvard University Press, 2009); Arne Bialuschewski, "Black People under the Black Flag: Piracy and the Slave Trade on the West Coast of Africa, 1718–1723," *Slavery and Abolition* 29 (2008): 461–75; and Jan Glete, *Warfare at Sea, 1500–1650: Maritime Conflicts and the Transformation of Europe* (New York: Routledge, 2000); and Ignacio Gallup-Diaz, *The Door of the Seas and Key to the Universe: Indian Politics and Imperial Rivalry in the Darien, 1640–1750* (New York: Columbia University Press, 2005). For global approaches see Alison Games, *The Web of Empire: English Cosmopolitans in an Age of Expansion, 1560–1660* (New York: Oxford University Press, 2008); Jerry Bentley, Renate Bridenthal, and Karen Wigen, eds., *Seascapes: Maritime Histories, Littoral Cultures, and Transoceanic Exchanges* (Honolulu: University of Hawai'i

Press, 2007); and Robert J. Antony, *Pirates in the Age of Sail* (New York: W.W. Norton, 2007). On pirate women, see David Cordingly, *Seafaring Women: Adventures of Pirate Queens, Female Stowaways, and Sailors' Wives* (New York: Random House, 2002). For a literary study of western pirate sexuality see Hans Turley, *Rum, Sodomy, and the Lash: Piracy, Sexuality, and Masculine Identity* (New York: New York University Press, 1999). For a more political angle, see Gabriel Kuhn, *Life Under the Jolly Roger: Reflections on Golden Age Piracy* (Oakland: PM Press, 2010). And for a geographical approach, Peter R. Galvin, *Patterns of Pillage: A Geography of Caribbean-based Piracy in Spanish America, 1536–1718* (New York: Peter Lang, 1999).

6   Essential is David F. Marley's, *Pirates of the Americas*, 2 vols. (Santa Barbara: ABC-CLIO, 2010). On French pirates, see Jean Pierre Moreau, *Pirates: flibuste et piraterie dans la Caraïbe et les mers du sud, 1522–1725* (Paris: Tallandier, 2006); and Anne Pérotin-Dumon, *La ville aux îles, la ville dans l'isle: Basse-Terre et Pointe-à-Pitre Guadeloupe, 1650–1820* (Paris: Karthala, 2000). A narrative of attacks on Venezuela's coast from the earliest French corsairs to Henry Morgan is Luis Britto García's *Señores del Caribe: Indígenas, conquistadores y piratas en el mar colonial* (Caracas: Fundación Tradiciones Caraqueñas, 2001). For attacks and responses in early Havana, see Alejandro de la Fuente, *Havana and the Atlantic in the Sixteenth Century* (Chapel Hill: University of North Carolina Press, 2008). For recent buccaneer studies see, for example, Diana and Michael Preston's *A Pirate of Exquisite Mind. Explorer, Naturalist, and Buccaneer: The Life of William Dampier* (New York: Berkley, 2004); Fabio López Lázaro, *The Misfortunes of Alonso Ramírez: The True Adventures of a Spanish American with 17th-Century Pirates* (Austin: University of Texas Press, 2011); Alexandre-Olivier Exquemelin, *Histoire des aventuriers flibustiers*, Réal Ouellet, ed. (Paris: Presses de l'Université Paris-Sorbonne, 2005); Anna Neill, "Buccaneer Ethnography: Nature, Culture, and Nation in the Journals of William Dampier," *Eighteenth-Century Studies* 33 (2000): 165–80; and Sandra Petrovich, *Henry Morgan's Raid on Panama: Geopolitics and Colonial Ramifications, 1669–1674* (Lewiston: Edwin Mellen, 2001). See also the superb study of Bermuda by Michael J. Jarvis, *In the Eye of All Trade: Bermuda, Bermudians, and the Maritime Atlantic World, 1680–1783* (Chapel Hill: University of North Carolina Press, 2010). Other recent contributions include Colin Woodard, *The Republic of Pirates, Being the True and Surprising Story of the Caribbean Pirates and the Man Who Brought Them Down* (New York: Harcourt, 2007); and Cruz Apestegui, *Pirates of the Caribbean: Buccaneers, Privateers, Freebooters and Filibusters* (London: Conway, 2002).

7   Harry Kelsey, *Sir John Hawkins: The Queen's Slave Trader* (New Haven: Yale University Press, 2003), and *Francis Drake: The Queen's Pirate* (New Haven: Yale University Press, 2000). See also James McDermott's excellent *Martin Frobisher, Elizabethan Privateer* (New Haven: Yale University Press, 2001).

8   Marcus Rediker, *Villains of All Nations: Atlantic Pirates in the Golden Age* (Boston: Beacon Press, 2004); Peter Linebaugh and Marcus Rediker, *The Many-Headed Hydra: Sailors, Slaves, Commoners and the Hidden History of the Revolutionary Atlantic* (Boston: Beacon, 2000); and Barry Clifford and Kenneth J. Kinkor, with Sharon Simpson, *Real Pirates: The Untold Story of the Whydah from Slave Ship to Pirate Ship* (Washington, DC: National Geographic, 2007).

9   See, for example, Bialuschewski's "Pirates, Black Sailors, and Seafaring Slaves in the Anglo-Maritime World, 1716–1726," *Journal of Caribbean History* 45 (Dec. 2011): 143–58; and "Between Newfoundland and the Malacca Strait: A Survey of the Golden Age of Piracy, 1695–1725," *Mariner's Mirror* 90 (May 2004): 167–86.

10 Mark Hanna, *Pirate Nests and the Rise of the British Empire, 1570–1640* (Chapel Hill: University of North Carolina Press, 2015); Jesse Cromwell, "Covert Commerce:

A Social History of Contraband Trade in Venezuela, 1701–1789," Ph.D. dissertation, University of Texas, Austin, 2012; and Cromwell, "Life on the Margins: (Ex)Pirates and Spanish Subjects on the Campeche Logwood Frontier, 1660–1716," *Itinerario* 33:3 (2009): 43–71; Linda Rupert, *Creolization and Contraband: Curaçao in the Early Modern Atlantic World* (Athens: University of Georgia Press, 2012); Wim Klooster, "Inter-imperial Smuggling in the Americas, 1600–1800," in Bernard Bailyn, ed., *Soundings in Atlantic History*, pp. 141–80 (Cambridge: Harvard University Press, 2009).

11 Carla Gardina Pestana, "Early English Jamaica without Pirates," *William & Mary Quarterly* 71:3 (July 2014): 321–60.

12 For a fresh overview, see Virginia W. Lunsford, *Piracy and Privateering in the Golden Age Netherlands* (London: Palgrave Macmillan, 2006). An excellent source that includes a description of Dutch attempts to settle Chile is Caspar van Baerle, *The History of Brazil under the Governorship of Count Johan Maurits of Nassau, 1636–1644*, Blanche T. van Berckel-Ebeling Koning, trans. and ed. (Gainesville: University Press of Florida, 2011). For Dutch contraband in the Caribbean after the Peace of Münster, see Wim Klooster, *Illicit Riches: Dutch Trade in the Caribbean, 1648–1795* (Leiden: KITLV, 1998).

13 Zacarias Moutoukias, *Contrabando y control colonial en el siglo XVII: Buenos Aires, el Atlántico y el espacio peruano* (Buenos Aires: CEAL, 1988).

14 See, most recently, James Walvin's *The Zong: A Massacre, the Law and the End of Slavery* (New Haven: Yale University Press, 2011).

15 For British policy just after the decree to suppress the slave trade, see Matthew McCarthy, *Privateering, Piracy and British Policy in Spanish America, 1810–1830* (Kingston: University of Hull, 2013).

16 Nina Gerassi-Navarro, *Pirate Novels: Fictions of Nation Building in Spanish America* (Durham: Duke University Press, 1999); Claire Jowitt, *The Culture of Piracy, 1580–1630: English Literature and Seaborne Crime* (Burlington: Ashgate, 2010); and Richard Frohock, *Buccaneers and Privateers: The Story of the English Sea Rover, 1675–1725* (Newark: University of Delaware Press, 2012).

17 Philip de Sousa, *Piracy in the Graeco-Roman World* (New York: Cambridge University Press, 2002).

18 See, for example, Peregrine Horden and Nicholas Purcell, *The Corrupting Sea: A Study of Mediterranean History* (New York: Oxford University Press, 2000).

19 Molly Greene, *Catholic Pirates and Greek Merchants: A Maritime History of the Mediterranean* (Princeton: Princeton University Press, 2010); Ayse Devrim Atauz, *Eight Thousand Years of Maltese Maritime History: Trade, Piracy, and Naval Warfare in the Central Mediterranean* (Gainesville: University Press of Florida, 2008); and Catherine Bracewell, *The Uskoks of Senj: Piracy, Banditry, and Holy War in the Sixteenth-Century Adriatic* (Ithaca: Cornell University Press, 2011). See also G.L. Weiss, *Captives and Corsairs: France and Slavery in the Early Modern Mediterranean* (Stanford: Stanford University Press, 2011); Alan G. Jamieson, *Lords of the Sea: A History of the Barbary Corsairs* (London: Reaktion Books, 2012); Adrian Tinniswood, *Pirates of Barbary: Corsairs, Conquests, and Captivity in the Seventeenth-Century Mediterranean* (New York: Riverhead Books, 2010); Nabil Matar, *Britain and Barbary, 1589–1689* (Gainesville: University Press of Florida, 2006); Jacques Heers, *The Barbary Corsairs: Warfare in the Mediterranean, 1480–1580* (London: Stackpole, 2003); Ramiro Feijoo, *Corsarios berberiscos: el reino corsario que provocó la guerra más larga de la historia de España* (Madrid: Carroggio/Belaqva, 2003); Robert C. Davis, *Christian Slaves, Muslim Masters: White Slavery in the Mediterranean, the Barbary Coast, and Italy, 1500–1800* (New York: Palgrave Macmillan, 2003); and Daniel J. Vitkus, *Piracy, Slavery, and Redemption* (New York: Columbia University Press, 2001).

20 See, for example, Mercedes García Arenal and Gerard Wiegers, *A Man of Three Worlds: Samuel Pallache, a Moroccan Jew in Catholic and Protestant Europe*, Martin Beagles, trans. (Baltimore: Johns Hopkins University Press, 2003); and Luis Salas Almela, *The Conspiracy of the Ninth Duke of Medina Sidonia (1641)*, Ruth MacKay, trans. (Leiden: Brill, 2013).

21 See, for example, Frank Lambert, *The Barbary Wars: American Independence in the Atlantic World* (New York: Hill & Wang, 2005); Joshua London, *Victory in Tripoli: How America's War with the Barbary Pirates Established the U.S. Navy and Shaped a Nation* (New York: Wiley, 2005); and Joseph Wheelan, *Jefferson's War: America's First War on Terror, 1801–1805* (Washington: Public Affairs, 2004).

22 Giancarlo Casale, *The Ottoman Age of Exploration* (New York: Oxford University Press, 2010).

23 Sebastian R. Prange, "A Trade of No Dishonor: Piracy, Commerce, and Community in the Western Indian Ocean, Twelfth to Sixteenth Century," *American Historical Review* 116:5 (Dec. 2011): 1269–1293. See also the work of Patricia Risso, including "Cross-Cultural Perceptions of Piracy: Maritime Violence in the Western Indian Ocean and Persian Gulf during a Long Eighteenth Century," *Journal of World History* 12:2 (2001): 293–319; and the various publications of Pius Malekandathil, including "From Merchant Capitalists to Corsairs: The Response of the Muslim Merchants of Malabar to the Portuguese Commercial Expansion (1498–1600)," *Portuguese Studies Review* 12:1 (2004): 75–96. For global views see Sugata Bose, *A Hundred Horizons: The Indian Ocean in the Age of Global Empire* (Cambridge: Harvard University Press, 2006), and the recent work of Sanjay Subrahmanyam.

24 Charles Davies, *The Blood-Red Arab Flag: An Investigation into Qasimi Piracy, 1797–1820* (Exeter: University of Exeter Press, 1997).

25 Robert J. Antony, ed., *Elusive Pirates, Pervasive Smugglers: Violence and Clandestine Trade in the Greater China Seas* (Hong Kong: Hong Kong University Press, 2010); Robert J. Antony, *Like Froth Floating on the Sea: The World of Pirates and Seafarers in Late Imperial South China* (Berkeley: University of California Press, 2003); and James F. Warren, *Iranun and Balangingi: Globalization, Maritime Raiding, and the Birth of Ethnicity* (Singapore: National University of Singapore Press, 2002).

26 Tonio Andrade, *Lost Colony: The Untold Story of China's First Great Victory over the West* (Princeton: Princeton University Press, 2011). See also the superbly documented work of José Eugenio Borao Mateo, *The Spanish Experience in Taiwan, 1626–1642: The Baroque Ending of a Renaissance Endeavor* (Hong Kong: Hong Kong University Press, 2009); and Cheng Wei-Chung, *War, Trade and Piracy in the China Seas, 1622–1683* (Leiden: Brill, 2013).

27 Glyndwr Williams, *Buccaneers, Explorers, and Settlers: British Enterprise and Encounters in the Pacific, 1670–1800* (Burlington: Ashgate, 2005), and *The Great South Sea: English Voyages and Encounters, 1500–1750* (New Haven: Yale University Press, 1997).

28 Benjamin Schmidt, *Innocence Abroad: The Dutch Imagination and the New World, 1570–1670* (New York: Cambridge University Press, 2006). Ignacio Gallup-Díaz, *The Door of the Seas and Key to the Universe: Indian Politics and Imperial Rivalry in the Darien, 1640–1750* (New York: Columbia University Press, 2005).

APPENDIX

Early Modern Pirates and Contemporary
European Monarchs

Spain	France	England	Portugal	Pirates
Ferdinand & Isabella (1469–1516)	Louis XII (1498–1515)	Henry VII (1485–1507)	Manoel I (1495–1507)	Oruç Barbarossa
				Jean Florin
Charles I (1516–56)	Francis I (1515–47)	Henry VIII (1509–47)	João III (1521–57)	François Le Clerc
				Jacques Sores
	Henri II (1547–59)	Edward VI (1547–53)		Hayreddin
				Seïer Reis
Philip II (1556–98)	Charles IX (1560–74)	Elizabeth I (1558–1603)	Sebastião (1557–78)	John Hawkins
				John Oxenham
	Henri III (1574–89)		Philip I (also Philip II of Spain) (1580–98)	Francis Drake
				Limahon
				Thomas Cavendish
Philip III (1598–1621)	Henri IV (1589–1610)	James I (1603–25)	Philip II (Philip III of Spain) (1598–1621)	Jacob Mahu
				Olivier van Noort
Philip IV (1621–65)	Louis XIII (1610–43)	Charles I (1625–49)	Philip III (Philip IV of Spain) (1621–40)	Joris van Speilbergen
				Jacques l'Hermite
		Cromwell Dictatorship (1649–60)	João IV (of Bragança) (1640–56)	Piet Heyn Diego el Mulato
				Christopher Myngs
				Koxinga
Charles II (1665–1700)	Louis XIV (1643–1715)	Charles II (1660–85)	Afonso VI (1656–83)	Henry Morgan l'Ollonais
		James II (1685–89)	Pedro II (1683–1706)	Bartholomew Sharp
				François Grogniet
		William & Mary (1689–1702)		William Dampier
				Henry Avery
Philip V (1700–46)	Louis XV (1715–74)	Anne (1702–14)	João V (1706–50)	William Kidd
				Edward Teach
		George I (1714–27)		Mary Read
				Ann Bonny
				Bartholomew Roberts

Note: The United Provinces of the Netherlands (after 1568) existed as a commonwealth led by parties, or factions, of burgher-oligarchs.

GLOSSARY OF TERMS

armadilla   Small Spanish naval squadron.

arquebus   Primitive sixteenth-century matchlock gun.

Arrr!   Pirate exclamation of contempt or frustration.

asiento   Slave trade monopoly granted by Spain to Dutch, French, or English suppliers after the mid-seventeenth century.

astrolabe   Device for measuring latitude by means of the sun's meridian altitude.

avería   Spanish ad valorem tax on merchandise shipped between Spain and the Americas, used to fund defense against pirates.

bagnio   North African jail where Christian prisoners were held until ransomed.

bey   North African governor with ties to Ottoman Turks and Mediterranean pirates.

biscocho   Spanish term for sea-biscuit, or "hard-tack," the early modern European sailor's staple food.

boucan   Barbecue prepared by renegades of Hispaniola and Tortuga in the seventeenth century.

brigantine   Small, two-masted sailing vessel popular with buccaneers (Spanish *bergantín*).

bumboe   Alcoholic beverage made from cane liquor and spices.

careen   Practice of hauling over ships to clean and repair underside.

castillo   Spanish term for "castle," referring specifically to fortresses in the American context.

cimarrón   Spanish term for runaway, usually referring to escaped slaves, as in Panama (English "maroon," French *marron*).

commission   Letter of reprisal issued by a monarch or crown representative to a privateer authorizing maritime aggression against a declared enemy (alt. "letter of marque," or Spanish *patente*).

corregidor   Local Spanish colonial official (alt. *alcalde mayor*).

corsario   Spanish term for privateers and pirates (English "corsair").

derrotero   Spanish term for sea chart, noting horizons, anchorages, shoals, etc. (English "waggoner").

ducat   Spanish money of account (*ducado*); the most common gold coin taken by pirates was the *escudo*, mistakenly called the "doubloon" by the English.

flibustier French term for buccaneers, derived from Dutch *vrijbuiter* (English "filibuster" or "freebooter").

flip Alcoholic beverage made from beer, sugar, and cane liquor, heated and served in tin cup (may have developed into modern eggnog).

fluyt Light and inexpensive Dutch trading vessel developed in 1595, most common in Baltic trade.

galibraza Swift Spanish war frigate developed in late sixteenth century for Indies run.

galleon Large ocean-going vessel developed in sixteenth century, perfected by Spanish.

galley Long, oared vessel common in Mediterranean Sea battles (e.g., Lepanto 1571).

guerrilla "Little war," a Spanish term used to refer to informal warfare, robbery, and hostage-taking.

jolly roger Black pirate flag with skull and crossed bones not common until early eighteenth century; earlier pirates normally flew flags of enemies to lure them closer before hoisting a red "attack" flag.

kaizoku See *wako*.

matelotage Practice of same-sex "mating" for legal and possibly sexual purposes among buccaneers of Hispaniola; *matelots* designated one another as heirs in case of accidental death.

musket Handheld, single-shot gun, successor of arquebus, predecessor of rifle.

outlier Late seventeenth-century English synonym for buccaneer, or pirate.

palenque Spanish term for stockade, but also applied to maroon settlements (see *cimarrón*, above).

patache Spanish term for small dispatch vessel (English "patax") usually accompanying larger galleons, frigates, etc.; similar vessels included barks, *chinchorros*, yachts.

pechelingue Spanish term for Dutch pirates and privateers, apparently derived from port of Vlissingen.

piece of eight Spanish silver coin divided into eight *reales* (Spanish *peso de a ocho* or *patacón*).

piragua Spanish American galley-like vessel made from extra-wide dugout canoes.

presidio Spanish term for garrisoned fort.

rancherías Spanish term for pearl fisheries, as on the islands of Margarita and Cubagua.

regua Spanish mule train carrying merchandise, slaves, silver, and gold across the Panamanian Isthmus.

rescate Practice of bartering for contraband in Spanish American colonies; practice of ransoming Christian captives from Berber corsairs in North Africa (Portuguese *resgate* usually referred to slave trading in Africa, with connotations of both barter and ransoming of war captives).

sack Pillage, rape, plunder, etc.; also English name for dry Spanish and Canarian white wine.

salamagundi Spicy pickled fish plate popular among Anglo-American pirates (French, *salmagondis*).

scurvy Deadly tissue-damaging disease caused by prolonged ascorbic acid (vitamin C) deprivation.

situado Onerous seventeenth- and eighteenth-century Spanish American impost used to pay for anti-pirate fortifications, military salaries, and so on in Panama, Cartagena, Havana, Florida, etc.

wako So-called dwarf pirates of the South China Sea, reputedly Japanese but often of mixed heritage.

zee-rover Dutch term for pirates, or "sea-rovers."

SELECT BIBLIOGRAPHY

Alsedo y Herrera, Dionisio de. *Piraterías y agresiones de los ingleses y de otros pueblos de Europa en la América Española desde el siglo XVI al XVIII*. Edited by D. Justo Zaragoza. Madrid: Imprenta de Manuel G. Hernández, 1883 [1740].

Anderson, J.L. "Piracy and World History: An Economic Perspective on Maritime Predation," *Journal of World History* 6:2 (Fall 1995): 175–99.

Andrade, Tonio. *Lost Colony: The Untold Story of China's First Great Victory over the West*. Princeton: Princeton University Press, 2011.

Andrews, Kenneth R. *The Spanish Caribbean: Trade and Plunder, 1530–1630*. New Haven: Yale University Press, 1978.

Antony, Robert J. *Pirates in the Age of Sail*. New York: W.W. Norton, 2007.

———. *Like Froth Floating on the Sea: The World of Pirates and Seafarers in Late Imperial South China*. Berkeley: University of California Press, 2003.

Antony, Robert J., ed. *Elusive Pirates, Pervasive Smugglers: Violence and Clandestine Trade in the Greater China Seas*. Hong Kong: Hong Kong University Press, 2010.

Apestegui, Cruz. *Pirates of the Caribbean: Buccaneers, Privateers, Freebooters and Filibusters*. London: Conway, 2002.

Atauz, Ayse Devrim. *Eight Thousand Years of Maltese Maritime History: Trade, Piracy, and Naval Warfare in the Central Mediterranean*. Gainesville: University Press of Florida, 2008.

Ayres, Philip, ed. *Voyages and Adventures of Captain Bartholomew Sharp and Others in the South Sea*. London: Walter Davis, 1684.

Baer, Joel H., ed. *British Piracy in the Golden Age: History and Interpretation, 1660–1730*. 4 vols. London: Pickering and Chatto, 2007.

Baerle, Caspar van. *The History of Brazil under the Governorship of Count Johan Maurits of Nassau, 1636–1644*. Translated and edited by Blanche T. van Berckel-Ebeling Koning. Gainesville: University Press of Florida, 2011.

Bahadur, Jay. *The Pirates of Somalia: Inside Their Hidden World*. New York: Pantheon, 2011.

Beal, Clifford. *Quelch's Gold*. Westport, CT: Praeger, 2007.

Bentley, Jerry, Renate Bridenthal, and Kären Wigen, eds. *Seascapes: Maritime Histories, Littoral Cultures, and Transoceanic Exchanges*. Honolulu: University of Hawai'i Press, 2007.

Benton, Lauren. *A Search for Sovereignty: Law and Geography in European Empires, 1400–1900.* New York: Cambridge University Press, 2010.

Bernal Ruiz, María del Pilar. *La toma del puerto de Guayaquil en 1687.* Seville: Escuela de Estudios Hispano-Americanos, 1979.

Bialuschewski, Arne. "Pirates, Black Sailors, and Seafaring Slaves in the Anglo-Maritime World, 1716–1726," *Journal of Caribbean History* 45 (Dec. 2011): 143–58.

———. "Black People under the Black Flag: Piracy and the Slave Trade on the West Coast of Africa, 1718–1723," *Slavery and Abolition* 29 (2008): 461–75.

———. "Pirates, Markets, and Imperial Authority: Economic Aspects of Maritime Depredations in the Atlantic World, 1716–1726," *Global Crime* 9 (2008): 52–65.

———. "Between Newfoundland and the Malacca Strait: A Survey of the Golden Age of Piracy, 1695–1725," *Mariner's Mirror* 90 (May 2004): 167–86.

Blom, Hans W., ed. *Property, Piracy and Punishment: Hugo Grotius on War and Booty in De Iure Praedae—Concepts and Contexts.* Leiden: Brill, 2009.

Borao Mateo, José Eugenio. *The Spanish Experience in Taiwan, 1626–1642: The Baroque Ending of a Renaissance Endeavor.* Hong Kong: Hong Kong University Press, 2009.

Bose, Sugata. *A Hundred Horizons: The Indian Ocean in the Age of Global Empire.* Cambridge: Harvard University Press, 2006.

Boxer, Charles R. *The Dutch Seaborne Empire, 1600–1800.* London: Hutchinson, 1965.

Bracewell, Catherine. *The Uskoks of Senj: Piracy, Banditry, and Holy War in the Sixteenth-Century Adriatic.* Ithaca: Cornell University Press, 2011.

Bradley, Peter T. *The Lure of Peru: Maritime Intrusion into the South Sea, 1598–1701.* New York: St. Martin's Press, 1989.

Britto García, Luis. *Señores del Caribe: Indígenas, conquistadores y piratas en el mar colonial.* Caracas: Fundación Tradiciones Caraqueñas, 2001.

Burg, Barry. *Sodomy and the Pirate Tradition: English Sea Rovers in the Seventeenth-Century Caribbean.* New York: New York University Press, 1984.

Burney, James. *A Chronological History of Voyages and Discoveries in the South Seas,* 5 vols. London: Luke Hansard and Sons, 1816.

Callander, John. *Terra Australis Cognita or Voyages to the Terra Australis,* 3 vols. New York: Da Capo Press, 1967 [1768].

Casale, Giancarlo. *The Ottoman Age of Exploration.* New York: Oxford University Press, 2010.

Cavendish, Thomas. *The Last Voyage of Thomas Cavendish, 1591–1592: The Autograph Manuscript of His Own Account of the Voyage, from the Collection of Paul Mellon.* Edited by David B. Quinn. Chicago: University of Chicago Press, 1975.

Cervantes, Miguel de. *Don Quixote.* Translated by J.M. Cohen. New York: Penguin Classics, 1950.

Cheng Wei-Chung. *War, Trade and Piracy in the China Seas, 1622–1683.* Leiden: Brill, 2013.

Cipolla, Carlo M. *Guns, Sails and Empires: Technological Innovation and the Early Phases of European Expansion, 1400–1700.* New York: Pantheon, 1965.

Clayton, Lawrence A. *Caulkers and Carpenters in a New World: The Shipyards of Colonial Guayaquil.* Athens: Ohio University Press, 1980.

———. "Local Initiative and Finance in Defense of the Viceroyalty of Peru: The Development of Self-Reliance," *Hispanic American Historical Review* 54:2 (May 1974): 284–304.

Clifford, Barry, and Kenneth J. Kinkor, with Sharon Simpson. *Real Pirates: The Untold Story of the Whydah from Slave Ship to Pirate Ship.* Washington, DC: National Geographic, 2007.

Cordingly, David. *Pirate Hunter of the Caribbean: The Adventurous Life of Captain Woodes Rogers.* New York: Random House, 2011.

Cordingly, David. *Under the Black Flag: The Romance and the Reality of Life among the Pirates.* New York: Random House, 1996.

Creighton, Margaret S., and Lisa Norling, eds. *Iron Men, Wooden Women: Gender and Seafaring in the Atlantic World, 1700–1920.* Baltimore: Johns Hopkins University Press, 1996.

Cromwell, Jesse. "Covert Commerce: A Social History of Contraband Trade in Venezuela, 1701–1789." Ph.D. dissertation, University of Texas, Austin, 2012.

———. "Life on the Margins: (Ex)Pirates and Spanish Subjects on the Campeche Logwood Frontier, 1660–1716," *Itinerario* 33:3 (2009): 43–71.

Dampier, William. *A New Voyage Round the World.* London: Adam and Charles Black, 1937 [1697].

Davies, Charles. *The Blood-Red Arab Flag: An Investigation into Qasimi Piracy, 1797–1820.* Exeter: University of Exeter Press, 1997.

Davis, Robert C. *Christian Slaves, Muslim Masters: White Slavery in the Mediterranean, the Barbary Coast, and Italy, 1500–1800.* New York: Palgrave Macmillan, 2003.

Donoso, Sebastián I. *Piratas en Guayaquil: Historia del asalto de 1687.* Guayaquil: El Universo, 2006.

Earle, Peter. *The Pirate Wars.* London: Methuen, 2003.

———. *The Sack of Panamá: Sir Henry Morgan's Adventures on the Spanish Main.* New York: Viking Press, 1981.

———. *The Treasure of the Concepción: The Wreck of the Almiranta.* New York: Viking Press, 1980.

Erauso, Catalina de. *Lieutenant Nun: Memoirs of a Basque Transvestite in the New World.* Translated by Michele Stepto and Gabriel Stepto. Boston: Beacon Press, 1996 [c. 1626].

Esquemeling, John. [A.O. Exquemelin]. *The Buccaneers of America.* Glorieta: Rio Grande Press, 1992 [1684].

Exquemelin, Alexandre-Olivier. *Histoire des aventuriers flibustiers.* Ed. Réal Ouellet. Paris: Presses de l'Université Paris-Sorbonne, 2005.

Feijoo, Ramiro. *Corsarios berberiscos: el reino corsario que provocó la guerra más larga de la historia de España.* Madrid: Carroggio/Belaqva, 2003.

Friedman, Ellen G. *Spanish Captives in North Africa in the Early Modern Age.* Madison: University of Wisconsin Press, 1983.

Frohock, Richard. *Buccaneers and Privateers: The Story of the English Sea Rover, 1675–1725.* Newark: University of Delaware Press, 2012.

Gage, Thomas. *Travels in the New World.* Edited by J. Eric S. Thompson. Norman: University of Oklahoma Press, 1958 [1648].

Gallup-Díaz, Ignacio. *The Door of the Seas and Key to the Universe: Indian Politics and Imperial Rivalry in the Darien, 1640–1750.* New York: Columbia University Press, 2005.

Galvin, Peter R. *Patterns of Pillage: A Geography of Caribbean-based Piracy in Spanish America, 1536–1718.* New York: Peter Lang, 1999.

Games, Alison. *The Web of Empire: English Cosmopolitans in an Age of Expansion, 1560–1660.* New York: Oxford University Press, 2008.

Gerassi-Navarro, Nina. *Pirate Novels: Fictions of Nation Building in Spanish America.* Durham: Duke University Press, 1999.

Gerhard, Peter. *Pirates on the West Coast of New Spain, 1575–1742.* Cleveland: Arthur H. Clark, 1960.

Glete, Jan. *Warfare at Sea, 1500–1650: Maritime Conflicts and the Transformation of Europe.* New York: Routledge, 2000.

Goslinga, Cornelis. *The Dutch in the Caribbean and on the Wild Coast, 1580–1680.* Gainesville: University of Florida Press, 1971.

Gosse, Philip. *The History of Piracy*. London: Longmans, Green, 1932.

———. *The Pirate's Who's Who: Giving Particulars of the Lives and Deaths of the Pirates and Buccaneers*. New York: Burt Franklin, 1968 [1924].

Greene, Molly. *Catholic Pirates and Greek Merchants: A Maritime History of the Mediterranean*. Princeton: Princeton University Press, 2010.

Hampden, John, ed. *Francis Drake, Privateer: Contemporary Narratives and Documents*. Tuscaloosa: University of Alabama Press, 1972.

Hanna, Mark. Pirate Nests and the Rise of the British Empire, 1570–1740. Chapel Hill: University of North Carolina Press, 2015.

Haring, Clarence H. *The Buccaneers in the West Indies in the XVIIth Century*. London: Methuen, 1910.

Hawkins, Richard. *Voyage into the South Sea* [1622 facsimile ed.]. Amsterdam: Da Capo Press, 1968.

Heers, Jacques. *The Barbary Corsairs: Warfare in the Mediterranean, 1480–1580*. London: Stackpole, 2003.

Hoffman, Paul E. *The Spanish Crown and the Defense of the Caribbean, 1535–1585: Precedent, Patrimonialism, and Royal Parsimony*. Baton Rouge: Louisiana State University Press, 1980.

Horden, Peregrine, and Nicholas Purcell. *The Corrupting Sea: A Study of Mediterranean History*. New York: Oxford University Press, 2000.

Howse, Derek, and Norman Thrower, eds. *A Buccaneer's Atlas: Basil Ringrose's South Sea Waggoner*. Berkeley: University of California Press, 1992.

Hrodej, Philippe. *L'amiral du Casse: L'élévation d'un Gascon sous Louis XIV*. Paris: Librairie de l'Inde, 1999.

Jameson, J. Franklin, ed. *Privateering and Piracy in the Colonial Period: Illustrative Documents*. New York: Macmillan, 1923.

Jamieson, Alan G. *Lords of the Sea: A History of the Barbary Corsairs*. London: Reaktion Books, 2012.

Jarvis, Michael J. *In the Eye of All Trade: Bermuda, Bermudians, and the Maritime Atlantic World, 1680–1783*. Chapel Hill: University of North Carolina Press, 2010.

Johnson, Charles. *A General History of the Pyrates*. London: J.M. Dent, 1972 [1724].

Jowitt, Claire. *The Culture of Piracy, 1580–1630: English Literature and Seaborne Crime*. Burlington: Ashgate, 2010.

Juárez Moreno, Juan. *Corsarios y piratas en Veracruz y Campeche*. Sevilla: Escuela de Estudios Hispano-Americanos, 1972.

Kelsey, Harry. *Sir John Hawkins: The Queen's Slave Trader*. New Haven: Yale University Press, 2003.

———. *Francis Drake: The Queen's Pirate*. New Haven: Yale University Press, 2000.

Kemp, Peter, and Christopher Lloyd. *Brethren of the Coast: The British and French Buccaneers in the South Seas*. London: Heinemann, 1960.

Kempe, Michael. "Even the Remotest Corners of the World: Globalized Piracy and International Law, 1500–1900," *Journal of Global History* 5:3 (2010): 353–72.

Klooster, Wim. *Illicit Riches: Dutch Trade in the Caribbean, 1648–1795*. Leiden: KITLV, 1998.

Konstam, Angus. *The World Atlas of Pirates*. New York: Lyons Press, 2009.

Kuhn, Gabriel. *Life Under the Jolly Roger: Reflections on Golden Age Piracy*. Oakland: PM Press, 2010.

Labat, Jean-Baptiste. *The Memoirs of Père Labat, 1693–1705*. Edited by John Eaden. London: Constable, 1931.

Lane, Kris. "Punishing the Sea Wolf: Corsairs and Cannibals in the Early Modern Caribbean," *New West India Guide* 77:3–4 (2003): 201–20.

———. *Quito 1599: City and Colony in Transition.* Albuquerque: University of New Mexico Press, 2002.

———. "Buccaneers and Coastal Defense in Late Seventeenth-century Quito: The Case of Barbacoas," *Colonial Latin American Historical Review* 6:2 (Spring 1997): 143–73.

Latimer, Jon. *Buccaneers of the Caribbean: How Piracy Forged an Empire.* Cambridge: Harvard University Press, 2009.

Leeson, Peter. *The Invisible Hook: The Economics of Pirates.* Princeton: Princeton University Press, 2009.

Linebaugh, Peter, and Marcus Rediker. *The Many-Headed Hydra: Sailors, Slaves, Commoners and the Hidden History of the Revolutionary Atlantic.* Boston: Beacon, 2000.

López Lázaro, Fabio. *The Misfortunes of Alonso Ramírez: The True Adventures of a Spanish American with 17th-Century Pirates.* Austin: University of Texas Press, 2011.

Lucena Salmoral, Manuel. *Piratas, bucaneros, filibusteros y corsarios en América: perros, mendigos y otros malditos del mar.* Madrid: Ed. MAPFRE, 1992.

Lunsford, Virginia W. *Piracy and Privateering in the Golden Age Netherlands.* London: Palgrave Macmillan, 2006.

Malekandathil, Pius. "From Merchant Capitalists to Corsairs: The Response of the Muslim Merchants of Malabar to the Portuguese Commercial Expansion (1498–1600)," *Portuguese Studies Review* 12:1 (2004): 75–96.

Marley, David F. *Pirates of the Americas.* 2 vols. Santa Barbara: ABC-CLIO, 2010.

———. *Pirates and Privateers of the Americas.* Santa Barbara: ABC-CLIO, 1994.

———. *Sack of Veracruz: The Great Pirate Raid of 1683.* Windsor: Netherlandic Press, 1993.

———. *Pirates and Engineers: Dutch and Flemish Adventurers in New Spain (1607–1697).* Windsor: Netherlandic Press, 1992.

Marx, Robert F. *Pirate Port: The Story of the Sunken City of Port Royal.* Cleveland: World, 1967.

Matar, Nabil. *Britain and Barbary, 1589–1689.* Gainesville: University Press of Florida, 2006.

McCarl, Clayton, ed. *Piratas y contrabandistas de ambas Indias, y estado presente de ellas (1693), por Francisco Seyxas y Lovera.* A Coruña (Spain): Fundación Pedro Barrié de la Maza, 2011.

McCarl, Clayton. "Carlos Enriques Clerque as Crypto-Jewish Confidence Man in Francisco de Seyxas y Lovera's *Piratas y contrabandistas* (1693)," *Colonial Latin American Review* 24.3. (Aug. 2015).

McCarthy, Matthew. *Privateering, Piracy and British Policy in Spanish America, 1810–1830.* Kingston: University of Hull, 2013.

McDermott, James. *Martin Frobisher, Elizabethan Privateer.* New Haven: Yale University Press, 2001.

Moreau, Jean Pierre. *Pirates: flibuste et piraterie dans la Caraïbe et les mers du sud, 1522–1725.* Paris: Tallandier, 2006.

Murphy, Martin. *Small Boats, Weak States, Dirty Money: Piracy and Maritime Terrorism in the Modern World.* New York: Columbia University Press, 2010.

Narborough, John. *An Account of Several Late Voyages to the South and North.* New York: Da Capo, 1969 [facsimile of 1694 London ed.].

Neill, Anna. "Buccaneer Ethnography: Nature, Culture, and Nation in the Journals of William Dampier," *Eighteenth-Century Studies* 33 (2000): 165–80.

Nuttall, Zelia, trans. and ed. *New Light on Drake: A Collection of Documents Relating to His Voyage of Circumnavigation, 1577–1580* (Hakluyt Society 2nd Series, No. 34). London: Hakluyt Society, 1914.

Palmer, Andrew. *The New Pirates: Modern Global Piracy from Somalia to the South China Sea*. London: I.B. Tauris, 2013.

Parry, John H. *The Spanish Seaborne Empire*. New York: Alfred A. Knopf, 1966.

———. *The Age of Reconnaisance*. New York: Mentor Books, 1963.

Pawson, Michael, and David Buisseret. *Port Royal, Jamaica*. Oxford: Clarendon Press, 1975.

Pennell, C.R., ed. *Bandits at Sea: A Pirates Reader*. New York: New York University Press, 2001.

Pérez Mejía, Angela. "Fronteras de la legalidad. Bucaneros en el siglo XVII," *Historia y sociedad* 8 (2002): 179–98.

Pérotin-Dumon, Anne. *La ville aux îles, la ville dans l'isle: Basse Terre et Pointe-à-Pitre Guadeloupe, 1650–1820*. Paris: Karthala, 2000.

———. "The Pirate and the Emperor: Power and the Law on the Seas, 1450–1850." In James D. Tracy, ed., *The Political Economy of Merchant Empires: State Power and World Trade, 1350–1750*. Cambridge: Cambridge University Press, 1991.

Pestana, Carla Gardina. "Early English Jamaica without Pirates," *William & Mary Quarterly* 71:3 (July 2014): 321–60.

Peterson, Mendel. *The Funnel of Gold*. Boston: Little, Brown, 1975.

Petrovich, Sandra. *Henry Morgan's Raid on Panama: Geopolitics and Colonial Ramifications, 1669–1674*. Lewiston: Edwin Mellen, 2001.

Phillips, Carla Rahn. *Six Galleons for the King of Spain: Imperial Defense in the Early Seventeenth Century*. Baltimore: Johns Hopkins University Press, 1986.

Poolman, Kenneth. *The Speedwell Voyage: A Tale of Piracy and Mutiny in the Eighteenth Century*. Annapolis: Naval Institute Press, 1999.

Prange, Sebastian R. "A Trade of No Dishonor: Piracy, Commerce, and Community in the Western Indian Ocean, Twelfth to Sixteenth Century," *American Historical Review* 116:5 (Dec. 2011): 1269–1293.

Preston, Diana and Michael. *A Pirate of Exquisite Mind. Explorer, Naturalist, and Buccaneer: The Life of William Dampier*. New York: Berkley, 2004.

Pritchard, James. *In Search of Empire: The French in the Americas, 1670–1730*. New York: Cambridge University Press, 2004.

Rankin, Hugh F. *The Golden Age of Piracy*. New York: Holt, Rinehart and Winston, 1969.

Rediker, Marcus. *Villains of All Nations: Atlantic Pirates in the Golden Age*. Boston: Beacon Press, 2004.

———. *Between the Devil and the Deep Blue Sea: Merchant Seamen, Pirates, and the Anglo-American Maritime World, 1700–1750*. Cambridge: Cambridge University Press, 1987.

Risso, Patricia. "Cross-Cultural Perceptions of Piracy: Maritime Violence in the Western Indian Ocean and Persian Gulf during a Long Eighteenth Century," *Journal of World History* 12:2 (2001): 293–319.

Ritchie, Robert C. *Captain Kidd and the War against the Pirates*. Cambridge: Harvard University Press, 1986.

Rogers, Woodes. *A Cruising Voyage Round the World*. Edited by G.E. Manwaring. New York: Longmans, Green, 1928 [1712].

Rupert, Linda. *Creolization and Contraband: Curaçao in the Early Modern Atlantic World*. Athens: University of Georgia Press, 2012.

Schmidt, Benjamin. *Innocence Abroad: The Dutch Imagination and the New World, 1570–1670*. New York: Cambridge University Press, 2006.

Shurz, William L. *The Manila Galleon*. New York: E.P. Dutton, 1939.

Skowronek, Russell K., and Charles R. Ewen, eds. *X Marks the Spot: The Archaeology of Piracy*. Gainesville: University Press of Florida, 2006.

Slater, Mary. *Cooking the Caribbean Way*. London: Spring Books, 1965.

Sluiter, Engel. "The Dutch on the Pacific Coast of America, 1598–1621." Ph.D. dissertation, University of California at Berkeley, 1937.

So, Kwan-Wai. *Japanese Piracy in Ming China during the 16th Century*. Ann Arbor: Michigan State University Press, 1975.

Sobel, Dava. *Longitude*. New York: Walker, 1995.

Sousa, Philip de. *Piracy in the Graeco-Roman World*. New York: Cambridge University Press, 2002.

Speilbergen, Joris van. *The East and West Indian Mirror, Being an Account of Joris Van Speilbergen's Voyage Round the World, 1614–1617*. Edited and translated by J.A.J.Villiers (Hakluyt Society 2nd Series, No. 18). London: Hakluyt Society, 1906 [1619].

Sugden, John. *Sir Francis Drake*. New York: Henry Holt, 1990.

Thompson, Janice E. *Mercenaries, Pirates, and Sovereigns: State-Building and Extraterritorial Violence in Early Modern Europe*. Princeton: Princeton University Press, 1994.

Thrower, Norman J., ed. *Sir Francis Drake and the Famous Voyage, 1577–1580: Essays Commemorating the Quadricentennial of Drake's Circumnavigation of the World*. Berkeley: University of California Press, 1984.

Tinniswood, Adrian. *Pirates of Barbary: Corsairs, Conquests, and Captivity in the Seventeenth-Century Mediterranean*. New York: Riverhead Books, 2010.

Turley, Hans. *Rum, Sodomy, and the Lash: Piracy, Sexuality, and Masculine Identity*. New York: NYU Press, 1999.

Unger, Richard W. *Dutch Shipbuilding before 1800*. Amsterdam: Van Gorcum, 1978.

Vitkus, Daniel J. *Piracy, Slavery, and Redemption*. New York: Columbia University Press, 2001.

Voigt, Lisa. *Writing Captivity in the Early Modern Atlantic: Circulation of Knowledge and Authority in the Iberian and English Imperial Worlds*. Chapel Hill: University of North Carolina Press, 2009.

Wafer, Lionel. *A New Voyage and Description of the Isthmus of America*. New York: Burt Franklin, 1970 [1699].

Walvin, James. *The Zong: A Massacre, the Law and the End of Slavery*. New Haven: Yale University Press, 2011.

Ward, Christopher. *Imperial Panama: Commerce and Conflict in Isthmian America, 1550–1800*. Albuquerque: University of New Mexico Press, 1993.

Warren, James F. *Iranun and Balangingi: Globalization, Maritime Raiding, and the Birth of Ethnicity*. Singapore: National University of Singapore Press, 2002.

Weiss, G.L. *Captives and Corsairs: France and Slavery in the Early Modern Mediterranean*. Stanford: Stanford University Press, 2011.

Wilbur, Marguerite Eyer. *Raveneau de Lussan: Buccaneer of the Spanish Main and Early French Filibuster of the Pacific*. Cleveland: Arthur H. Clark, 1930.

Williams, Glyndwr. *The Great South Sea: English Voyages and Encounters, 1500–1750*. New Haven: Yale University Press, 1997.

Wolf, John B. *The Barbary Coast: Algiers under the Turks, 1500–1830*. New York: W.W. Norton, 1979.

Woodard, Colin. *The Republic of Pirates, Being the True and Surprising Story of the Caribbean Pirates and the Man Who Brought Them Down*. New York: Harcourt, 2007.

Wright, Irene A., ed. *Spanish Narratives of the English Attack on Santo Domingo, 1655*. London: Royal Historical Society, 1926.

INDEX